INDEX OF

PACIFIC NORTHWEST PORTRAITS

INDEX OF
PACIFIC NORTHWEST PORTRAITS

EDITED BY MARION B. APPLETON

Published for PACIFIC NORTHWEST LIBRARY ASSOCIATION, REFERENCE DIVISION
by the UNIVERSITY OF WASHINGTON PRESS
SEATTLE AND LONDON

Library of Congress Cataloging in Publication Data

Appleton, Marion Brymner.
    Index of Pacific Northwest portraits.

    Bibliography: p.
    1. Northwest, Pacific--History--Portraits--Indexes.
2. Portraits, American--Indexes. I. Pacific North-
west Library Association. Reference Division.
II. Title.
Z1251.N7A63   016.757'9'09795   70-38982
ISBN 0-295-95179-6

PREFACE

The idea of compiling an index of "all available Northwest historical pictures"* was broached initially at the 1938 Pacific Northwest Library Association annual conference. However, it was not until 1949 that the project was firmly established, with the appointment of five state chairmen to work with the regional chairman on book selection and preliminary indexing. In the early 1950's the project was redefined as a portrait index only, as the majority of the illustrations submitted were portraits.

The completed portrait index lists the names of over twelve thousand men and women identified with the history of the Pacific Northwest: Alaska, British Columbia, Idaho, Montana, Oregon and Washington. It ranges in time from the years of early exploration to the first quarter of the twentieth century; selective indexing of the period from the twenties to the present consists mainly of portraits in serial publications. It includes portraits of Indians, explorers, pioneers and others who developed the region, and Easterners who influenced the West; also, there are a few portraits of individuals who lived in areas bordering the Northwest: the Mormons of Utah, the Sioux east of Montana.

Some of the illustrations indexed are not formal portrait photographs; it seemed preferable to include a "candid" photo, or a reproduction of drawing, painting or sculpture rather than no likeness at all. Several sources of portraits of one individual may be included.

The three hundred twenty-four titles selected for the project are enumerated in the Bibliography of Books Indexed, in an alphabetical arrangement by key letters. Several additional lists are provided: an alphabetical listing by author, and regional lists classified by state and province.

Although the Index is not a biographical reference, in many instances biographical information, often including an autograph, is given in connection with the portrait.

Hopefully, this first regional portrait index will call forth numerous suggestions of additional names and sources that might be incorporated in a future supplement.

MBA

Picture Indexing Committee 1970-71
Joy N. Smith, Chairman
Marion B. Appleton
Lorraine Schluter
Chloe T. Sivertz

* PNLA Quarterly 3:80 October 1938 in report presented by Elizabeth
  Henry Albertson

CONTENTS

PREFACE   iii

ABBREVIATIONS; A NOTE ON USING THE INDEX   vi

INDEX OF PACIFIC NORTHWEST PORTRAITS   1 - 174

BIBLIOGRAPHY OF BOOKS INDEXED   175

ALPHABETICAL LIST OF BOOKS INDEXED   196

REGIONAL LISTS OF BOOKS INDEXED

        Pacific Northwest   203

        Alaska   204

        British Columbia   205

        Idaho   206

        Montana   206

        Oregon   207

        Utah   208

        Washington   208

INDEX OF

PACIFIC NORTHWEST PORTRAITS

ABBREVIATIONS

fol.   : following

front. : frontispiece

no.   : number

pt.   : part

suppl. : supplement

unp.   : unpaged

A NOTE ON USING THE INDEX

The portrait index is arranged alphabetically by name of individual, followed by volume and page notation and key letters referring to the Bibliography of Books Indexed, where author, title and facts of publication are given.

Spelling and form of the name of an individual occasionally vary from source to source, or even within a single source. When this happens, in the absence of a final authority a logical choice between forms has been made, with cross indexing of variant forms.

When there are two or more identical names, repetition of the name is avoided by substituting an unbroken line; usually, but not always, this indicates the references are to one person.

Birth and death dates are given occasionally to differentiate between individuals with identical names.

214-215   Page notations of this type indicate that the portrait appears in a group of illustrations between pages 214 and 215.

*   An asterisk before an author's name in the Bibliography of Books Indexed indicates that Pacific Northwest portraits only have been indexed in the volume.

INDEX

OF

PACIFIC NORTHWEST PORTRAITS

NAME	PAGE	KEY	NAME	PAGE	KEY
Abbot, Henry Larcom	44:front.	OHQ	Adair, Mrs. John, see		
Abbott, Edward C	1:307	ACR	Adair, Berthina Angelina (Owens)		
Abbott, Harry Braithwaite	4:57	BCF	Adam, George N	318	JNT
————	fol. pt. 1	SHB	Adam, William	4:550	PH
Abbott, John J C	227, 302	GI	Adama, F W	2:front. 1924	BCHA
Abbott, Twyman Osmand	2:26	HHT	Adams, A Hugh	1941-42:65	OO
————	13 no. 4:421	MWH	Adams, A O	37	MG
Abel, A M	1924:160	WSP	Adams, Augusta, see		
Abel, W H	21	LT	Young, Augusta (Adams)		
Abel, William M	2:179	SMS	Adams, Charles Francis	211	BOO
Abercrombie, Esther, see			Adams, E Arlita (Hewitt)	3:449	BHS
Thompson, Esther (Abercrombie)			Adams, E M	2:231	SMS
Abercrombie, William R	fol. 207	SHI	Adams, Foster	177	PL
Aberdeen, John Campbell Gordon, 7th Earl of			Adams, Mrs. Frank E , see		
	1897:102	YB	Adams, E Arlita (Hewitt)		
Abernethy, George	88	AC	Adams, Fred W	1945-46:85	OO
————	2:168	FI	Adams, Frederick E	2:291	CHW
————	1:127	GP	Adams, J C	3:1376	SM
————	3:286	LH	Adams, John	44	CBC
————	1:12	NH	Adams, John D	3:531	HHI
————	1:12	PMO	Adams, Lottie, see		
————	48 no. 3:78	PN	Peltier, Lottie (Adams)		
————	2:280	SH	Adams, Louis J	2:458	PMO
————	13	TUR	Adams, Louis Rudolph	3:1047	FH
Abernethy, Sarah F (Gray)	3:313	LHC	Adams, Orville	287	BHSS
Abernethy, William	3:312	LHC	Adams, Sarah Elizabeth, see		
Abernethy, Mrs. William, see			Brigham, Sarah Elizabeth (Adams)		
Abernethy, Sarah F (Gray)			Adams, Mrs. Tom, see		
Abraham, Father, see			Martin, Josephine (Rider) Adams Wright		
Father Abraham			Adams, W L	13:front.	WBP
Abrahams, Mrs.	2:19 1924	BCHA	————	14:32	WBP
Abrahamson, John C	2:224	SMS	————	front.	WRE
Abrams, C J	39	MG	Adams, W Lloyd	3:484-485	BEA
Abrams, Milton	24:272	PNLA	Adams, William	2:front. 1924	BCHA
Abrams, Sarah	1:210-211	GP	————	1897:106	YB
Abrams, W E	39	MG	Adams, William L	2:31	HWW
Achabal, Adolfo James	3:111	BEA	————	1:584	NH
Achurch, Samuel	4:165	BCF	Adams, William P	2:36	SMS
Ackerman, Ike	1:154-155	EPD	Adamson, Anna M , see		
Ackerman, W A	1924:144	WSP	Terrill, Anna M (Adamson)		
Ackerson, John W	1:138	HHT	Adamson, James	4 no. 2:86	BCH
Ackerson, Mrs. John W	1:138	HHT	Adamson, John	2:870	FH
Ackley, Daniel W	189	MSG	Adamson, Joseph Warren	3:370	BEA
Acton, J H	456	AG	Adamson, Rainie, see		
Adair, Berthina Angelina (Owens)	2:426	NH	Small, Rainie (Adamson)		
Adair, Hugh R	1941:52	EN	Adelmann, Richard C	2:676	FH
Adair, Irvin M	2:193	CHW	————	2:137	HHI
Adair, John	2:257	BCF	Adkison, Hattie (Brown)	1:154-155	EPD

Adolphe, Flathead chief   fol. 512   BUR
Agassiz, L   N   3:615   BCF
Agassiz, Louis A   3:615   BCF
Agen, John Bernard   3:729   BHK
Agnes George (Umatilla Indian) 212   AI
Agur, Robert H   fol.pt.1   SHB
Ah Loy   374   BR
Ah Moon   374   BR
Ahern, George Patrick   58 no.3:143   PN
Aiken, Clara B   , see
    Fisher, Clara B   (Aiken)
Aiken, N   J   298   BHSS
Ainslie, George   293   DSW
Ainsworth, George Jennings 3:195   GP
                                 215   LDM
Ainsworth, John C   98   BOO
_____   1:258   GP
_____   2:79   GP
_____   31   LDM
_____   1:135, 655   LHC
_____   353   QT
Ainsworth, L   S   2:601   LHC
Airey, Robert   172   LDM
Aitchison, James Nelson   3:895   BCF
Aitken, George M   1935-36:50   OO
Akins, Sage   30   THI
Alab-lernot, see
    Tolo (Nez Percé Indian)
Alastra, Jose   3:883   HHI
Alber, N   Ray   1935-36:51   OO
                                 1937-38:62-63   OO
Albers, William   3:359   LHC
Alberson, Letha   63:321   OHQ
Albert, J   H   1:553   CHW
Albert, Lester F   19:14 1943-44   IH
Albert, M   F   2:891   HHI
Albertson, Arthur Freeman   3:541   HHT
_____   1910:2   TDL
_____   13:118 1908   WBP
_____   14:front. 1909 WBP
Albertson, Robert Brooke   3:419   BHS
_____   5:248   SH
_____   1895-96:81   SSS
Albi, Joseph A   255   GG
Albright, Jacob   2:1279   SM
Aldecoa, Domingo   3:737   HHI
Aldecoa, Marcelino   3:829   HHI
Alden, George H   6:26 1906   WDT
Alderman, Albert L   1:144   NH
Alderson, William W   214   LHM
_____   5:313   MC
_____   2:359   SMS
Aleb-Pernot, see
    Tolo (Nez Percé Indian)
Alec Pierre (Spokan Indian) 58   LC
Alee, Flathead chief   64   PI
                                 84   PIW
Alers-Hankey, Gerald Cramer fol.pt.2   SHB

Alexander, Pend d'Oreille chief
                                 fol. 512   BUR
Alexander, Dorothy L   34 no.1:32   PNLA
Alexander, Elmer E   1:343   HH
Alexander, George   3:399   BCF
_____   1945-46:65   OO
_____   fol. title page SHB
Alexander, Ivan Winfred   4:631   PH
Alexander, J   48   LS
Alexander, J   H   173   PL
Alexander, J   W   19:160 1914   WBP
Alexander, James J   184   E
Alexander, James Newton   2:509   SMS
Alexander, Lucy A   , see
    Thomas, Lucy A   (Alexander)
Alexander, Moses   343   DSW
_____   2:282-283   EPD
_____   594   IHI
Alexander, Richard Henry   3:829   BCF
_____   fol.pt.1   SHB
Alexander, Tom   2:front.   BCHA
Alexander, Mrs. William, see
    Stirling, Sarah (Livingston)
Alfonso, Marie   26:42 1925   WDT
Alge, O   295   E
Alger, Hollis   2:645   GP
Alisky, Charles Adolph   2:667   GP
_____   560   SHP
Alla, Alexander   3:1752   SM
Allaeys, Honore   326, 366   PI
_____   436   PIW
Allard, Jason   16   NF
Allard, Ovid   16   NF
Allen, Alfred E   1895-96:83   SSS
Allen, Andrew   69:314   OHQ
Allen, B   F   2:433   PMO
Allen, Beulah, see
    Webb, Beulah (Allen)
Allen, Billy   2:464-465   EPD
Allen, D   D   203   PSW
Allen, E   C   1937-38:62-63   OO
_____   1941-42:65   OO
_____   1945-46:85   OO
Allen, E   T   51 no.2:51   PN
Allen, Edward Jay   132   MP
_____   94   WCS
Allen, Edward W   1924:161   WSP
Allen, Emma, see
    Chambard, Emma (Allen)
Allen, Eugene C   front.   BK
Allen, Eugenia, see
    Keeney, Eugenia (Allen)
Allen, Frank   1905-06:[67]   RLW
Allen, Frank P   , Jr.   unp.   VU
Allen, H   E   1905-06:[28]   RLW
Allen, H   Eugene   2:467   BHK
_____   1:334   BHS
Allen, H   H   2:274   NH

Allen, Harry Mortimer 2:1240 SM
Allen, Henry Coburn 36:20 1935 WDT
Allen, Henry T fol. 207 SHI
Allen, Herman 19 LT
Allen, Jack E 1935-36:50 OO
Allen, Mrs. Janet 2:123 BCF
Allen, John B 4:388 SH
Allen, Kenneth S 24:147 PNLA
Allen, L F 1931-32:41 OO
Allen, Mary A (Settlemier) 1:588 PMO
Allen, Patrick A 4:965 BCF
Allen, Percy G 3:943 LHC
Allen, Pliny L [106] RLX
Allen, Raymond B 120-121 GA
    50:5 1949 WDT
Allen, Samuel 1:572 NH
    1:588 PMO
Allen, Mrs. Samuel, see
    Trimble, Sarah (Benson) Allen
Allen, Sarah (Benson), see
    Trimble, Sarah (Benson) Allen
Allen, Thomas B 1:588 PMO
Allen, Mrs. Thomas B , see
    Allen, Mary A (Settlemier)
Allen, Wiley B 1:428 PMO
Allen, William A 1941:52 EN
    2:1069 SM
Allen, William Burton 14 no. 1:11 MWH
Alley, Benjamin F 1895:76 OO
Alley, Frank E 165 PL
Alley, J N 22 SPI
Allison, John Fall fol. title page SHB
Allison, L L 43 no. 2:136-137 PN
Allison, Ruhannah (Hedgecock) 3:978-979 FH
Allison, Mrs. Susan L 2:front. 1924 BCHA
Allison, William B 3:978-979 FH
Allison, Mrs. William B , see
    Allison, Ruhannah (Hedgecock)
Allison, William H 300 LDM
Allred, Paulinus H 146 GL
Allstrum, Esther 2:503 HHT
Allyn, Frank 2:313 HH
    2:26 HHT
    3:285 HHT
Almy, Helen M (Winsoer) 2:1231 SM
Almy, James S 2:1231 SM
Almy, Mrs. James S , see
    Almy, Helen M (Winsoer)
A-lom-pum (Cayuse Indian) 1:578, 579 PMO
Alquema, Santiam chief 7 BD
Alston, Edward G 1897:43, 124 YB
Altman, Francis 383 SCH
Alvensleben, Constantin Alvo von
    fol. pt. 2 SHB
Alvord, Benjamin 65:64 OHQ
Alvord, David D 2:757 HHI
Alvord, Dorothy 27:23 PNLA
Alvord, Elisha Henry 3:387 BHS
Alvord, Thomas M 2:142 NH

Alward, H V 24:64 1919 WBP
    25:128 1920 WBP
    26:128 1921 WBP
Amadeus, Mother 247 PIW
Amera, Charles 2:368-369 EPD
Ames, Edwin Gardner 2:125 BHK
    3:62 BHS
    5:416 SH
Ames, James Almond 2:445 HHI
Ames, Oakes 76 BOO
    32 QT
Amonson, Carl 1152 SIH
Amos, John B 3:1674 SM
Amundsen, Roald 146 BET
    260 KI
    front. KU
Amy, John P 1:554 PHP
Anderburg, Matilda, see
    Larson, Matilda (Anderburg)
Andersen, William Lee 3:441 BEA
Anderson, A 77 AG
Anderson, A C 232 MHN
    18 NF
    71 WTH
Anderson, A M 201 E
Anderson, A W [94] RLX
Anderson, Agnes (Healy) unp. WD
Anderson, Alexander Caulfield 56 DC
    fol. title page SHB
    1897:18 YB
Anderson, Alexander J 18-19 GA
    296 NM
Anderson, Mrs. Alfred H , see
    Anderson, Agnes (Healy)
Anderson, Amy 3:290-291 PH
Anderson, Andrea 222 FF
Anderson, Andrew 4:155 BHK
Anderson, Andrew Bjrring 305, 328 GL
Anderson, Mrs. Andrew Bjrring, see
    Anderson, Hannah (Evans)
Anderson, Andrew Rasmus 222 GL
Anderson, Mrs. Andrew Rasmus, see
    Anderson, Mary Ann (Pederson)
    Anderson, Nelsina M (Anderson)
Anderson, Anna, see
    Johnson, Anna (Anderson)
Anderson, Arthur 1941:69 EN
    3:290-291 PH
Anderson, C F 43 no. 2:136-137 PN
Anderson, C G W 76 SS
Anderson, C M 39 MG
Anderson, Caspar H 167 LDM
Anderson, Charles H 3:318 PH
Anderson, Charlotte C , see
    Bender, Charlotte C (Anderson)
Anderson, David F 1:301 HH
Anderson, Donald K 50:22 1949 WDT
Anderson, Edward 3:290-291 PH

Anderson, Eli K — 1:156 — NH
Anderson, Elizabeth Holgate (Carr) — 3:340 — PH
Anderson, Elmer — 64 — RSA
Anderson, Mrs. Elmer J — 6:408-409 — MC
Anderson, Elof — 3:1294 — FH
Anderson, Elof — 2:110 — FSB
Anderson, G H — 41 — MG
Anderson, George A , Jr. — 3:631 — HHT
Anderson, George Burford — 4:781 — BCF
Anderson, George Edgar — 4:476 — PH
Anderson, Geraldean — 67 — MG
Anderson, Graebert — 94 — SS
Anderson, Gust — 1931-32:41 — OO
Anderson, Guy L — 135 — MLO
Anderson, H E — 3:359 — BH
Anderson, H N — 2:153 — HWW
Anderson, Hannah (Evans) — 329 — GL
Anderson, Herman — 4:185 — BHK
Anderson, J F — 184 — SS
Anderson, J G — 4:87 — BCF
Anderson, J R — 2:293 — BCF
Anderson, J R — 2:front.1924 — BCHA
Anderson, James — 2:531 — GP
Anderson, James L — 378 — LDM
Anderson, James M — 224 — GL
Anderson, James T — 6:408-409 — MC
Anderson, James W — 1924:144 — WSP
Anderson, John C — 134 — CBC
Anderson, Karl — 3:290-291 — PH
Anderson, Katherine — 6:74 — PNLA
Anderson, Levi — 1:592-593 — GP
Anderson, Louis C — 4:195 — BHK
Anderson, Martha — 12 — SS
Anderson, Martin — 680 — SIH
Anderson, Mary Ann (Pederson) — 326 — GL
Anderson, Mathew — 3:340 — PH
Anderson, Mrs. Mathew, see
    Anderson, Elizabeth Holgate (Carr)
Anderson, Minnie — 12 — SS
Anderson, Nelsina M , see
    Anderson, Nelsina M (Anderson)
Anderson, Nelsina M (Anderson) — 327 — GL
Anderson, Nils — 4:655 — PH
Anderson, O A — 316 — LDM
Anderson, O J — 1:372 — HHT
Anderson, Olaf — 3:290-291 — PH
Anderson, Ole A — 1128 — SIH
Anderson, Oscar — 78 — SS
Anderson, Ossian — 3:290-291 — PH
Anderson, Peter — 2:1048 — SM
Anderson, Robert — 52 — CBC
Anderson, Sarah Jane (Sturgis) — 3:657 — GP
Anderson, Sten — 3:290-291 — PH
Anderson, Thomas McArthur — 1:580-581 — GP
Anderson, Thomas McArthur — 3:633 — GP
Anderson, V S — 138 — HIT
Anderson, W D E — Feb.1906:62 — TDL

Anderson, W Scott — 2:846 — FH
Anderson, William H — 3:1219 — FH
Anderson, Mrs. William Reese, see
    Anderson, Sarah Jane (Sturgis)
Andrae, Oswald — 3:755 — LHC
Andreason, Hyrum — 224 — GL
Andres, R G — 39 — MG
Andrew, F W — 195 — AT
Andrewartha, Bertha Irene — 3:203 — HHI
Andrewartha, Harriet H — 3:202 — HHI
Andrewartha, Mrs. John, see
    Andrewartha, Harriet H
Andrews, Charles H — 3:1010 — FH
Andrews, E W — unp. — VU
Andrews, Frank E — 1931-32:41 — OO
Andrews, G P — 1:unp.1900-01 — WDT
Andrews, Guy — 3:213 — HWW
Andrews, Jane (Mansell) — 3:539 — HHI
Andrews, Lena, see
    Zielinski, Lena (Andrews)
Andrews, Thomas — 3:539 — HHI
Andrews, Mrs. Thomas, see
    Andrews, Jane (Mansell)
Andrus, Harry E — 2:375 — SMS
Angel, Texas — 3:991 — FH
Angeline, Princess — 89 — AG
Angeline, Princess — 1:84 — BHS
Angeline, Princess — 1:114 — HWW
Angeline, Princess — 614-615 — USCI
Angeline, Princess — unp. — VU
Angell, Earle F — 2:616 — SMS
Angell, Homer D — 1931-32:41 — OO
Angell, Homer D — 1935-36:51 — OO
Angell, Homer D — 1937-38:62 — OO
Angell, Homer D — 1943-44:13 — OO
Angell, Homer D — 1945-46:13 — OO
Angell, Mary Ann, see
    Young, Mary Ann (Angell)
Angerstein, L E — 372 — LDM
Angus, R B — 122,220,302 — GI
Ankeny, Alexander P — 106 — LDM
Ankeny, Henry — 2:29 — CHW
Ankeny, Levi — 1905-06:[32] — RLW
Ankeny, Levi — [81] — RLX
Ankeny, Levi — 19:176 1914 — WBP
Ann, Poka-Billy, see
    Poka-Billy Ann
Annett, William C — 2:603 — FH
Anscomb, H — 3:14 1925 — BCHA
Anstie, W A — fol.pt.2 — SHB
Antrim, Ray L — 1937-38:62-63 — OO
Apash-Wyakaikt, see
    Looking Glass, Sr., Nez Percé chief
Appelhagen, Sophia D , see
    Jaeger, Sophia D (Appelhagen)
Apperson, E C — 2:247 — CHW
Apperson, E C — unp. — SOU
Apperson, H B — 1924:161 — WSP

Appleby, Nellie, see
   Van Eaton, Nellie (Appleby)
Appleby, Stephen   58 no.4:190   PN
                         1910:43   TDL
Applegate, Albert Dean   2:139   CHW
Applegate, Jesse   55 no.4:173   PN
Applegate, Moray Lindsay 58:5   OHQ
Applegate, O   C   311   BN
Applequist, "Hack"   393   BHSS
Aram, Clara, see
   Fitzgerald, Clara (Aram)
Aram, Mrs. John, see
   Aram, Sarah Elizabeth (Barr)
Aram, Sarah Elizabeth (Barr) 2:464-465 EPD
Archabal, John B   2:107   HHI
Archer, Mary, see
   Latham, Mary (Archer)
Archer, Samuel   2:113   BCF
Archer, Sarah E   , see
   Pope, Sarah E   (Archer)
Archibald, Adam G   2:74   MCC
Arestad, Sverre   50:39 1949   WDT
Argyle, Albert   2:front.1924 BCHA
Argyle, Thomas   2:113   BCF
Ariss, E   Augusta   144   LHN
Arkwright, May, see
   Hutton, May (Arkwright)
Arlee, Flathead chief, see
   Alee, Flathead chief
Ar-lo-quat, see
   Ollokot, Nez Percé chief
Armbrust, C   M   48   LS
Armon, Esther de, see
   Taylor, Esther (DeArmon)
Armstrong, A   P   1:192   PMO
Armstrong, F   A   103   LHN
Armstrong, Francis K   2:6   SMS
Armstrong, J   C   2:139   BCF
Armstrong, J   W   219   PSW
Armstrong, Katherine (Moore) 3:841   LHC
Armstrong, Leo L   260   GG
Armstrong, Mrs. Mary J   31   THI
Armstrong, Obadiah   3:393   HHI
Armstrong, Robert J   211   GG
Armstrong, Thomas J   3:840   LHC
Armstrong, Mrs. Thomas J   , see
   Armstrong, Katherine (Moore)
Armstrong, Thomas Joseph 3:293   BCF
Armstrong, William Henry 3:223   BCF
                        fol.pt.1   SHB
Armstrong, William J   2:141,337 BCF
                        3:537   BCF
Arnett, Telitha J   , see
   Ellis, Telitha J   (Arnett) Stafford
Arnett, W   F   135   MLO
Arnold, Alford A   3:1472   SM
Arnold, Green   1:264   NH
Arnold, H   W   1924:65   WSP

Arnold, L   C   157   AI
Arnold, Melvin L   32 no.4:28   PNLA
Arnold, Morris A   2:189   BHK
                        3:363   BHS
Arnold, R   D   3:103   HHI
Arntson, John M   120   SS
                      May 1907:38 TDL
Arnzen, Clem   1:282-283   EPD
Arrapeen, Ute chief   133   BHI
Arrington, Noah Wesley 3:177   BEA
Arthuis, Paul T   251   GG
                      10   SCH
Arthur, Catherine, see
   Davey, Catherine (Arthur)
Arthur, Edward B   3:23   HHI
Arthur, Jesse   2:253   HH
Arthur, John   3:443   BHS
                      2:325   HH
                      Feb.1906:44 TDL
                      1923:76   WSP
Arthur, Sarah Angeline, see
   Robinson, Sarah Angeline (Arthur)
Arthurs, John A   3:1534   SM
Asbridge, Joseph L   2:522   SMS
Asbury, D   I   unp.   SOU
Ash, Clarence E   1939-40:30 OO
Ash, John   2:337   BCF
Ashby, Edna, see
   Cochran, Edna (Ashby)
Ashcroft, Albert Edward fol.pt.2   SHB
Ashley, James M   4:106   MC
                      6:143   MC
                      58 no.2:83   PN
                      1:410   SMS
Ashton, Araminta (Lawrence) 333   GL
Ashton, Esther Ann, see
   Powell, Esther Ann (Ashton)
Ashton, James Martin   3:5   BH
                      192   E
                      2:247   HH
                      4:465   PH
                      1:584   PHP
                      5:44   SH
                      May 1907:39 TDL
                      1924:161   WSP
Ashton, Thomas   73   GL
Ashton, Mrs. Thomas, see
   Ashton, Araminta (Lawrence)
Ashwell, G   R   2:139   BCF
Ashwell, John H   2:front.1924 BCHA
Askren, Thomas Merle 3:235   PH
Askren, W   D   1924:9   WSP
Aspling, Charles E   2:336   SMS
Aspling, Thomas   6:374   MC
Aspray, Joseph   39   MG
Aspray, Melvin   37   MG
Asselstine, George H 2:564   SMS
Astington, Mary, see
   Kirkham, Mary (Astington)

Astor, John Jacob, 1763-1848 21   BF
                               73   BHI
_____   1:108   BS
_____   1:342   CAF
_____   1:98,308   CAFT
_____   205   CHO
_____   1:37   CHW
_____   22   CIR
_____   64   DSW
_____   1:176   FI
_____   fol. 56   FRA
_____   50   GI
_____   1:42-43   GP
_____   2:232   LH
_____   1:47   LHC
_____   1:326   SH
Astor, John Jacob, 1822-1890 22   CIR
Astor, William Backhouse   23   CIR
Athanase (Carrier Indian)   23   MHN
Atkins, Henry A   unp.   SEA
Atkins, Penelope, see
    Pitt, Penelope (Atkins)
Atkins, Thomas Edward   3:383   BCF
Atkinson, Amos Barnes   4:1023   BCF
Atkinson, C   R   26:48 1925 WDT
Atkinson, George E   1:134   HHT
Atkinson, George Henry   1:368   GP
_____   3:97   GP
_____   1:433   LHC
_____   2:348   PMO
Atkinson, Mrs. George Henry, see
    Atkinson, Nancy (Bates)
Atkinson, John   2:748   FH
Atkinson, John D   1905-06:[36] RLW
                              [79]   RLX
Atkinson, John Milton Eddy   3:943   BHS
Atkinson, Morton E   1941:458   EN
Atkinson, Nancy (Bates)   2:348   PMO
Atkinson, Ralph W   4:547   BCF
Atkinson, Reilly   3:31   BEA
Attix, Frederick F   2:45   SMS
Atwater, Ben   76   HEG
Atwell, Francis   193   E
Atwell, Frank Charles   2:249   LHC
Atwell, H   C   1:360   GP
Atwood, Albert   4   AC
                              front.   AG
                              28   PC
Aubert, Casimir   1:204   MCC
Aubury, Lewis E   419, 437   PL
Auld, James Currie   2:647   SMS
Ault, Harry   55 no.4:151 PN
Austin, A   E   252   PSW
Austin, Charles Henry   2:974   SM
Austin, Emma (Grace)   335   GL
Austin, George   291   GL
Austin, James W   3:877   SMS
Austin, John   211   GL

Austin, Mrs. John, see
    Austin, Emma (Grace)
Austin, Lonnie   1 no.4:310 WM
Austin, R   L   2:405   HH
Avery, A   G   1924:96   WSP
Avery, Alexander Gordon   3:387   HHT
Avery, Henry H   981   LHM
Avery, J   C   1:596   NH
Avey, Oliver H   2:772   FH
                              2:451   HHI
Axline, George Andrew   1:216   FSB
Axtell, Abram   3:589   GP
Ayer, Charles H   1:451   HH
Ayer, Fred C   26:48 1925 WDT
Ayer, Robert   1905-06:[57] RLW
Ayers, Roy E   3:1693   SM
Aylesworth-Edsall, Mrs. Ella 6:338   MC
Azcuenaga, Antonio   3:247   HHI

B

Babb, Mrs. Daisy T   32   THI
Babbidge, John W   126   LDM
Babbidge, S   R   283   LDM
Babbitt, Charles E   3:215   BEA
Babcock, Albert L   211   MI
                              2:1215   SM
                              2:241   SMS
Babcock, Edward Coddington   3:1308   SM
Babcock, Fred Jason   1941:163   EN
Babcock, O   L   1941-42:65 OO
Babcock, Paul   3:1759   SM
Babson, Sydney G   70:51,55   OHQ
Bach, E   W   630   MI
Bach, Thomas C   4:110   MC
                              1:428   SMS
Bachelder, Frederick S   3:1486   SM
Bachelder, J   M   1:566   BH
Backus, Clyde J   3:207   BH
Backus, Manson Franklin   3:537   BHK
                              4:737   PH
                              5:100   SH
                              10:36 1905 WBP
                              24:80 1919 WBP
                              1 no.8:17   WN
Bacon, Alice (Reid)   3:491   BEA
Bacon, E   G   1:372   HHT
Bacon, Ellen D   (Bartlett) 1:11   D
Bacon, Mrs. George W   , see
    Bacon, Ellen D   (Bartlett)
Bacon, John M   1:208   NH
Bacon, Thomas Clyde   3:491   BEA
Bacon, Mrs. Thomas Clyde, see
    Bacon, Alice (Reid)
Badolato, Frank N   2:847   BHK
Baer, Edward Sherman   3:1698   SM

Baer, Harry F	202	E
Baer, Louis F	203	E
Bagley, Alice (Mercer)	1:91	BHK
Bagley, Clarence Booth	220	AC
———	1:front.,219	BHK
———	1:front.	BHS
———	458	MP
———	51 no.4:178	PN
Bagley, Mrs. Clarence Booth, see		
Bagley, Alice (Mercer)		
Bagley, Daniel	93	AG
———	1:82	BHK
———	2:199	BHK
———	2:front.	BHS
———	18-19	GA
———	52 no.2:62	PN
———	4:368	SH
Bagley, Mrs. Daniel, see		
Bagley, Susannah (Rogers)		
Bagley, Henry B	2:349	HH
Bagley, Herman Beardsley	2:145	BHK
Bagley, Susannah (Rogers)	1:83	BHK
Bagshaw, Clarence	176-177	GA
Bailey, Barbara A (Clary)	2:691	GP
Bailey, Benjamin	fol. title page	SHB
Bailey, Frank T	3:1748	SM
Bailey, Henry	260	LDM
Bailey, J O	1931-32:40	OO
———	1935-36:34	OO
———	1937-38:7	OO
———	1939-40:7	OO
———	1941-42:14	OO
———	1943-44:21	OO
———	1945-46:33	OO
Bailey, Joseph	2:690	GP
———	25:186	OHQ
Bailey, Mrs. Joseph, see		
Bailey, Barbara A (Clary)		
Bailey, Lester A	230	LDM
Bailey, Robert	4:863	BCF
Bailey, Robert Edward	3:306	BEA
Bailey, Robert Gresham	429	BR
———	32	THI
Bailey, Mrs. Robert Gresham	32	THI
Bailey, William Benjamin Valentine		
	fol.pt.2	SHB
Baillargeon, Cebert	4:421	BHK
Baillargeon, Joseph A	4:115	BHK
———	4:429	PH
Baillie, Alex	1:534	HHT
Baillie-Begbie, Matthew, see		
Begbie, Matthew Baillie		
Bain, Jack	1945-46:85	OO
Bain, James R	1945-46:92	OO
Bainbridge, William	29	CIR
Baird, Alexander K	6:426	MC
Baird, David	1945-46:73	OO
Baird, David E	2:512	SMS

Bakeman, Charles H	1:491	HH
Baker, C H	1895:106	OO
Baker, Daniel W	486	PL
Baker, Dorsey S	139	BOO
———	1:25	HH
———	4:242	SH
———	1 no.11:11	WN
Baker, Edward Dickinson	2:576a	CGO
———	4:312	LH
———	2:114	PMO
———	44 no.3:113	PN
———	178	WRE
Baker, Emma, see		
Galloway, Emma (Baker)		
Baker, Frank	206	BHSS
Baker, Frank C	1:86	PMO
Baker, Frank R	2:200	PHP
———	1895-96:83	SSS
Baker, Frank Whitney	2:275	BHK
———	3:153	BHS
———	3:55	PH
———	50 no.1:2	PN
———	5:202	SH
———	unp.	VU
Baker, George H	1905-06:[49]	RLW
Baker, Horace B	3:731	HHI
Baker, Mrs. Horace B , see		
Baker, Letitia Sarah (Kirby)		
Baker, Howard F	3:625	HHI
Baker, I G	400	LHM
Baker, James	fol.pt.1	SHB
———	1897:104	YB
Baker, John Sherman	2:271	HH
———	3:51	HHT
———	13 no.4:416	MWH
———	5:222	SH
Baker, Lena Tacoma, see		
Johnston, Lena Tacoma (Baker)		
Baker, Letitia Sarah (Kirby)	3:731	HHI
Baker, M	1:216	NH
Baker, Mabel	410	BHSS
Baker, Richard H	3:647	BCF
Baker, Sarah Louisa (Denny)	1:126	HHT
Baker, Thomas T	2:1056	SM
Baker, Valentine Hyde	fol.pt.2	SHB
Baker, W E	431	LDM
Baker, William	1:126	HHT
Baker, Mrs. William, see		
Baker, Sarah Louisa (Denny)		
Balabanoff, Ivan P	3:111	BH
Balch, Anna, see		
Hamilton, Anna (Balch) Stump Morrell		
Balch, Glenn	25:34	PNLA
Balch, John Lewis	3:168	BEA
Balch, John W	221	LDM
Balch, Lafayette	1:63	BH
———	3:132	SH
Balderree, W W	1945-46:85	OO

Baldock, R   H   1945-46:37   OO
Baldwin, Clement J   2:15   SMS
Baldwin, Elias J   261   QT
Baldwin, Mrs. James T   854   SIH
Baldwin, Robert L   front.   BM
Balentine, U   S   1937-38:62   OO
          1939-40:15   OO
———
Balfe, John J   255   GG
Ball, A   Harvey   3:547   HHI
Ball, Henry Maynard   2:191   BCF
          1897:43,124,135   YB
Ball, Jennie (Claflin)   3:838   SMS
Ball, Jesse B   1:484   NH
Ball, Mary, see
   Washington, Mary (Ball)
Ball, Robert John   1941:390   EN
          3:837   SMS
Ball, Mrs. Robert John, see
   Ball, Jennie (Claflin)
Ball, Rose, see
   Ellsworth, Rose (Ball)
Ball, Walter J   4:275   BHK
Ball, William   142   GL
Ball, Mrs. William   113   GL
Ball, William, Jr.   224   GL
Ballaine, John Edmund   6:228   SH
          1895-96:147
Ballantine, James W   413   IHI
Ballantyne, Zechariah   3:1073   FH
Ballard, David W   242   DL
Ballard, Levi W   2:142   NH
          35   PSW
Ballard, William Rankin   2:159   BHK
Ballinger, Harry   1924:129   WSP
Ballinger, Richard Achilles   2:775   BHK
          479   PL
          48 no.3:91   PN
          unp.   SEA
          58   SSP
          unp.   VU
Balmer, Thomas   36:19 1935   WDT
Bane, Louisa E   R   , see
   Bennett, Louisa E   R   (Bane)
Bangs, Benton   393   BHSS
Bangs, Nathan   26   AC
Banks, John   410   FF
Banks, L   A   107   AG
Bannick, C   G   14, 59   SSP
Banning, Phineas T   261   QT
Bannock, Julia   9   SPI
Bannon, Patrick J   2:861   LHC
Baranoff, Alexander Andrevitch   front.   AN
          43   BET
          278-279   HU
Barber, A   W   147, 158   PL
Barber, John Manning   3:1475   SM
Barcelo, Peter   221, 364   PI
          432   PIW

Barclay, Forbes   1:667   LHC
Barclay, Mrs. Forbes, see
   Barclay, Maria (Pambrun)
Barclay, George Neville   fol.pt.1   SHB
Barclay, Maria (Pambrun)   1:422   PMO
Barclay, R   Proctor   2:390   SMS
Barge, B   F   1895-96:83   SSS
Barkdull, Stewart   3:134   BEA
Barker, Burt Brown   66:342   OHQ
Barker, Rosa Viola, see
   Beall, Rosa Viola (Barker)
Barker, Samuel, Jr.   2:1277   SM
Barker, Simon B   2:471   LHC
Barker, William Morris   31   JP
Barkhousen, H   S   419   JNT
Barkhousen, Mrs. H   S   , see
   Barkhousen, Julia
Barkhousen, Julia (daughter of Chief
   Sehome)   419   JNT
Barkhuff, W   D   204   BHSS
Barkley, Charles William   6 no.1:32   BCH
Barkley, Henry L   1895:111   OO
Barkley, Robert   3:14 1925   BCHA
Barlow, Orin Watts   3:441   HHT
Barlow, Samuel Kimbrough   1:324   NH
Barnaby, Joseph Robert   2:665   BHK
Barnard, A   W   373   LHM
Barnard, Francis Jones   66   KB
          fol. title page   SHB
          1897:42   YB
Barnard, Frank   287   BHSS
Barnard, Frank J   255   BHSS
Barnard, H   G   1911:70-71   YB
Barnard, James   3:681   HHI
Barnard, William Edward   18-19   GA
Barnes, Charles   79   GL
Barnes, Clarence L   219   BHSS
Barnes, Ellis W   1935-36:51   OO
          1937-38:62-63   OO
Barnes, Erle J   1 no.6:27   WN
Barnes, Frank Grant   3:173   LHC
Barnes, John Piper   2:968   SM
Barnes, Joseph I   848   SIH
Barnes, Pierre   2:579   BHK
Barnes, Silas Parker   54   GL
Barnet, E   J   41   MG
Barnett, Charles Clinton   1941:106   EN
          3:63   PH
Barnett, Eugene   29   LT
Barney, Harriet, see
   Young, Harriet (Barney)
Barnhart, T   C   41   MG
Barnston, J   G   2:337   BCF
Barnum, Emeline, see
   Robinson, Emeline (Barnum)
Barnum, Ward   206   BHSS
Barr, Eric L   50:23 1949   WDT

Barr, Mary Jane, see
    Beezley, Mary Jane (Barr)
Barr, Sarah Elizabeth, see
    Aram, Sarah Elizabeth (Barr)
Barrell, Joseph   2:88   LH
Barret, Anthony H   165   LHM
                                 4:148   MC
Barrett, Alice E   (Cook) 2:900-901   SM
Barrett, Charles A   2:622   NH
Barrett, George J   2:443   PMO
Barrett, J   F   2:501   LHC
Barrett, Martin   2:900-901   SM
Barrett, Mrs. Martin, see
    Barrett, Alice E   (Cook)
Barrie, Robert   170   GV
Barrington, Edward, Sr.   54   LDM
Barrington, Edward M   357   LDM
Barrington, Edward J   247   GG
Barron, James Thomas   3:89   GP
Barry, Alex G   1945-46:85   OO
Bartell, Jeff   42   LT
Bartle, Philip J   2:507   CHW
Bartlett,   (Captain)   163   LDM
Bartlett, E   L   169   BET
Bartlett, Ellen D   , see
    Bacon, Ellen D   (Bartlett)
Bartlett, F   A   1905-06:[57]   RLW
Bartley, Paris B   3:682   SMS
Barton, E   M   277   IHI
Barton, Ira David Sankey   4:535   BCF
Barton, Tirzah, see
    McMillen, Tirzah (Barton)
Bash, Mary I   36:25 1935   WDT
Bashford, James O   1910:33   TDL
Bassett, George W   1905-06:[79]   RLW
Bassett, J   D   1905-06:[65]   RLW
                                 [117]   RLX
Bassett, Wilbur F   264   DD
                                 166   DSW
Bast, Beatrice, see
    Broesamle, Beatrice (Bast)
Bast, Casper   3:263   HWW
Bast, Celia   3:263   HWW
Bast, Clara   3:263   HWW
Bast, Ellen, see
    Diggs, Ellen (Bast)
Bast, Frances   3:263   HWW
Bast, Genevieve   3:263   HWW
Bast, John H   3:263   HWW
Bast, Mrs. John H   , see
    Bast, May O   (Russell)
Bast, May O   (Russell) 3:263   HWW
Bast, Mildred   3:263   HWW
Bast, Theresa   3:263   HWW
Basye, John F   T   3:565   HHI
Basye, Mrs. John F   T   , see
    Basye, Mary Albertine (Brown)
Basye, Mary Albertine (Brown) 3:565   HHI

Bate, Mark   2:front.1924   BCHA
                                 74   KB
Bateman, Myron Thomas   1943:219   ENC
Batens, Francis X   370   PI
                                 442   PIW
Bates, Annie   110-111   HCM
Bates, Charles O   194   E
                                 3:451   HHT
                                 1917:front.   WSP
Bates, E   G   3:643   LHC
Bates, Nancy, see
    Atkinson, Nancy (Bates)
Battle, Alfred   2:919   BHK
                                 3:51   BHS
                                 1924:145   WSP
Battleson, Benjamin W   2:111   CHW
Bauer, Harry C   18:9   PNLA
                                 50:22 1949   WDT
Bauer, Julia H   78   BE
Baughman, E   G   271   LDM
Baughman, E   W   34   LDM
Baum, Frank M   1895-96:115   SSS
Baxter, Chauncey L   1924:81   WSP
Baxter, Ernest C   2:592   SMS
Baxter, Fred Hudson   3:589   BHK
Baxter, James   558   IHI
Baxter, Portus   3:159   BHS
Baxter, Sutcliffe   3:515   BHS
Baxter, Truman Smith   4:155   BCF
Bayley, Elizabeth (Harpole) 1:512   NH
Bayley, J   R   1:512   NH
Bayley, Mrs. J   R   , see
    Bayley, Elizabeth (Harpole)
Baylis, William   4:281   BCF
Bayne, Stephen Fielding   45   JP
Beach, Elizur   4:68   MC
                                 5:329   MC
Beach, Jarvis Varnel   2:621   LHC
Beach, S   C   1895:93   OO
Beach, W   G   243   BHSS
Beach, William M   [124]   RLX
Beachley, Mrs. Kate C   6:410-411   MC
Beachley, William P   6:410-411   MC
Beachy, Hill   164   BHSI
Beal, G   W   931   LHM
Beal, Merrill D   3:519   BEA
Beall, Rosa Viola (Barker) 642   LHM
Beall, Thomas J   314, 334   BR
                                 152   DSW
                                 1:117   HHI
                                 38   LC
                                 192   MCO
Beall, William J   643   LHM
Beall, Mrs. William J   , see
    Beall, Rosa Viola (Barker)
Beam, Jennie, see
    Haskins, Jennie (Beam)
Bean, C   W   1895-96:121   SSS

Bean, Charles F   2:1243   SM
Bean, Henry J   1931-32:8   OO
_____   1935-36:34   OO
_____   1937-38:7   OO
_____   1939-40:7   OO
Bean, John   647   MI
Bean, Mary J   , see
   Hayden, Mary J   (Bean)
Bean, Robert Sharp   1:639,641   CHW
   1:28   PMO
Beard, William George   1:408   PHP
Beardsley, Arthur F   2:653   CHW
Beardsley, Mrs. Arthur F   , see
   Beardsley, Cora A   (Miller)
Beardsley, Cora A   (Miller) 2:653   CHW
Beardsley, George O   1924:65   WSP
Bearfighter, Basil   6:432-433   MC
Beary, Samuel L   1:192   PMO
Beasley, George M   2:1116   SM
Beasley, Phoebe, see
   Chapman, Phoebe (Beasley) Dill
Beattie, Archibald Murray   3:503   BCF
Beattie, Frank   127   PSW
Beattie, James H   36   PSW
Beattie, R   Kent   215   BHSS
Beattie, Robert E   fol.pt.2   SHB
Beatty, Edward W   380   GI
   244   SC
Beatty, Henry   104   GI
Beaulieu, Leo V   3:1809   SM
Beaven, Robert   2:335,337   BCF
_____   52   JAC
_____   96   KB
_____   fol.pt.1   SHB
_____   1897:64   YB
_____   1911:70-71   YB
Beaver Dick, see
   Leigh, Richard
Bebb, Charles Herbert   2:353   BHK
_____   3:115   BHS
_____   6:68   SH
_____   1 no.3:23   WN
Bech, George   92   SS
Bechdolt, Adolph Frederick
   1:unp.1900-01   WDT
Bechtold, Frank   3:1686   SM
Beck, Clarence Hunter de, see
   DeBeck, Clarence Hunter
Beck, George Ward de, see
   DeBeck, George Ward
Beck, Jacob   3:551   HWW
Beck, John   262   GL
Beck, Josiah Francis   2:928   SM
Beck, Martha, see
   Elvrum, Martha (Beck)
Beck, T   Romeyn   45   DW
Beck, William   2:283   GP
Beck, William W   48   LS

Becker, Charles   67 no.3:cover,212   OHQ
Becker, Ernest J   255   GG
Becker, Ray   58   LT
_____   59 no.2:90,96   PN
Beckett, Ernest William   4:497   BCF
Beckingham, C   L   59   SSP
Beckley, Henry   1895:76   OO
Beckmann, Florence, see
   Smeed, Florence (Beckmann)
Beckroge, Catherine M   , see
   Cleary, Catherine M   (Beckroge) Elfers
Becktell, W   C   3:283   LHC
Becwar, Andrew J   3:1819   SM
Bedford, Charles   2:384   PHP
Bedford, Clifton C   3:955   FH
Beebe, Albert H   [134]   RLX
Beebe, Charles F   1:574-575   GP
   2:541   LHC
Beecher, Charles McCulloch   4:935   BCF
Beede, John E   536   SIH
Beekman, Benjamin B   1941:5   EN
Beekman, Cornelius C   1:641   CHW
_____   1941:3   EN
Beem, Martin   4:100   MC
Beeman, Rufus H   256   SIH
Beernink, Harry Joseph   4:699   PH
Beers, Alexander   459   AG
Beetham, Edward   4 no.2:86   BCH
Beezley, Joseph   1:464   NH
Beezley, Mrs. Joseph, see
   Beezley, Mary Jane (Barr)
Beezley, Mary Jane (Barr)   1:464   NH
Begbie, Matthew Baillie   2:653   BCF
_____   11 no.1:1   BCH
_____   15 no.1-2:91   BCH
_____   28   KB
_____   38   LCT
_____   22, 25   NF
_____   fol.pt.1   SHB
_____   23   WSE
_____   1897:135   YB
_____   1911:70-71   YB
Beggs, Mrs. S   R   88   AC
Behnsen, Frederick William 1911:70-71   YB
Behrendt, Paul   2:130   SMS
Beidler, J   X   5:210   MC
Belcourt, Georges Antoine   1:138   MCC
Belknap, Leland V   3:615   LHC
Belknap, Webster C   2:253   HH
_____   1895-96:63   SSS
Bell, Augustus V   136-137   SRW
Bell, C   A   1:917   LHC
Bell, Charles E   4:70   MC
Bell, George   fol.pt.2   SHB
Bell, Henry Allyrdice   3:751   BCF
Bell, James E   172   E
Bell, Jane, see
   Coble, Jane (Bell)

Bell, John Colgate   1:200   NH
Bell, Mrs. John Colgate, see
     Bell, Sarah E   (Ward)
Bell, Robert Norman   2:379   HHI
Bell, Samuel   6:330-331   MC
Bell, Sarah E   (Ward)   1:200   NH
Bell, T   H   [121]   RLX
Bell, Tom, see
     Beall, Thomas J
Bell, W   R   130   E
Bell, William D   6:330-331   MC
Bell, William Nathaniel   1:75   BHK
     2:824   BHS
Bellefleur, Irene (Duffy)   2:631   SMS
Bellefleur, W   M   2:631   SMS
Bellefleur, Mrs. W   M   , see
     Bellefleur, Irene (Duffy)
Bellinger, Charles Byron   1:563   CHW
     1:556   GP
     93   PL
     322   SHP
Bellinger, G   C   1945-46:66   OO
Bellinger, Jacob Herkimer   1:295   HH
Belnap, Joseph   3:1098   FH
Belnap, R   Stanton   3:1098   FH
Belshaw, R   E   50:35 1949   WDT
Belt, Harry H   1931-32:8   OO
     1935-36:34   OO
     1937-38:7   OO
     1939-40:7   OO
     1941-42:14   OO
     1943-44:21   OO
     1945-46:33   OO
Belton, Howard C   1939-40:15   OO
     1941-42:62   OO
     1943-44:75   OO
     1945-46:82   OO
Belyea, Harry Allen   3:319   BCF
Bemis, Charles A   2:90-91   EPD
Bemis, Mrs. Charles A   , see
     Bemis, Polly (Nathoy)
Bemis, Polly (Nathoy)   475   BR
     2:90-91   EPD
Benadom, W   O   368   AG
Bender, Charlotte C   (Anderson)
     2:315   HWW
Bender, Frank   2:42   SMS
Bender, John F   2:314   HWW
Bender, Mrs. John F   , see
     Bender, Charlotte C   (Anderson)
Bender, John R   290   BHSS
Bendire, Charles Emil   66:234   OHQ
Bendrodt, J   P   330   LDM
Benedict, Isabella, see
     Robie, Isabella (Benedict)
Benedict, Samuel   464   SIH
Benedicta, Sister   348   PI
Benediktson, Indridi   1943:242   ENC

Benefiel, Edith   207   BHSS
Bengston, O   H   1945-46:85   OO
Benham, Allen R   26:49 1925   WDT
Benjamin, A   O   307   LDM
Benjamin, Edward H   432   PL
Benjamin, Rial   136   AG
Benn, Edmund Burke   1905-06:[63]   RLW
Benn, Samuel   3:407   HWW
     47 no.1:11   PN
     1 no.12:28   WN
Bennet, Howard G   3:688   SMS
Bennett, Alden J   765   MI
Bennett, C   F   375   AG
Bennett, Charles E   1112   SIH
Bennett, Emma, see
     Just, Emma (Bennett)
Bennett, Foster   2:352   PMO
Bennett, George   28:311   OHQ
Bennett, J   E   1931-32:40   OO
Bennett, James Abner   2:238   NH
Bennett, Mrs. James Abner, see
     Bennett, Louisa E   R   (Bane)
Bennett, John James   1:96   FSB
Bennett, Louisa E   R   (Bane)
     2:238   NH
Bennett, Mary E   (Wilburn)
     864   SIH
Bennett, Nelson   1:534   HHT
     3:4   HHT
     2:518   NH
Bennett, Percy J   864   SIH
Bennett, Mrs. Percy J   , see
     Bennett, Mary E   (Wilburn)
Bennett, R   H   C
     1937-38:62-63   OO
Bennett, Robert A   1943-44:77   OO
     1945-46:85   OO
Bennett, Walter E   2:169   SMS
Bennett, William Andrew Cecil
     252   JAC
Bennett, William D   1937-38:62   OO
Bennetts, Benjamin Harvey   1941:269   EN
Bennie, D   J   , Jr.   153   SS
Bennighoff, George F   3:1559   SM
Benson, Annie F   (Newland)   304   SIH
Benson, Benny   156   BET
Benson, Charles D   304   SIH
Benson, Mrs. Charles D   , see
     Benson, Annie F   (Newland)
Benson, Edwin F   1 no.4:259   WM
Benson, Frank W   58   TUR
Benson, Freeland Howe   180   SRW
Benson, H   C   456   AG
Benson, Henry D   4:355   BCF
Benson, Henry Kreitzer   6:31 1906   WDT
Benson, Henry Victor   4:85   BHK
Benson, Sarah, see
     Trimble, Sarah (Benson) Allen

Benson, Simon   2:89   LHC
    66:250   OHQ
Benson, Theodore J   2:237   SMS
Bent, William   88   NL
Benton, Joel R   unp.   HOF
Benton, Sidney S   1:604   NH
Benton, Thomas Hart   1:148   GP
    3:126   LH
    1:476   PMO
    2:222   SH
Bentz, Mrs. Charles   1:154-155   EPD
Bergan, Mrs. Erling, see
    Bergan, Sarah Inez (Cochran)
Bergan, Sarah Inez (Cochran)   2:24   CPD
Berger, Jacob   273   HA
Bering, Vitus   51   CIR
Berkin, John   2:380   SMS
Berkin, William   2:10   SMS
Bermingham, John   53   LDM
Bernard, Reuben F   187   AI
    7   BSC
    10:29 1925-26   IH
Bernards, Hubert   2:436   PMO
Berrett, William T   3:143   BEA
Berry, A   Marcellus   3:601   BHS
Berry, Albert C   3:914   SMS
Berry, Alice H   (Miller)
    4:929   BCF
Berry, Frederick William   2:597   GP
Berry, Mrs. Harry A   , see
    Berry, Alice H   (Miller)
Berry, James A   2:637   HHI
Berry, Rogers W   3:1506   SM
Berry, Samuel H   1905-06:[28]   RLW
Berryman, Clay S   205   E
Bertha, Sister   290   PI
Bertonneau, Louis L   206   E
Bertrand, George J   247   GG
Bertrand, James   7, 40   JNT
Bessette, Charles H   1941:193   EN
Best, Charles Sumner   3:999   BHS
Best, Frank Ellison   4:317   BHK
Best, Mrs. Gertrude D   1 no. 11:19   WN
Best, James A   1935-36:50   OO
    1937-38:62   OO
    1939-40:15   OO
    1941-42:62   OO
    1943-44:75   OO
Best, Oly M   2:369   SMS
Betchard, Frank, Jr.   3:609   BH
Bettinger, A   177   PL
Betz, Jacob   3:255   HHT
Bevans, Daisy B   1937-38:62-63   OO
Beveridge, James   3:271   BCF
Beverly, Hugh   135   MLO
Beverly, John   1:337   HH
Bevington, Thomas Forsythe   6:154   SH
Bewley, Lorinda, see
    Chapman, Lorinda (Bewley)

Bexell, John Andrew   2:681   CHW
Beyerle, Arlen C   3:73   BEA
Beyerle, Tuck, see
    Beyerle, Arlen C
Beynon, William   298   LDM
Bibb, Mary E   (Morris) Longanecker
    544   SIH
Bibb, Robert M   544   SIH
Bibb, Mrs. Robert M   , see
    Bibb, Mary E   (Morris) Longanecker
Bibbins, C   D   207   E
Bibee, George W   43   PL
Bickford, W   C   1935:5   S
    1936:3   S
    1937:3   S
Bickford, Walter Mansur   1941:31   EN
    393   MI
    2:12   SMS
Bickmore, J   Grant   3:15   BEA
Bicknell, Lillian Charlotte, see
    Craner, Lillian Charlotte (Bicknell)
Bicknell, Richard Frederick   2:95   HHI
Biddle, Harriet B   , see
    Campbell, Harriet B   (Biddle)
Bidges, J   T   1895:107   OO
Bidwell, John   52   GR
Biedler, John X   298   BV
    174   SW
Biel, Charlie   1:189   ACR
Bielby, John   248   SIH
Bielenberg, Nicholas J   552   MI
    2:960   SM
Bieri, William G   43 no. 2:136-37   PN
Big Belly   1:206   ACR
Big Ignace, see
    Old Ignace (Flathead Indian)
Big Jennie, see
    Allen, Mrs. Janet
Big Nose, Yakima chief   57   AI
Big Nose George   278-279   KO
Big Thunder, see
    James, Nez Percé chief
Bigelow, Harry A   3:493   BHS
    6:76   SH
Bigelow, I   N   861   HI
Bigelow, Lucy, see
    Young, Lucy (Bigelow)
Biggs, D   E   1895-96:115   SSS
Biggs, M   A   1945-46:93   OO
Biggs, Marion R   355   PL
Bigham, Christine Anna (Kuoni)   621   IHI
Bigham, Samuel W   621   IHI
Bigham, Mrs. Samuel W   , see
    Bigham, Christine Anna (Kuoni)
Bigler, Earle S   unp.   SAA
Biglow, Raymond   195   GG
Bihler, Charles S   1:576   PHP
Biles, John C   4:704   PH
Bilger, William L   1943:127   ENC

Bill, Mr., see
   Ka-koop-et
Billings, Charles W   3:581   HHT
Billings, Frederick   120   BOO
                       400   QT
_____
Billings, William   1:432   NH
Billingsley, J   D   1931-32:40   OO
Billups, John W   160   SIH
Billups, Mrs. John W   , see
   Billups, Rhoda C   (Farmer)
Billups, Rhoda C   (Farmer) 160   SIH
Billy The Kid, see
   McCarty, Henry
Bilyeu, Joseph S   3:1408   SM
Binge, William Frederick Phillip
              1941:134   EN
Bingham, C   E   26:128 1921   WBP
_____   27:97 1922   WBP
_____   35:30 1930   WBP
_____   36:front. 1931   WBP
Bingham, Herbert E   3:853   BCF
Bingham, John   2:253   GP
Bingham, Marion   18:9   PNLA
Binns, S   C   4 no.2:86   BCH
Birch, Arthur N   2:191   BCF
              1897:135   YB
_____
Bird, J   T   39   MG
Bird, James   10:36   MC
Bird, John   1:548   NH
Bird, Mabel M   , see
   Holman, Mabel M   (Bird)
Birds, Samuel B   3:553   BCF
Birnie, James   2:334   LH
_____   1:644   NH
Birrer, Frank P   3:1644   SM
Bishop, Clarence   67:204   OHQ
Bishop, Edgar L   6:416-417   MC
Bishop, Edward K   1 no.8:17   WN
Bishop, John F   5:323   MC
_____   2:890   SM
Bishop, Louis   32   THI
Bishop, William   1905-06:[67]   RLW
Bistline, Francis Marion   3:312   BEA
Bittner, Godfrey E   235   GG
Bixler, Henry S   1:372   HHT
Blaauw, John   129   SS
Black, A   H   2:441   PMO
Black, Frank D   2:249   BHK
_____   unp.   SEA
Black, Henry F   352   SIH
Black, Mrs. Henry F   , see
   Black, Melvina (Hambelton)
Black, James   70:224   OHQ
Black, John H   248   SIH
Black, Leander M   243   LHM
_____   5:315   MC
Black, Melvina (Hambelton) 352   SIH
Black, Robert Grant   3:537   GP

Black, Roy L   2:289   HHI
Black Eagle, Nez Percé chief   136   AI
Blackburn, David O   416   LDM
Blackman, Alanson A   2:454   NH
Blackman, Elhanan   2:454   NH
Blackman, Henry   2:478   NH
Blackman, Hyrcanus   2:454   NH
Blackman, Rollin E   49   PSW
Blackmore, E   A   1905-06:[56]   RLW
_____   [120]   RLX
Blackstock, Mary (Isaac)   4:479   BCF
Blackstock, Robert   4:479   BCF
Blackstock, Mrs. Robert, see
   Blackstock, Mary (Isaac)
Blackstone,   (Captain) 163   LDM
Blackwell, Alice E   (Bliven) 3:83   HHT
Blackwell, William B   3:82   HHT
Blackwell, Mrs. William B   , see
   Blackwell, Alice E   (Bliven)
Blagen, N   J   2:123   HWW
Blain, Leighton E   2:408   CHW
Blain, Mrs. Leighton E   , see
   Blain, Mary (Miller)
Blain, Mary (Miller)   2:409   CHW
Blaine, David Edwards   92   AG
_____   44 no.2:62   PN
_____   47 no.1:6   PN
_____   5:256   SH
Blaine, Elbert F   2:796   BHS
_____   3 no.8:423   PM
_____   5:360   SH
Blaine, Samuel Edward   1941:153   EN
_____   2:650   FH
Blair, Gilbert   fol. pt. 2   SHB
Blair, John L   [101]   RLX
Blair, John W   2:1025   SM
Blair, Wesley A   4:769   BCF
Blake, Henry N   5:253   MC
Blakeley, Charles P   1140   LHM
_____   372   MI
Blakeley, Mrs. Charles P   , see
   Blakeley, Elizabeth (Downing)
Blakeley, Elizabeth (Downing) 1140   LHM
Blakeley, George Clarence   2:209   LHC
Blakely, Dick   2:144-145   EPD
Blaker, A   M   1905-06:[70]   RLW
Blakeslee, George C   208   E
Blakeslee, Glenn B   2:172   SMS
Blakeslee, Mrs. Glenn B   , see
   Blakeslee, May (Trowbridge)
Blakeslee, May (Trowbridge) 2:172   SMS
Blalock, Nelson Gales   2:25   HH
_____   3:691   LHC
_____   1:384   NH
_____   1905-06:[28]   RLW
_____   5:376   SH
Blalock, Yancey C   749   HI
Blanchard, Dean   160   LDM

Blanchard, Jonathan 6:292 MC
Blanchet, Augustine Magloire Alexander
                                        268 EW
_____   3:422 LH
_____   1:40 NH
_____   9 OP
_____   front. OPC
_____   2:164 SH
Blanchet, Francis Norbert 268 EW
_____   1:208-209 GP
_____   3:422 LH
_____   140 MHC
_____   9, 123 OP
_____   front., 12 OPC
_____   1:524 PMO
_____   40 SG
_____   2:164 SH
Bland, Bert 27 LT
Bland, O   C 31 LT
Bland, Robert 2:front. 1924 BCHA
Blandford, H   S 108 BHSS
Blangy, Albert Francis 3:386 PH
Blank, E   L 172-173 HA
Blankenship, James 2:24 CPD
Blankenship, Nancy Louisa (Cochran)
                                        2:24 CPD
Blanshard, Richard 1:510 BCF
_____   2:277 BCF
_____   14 no. 1-2:1, 12 BCH
_____   fol. title page SHB
_____   1897:63 YB
_____   1911:70-71 YB
Blaser, Ernest 3:211 BEA
Blattner, Frank S 3:501 HHT
_____   6:62 SH
_____   May 1907:39 TDL
Blethen, Alden J 3:9 BHS
_____   unp. VU
Blethen, Clarence B 2 no. 1:12 WN
Blewett, John L 184 SIH
Blewett, Mrs. John L   , see
    Blewett, Lily M   (Peer)
Blewett, Lily M   (Peer) 184 SIH
Bliven, Alice E   , see
    Blackwell, Alice E   (Bliven)
Blood, Mrs. James (Piegan Indian) 111 VT
Blossom, Leonora 1:210-211 GP
Blue, Teddy, see
    Abbott, Edward C
Bluhm, Conrad 140 PSW
Blumauer, Mollie (Radelsheimer) 1:306 PMO
Blumauer, Simon 1:306 PMO
_____   2:343 PMO
Blumauer, Mrs. Simon, see
    Blumauer, Mollie (Radelsheimer)
Blumauer, Sol 1:138 PMO
Blyth, David 109 PSW
Blyth, John 2:557 HHI
Blythe, S   F 1:917 LHC

Blythe, Mrs. S   F 1:917 LHC
Boardman, H   L unp. SOU
Boardman, John M 1941:24 EN
Boardman, S   H 1945-46:198 OO
Boarman, Marcus 243 GG
Boatman, Robert Thornton 2:287 SMS
Boatman, Willis 1:149 BH
Boatman, Mrs. Willis 1:149 BH
Bock, Adolf 1943:174 ENC
Bodden, Jacob C 2:199 SMS
Bode, Minnie M 2:273 PMO
Bodisco, Vlademar 278-279 HU
Bodman, Mary H   , see
    Strowbridge, Mary H   (Bodman)
Boecklin, August von, see
    Von Boecklin, August
Boeing, William Edward 1:487 BHK
_____   45 no. 2:41 PN
_____   unp. WD
Boelling, Mary Christiana Lydia, see
    Flavel, Mary Christiana Lydia (Boelling)
Boesmann, Richard 209 E
Boetzkes, Ottilie G 6:28 1906 WDT
Bogan, James 415 LDM
Bogert, J   V 5:315 MC
Boggs, Beaumont 3:14 1925 BCHA
Bogue, John C 3:1249 SMS
Bohler, J   F 319, 473 BHSS
Bohler, Roy 393, 473 BHSS
Boise, Reuben Patrick 66:4 OHQ
_____   82 WRE
Boivin, Harry D 1935-36:51 OO
_____   1937-38:62-63 OO
_____   1939-40:30 OO
_____   1941-42:65 OO
Bole, W   Norman 106 KB
Bolinger, W   A 1905-06:[57] RLW
Boller, Samuel J 3:865 HHI
Bolles, Frederick 134 LDM
Bolton, Frederick E 120-121 GA
_____   26:49 1925 WDT
Bompas, W   C 10 PJ
Bone, Hannah (Slater) 119 GL
Bone, Homer T 53 no. 2:75 PN
Bone, John 339 GL
Bone, Mrs. John, see
    Bone, Hannah (Slater)
Bone, W   H 2:front. 1924 BCHA
Bone, William 194 GL
Boner, William Henry 6:150 SH
Bonham, B   F 1:553 CHW
Bonn, Frederick 429 AG
Bonnell, Charles R 197 PMT
Bonnell, S fol. pt. 2 SHB
Bonner, John W 1941:473 EN
Bonneville, Benjamin Louis Eulalie de
                                        101 BF
_____   74 BHI
_____   74 BHSI

14

_____	2:648	CAFT
_____	65	CIR
_____	98	DSW
_____	3:175	MC
_____	1:88	PH
_____	247	WCS
Bonney, Lyman Walter	2:816	BHS
Bonney, Mary E , see		
Shorey, Mary E (Bonney)		
Bonney, Sherwood	1:125	BH
Bonney, Mrs. Sherwood	2:1227	BH
Bonney, William H , see		
McCarty, Henry		
Bonney, William Pierce	1:front.	BH
	3:727	BH
Bonney, Zaidee E	64	PC
Bonsall, Annie (Botterill)	3:963	BCF
Bonsall, Henry	3:963	BCF
Bonsall, Mrs. Henry, see		
Bonsall, Annie (Botterill)		
Bonson, Lewis Francis	2:113	BCF
	4:11	BCF
Bonson, Robert Forrest	4:603	BCF
Boole, George	unp.	VU
Boomer, A H	76	DL
Boon, Al	1937-38:62-63	OO
Boone, D	393	BHSS
Boone, H M	1905-06:[49]	RLW
	[102]	RLX
Boone, Ralph	393	BHSS
Boone, W E	1:115	HH
Boone, William Judson	2:779	FH
	1:124	FSB
	15:130 1935-36	IH
Boorman, Benjamin J	3:744	SMS
Boose, Arthur	[49]	HN
Booth, George Paton, see		
Booth, John Paton		
Booth, James Henry	372	PL
Booth, Joel C	1931-32:40	OO
	1939-40:15	OO
	1941-42:62	OO
	1943-44:75	OO
	1945-46:82	OO
Booth, John Paton	2:337	BCF
	fol. pt. 1	SHB
	1897:105	YB
	1911:70-71	YB
Booth, Robert A	237	PL
	2:456	PMO
Booth, Robert F	1905-06:[55]	RLW
	[93]	RLX
Boothley, J S	1895:97	OO
Boppell, Charles J	140	PSW
Borah, William Edgar	313	DSW
	1:8	FSB
	3:4	HHI
	375	IHI
	56 no. 1:24	PN

_____	56 no. 4:148, 152	PN
_____	58 no. 3:121, 124	PN
Borde, H	2:front. 1924	BCHA
Bordeaux, Joseph	4:135	BHK
Bordeaux, Thomas	2:64	PHP
Borden, Mary Frances	34 no. 4:46	PNLA
Boren, Carson Dobbins	1:77	BHK
	2:852	BHS
Boren, Louisa, see		
Denny, Louisa (Boren)		
Boren, Mary Ann, see		
Denny, Mary Ann (Boren)		
Borglum, Gutzon	57	IN
_____	59 no. 3:122	PN
Borie, Fanchon	1 no. 5:379	WM
Bories, Emil	2:289	HH
	2:348	PMO
Borland, Earl	60	AL
Borst, Jeremiah W	1:271	BHK
	1:492	NH
Borst, Joseph W	3:165	BHS
Borthwick, Alexander E	3:603	GP
Borup, David Clarence	3:5	BEA
Boscowitz, J	2:293	BCF
Bostock, Hewitt	1897:110	YB
	1911:70-71	YB
Bostwick, May L , see		
Stranahan, May L (Bostwick)		
Boswell, Nathaniel K	276	SW
Botterill, Annie, see		
Bonsall, Annie (Botterill)		
Bottolfsen, Clarence A	17:5	IH
	19:front.	IH
Bottorf, Jacob K	6:424-425	MC
Boucher, Jem	281	MHN
Boucher, Robert Beauchamp	fol. pt. 2	SHB
Boultbee, Herbert N	4:543	BCF
Bound, Margaret, see		
Thorp, Margaret (Bound)		
Bounds, J L	314	BR
Bourget, Ignace	xvi	SG
Bourke, David D	3:549	BCF
Bourne, J B E	3:427	LHC
Bourne, Jonathan	68:212	OHQ
	69:197	OHQ
Bourquin, George M	2:1270	SM
Bousfield, Frederick H	20-21	RA
Boutelle, Henry Moss	58	SRW
Bowden, Angie (Burt)	1:13	D
Bowden, Edmund	3:789	BHK
Bowden, Mrs. Edmund, see		
Bowden, Angie (Burt)		
Bowen, Ozra A	1905-06:[28]	RLW
	1895-96:59	SSS
Bowen, William J	2:425	HH
Bower, James E	3:1131	FH
Bower, Mrs. James E , see		
Bower, Sarah (Land)		
Bower, Sarah (Land)	3:1131	FH

Bowerman, Guy Emerson	2:355	HHI
Bowerman, Jay	60	TUR
Bowers, Cy	135	MLO
Bowers, D P	1905-06:[57]	RLW
Bowers, Henry	3:1071	BHS
Bowers, John	20	WOY
Bowker, Martha, see		
Young, Martha (Bowker)		
Bowlby, Wilson	1:256	NH
_____	232	SIH
Bowles, Charles D	2:119	LHC
Bowman, Alonzo Costello	3:245	BHK
	1:223	HH
_____ Bowman, Frank C	3:1052	FH
Bowman, Henry	1:588	NH
Bowman, Joseph Henry	3:93	BCF
Bowman, Maggie (Manual)	189	BR
Bowmer, Angus	34 no. 4:55	PNLA
Bown, Ella M , see		
Cole, Ella M (Bown)		
Bown, Joseph	2:786-787	FH
Bown, Mrs. Joseph, see		
Bown, Temperance Statira (Hall)		
Bown, Statira Temperance (Hall), see		
Bown, Temperance Statira (Hall)		
Bown, Temperance Statira (Hall)		
	2:786-787	FH
Bowser, Mrs. F	2:front. 1924	BCHA
Bowser, Francis	3:119	BCF
Bowser, William John	2:547	BCF
	4:751	BCF
_____	166	JAC
_____	fol. pt. 1	SHB
_____	1911:6-7, 70-71	YB
Boyce, Mrs. A C	2:front. 1924	BCHA
Boyce, B F	fol. pt. 1	SHB
Boyce, Edward	58 no. 1:16	PN
Boyce, Robert W	unp.	VU
Boyd, Albert E	228	HA
Boyd, "Bus", see		
Boyd, R M		
Boyd, George W	68	LDM
Boyd, James W	184	SIH
Boyd, R M	117, 293	KI
Boyd, Robert	68	PSW
Boyd, Thomas M	77	PSW
Boydstun, Neal	3:140	BEA
Boydstun, William Bartlett	3:140	BEA
Boyer, Alfred	872	SIH
Boyer, Mrs. Alfred, see		
Boyer, Ella (Haney)		
Boyer, C O	450	AG
Boyer, Ella (Haney)	872	SIH
Boyle, Candace M , see		
Hartness, Candace M (Boyle)		
Boyle, Catharine, see		
Waterman, Catharine (Boyle)		
Boyle, Daniel	1941:474	EN
Boyle, R L	2:395	HH

Bozeman, John M	2:front.	HBT
Brabant, August Joseph	2:344	MCC
Brabant, F H	3:14 1925	BCHA
Brace, Howard J	3:757	HHI
Brace, John Stewart	3:845	BHS
Brackel, Henry L	6:29 1906	WDT
Brackett, George	1:460	NH
Brackett, Oscar	3:1007	SMS
Brackett, William Henry	1943:51	ENC
Bradbury, C A	1:440	NH
Bradbury, William A	3:1054	FH
Braden, John	2:front. 1924	BCHA
_____	1897:106	YB
Braden, William Robert	fol. pt. 1	SHB
	1911:70-71	YB
Bradford, Donald	15 no. 2:154	MWHN
Bradford, Purlia Cordelia, see		
Womack, Purlia Cordelia (Bradford)		
Bradford, W M	2:233	SMS
Bradley, Abram Lincoln	2:492	SMS
Bradley, C C	1939-40:30	OO
	1941-42:65	OO
Bradley, Cyrus	2:307	HH
Bradley, Henry	1:261	BH
Bradley, James Guy	3:57	BEA
Bradley, James H	unp.	HOF
_____	3:201	MC
_____	1:214	SMS
Bradley, James M	892	SIH
Bradley, James N	2:164	HHT
Bradley, John	1:71	BH
Bradley, Joseph W	36:32 1931	WBP
Bradley, Lawson G	2:181	CHW
Bradley, Lee R	1905-06:[55]	RLW
Bradley, Levi	30	SSP
Bradley, Luther P	2:192	PHP
Bradley, W R	1910:3	TDL
Bradsberry, Frank	[136]	RLX
Bradshaw, Charles M	1:360	NH
Brady, Edward	3:213	BHS
_____	1924:81	WSP
Brady, J A	1072	SIH
Brady, James H	1:front.	FSB
Brady, John G	203	JA
_____	252, 259	PSW
Brady, Phil	1937-38:62-63	OO
_____	1939-40:30	OO
_____	1941-42:65	OO
_____	1943-44:77	OO
_____	1945-46:85	OO
Brady, Thomas J	151, 167	OB
Braffett, Mark	182-183	KO
Brain, Jane Mariah, see		
Vaughn, Jane Mariah (Brain)		
Braman, J D	unp.	SEA
Bramlett, Sanford	314	BR
Brand, James T	1941-42:14	OO
_____	1945-46:33	OO

16

Branin, Alvertis	2:416	PHP	Brickell, E J	2:133	HH
Brannan, Joseph	2:178	NH	Bridge, Albert W	3:215	BH
Branson, I N	unp.	SOU	Bridger, Anna (Nicholson)	2:873	HHI
Branstetter, Joseph	202	HIT	Bridger, James	92	AM
Brantly, Theodore	4:109	MC	_____	59	BHI
	6:386	MC	_____	140	DW
Brasier, Robert T	6:382-383	MC	_____	1:566	FH
Bratt, E C	1905-06:[46]	RLW	_____	55	FM
_____	[96]	RLX	_____	1:44	GP
Brauti, Erling L	1941-42:63	OO	_____	16	GR
Bray, A F	561	MI	_____	2:207	HBT
Bray, Benjamin C	2:829	FH	_____	3:181	MC
Bray, Mrs. Benjamin C , see			_____	1:115	SMS
Bray, Frances (Hopkins)			Bridger, John A	2:873	HHI
Bray, Charles H	2:1272	SM	Bridger, Mrs. John A , see		
Bray, Frances (Hopkins)	2:829	FH	Bridger, Anna (Nicholson)		
Bray, J W	3:287	BH	Bridges, J B	1923:16	WSP
Bray, Matt	234	FF	Bridges, Robert	2:877	BHK
Brayman, Mason	60 no.2:80	PN	_____	57 no.4:155	PN
Braymer, A A	2:842	BHS	_____	40	SA
Brazeau, S D	37	MG	Briggs, Albert	1:88	NH
Brechbill, John M	2:1106	SM	Briggs, Azer R	284	GL
Breck, John Malcolm, Jr.	1:198	PMO	Briggs, Benjamin F	3:133	BHS
Breck, John Malcolm, Sr.	94	LDM	Briggs, Burdice J	3:1063	FH
	1:188	PMO	_____	382	IHI
Breckenridge, Catherine, see			_____	1924:41	WSP
Randolph, Catherine (Breckenridge)			Briggs, E D	2:429	PMO
Breckenridge, Loyal Leverton 3:77		BEA	Briggs, Harry C	3:439	BCF
Breckon, William F	3:925	FH	Briggs, Samuel	81	GL
Bredes, Flora A , see			Briggs, Thomas L	2:267	BCF
Walker, Flora A (Bredes)			Briggs, Wallace W	1 no.1:9	WN
Breedlove, John C	3:337	HHT	_____	1 no.6:10	WN
Breen, Martin J	151, 159	OB	Briggs, William Irving	fol.pt.2	SHB
Bremer, William	4:95	BHK	Brigham, Mrs. E F , see		
Bremmer, Fred	232	BR	Brigham, Sarah Elizabeth (Adams)		
Bremner, G A	32	JNT	Brigham, Sarah Elizabeth (Adams)		
Brengman, John P	884	SIH		1:242	PMO
Brennan, William H	2:352	SMS	Brighouse, Samuel	2:431	BCF
Brennen, W J	3:822	SMS	_____	4:343	BCF
Brenner, J J	3:479	HWW	_____	112	KB
Brents, Thomas Hurley	5:306	SH	Bright, John B	3:35	BCF
Brevig, E P	43 no.2:137	PN	Bright, S A	115	AG
Brew, Chartres	2:191	BCF	Brinckerhoff, H	242	LDM
	14 no.1-2:63	BCH	Brining, John	3:147	PH
_____	86	HEH	Brinton, Caleb	58	BR
_____	70	RA	Brinton, Wilmer B	3:381	BHK
_____	1897:135	YB	Brislawn, Joseph W	43 no.1:17	PN
Brewer, Henry Bridgman	29:288	OHQ	Bristol, William Coleman	2:377	GP
Brewer, J F	2:121	HH	_____	271	PL
Brewer, L V	3:215	BHK	Bristow, Elijah	1:363	CHW
Brewer, Thomas Howard	136-137	SRW	Bristow, Mrs. M J	1:120	NH
Brewitt, Herbert	May 1907:68	TDL	Brittain, J C	215	LDM
Brewster, Harlan Carey	179	JAC	Broadbent, Eliza Ann, see		
	1911:70-71	YB	Fjeld, Eliza Ann (Broadbent)		
Brewster, Horace	1:48	ACR	Broadbent, Joseph	227, 276	GL
Brewster, James Raleigh	4:529	PH	Broadbent, Mrs. Joseph, see		
Breyman, Arthur H	3:324	GP	Broadbent, Sarah (Dixon)		
Brice, Pat	191	BR	Broadbent, Sarah (Dixon)	120	GL

Broadbrooks, Clarence E 3:941 SMS
Broadwater, Charles A front. MI
Brodbeck, L C 4:491 PH
Brodie, D A 202 BHSS
Brodie, James 3:1571 SM
Broesamle, Mrs. Albert P , see
  Broesamle, Beatrice (Bast)
Broesamle, Beatrice (Bast) 3:263 HWW
Bronaugh, Earl C 1931-32:41 OO
Bronaugh, Earl C , Jr. 2:113 GP
Bronaugh, Earl C , Sr. 2:183 GP
  548 SHP
Broncho, Daniel 386 BF
Brondel, John Baptist front.,364,366 PI
  424,432,436 PIW
Bronelson, Anna, see
  Worlton, Anna (Bronelson)
Brong, Elias 2:335 GP
Bronn, Fred W 1945-46:93 OO
Bronson, Adolph 3:629 BHK
Bronson, Ira 1910:116 WSP
Bronson, W E 1905-06:[47] RLW
Brooke, E G 4:83 MC
Brooke, George Smith 2:470 NH
  6:30 SH
  8:104 1903 WBP
Brookes, A M 2:660 NH
Brookes, James 4:677 BCF
Brooks, Alfred Hulse fol.207 SHI
Brooks, B F 401 AG
Brooks, Bert 393 BHSS
Brooks, John E 1:544 NH
Brooks, John W 340 LDM
Brooks, Joseph 3:1120 SMS
Brooks, Nelson B 3:14 PH
  1924:145 WSP
Brooks, William 64:42 OHQ
Brophy, John William 2:427 SMS
Brophy, Patrick J 2:424 SMS
Brophy, T D'Arcy 260 GG
Brophy, Thomas 896 SIH
Brose, Augusta (Domroes) 3:1247 FH
Brose, Robert 3:1247 FH
Brose, Mrs. Robert, see
  Brose, Augusta (Domroes)
Brosnan, Jeremiah 69:118 OHQ
Brosnan, Mrs. Jeremiah, see
  Brosnan, Mary (Gafney)
Brosnan, Mary (Gafney) 69:118 OHQ
Brother Van, see
  Van Orsdel, William Wesley
Brotton, Philip Mina 3:541 BH
Broughton, George 2:611 LHC
Broughton, William Robert 1911:70-71 YB
Brouillet, John Baptist Abraham 268 EW
  3:422 LH
  1:40 NH
  1:524 PMO

  2:164 SH
Brower, W J unp. SOU
Brown, A N [85] RLX
Brown, Amelia Lorene (Spalding) 310 DS
  144 WMW
Brown, Amos 1:661 BHK
  2:756 BHS
  5:238 SH
Brown, Beriah unp. SEA
Brown, C G 1905-06:[51] RLW
  [96] RLX
Brown, Califernia, see
  Charlton, Calla (Brown)
Brown, Carl Elliott 3:11 BEA
Brown, Charlotte (Norrise) 2:475 HH
Brown, Christopher 4:1113 BCF
Brown, Clara 20 RO
Brown, Clarissa (Browning) 1:380 NH
Brown, Mrs. Clark, see
  Brown, Tabitha (Moffett)
Brown, Clifford W 2:565 CHW
Brown, David E 3:59 BCF
Brown, Edwin Jay 3:109 BHS
  unp. SEA
  5, 58 SSP
Brown, Eli 2:19 DN
Brown, Elizabeth (Harrison) 1:154-155 EPD
Brown, Ellsworth Lincoln 1895-96:63 SSS
Brown, Francis H 3:1035 BHS
Brown, Fred R 2:51 HWW
Brown, George H 2:465 HH
Brown, Mrs. George H , see
  Brown, Charlotte (Norrise)
Brown, George N 1931-32:8 OO
Brown, H D 400 AG
Brown, Hattie, see
  Adkison, Hattie (Brown)
Brown, Herbert W 3:718 SMS
Brown, Hiram 35 LDM
Brown, Hugh Leeper 1:380 NH
Brown, Mrs. Hugh Leeper, see
  Brown, Clarissa (Browning)
Brown, J 97 DH
Brown, Mrs. J G 2:front.1924 BCHA
Brown, J Henry 1:596 GP
Brown, John 67 GL
Brown, Mrs. John, see
  Brown, Amelia Lorene (Spalding)
Brown, John, Jr. 210 E
Brown, John Cunningham fol. title page SHB
Brown, John George 110-111 HCM
  50 KY
Brown, John Griest 1941:339 EN
Brown, John W 287 LDM
Brown, Jonas W 195 DSW
  2:667 FH
Brown, Kenneth 6:420-421 MC
Brown, Lizzie, see
  Kindred, Lizzie (Brown)

Brown, Lorenzo D	3:177	HHI	Bruncell, Louisa Catharine, see
Brown, Louie	41:154	OHQ	Johnson, Louisa Catharine (Bruncell)
Brown, Loyal P	154	AI	Brundage, Hiram
_____	339	BR	Bruns, Edwin (Eddie)
	1:90-91	EPD	Bryan, Arthur W
Brown, Mary Albertine, see			Bryan, Enoch Albert
Basye, Mary Albertine (Brown)			
Brown, Michael	3:1764	SM	Bryan, Robert Bruce
Brown, Michael Costin	3:1109	BCF	Bryan, Thomas James
Brown, N R	41	MG	Bryan, William
Brown, Newal A	118	GL	Bryan, William J
Brown, Newell Jonathan	185	IHI	Bryan, William Jennings
Brown, Peter E	3:835	HHI	
Brown, Robert	2:257	BCF	Bryant, Frank Millwood
Brown, Mrs. Rollin C , see			Bryant, Harry H
Brown, Elizabeth (Harrison)			Bryant, J C
Brown, Sam H	1931-32:40	OO	Bryant, John M
Brown, Samuel Albert	2:851	LHC	Bryant, Melvin B
Brown, Sarah (Stoddard)	108	GL	Bryant, W J
Brown, Sherman D	269	LDM	Bryden, John
Brown, Tabitha (Moffett)	1:388	GP	Brydone-Jack, William Disbrow
Brown, W M	2:337	BCF	
	97	DH	Brygger, Johan
Brown, Warren Harrington	3:129	BEA	Brymner, George Douglas
Brown, Wesley	1905-06:[54]	RLW	_____
Brown, William Carey	8	BSC	Brymner, James Greenshields
	10:30	IH	Bryon, William
Brown, William Harold	3:625	BCF	Bryson, Dean
Browne, David G	360	MI	Bryson, Edwin R
_____	2:1135	SM	Bryson, Herbert C
	3:954	SMS	Buchanan, D
Browne, George	2:26	HHT	Buchanan, Daniel E
_____	3:21	HHT	Buchanan, J K
	1:496	PHP	Buchanan, James C
	5:162	SH	Buchanan, Richard T
Browne, Guy C	27:97 1922	WBP	Bucholtz, Otto
	31:front.1926	WBP	Buchtel, Joseph
Browne, Hazel	207	BHSS	Buck, Amos
Browne, Irma	207	BHSS	Buck, D W
Browne, J J	255	BHSS	Buck, Lyle M
_____	1:37	HH	Buck, N K
	2:62	NH	Buck, Ole
	1905-06:[28]	RLW	Buck, Mrs. Orville
Browne, James	3:1137	FH	Buck, S J
Browne, Joe A	91	LHM	Buck, Sam R
Brownell, Francis H	1924:96	WSP	Buck, Storey
Brownell, George C	1895:82	OO	Buckalew, Mrs. Garrett, see
_____	367	PL	McCarver, Julia Ann (McCoy) Buckalew
	2:457	PMO	Buckalew, Julia Ann (McCoy), see
Browner, George H	190	LDM	McCarver, Julia Ann (McCoy) Buckalew
Brownfield, Curtis D	161	LDM	Buckingham, Harriet Talcott, see
Browning, Clarissa, see			Clarke, Harriet Talcott (Buckingham)
Brown, Clarissa (Browning)			Buckley, Charles Everett
Bruce, Henry	2:113	BCF	Buckley, Frank Llewelyn
Bruce, James	1:184	NH	Buckley, William B
Bruckhauser, John Peter	1941:191	EN	Bucklin, E F
Bruckman, F A	3:951	LHC	Buckman, Thomas
Brughier, John (Sioux Indian) 166		KY	Bucknam, S W

Right column entries:

Brundage, Hiram	5:323	MC
Bruns, Edwin (Eddie)	283	JNT
Bryan, Arthur W	290	BHSS
Bryan, Enoch Albert	XVI, 483	BHSS
	12	LW
Bryan, Robert Bruce	1908:15	WAP
Bryan, Thomas James	2:1169	SM
Bryan, William	126	HIT
Bryan, William J	36	LDM
Bryan, William Jennings	310	DSW
	175	SCH
Bryant, Frank Millwood	4:577	BCF
Bryant, Harry H	2:600	HHI
Bryant, J C	122	WSE
Bryant, John M	3 no.4:239	BCH
Bryant, Melvin B	2:601	HHI
Bryant, W J	409	LDM
Bryden, John	1897:106	YB
Brydone-Jack, William Disbrow	fol.pt.1	SHB
Brygger, Johan	3:1011	BHS
Brymner, George Douglas	3:85	BCF
	fol.pt.2	SHB
Brymner, James Greenshields	4:573	BCF
Bryon, William	212	DL
Bryson, Dean	1943-44:77	OO
Bryson, Edwin R	2:15	CHW
Bryson, Herbert C	1924:128	WSP
Buchanan, D	1905-06:[28]	RLW
Buchanan, Daniel E	181	LDM
Buchanan, J K	224	PSW
Buchanan, James C	2:627	BHK
Buchanan, Richard T	2:164	HHT
Bucholtz, Otto	439	LDM
Buchtel, Joseph	2:238	NH
Buck, Amos	7:119	MC
Buck, D W	735	LHM
Buck, Lyle M	290	BHSS
Buck, N K	1924:128	WSP
Buck, Ole	278-279	KO
Buck, Mrs. Orville	115	CBC
Buck, S J	357	AG
Buck, Sam R	1924:49	WSP
Buck, Storey	1905-06:[79]	RLW
Buckley, Charles Everett	3:571	BH
Buckley, Frank Llewelyn	fol.pt.2	SHB
Buckley, William B	3:491	HHT
Bucklin, E F	297	LDM
Buckman, Thomas	1895:89	OO
Bucknam, S W	298	LDM

Buckner, Hubbard T	3:769	BHK		Burgeson, Charles F	3:561	HHT
Budd, Ralph	150	LBT		Burgess, Eliza, see		
————	54 no.3:108	PN		Young, Eliza (Burgess)		
————	2 no.1:15	WN		Burgess, Felix	3:1129	FH
Buddle, Edward	195	GG		Burgess, Harrison	74	GL
Budge, Alfred	2:715	FH		Burk, James A	1905-06:[28]	RLW
————	1:172	FSB		Burke, Alonzo Francis James	3:403	PH
Budge, William	3:1303	FH		Burke, Caroline E (McGilvra)	2:9	BHK
————	602	IHI		Burke, George B	1910:2	TDL
Budlong, John	1:372	HHT		Burke, John	3:133	GP
Buffalo Horn (Bannock Indian)	166	KY		Burke, Martha Jane (Canary)	252	BR
Buffelen, John	3:367	BH		————	195	FM
Buffum, Fred G	177	PL		————	328	SW
Bulger, Martin	39	LDM		Burke, Martin	366	JNT
Bulger, William	165	GG		Burke, Mary A (Devlin)	3:75	GP
Bulkley, Charles S	81	WOY		Burke, Thomas	2:front.	BHK
Bull, Moses	1895-96:83	SSS		————	733	HI
Bull, Olof	110	SS		————	3 no.8:426	PM
Bull, Vernon D	1935-36:51	OO		————	5:30	SH
————	1937-38:62-63	OO		————	1 no.3:158	WM
————	1939-40:30	OO		Burke, Mrs. Thomas, see		
————	1941-42:65	OO		Burke, Caroline E (McGilvra)		
————	1943-44:77	OO		Burke, Thomas	3:75	GP
————	1945-46:85	OO		Burke, Mrs. Thomas, see		
Bullard, Bill	234	FF		Burke, Mary A (Devlin)		
Bullard, Charles Jackson	2:869	FH		Burke, W E	1895:109	OO
Bullard, John Gilman	2:619	SMS		————	1931-32:40	OO
Bullard, Massena	327	MI		————	1935-36:50	OO
Bullard, William Mason	147	MI		————	1937-38:62	OO
Bullene, George W	129	LDM		————	1939-40:15	OO
Bullitt, A Scott	3:749	BHK		————	1941-42:62	OO
————	4:431	PH		————	1943-44:75	OO
————	1 no.8:8	WN		————	1945-46:82	OO
Bunce, Fanny	258	FF		Burkhart, Henry W	1:480	PHP
Bunce, Helen	258	FF		Burkhart, Joseph E	6:397	MC
Bundy, O C	696	LHM		Burkhart, William E	3:405	BH
Bunger, Myrtle (Ryan)	1941:172	EN		Burkheimer, Clark M	1924:128	WSP
Bunger, William John	1941:172	EN		Burkheimer, Dean	1924:65	WSP
Bunnell, Charles E	406-407	HU		Burleigh, Andrew Faulk	685	HI
Bunnell, Mrs. Gertrude	31	THI		Burley, Robert M	2:921	LHC
Bunster, Arthur	1897:43	YB		Burmeister, Henry	2:1022	SM
Bunyan, Paul	passim	MT		Burn, William J	177, 241	PL
————	passim	SPB		Burnett, Blanche, see		
————	front.	STPB		Parker, Blanche (Burnett)		
————	passim	TP		Burnett, George H	2:front.	CHW
Buob, Mary	98	RO		————	1:86	PMO
Burbank, Augustus R	2:254	NH		Burnett, James D	1:332	NH
————	unp.	SOU		Burnett, John	1:278	NH
Burbank, Mrs. Augustus R , see				Burnett, Mrs. John, see		
Burbank, Mary E (Eckles)				Burnett, Martha (Hinton)		
Burbank, Eva L	2:250	NH		Burnett, Martha (Hinton)	2:238	NH
Burbank, Mary E (Eckles)	2:250	NH		Burnett, Peter Hardeman	34	GR
Burch, B F	1:184	NH		————	1:723	LHC
Burchett, William John	1941:236	EN		————	141	OP
Burd, Henry A	36:22 1935	WDT		————	124	OPC
————	50:52 1949	WDT		Burningham, Harry M	3:217	BEA
Buren, Michael J	2:533	HHT		Burns, A M	132	LDM
Burge, Andrew J	377	MP		Burns, Charles Y	211	E

Burns, Cyrus R   2:211   HH
Burns, Dominic   fol.pt.2   SHB
Burns, F   J   37   MG
Burns, Frank Leonard   3:1445   SM
Burns, H   C   unp.   SOU
Burns, H   G   20:80 1915   WBP
Burns, Jimmie   58   BR
Burns, Mary, see
    Rankin, Mary (Burns)
Burns, Shipmate, see
    Burns, Jimmie
Burns, William   4:993   BCF
Burnt Charley   1:9   BH
Burpee, Lawrence J   22   LBT
Burr, Hugh   4:393   BCF
Burrell, Martin   fol.pt.1   SHB
                                   1911:70-71   YB
Burrell, Walter Frazar   3:279   GP
Burrows, A   E   125   AG
Burrows, Albert   1895-96:85   SSS
Burrows, Julius Caesar   60 no.3:158   PN
Burt, Angie, see
    Bowden, Angie (Burt)
Burt, C   L   2:953   HHI
Burt, Mrs. C   L   , see
    Burt, S   M   (Guffey)
Burt, George W   3:1544   SM
Burt, S   M   (Guffey) 2:953   HHI
Burton, E   M   2:773   GP
Burton, Georgiana M   , see
    Pittock, Georgiana M   (Burton)
Burton, Helen   1:210-211   GP
Busch, Ernest C   2:88   SMS
Bush, A   S   1895-96:85   SSS
Bush, Asahel   1:415,641   CHW
_____   1:212   NH
_____   58 no.2:70   PN
_____   16   TO
_____   front.,82   WRE
Bush, Barbara A   (Evans) 191   GL
Bush, Edward C   6:442-443   MC
Bush, James H   473   IHI
Bush, Mrs. John, see
    Bush, Barbara A   (Evans)
Bush, Richard L   284   GL
Bushby, Arthur Thomas   2:141   BCF
_____   131   DC
_____   fol. title page   SHB
_____   1897:43,124   YB
Bushby, George Gordon   2:front. 1924   BCHA
_____   fol.pt.2   SHB
Bushman, John   347   GL
Bushman, Mrs. John, see
    Bushman, Lois A   (Smith)
Bushman, Lois A   (Smith) 347   GL
Bushman, Martin   52   GL
Bushman, Martin Benjamin 305, 346 GL
Bushnell, Estella A   , see
    Kellogg, Estella A   (Bushnell)

Bushnell, William E   86   LDM
Busk, Charles W   fol.pt.1   SHB
Buskens, Peter   491   SCH
Buskett, William C   6:52   MC
Bussell, Charles B   3:207   BHS
                                   6:190   SH
Busy Wolf, Crow chief   216, 248   PIW
Butcher, Daniel   6:350   MC
Bute, 3rd Earl of, see
    Stuart, John, 3rd Earl of Bute
Butler, George   117   KI
Butler, Hillory   717   HI
                                   1:500   NH
Butler, Ira F   M   1:524   NH
Butler, J   B   V   2:629   CHW
Butler, J   C   10 no.3:198   BCH
Butler, J   S   1:365   HHI
Butler, James E   330   LDM
Butler, Lewis S   2:99   SMS
Butler, N   F   219   PSW
Butler, N   L   1895:79   OO
Butler, Nicholas Murray   50 no.3:104   PN
Butler, Pierce   254   LBT
Butler, Portia E   , see
    Mulkey, Portia E   (Butler)
Butler, Mrs. R   2:front.1924   BCHA
Butler, Robert   2:113   BCF
Butler, Thomas J   1:365   HHI
Butt, Clarence   2:430   PMO
Buttelmann, John G   3:1400-1401   SM
Buttelmann, Nicholas H   3:1400-1401   SM
Butter, James B   6:442-443   MC
Butter, Mrs. James B   6:438-439   MC
Buxton, Henry   1:496   NH
Buxton, John   2:811   HHI
Buxton, Mrs. John, see
    Buxton, Mary A   (Pond)
Buxton, Mary A   (Pond) 2:811   HHI
Buyken, George H   3:361   BHK
Byer, John H   3:955   BHS
Byerly, Oliver   1905-06:[61]   RLW
                                   [121]   RLX
Byers, Horace Greeley   1:unp. 1900-01   WDT
_____   6:23 1906   WDT
Byers, Ovid Ambrose   92   SRW
Byers, W   D   447   LDM
Byles, Charles N   1:636   NH
Bynon, Allan A   1931-32:41   OO
_____   1935-36:50   OO
Byrne, Gerald E   4:646   PH
Byrne, Harry B   3:1717   SM
Byrom, John   246   AI

                         C

Cade, E   W   3:375   BH

Cade, George E	3:507	BCF
Cade, John B	3:599	BCF
Cady, William P	1937-38:62-63	OO
Caesar, Philip Vanderbilt	1:379	HH
Cage, Milton G	2:654	FH
Cahill, William E	3:151	PH
Cain, Denis	2:257	BCF
Caine, Elmer Ellsworth	3:103	BHS
_____	6:224	SH
_____	unp.	VU
Calamity Jane, see		
Burke, Martha Jane (Canary)		
Calbreath, John F	1895:78	OO
_____	unp.	SOU
Calder, Donald	3:1413	SM
Calder, W L A	2:17	SMS
Calderhead, J H	4:148	MC
Caldwell, Hugh M	50	PIG
_____	unp.	SEA
_____	58	SSP
Caldwell, Samuel	191	JNT
Calhoun, George V	1:336	NH
Calhoun, Henry J	2:242	SMS
Calhoun, James	110-111	HCM
Calhoun, Mrs. James	110-111	HCM
California Jim	front.	BI
Calkins, C C	3 no. 4:308	PM
Calkins, William H	1:121	HH
_____	3 no. 2:213	PM
Callanan, Michael	fol. pt. 1	SHB
_____	1911:70-71	YB
Callaway, James E	789	LHM
Callaway, Ned H	1941-42:65	OO
_____	1943-44:77	OO
_____	1945-46:85	OO
Callicum, Nootka chief	1:128	BCF
Callow, A L	2:175	HH
Callow, William	1895-96:85	SSS
Calvert, J L	1895:91	OO
Calvert, James Henderson	6:132	SH
Calvin, Edward M	6:401	MC
Calvin, Kate	6:386	MC
Cambie, Henry J	184	GI
Cameron, C C	2:605	CHW
Cameron, Cariboo, see		
Cameron, John A		
Cameron, Daniel	633	SIH
Cameron, David	2:653	BCF
_____	fol. pt. 1	SHB
_____	1897:135	YB
_____	1911:70-71	YB
Cameron, Duncan	2:1121	SM
Cameron, Frances	66	MG
Cameron, James Edwin	3:803	LHC
Cameron, Jessie	2:front. 1924	BCHA
Cameron, John A	2:83	BCF
Cameron, Samuel J	[120]	RLX
_____	6:120	SH

Cameron, Solomon	fol. pt. 2	SHB
Cameron, Theodoric	2:452	PMO
Cameron, W G	2:front. 1924	BCHA
Cameron, Mrs. W G	2:front. 1924	BCHA
Cameron, William T	2:441	HWW
Camp, Edgar Boyd	2:1152	SM
Camp, Norman H	42	HIT
Campbell, Alexander Colin	2:178	NH
Campbell, Amasa B	369	IHI
Campbell, C Stuart	4:817	BCF
Campbell, Caroline (Osborn)	3:154	BEA
Campbell, Charles Albert	3:154	BEA
Campbell, Mrs. Charles Albert, see		
Campbell, Caroline (Osborn)		
Campbell, Daniel	2:647	HWW
Campbell, Donald Kenneth	fol. pt. 2	SHB
Campbell, E O	252	PSW
Campbell, Finlay	2:257	BCF
Campbell, Fremont	2:265	HH
_____	13 no. 3:293	MWH
_____	6:116	SH
_____	May 1907:39	TDL
Campbell, Hamilton	1:422	PMO
Campbell, Mrs. Hamilton, see		
Campbell, Harriet B (Biddle)		
Campbell, Harriet B (Biddle)	1:422	PMO
Campbell, Harriet Elizabeth Cook, see		
Young, Harriet Elizabeth Cook (Campbell)		
Campbell, Horace	379	LDM
Campbell, J E	288	LDM
Campbell, J G	1895-96:65	SSS
Campbell, James U	1931-32:8	OO
_____	1935-36:34	OO
_____	1937-38:7	OO
Campbell, John A	2:265	BHK
Campbell, John Bell	3:477	BCF
Campbell, John L	1941:471	EN
Campbell, John S	3:1155	SMS
Campbell, Kathleen	24:272	PNLA
Campbell, Levi N	130	DT
Campbell, Louis D	2:176	PHP
Campbell, Louis L	132	DT
Campbell, Mabel (Lindstadt)	2:345	SMS
Campbell, Mrs. Nigel H , see		
Campbell, Mabel (Lindstadt)		
Campbell, Prince Lucien	2:4	CHW
Campbell, Mrs. Sarah	30	THI
Campbell-Johnston, Ronald Campbell		
_____	3:245	BCF
Campo, Henry	23	BSC
_____	10:45	IH
Campo, Joe, see		
Campo, Henry		
Canaday, H A	1939-40:30	OO
Canary, Martha Jane, see		
Burke, Martha Jane (Canary)		
Canavan, Harold Worsley Ebbs	4:215	BCF
Canby, E R S	1:68	NH

Cane, Captain	43	SPI	
Canestrelli, Philip	160	PI	
Canfield, F A , see			
Heron, F A (Canfield)			
Canfield, Francis Orra	4:1005	BCF	
Canfield, H W	266	BHSS	
_____	1924:96	WSP	
Canfield, Oscar	87	CW	
Canfield, William D	2:60	PMO	
Canfield, Mrs. William D	2:60	PMO	
Cann, A E	401	LDM	
Canney, A J	107	PSW	
Cannon, A M	2:37	HH	
_____	1:148	NH	
_____	4:294	SH	
Cannon, Charles Wesley	15 no.6:656	MWHN	
Cannon, Edward James	6:176	SH	
Cannon, George Q	117	CWW	
Cantwell, J C	1895-96:85	SSS	
Cantwell, John C	fol.207	SHI	
Cantwell, Thomas	167	OB	
Capilano, Joe	58 no.2:96	PN	
Caplice, John	229	LHM	
_____	6:451	MC	
_____	784	MI	
Captain Jack, see			
Kintpuash, Modoc chief			
Captain Jim	302	FF	
Card, Charles Ora	59 no.1:13	PN	
Card, Ernest	May 1907:39	TDL	
Cardiff, Ira D	483	BHSS	
Cardiff, Leonard	3:337	BEA	
Cardoner, Damian	1136	SIH	
Cardwell, B P	1895:107	OO	
Cardwell, Ed	287	BHSS	
Cardwell, Edward	660	MI	
Cardwell, J R	1:352	GP	
Carey, Charles Henry	front.	CHO	
_____	43:front.	OHQ	
Carfrae, William	4 no.2:86	BCH	
Carkeek, Morgan James	2:179	BHK	
Carlin, W P	110-111	HCM	
Carlisle, John Howe	3:309	BCF	
Carlson, Ruth	42:32 1930	WSGP	
Carlson, William H	18:9	PNLA	
_____	26:18	PNLA	
Carlyle, Callie Augusta (Holbrook)			
_____	3:263	HHI	
Carlyle, M W	3:215	HHI	
Carlyle, W H	3:263	HHI	
Carlyle, Mrs. W H , see			
Carlyle, Callie Augusta (Holbrook)			
Carlyon, Philip Henry	[122]	RLX	
_____	1 no.3:8	WN	
Carmack, George	114	BET	
Carmack, Mrs. George, see			
Carmack, Kate			
Carmack, Kate	114	BET	

Carman, Joseph Lincoln	1941:388	EN	
_____	3:123	HHT	
_____	6:74	SH	
Carmony, Fred A	3:1088	SMS	
Carnahan, D T	53	PSW	
Carnahan, Harry A	6:404-405	MC	
Carne, Fred	2:front.1924	BCHA	
Carney, Byron G	1935-36:50	OO	
_____	1937-38:62	OO	
Carnochan, Robert A	2:1229	SM	
Carolan, Thomas W	247	GG	
Caron, Mother	364	PIW	
Carothers, Thomas H	556	SIH	
Carpenter, Charles	2:366	NH	
Carpenter, Frank	4:156	MC	
_____	21:96 1916	WBP	
Carpenter, Horace	46:292	OHQ	
Carpenter, Hubert Vinton	215, 430	BHSS	
_____	1943:12	ENC	
Carpenter, Ida	4:156	MC	
Carpenter, John R	3:121	HHI	
Carpenter, M S	4:100	MC	
Carper, Howard Page	3:379	BCF	
Carr, Anthony	1:98	HHT	
Carr, C G	15	SSP	
Carr, Calvin J	3:691	HHT	
Carr, Edmund	1:207	BHK	
Carr, Elizabeth	2:front.1924	BCHA	
Carr, Elizabeth Holgate, see			
Anderson, Elizabeth Holgate (Carr)			
Carr, Emily	2:front.1924	BCHA	
Carr, Eugene	May 1907:39	TDL	
Carr, Howard	1:98	HHT	
Carr, James Wellington	3:195	PH	
_____	1924:113	WSC	
Carr, Job	1:98	HHT	
_____	157	PMT	
Carr, Mrs. Job, see			
Staley, Mrs. Rebecca (Rittman) Carr			
Carr, John H	475	AG	
Carr, Lucie (Whipple)	1:195	BHK	
_____	1:140	BHS	
_____	1:208	HWW	
Carr, Marietta, see			
Mahon, Marietta (Carr)			
Carr, Mrs. Ossian J , see			
Carr, Lucie (Whipple)			
Carrall, Richard William Weir	96-97	SHL	
_____	1897:42	YB	
Carrey, Brad	2:48-49	EPD	
Carrico, Emerson H	1924:128	WSP	
Carrigan, M J	22	PIG	
Carrigan, Virginia	66	MG	
Carrington, Henry B	2:41	HBT	
Carrington, Herbert D	6:26 1906	WDT	
Carroll, Charles	1:124	D	
Carroll, Harry W	2:695	BHK	
_____	1895-96:122	SSS	

Carroll, James — 1943:210 — ENC
Carroll, James C — 3:195 — BHS
_____ — 150 — LDM
_____ — 56 no.2:69 — PN
Carroll, John D — 908 — SIH
Carroll, John E — unp. — SEA
Carroll, John Patrick — 3:1721 — SM
Carroll, John Valentine — 2:578 — SMS
Carroll, M — 191 — LHM
Carroll, Patrick Pittman — 3:1059 — BHS
Carroll, Thomas — 2:127 — HH
Carroll, Thomas H — 1167 — LHM
Carsner, R J — 1931-32:40 — OO
Carson, Allan G — 1941-42:65 — OO
Carson, Mrs. C — 2:front.1924 — BCHA
Carson, Christopher, see
   Carson, Kit
Carson, Glenn O — 3:485 — BHK
Carson, John — 1:163 — BH
_____ — 1:476 — NH
Carson, John H — 1943-44:75 — OO
_____ — 1945-46:82 — OO
Carson, Joseph K , Jr. — 3:511 — LHC
Carson, Kit — 74 — BHI
_____ — 2:680 — CAFT
_____ — 102 — CIR
_____ — 97 — DSW
Carson, Luella Clay — 1:402-403 — GP
Carstens, Ernest — 3:319 — BHS
Carstens, Thomas — 3:275 — HHT
_____ — 5:398 — SH
Cartee, LaFayette — 192 — DSW
Carter, Clara M — 139 — PJ
Carter, George P — 2:front.1924 — BCHA
Carter, Harriet (Wood) — 278 — GL
Carter, Henry — 285 — LDM
Carter, J E — 2:463 — BCF
Carter, James Perry — 278 — GL
Carter, Mrs. James Perry, see
   Carter, Harriet (Wood)
Carter, John, see
   Maxwell, C L
Carter, Naamah Kendell Jenkins, see
   Young, Naamah Kendell Jenkins (Carter)
Carter, Ross — 34 no.1:28 — PNLA
Carter, Roy E — 1935-36:51 — OO
_____ — 1937-38:62-63 — OO
_____ — 1939-40:30 — OO
_____ — 1941-42:65 — OO
Carter, Thomas — 437 — CHO
_____ — 1:210-211 — GP
Carter, Thomas H — 5:71 — MC
_____ — 181 — MI
_____ — 160 — PIW
_____ — 2:912 — SM
Carter, Tolbert — 1895:78 — OO
Carter, William A — 2:439 — PMO
Carter, William D — 2:front.1924 — BCHA

Carter-Cotton, Francis Lovett
_____ — 1897:106 — YB
_____ — 1911:70-71 — YB
Cartwright, Mrs. C M , see
   Cartwright, Charlotte (Terwilliger) Moffett
Cartwright, Charlotte (Terwilliger) Moffett
_____ — 2:509 — GP
Cartwright, W R — 2:818 — FH
Carty, James — 69:105 — OHQ
Carty, Maria (Curran) — 69:105 — OHQ
Caruana, Joseph M — 11 — CK
_____ — 23 — JJ
Carvalho, Solomon Nunes — 104 — CIR
Carver, Bill — 86-87 — KO
Cary, Alice Elma — 2:541 — CHW
Cary, C B (Taylor) — 1:572 — NH
Cary, Clara (Vaughn) — 2:541 — CHW
Cary, Ed — 2:541 — CHW
Cary, Mrs. Ed, see
   Cary, Clara (Vaughn)
Cary, Miles S — 1:572 — NH
Cary, Mrs. Miles S , see
   Cary, C B (Taylor)
Case, Charles Monodus — 3:351 — BH
Case, Frank E — 3:909 — BHK
Case, Ira H — 1:592 — PHP
Case, John Franklin — 3:1315 — SM
Case, Otto Albert — 4:295 — BHK
Case, Samuel — 2:286 — NH
Casement, J S — 38 — DH
Casey, J E — 187 — PL
Casey, James P — 936 — SIH
Casey, John N — 3:961 — LHC
Casey, John T — 3:413 — BHS
Casey, Thomas L — 47 no.2:39 — PN
Casey, Timothy — 3:1127 — BCF
Cash, Eliza J , see
   Kenedy, Eliza J (Cash) Abernathy
Casimir, Kwantlen chief — 6 — NF
Casorsa, John — unp. — SHB
Cassagranda, Ben — 17 — LT
Cassidy, Butch, see
   Parker, George LeRoy
Cassidy, George, see
   Parker, George LeRoy
Cassidy, Mike — 86-87 — KO
Castleman, I J (Davis) Evans
_____ — 1:488 — NH
Castleman, Philip F — 1:488 — NH
_____ — 1:366 — PMO
Castleman, Mrs. Philip F , see
   Castleman, I J (Davis) Evans
Castleman, Samuel John — 3:179 — BCF
Castner, John K — 2:1076-1077 — SM
Cataldo, Joseph M — 4 — BO
_____ — fol.512 — BUR
_____ — 3 — CK

_____ 2:368-369 EPD
_____ 2:104 FI
_____ 63 GG
_____ 18 JJ
_____ 52, 364 PI
_____ 32, 432 PIW
_____ 9 SCH
_____ front. WJ
Caten, Emma 394-395 MCK
Cates, Mrs. E A 1:584 NH
Cathcart, Isaac 1:43 HH
_____ 1:444 NH
Cation, A M 219 PSW
Catlin, Charles B 6:408-409 MC
Catlin, Mrs. Emma S 6:408-409 MC
Catlin, George 20 AC
_____ 106 CIR
Catlin, James K 6:408-409 MC
Catlin, John 1:632 NH
_____ 1895-96:87 SSS
Catlin, John B 7:117 MC
Catlin, John S 6:408-409 MC
Catlin, Russell 2:73 CHW
Catlin, Thomas W 6:374 MC
Catlin, Truman C 2:143 HHI
Catlin, William E 6:408-409 MC
Catlin-Edwards, Mrs. Mary 6:408-409 MC
Cattanach, George 2:442 PMO
Catterson, T L 41 MG
Caufield, J R 1935-36:51 OO
_____ 1939-40:30 OO
_____ 1941-42:65 OO
Caughran, Josephus D 13 no.3:297 MWH
Cavanah, Frank P 1:84 FSB
Cavanaugh, Fred B 2:655 BHK
Cavanaugh, Samuel 3:225 BHK
Cavanaugh, Thomas H 51 no.4:179 PN
Cavaney, Peter Edward 2:858 FH
_____ 2:58 FSB
_____ 2:361 HHI
Cave, Cecil 290 BHSS
Caven, Thomas Donald fol.pt.1 SHB
_____ 1911:70-71 YB
Cavender, Charles A 1:540 PHP
Cavendish, Thomas 1:236 LH
Cawley, Dan 60 SHO
Cawley, Samuel Arthur 3:629 BCF
_____ 1911:70-71 YB
Cecil, George H 44 no.4:147 PN
Celiast, daughter of Coboway, Clatsop
   chief, see
      Smith, Helen (Indian name: Celiast)
Ceperley, Henry Tracy 3:31 BCF
_____ fol.pt.1 SHB
Cessford, James 2:front.1924 BCHA
Chaboneau (Charbonneau), Mrs. Toussaint, see
      Sacajawea (Shoshone Indian)
Chadsey, G W 2:139 BCF

Chadsey, Mrs. George 2:front.1924 BCHA
Chadsey, Mrs. William 2:front.1924 BCHA
Chadwick, Mary Ann, see
   Hull, Mary Ann (Chadwick)
Chadwick, Stephen F 1924:41 WSP
Chadwick, Stephen Fowler 1:681 CHW
_____ 1:304 NH
_____ 40 TUR
Chadwick, Stephen James 55 no.3:113,116 PN
_____ 1 no.8:8 WN
_____ 1911:106 WSP
_____ 1924:front. WSP
Chadwick, W F 323 LHM
Chadwick, W W 1943-44:77 OO
_____ 1945-46:85 OO
Chaffey, George 321 QT
Chaffin, Elijah 879 LHM
Chaffin, Samuel O 7:122 MC
Challacombe, Nicholas B 3:11 HWW
Chambard, Emma (Allen) 836 SIH
Chambard, Louis 836 SIH
Chambard, Mrs. Louis, see
      Chambard, Emma (Allen)
Chamberlain, Mrs. A E
_____ 1:210-211 GP
Chamberlain, Fred J 48:211 1936 WSGP
Chamberlain, George Earle 1:681 CHW
_____ 335 PL
_____ 51 no.2:54 PN
_____ 56 TUR
Chamberlain, H E 4 no.8:3 C
Chamberlain, Horace Lorenzo 1:100 FSB
Chamberlain, Martin N 50:22 1949 WDT
Chamberlain, P B 78 BE
Chamberlin, Albert Victor 1943:95 ENC
Chamberlin, Ellen Jeannette 1941:85 EN
Chamberlin, Martin L 1:332 NH
Chambers, Andsworth H 1:576 NH
Chambers, Frank Leslie 2:273 CHW
Chambers, H M 390 BHSS
Chambers, Mrs. Mary A 1:404 NH
Chambers, W M 2:175 HH
Chambers, Walter 2:front.1924 BCHA
Chambreau, Edward 70:133 OHQ
Cham-e-sup-um (Yakima Indian) 124 SK
_____ 128 SKA
Champion, Benjamin Hiram 4:757 BCF
Champney, Edouard Frere 6:106 SH
Chandler, George 29 SCC
Chandler, Melissa D , see
      Thayer, Melissa D (Chandler)
Chandler, William M 2:596 NH
Chandler, William P 22 HIT
Chaney, George H 1937-38:62-63 OO
_____ 1939-40:15 OO
Chant, C S B 212, 213 E
Chapin, A B 374 AG
Chapin, George 2:562 HHI

Chapin, Willard Hart	2:299	GP	
Chaplin, Daniel	1:264	NH	
Chapman, C C	1939-40:30	OO	
Chapman, Charles E	304	SIH	
Chapman, Mrs. Charles E , see			
Chapman, Phoebe (Beasley) Dill			
Chapman, Mrs. E L , see			
Chapman, Lorinda (Bewley)			
Chapman, Mrs. Emma J	30	THI	
Chapman, Harra D	2:352	PMO	
Chapman, Horace P	1935:5	S	
	1936:3	S	
	1937:3	S	
Chapman, J A	306	AC	
Chapman, John W	3:1162	FH	
	14	PJ	
Chapman, John William	2:60	SMS	
Chapman, Lorinda (Bewley)	55	CW	
	1:52	NH	
	1:62	PMO	
Chapman, Mary Ann, see			
O'Farrell, Mary Ann (Chapman)			
Chapman, Phoebe (Beasley) Dill	304	SIH	
Chapman, W O	4:411	PH	
	May 1907:39	TDL	
Chapman, William	1:428	NH	
Chapman, William Williams	1:206-207	GP	
	3:219	GP	
	1:64	NH	
	2:331	PMO	
	22	SHP	
Chapman, Winfield S	2:352	PMO	
Chapple, Stanley	50:31 1949	WDT	
Charbonneau, Mrs. Toussaint, see			
Sacajawea (Shoshone Indian)			
Charles II, King of Great Britain and			
Ireland	1:252	LH	
	18	MH	
Charles, Alex	131	JNT	
Charles, C M	3:685	BH	
Charles, Mrs. C M , see			
Charles, Helen (Hill)			
Charles, Fannie G	3:685	BH	
Charles, Helen (Hill)	3:685	BH	
Charles, William	3:19	BCF	
Charley, Bill	41:154	OHQ	
Charlie Shaplish, see			
Whirlwind (Umatilla Indian)			
Charlot, Flathead chief	66	PI	
Charlotte, Sophia, consort of George III,			
King of Great Britain and Ireland	282	MV	
Charlton, A D	1:133	HH	
Charlton, Califernia (Brown), see			
Charlton, Calla (Brown)			
Charlton, Calla (Brown)	973	HIO	
Charlton, Mrs. James, see			
Charlton, Calla (Brown)			
Chase, George	60	SHO	
Chase, Truman A	1939-40:30	OO	
	1941-42:65	OO	

	1943-44:77	OO	
	1945-46:85	OO	
Chastek, Chester John	3:311	PH	
Chatham, 2d Earl of, see			
Pitt, John			
Chatterton, James T	309	LDM	
Chattin, Robert P	3:1033	FH	
Chattin, William Carson	101	AG	
Chauvin, Joseph	2:1177	SM	
Chealander, Godfrey	12, 75	DA	
	1 no. 4:330	WM	
Cheasty, Edward Caamano	5:342	SH	
Chee-che-ka (Cowichan Indian)	47	HF	
Cheek, Harry	293	KI	
Cheesman, Henry	2:78	SMS	
Cheetham, Neal	1895-96:87	SSS	
Cheetsamahoin, see			
Chetzemoka, Clallam chief			
Chemin, Louis Francis	3:775	GP	
Cheney, D Rufus	1943:6	ENC	
Cheney, William H	2:655	SMS	
Cherry, C C	409	LDM	
Cherry, Norene	42:32 1930	WSGP	
Cherry, P J	290	BHSS	
Chesnut, James D	47 no. 4:120	PN	
Chessman, Merle R	1943-44:75	OO	
	1945-46:82	OO	
Chessman, William A	292	MI	
Chetzemoka, Clallam chief	1:76	NH	
	9	WCS	
Chevigny, Hector	383	SCH	
Chew, R S	278-279	HU	
Chilberg, Andrew	3:15	BHS	
	1:181	HH	
	4	SS	
Chilberg, Benjamin A	287	HA	
Chilberg, John Charles	48	SS	
Chilberg, John Edward	May 1907:37	TDL	
	June 1909:30	TDL	
	unp.	VU	
	17:97 1912	WBP	
	1 no. 4:250	WM	
Child, George N	305	GL	
Childs, Amy Allen, see			
Ellison, Amy Allen (Childs)			
Childs, Charles	1939-40:15	OO	
	1941-42:62	OO	
Chilton, Jennie M , see			
Morris, Jennie M (Chilton) Pearce			
Chindgren, H H	1931-32:41	OO	
	1939-40:30	OO	
	1941-42:65	OO	
	1943-44:77	OO	
	1945-46:85	OO	
Chinnock, James T	1931-32:41	OO	
	1935-36:50	OO	
Chirouse, Father	3:240	SH	
Chisholm, Donald	4:65	BCF	
Chittenden, Hiram Martin	1:front.	CAFT	

_____	57 no. 2:75	PN
	38	SA
Choisser, Joe E	3:1003	SMS
Chouteau, Charles	unp.	HOF
	3:201	MC
	1:214	SMS
Chouteau, Jean Pierre	115	CIR
Chouteau, Pierre, see		
Chouteau, Jean Pierre		
Chouteau, Pierre (Cadet)	2:674	CAFT
Chovil, Frederick William	3:311	BH
Chowning, Charles William	3:811	SMS
Christ, Henry	3:545	GP
Christensen, Christian	177	PL
Christensen, Hannah, see		
Jones, Hannah (Christensen)		
Christensen, J P	208	LS
Christensen, Mrs. J P	208	LS
Christensen, Lars	204	SS
Christensen, Mrs. Lars	204	SS
Christensen, Mathilde, see		
Prestbye, Mathilde (Christensen)		
Christian, Joseph	fol. title page	SHB
Christiansen, James	180	LDM
Christiansen, James, Jr.	418	LDM
Christie, Alexander	206	OPC
	xii	SG
Christie, Alexander S	3:1480	SM
Christie, Kenneth	3:1650	SM
Christie, William	1:372	HHT
Christien, Louis	3:835	BCF
Christler, Leonard Jacob	2:640	SMS
Christof, N A	88	SS
Christopher, C J	1924:65	WSP
Christopher, Thomas	6:162	SH
Chumasero, William	325	LHM
	14 no. 1:63	MWH
Church, Daniel W	2:251	HHI
Church, Irving W	3:694	SMS
Church, K Y	291	E
Church, Peronne Hall, see		
North, Peronne Hall (Church)		
Church, Phil E	50:43 1949	WDT
Church, S T	108	LDM
Churchill, Elsa	1 no. 3:168	WM
Churchill, Frederick Arthur	2:121	HH
Churchill, John	34	MH
Clabon, Arthur Bryant	3:529	BCF
Claessens, William	62	PI
	96	PIW
Claflin, Jennie, see		
Ball, Jennie (Claflin)		
Clagett, William H	247	BHSI
	58 no. 4:171	PN
Clah, see		
McKay, Philip (Tsimshian Indian)		
Clair, Harry C , Jr.	2:391	LHC
Clancey, Charles E	171	LDM
Clancy, John	20	WOY
Clancy, William	3:1520	SM
Clapp, Cyrus F	2:550	NH
	1905-06:[42]	RLW
Clapp, Joseph Malcolm	3:469	BHS
Clapperton, J	2:293	BCF
Clark, Ace	393	BHSS
Clark, Adelbert B	2:532	PHP
Clark, Allan	71	IN
Clark, Mrs. Arthur Lawrence, see		
Clark, Ethel Frances (Savage)		
Clark, Bert J	unp.	SOU
Clark, C W	1937-38:62	OO
	1939-40:15	OO
	1941-42:62	OO
Clark, Chase Addison	3:28	BEA
	18:front., 53	IH
Clark, Dan Elbert	57:351	OHQ
	1945-46:173	OO
Clark, David	15	GL
Clark, Mrs. David, see		
Clark, Myra (Williams)		
Clark, Elizabeth C , see		
Kelly, Elizabeth C (Clark)		
Clark, Ethel Frances (Savage)	1:104	HWW
Clark, Everett P	unp.	SAA
Clark, Frances Ellen	1:104	HWW
Clark, Frank	1:245	BH
	1:306	HHT
Clark, Mrs. Frank	1:306	HHT
Clark, Geneva, see		
Evans, Geneva (Clark)		
Clark, H William	1905-06:[66]	RLW
Clark, Henry S	909	LHM
Clark, Mrs. Henry S , see		
Clark, Laura (Roberts)		
Clark, Isaac Alonzo	2:43	HH
Clark, James	28	GL
Clark, Jane (Stevenson)	352	GL
Clark, Jim	176-177	GA
Clark, John Arthur	3:843	BCF
Clark, Joseph Addison	3:28	BEA
Clark, Joseph Kithcart	467	MI
Clark, Laura (Roberts)	908	LHM
Clark, Louis	200	SIH
Clark, Myra (Williams)	26	GL
Clark, Peter F	3:21	HWW
Clark, Ray W	3:555	BH
Clark, Robert S	727	LHM
Clark, Robert William	3:447	BCF
Clark, Samuel K	3:775	HHI
Clark, T J V	1:488	NH
Clark, William	26	AC
	64	AM
	33	BF
	65	BHI
	40	BHSI
	403	BR

_____	1:96	BS
_____	1:54	CAFT
_____	1:288a	CGO
_____	171	CHO
_____	118	CIR
_____	1:34	CP
_____	43	DSW
_____	1:120	FI
_____	16	FW
_____	105	GBS
_____	front.	GE
_____	229	GL
_____	1:54-55	GP
_____	174	LBT
_____	64-65	LCRH
_____	2:134	LH
_____	1:44	LHC
_____	1:287	SH
_____	1:35,79	WT

Clark, Mrs. William, see
   Clark, Jane (Stevenson)
Clark, William (Billy) 153 JNT
Clark, William A 364 MI
Clark, William Andrews 87 LHM
_____ 4:77 MC
_____ 261 QT
_____ 2:854 SM
_____ 1:372 SMS
Clark, William R 139 LDM
Clark, William Spencer 1941:361 EN
Clarke, Charles Henry 3:679 BHK
Clarke, Harriet Talcott (Buckingham)
 1:416 PMO
Clarke, John L 3:13 BEA
Clarke, Malcolm 2:329 MC
 1:238 SM
Clarke, Samuel A 1:front. CP
 1:416 PMO
 2:340 PMO
Clarke, Mrs. Samuel A , see
   Clarke, Harriet Talcott (Buckingham)
Clarke, Susanna Gertrude, see
   Mellon, Susanna Gertrude (Clarke)
Clary, Barbara A , see
   Bailey, Barbara A (Clary)
Clary, Charles 6:140 SH
Clatterbuck, M B 1945-46:61 OO
Claudet, Francis G 2:141 BCF
 2:front.:1924 BCHA
 20, 88 RA
Clausen, Charles W 1905-06:[38] RLW
 [80] RLX
Clausen, F C 2:581 LHC
Clawson, Fannie, see
   Grover, Fannie (Clawson)
Clay, Margaret 27:23 PNLA
Clayberg, John Bertrand 728 MI
Clayson, Charlotte Louise, see
   Snook, Charlotte Louise (Clayson)

Clayton, William front. CWC
Clearman, Fred 134 MLO
Cleary, Beverly 32 no.4:28 PNLA
_____ 33 no.1:26 PNLA
Cleary, Catherine M (Beckroge) Elfers
 450-451 SIH
Cleary, Mrs. Philip, see
   Cleary, Catherine M (Beckroge) Elfers
Cleaver, Charles Henry 3:353 HWW
Cleeton, T J 1895:93 OO
Clegg, Frances A , see
   Pickett, Frances A (Clegg)
Cleland, John Bryson 2:831 LHC
Clem, Jacob 2:453 PMO
Clemens, John 202 BHSS
Clements, Albert I 3:1470 SM
Clements, Edward 375 LDM
Clemes, Art fol. title page SHB
Cleveland, A A 430 BHSS
Click, Orie W 320 SIH
Cliff, Charles Edwin 3:97 BCF
Clifford, John E 2:372 SMS
Clifford, M L May 1907:39 TDL
Clift, David H 24:272 PNLA
Clifton, David 3:1059 BCF
Cline, Charles Edward 1895-96:89 SSS
Cline, Frank Charles 1941:196 EN
Cline, George L 3:427 BH
Cline, V E 1107 LHM
Clinton, Gordon S 24:272 PNLA
_____ unp. SEA
Clinton, Robert Lee 3:1464 SM
Clise, J W unp. VU
Clizer, William A 206 BHSS
Cloes, James W [128] RLX
_____ 1895-96:87 SSS
Clothier, Harrison 1905-06:[28] RLW
Clough, C F 1:205 HH
Clough, William H 196 LDM
Clute, John Stillwell 126 KB
Clyman, James 16 GR
Coal Tyee (Salish Indian) 128 CAA
Coalman, Stephen Davis 60:9 OHQ
Coate, L A 14:112 1909 WBP
Coate, William 1905-06:[60] RLW
Coates, Albert Lindy 3:393 BEA
Coates, Grace Stone 13 no.1:ix F
Coates, Harry 251 LDM
Coates, Sydney N 2:745 BHK
Coatham, William C 3:783 BCF
Coats, Alfred F 5:392 SH
Cobb, Charles Henry 4:525 PH
_____ 5:198 SH
Cobb, Irvin 1:231 ACR
Cobb, John N 26:50 1925 WDT
Coble, Mrs. Charles Edward, see
   Coble, Jane (Bell)
Coble, Jane (Bell) 16 LS

Cobleigh, William 6:394 MC
Coburn, Chester P 273 DSW
    ——— 522 IHI
Cochran, Ann (Lowry) 2:24 CPD
Cochran, Billy 82 NL
Cochran, Edna, see
    McCoy, Edna (Cochran)
Cochran, Edna (Ashby) 2:24 CPD
Cochran, Effie Ruth, see
    Montague, Effie Ruth (Cochran)
Cochran, J A 2:498 NH
Cochran, J Robert 2:24 CPD
Cochran, Mrs. J Robert, see
    Cochran, Edna (Ashby)
Cochran, Jane (Orr) 2:24 CPD
Cochran, Jesse F 2:217 HH
Cochran, John Eakin 1:45-46 CPD
Cochran, Mrs. John Eakin, see
    Cochran, Nancy Emmaline (Pickard)
Cochran, Martha Elizabeth 2:24 CPD
Cochran, Mary Jane, see
    Sheets, Mary Jane (Cochran)
Cochran, Nancy Emmaline (Pickard) 2:24 CPD
Cochran, Nancy Louisa, see
    Blankenship, Nancy Louisa (Cochran)
Cochran, Robert Lusk 2:24 CPD
Cochran, Sarah Inez, see
    Bergan, Sarah Inez (Cochran)
Cochran, Sarah Texanna, see
    Kittrell, Sarah Texanna (Cochran)
Cochran, Sidney Luther 2:24 CPD
Cochran, William L 2:24 CPD
Cochrane, Bell 1:419 BHK
Cochrane, Sarah, see
    Coshaw, Sarah (Cochrane)
Cocking, James Goldsworthy 1943:200 ENC
Cockrill, Vard A 723 LHM
Codd, A N 37 MG
Codd, Ambrose W 235 GG
Codd, James E 247 GG
Codd, Joseph W 235 GG
Codd, Nicholas 1941:406 EN
Cody, William F 309 VT
Coe, Charles 1:911 LHC
Coe, Eugene F 101 LDM
Coe, H C 125 LDM
Coe, Henry Waldo 2:301 LHC
Coe, Lawrence W 50 LDM
Coe, Mrs. Mary 1:911 LHC
Coe, Nathaniel 1:911 LHC
Coe, Mrs. Nathaniel, see
    Coe, Mrs. Mary
Coey, Charles P 1905-06:[28] RLW
Coey, W S 214 E
Coffee, William Buckingham 3:643 BH
Coffey, Alexander Brainard
    1:unp. 1900-01 WDT
Coffey, Elisabeth A , see
    Van Vleet, Elisabeth A (Coffey)

Coffin, Charlotte Irene (Quivey)
    3:462 BEA
Coffin, Franklin Rayle 3:462 BEA
Coffin, Mrs. Franklin Rayle, see
    Coffin, Charlotte Irene (Quivey)
Coffin, Harvard Stanley 1941:409 EN
Coffin, Mrs. Lucinda 1:219 GP
Coffin, Sherman M 3:53 HHI
Coffin, Stephen 437 CHO
    ——— 1:206-207,574-575 GP
    ——— 1:320 NH
    ——— 2:331 PMO
Coffin, Mrs. Stephen, see
    Coffin, Mrs. Lucinda
Coffman, D T 34:54 1929 WBP
Coffman, Harry Canby 1:unp. 1900-01 WDT
    ——— 6:27 1906 WDT
Coffman, Noah B 5:196 SH
    ——— 23:32 1918 WBP
    ——— 24:front.1919 WBP
Coghlan, Arthur J 225 LDM
Cogswell, C A 1895:81 OO
Cogswell, Ira 3:327 HHT
Cogswell, Myron J 3:326 HHT
Cogswell, Sherman T 3:904 SMS
Cohen, Arthur G 1924:64 WSP
Cohen, Benjamin I 1:519 GP
Cohn, Harry 1941:490 EN
Coiner, B W 1:283 HH
Coiner, Charles Warren 3:323 BEA
Coit, Hannah Lawton, see
    Easterbrook, Hannah Lawton (Coit)
Colburn, Gracie 207 BHSS
Coldicutt, Thomas Davis 3:499 BCF
Cole, Clarence 1895:110 OO
Cole, Ella M (Bown) 2:736 FH
Cole, Fern Morton 3:93 BEA
Cole, Fred 439 LDM
Cole, George E 1:49 HH
    ——— 21 MAG
    ——— 30 ME
    ——— 34 no.4:400-401 PN
    ——— [47] RLX
    ——— unp. SE
Cole, Margaret, see
    Stewart, Margaret (Cole)
Cole, Orric 2:736 FH
Cole, Mrs. Orric, see
    Cole, Ella M (Bown)
Colegrove, Frederick Welton
    1:unp.1900-01 WDT
Coleman, Ann, see
    Smith, Ann (Coleman)
Coleman, J A 1926:24 WSP
Coleman, John A 3:1800 SM
Coleman, Lewis 2:982 SM
Coleman, Mrs. Prime, see
    Coleman, Sarah (Thornton)

Coleman, Rebecca, see
    Evans, Rebecca (Coleman)
Coleman, Sarah (Thornton)   352   GL
Coleman, William   2:1028   SM
Coleman, Z   Y   284   E
Coles, Samuel   [131]   RLX
Colkett, W   J   1 no.2:92   WM
Collett, Sylvanus   64   GL
Collier, E   C   14   SSP
Collier, Henry E   3:569   LHC
Collier, John A   3:593   LHC
Collier, William Hoyle   278   LDM
Collin, G   H   1895-96:89   SSS
Collins, D   J   3:279   BH
Collins, Emily, see
    Hunsaker, Emily (Collins)
Collins, Everell Stanton   1943:1   ENC
Collins, Henry W   215   E
Collins, I   S   41   MG
Collins, John   2:49   HH
_____   unp.   SEA
                              5:132   SH
Collins, John A   3:1056   SMS
Collins, John Blatchford   2:1250   SM
Collins, Joseph R   648   SIH
Collins, Josiah   5:394   SH
                              unp.   VU
Collins, Steve Thomas   3:187   BEA
Collins, T   E   4:72   MC
Collins, Thomas M   2:612   SMS
Collister, George   2:827   FH
                              2:28   FSB
Collister, R   421   LDM
Colliver, Samuel Nuel   3:987   BHS
Collyer, Joseph   319   LDM
Collyer, Samuel   1:534   HHT
                              34:132 1929 WBP
Colman, James Manning   6:204   SH
Colman, James Murray   2:49   BHK
_____   1:55   HH
                              333   HI
_____   51   PIG
                              4:236   SH
Colman, Laurence J   3:200   PH
Colnett, James   1:144   BCF
Colson, Samuel   257   LDM
Colt, Cornelius Chapman   2:229   GP
Colton, M   O   155   SS
Coluccio, Larry   3:889   BHK
Colvig, George W   2:447   PMO
Colwell, J   Irving   3:121   BHK
Coman, Edwin Truman   266   BHSS
                              5:228   SH
_____   9:44   WBP
                              10:front.   WBP
_____   20:96   WBP
                              24:80   WBP
Combs, Charles H   1945-46:93   OO

Comeford, J   P   2:290   NH
Comegys, George   1905-06:[28] RLW
Comerford, Mrs. J   A   1:372   HHT
Comfort, George   5:313   MC
Compton, Nolia   42:32 1930   WSGP
Comstock, G   M   15   SSP
Comstock, Ross J   2:101   HHI
Concomly, Chinook chief   1:480   SH
Condit, E   H   1945-46:85   OO
Condit, Elbert N   74   PSW
Condit, J   H   252, 284   PSW
Condon, Edward P   215   GG
Condon, Herbert T   120-121   GA
                              36:24 1935   WDT
                              50:21,23 1949 WDT
Condon, J   R   39   MG
Condon, John J   247   GG
Condon, John Leo   1943:135   ENC
Condon, John T   120-121   GA
                              1:unp. 1900-01 WDT
                              6:27 1906   WDT
                              26:50 1925   WDT
Condon, R   W   1905-06:[48] RLW
_____   [99]   RLX
Condon, Thomas   67:4   OHQ
Condon, William J   261   GG
Condron, John   216   E
                              1:168   FSB
Cone, A   W   1:372   HHT
Cone, Mrs. Belle   1:154-155   EPD
Conger, John S   2:409   CHW
Conger, Mrs. John S   , see
    Conger, Sarah E   (Rickard)
Conger, Sarah E   (Rickard) 2:409   CHW
Congle, John B   1:304   NH
Congleton, J   F   [111]   RLX
Conibear, Hiram B   74-75   GA
                              2 no.6:31   W
Conley, Frank   2:343   SMS
Conley, James   118   BR
Conlon, James   1941:225   EN
Conn, Virgil   1895:92   OO
Connell, E   DeWitt   2:613   GP
                              2:871   LHC
Connell, F   P   [114]   RLX
Connell, Michael J   336   MI
Connelly, Edward M   260   GG
Connelly, Frank B   1941:245   EN
                              2:9   SMS
Conner, Charles R   108   BHSS
Conner, Eddie (Nez Percé Indian) 232   BR
Conner, Francis   62   LDM
Conner, Herbert S   1895-96:117 SSS
Conner, John Thomas   7:219   MC
Conner, Louise Ann   413   JNT
Conner, Patrick E   86   AI
Connick, John T   141   LDM
Connolly, Amelia, see
    Douglas, Amelia (Connolly)

Connor, M Joseph	3:663	GP
Connor, Patrick Edward	276	HCC
Connor, R C	376	LDM
Conover, Joseph B	2:581	HHI
Conrad, C E	400	LHM
Conrad, Chesley T	2:392	PHP
Conrad, Ernest M	50:22 1949	WDT
Conrad, Joseph D	2:970	SM
Conrad, William G	403	LHM
_____	2:994	SM
Conrardy, Lambert	70:323	OHQ
Considine, John W	2 no.1:29	WM
Conte, William R	32 no.3:34	PNLA
Conway, Edmund	10 no.3:198	BCH
Conway, Mike	217	E
Conway, T R	1945-46:44	OO
Cook, Alice E , see		
Barrett, Alice E (Cook)		
Cook, Charles W	5:350	MC
_____	2:949	SM
Cook, Francis H	1:235	HH
_____	2:534	NH
Cook, James	1:105	BCF
_____	2:149	BCF
_____	128	CIR
_____	16	FW
_____	50, 59	GBS
_____	34	GI
_____	1:25	GP
_____	14	GV
_____	3	LDM
_____	1:256	LH
_____	1:96	SH
_____	fol. title page	SHB
_____	1897:17	YB
_____	1911:70-71	YB
Cook, James H	2:183	HBT
Cook, James W	2:73	GP
_____	2:109	LHC
Cook, John W	2:793	HHI
Cook, Mrs. John W , see		
Cook, Laevenia Coffey		
Cook, Joseph	3:153	HHI
Cook, Laevenia Coffey	2:793	HHI
Cook, Mary Anna, see		
Thompson, Mary Anna (Cook)		
Cook, Millie Grace, see		
Tanner, Millie Grace (Cook)		
Cook, Milton L	6:301, 388	MC
Cook, Vining A	6:415	MC
Cook, William T	2:616	NH
Cooke, Charles P	1:268	NH
Cooke, Edwin N	1:356	NH
Cooke, Mrs. Edwin N , see		
Cooke, Eliza (Vandercock)		
Cooke, Eliza (Vandercock)	1:356	NH
Cooke, Jay	1:166	HHT
_____	400	QT

Cooke, Richard Plunkett	3:793	BCF
Cookson, Frank	242	LDM
Cooley, John Diodate	4:305	BHK
Coolidge, C A	44:338	OHQ
Coolidge, Sherman	14	TMP
Coon, Charles Edward	1905-06:[52]	RLW
_____	[84]	RLX
_____	5:230	SH
Coon, L H	1895-96:89	SSS
Coon, Sam	55 no.2:57, 61	PN
Coon, Shirley	36:21 1935	WDT
Coon, T R	1895:109	OO
Cooper, Songhees chief	fol. pt. 1	SHB
Cooper, Jacob Calvin	unp.	SOU
Cooper, James	1897:18	YB
Cooper, John B	3:1109	FH
Cooper, Thomas H	1895:96	OO
Cooper, Walter	77	LHM
_____	5:314	MC
_____	790	MI
_____	2:1012	SM
Cooper, Mrs. Walter	6:325	MC
Coopman, Amat A	366, 376	PI
_____	436, 442	PIW
Cooter, John E	1935-36:51	OO
Cope, F Thomas	3:215	BCF
Coplen, Benjamin Franklin	2:385	HH
Coppedge, William H	3:65	HHI
Copple, Simpson	1:917	LHC
Corbaley, Richard	1:192	NH
Corbett, D G	37	MG
Corbett, Elijah	1:372	PMO
Corbett, Emma (Ott), see		
Ray, Emma (Ott) Corbett		
Corbett, Felix (Nez Perce Indian) 414		DS
Corbett, Harry L	1935-36:50	OO
Corbett, Henry Jagger	2:22	PMO
Corbett, Henry Ladd	2:295	PMO
Corbett, Henry Winslow	447	CHO
_____	1:584-585	GP
_____	2:24	GP
_____	1101	HIO
_____	1:423	LHC
_____	1:416	NH
_____	1:16	PMO
_____	2:336	PMO
_____	58	SHP
Corbin, Daniel Chase	191	BOO
_____	3:172	FI
_____	5:138	SH
Corbould, Gordon Edward	130	KB
Corbus, Jesse	97	DH
Corcoran, Paul	18	HCA
Cordon, Guy	1945-46:13	OO
Cordray, John F	June 1891:481	PM
Corkery, Francis	491	SCH
Corlies, W H R 231		JA
Corlies, Mrs. W H R 231		JA

Corliss, Charles William	3:1065	BHS
Cornelius, Bessie J	, see
   Rudene, Bessie J	(Wallace)
   Cornelius
Cornelius, Charles W	2:437	GP
   	1:428	PMO
Cornelius, Thomas R	1:212	NH
   	66:136	OHQ
Cornell, Daniel I	3:143	HHT
Cornett, Marshall E	1941-42:62	OO
   	1943-44:75	OO
   	1945-46:82	OO
Corning, Dale	32 no.1:25	PNLA
Cornoyer, Narcisse A	1:72	NH
   	70:167	OHQ
Cornwall, Clement Francis	2:281	BCF
   	56	KB
   	fol.pt.1	SHB
   	1897:63	YB
   	1911:70-71	YB
Cornwall, Frederick Temple	fol.pt.2	SHB
Corrigan, Dorothy	30 no. 4:cover	PNLA
   	31:50	PNLA
Corser, Harry Prosper	5	CTL
Corson, G	W	48	LHN
Cort, William C	6:420-421	MC
Cortés, Hernando	1:188	LH
   	1:47	SH
Corwin, Mrs. George A	32 no.1:24	PNLA
Corwin, John W	2:251	SMS
Corwith, John E	23	DH
Cory, Hester A	, see
   Davis, Hester A	(Cory)
Cosgrove, John	119	LDM
Cosgrove, Samuel Goodlove	47	MAG
   	98	ME
   	34 no.4:400-401	PN
   	1905-06:[28,69]	RLW
   	unp.	SE
   	5:232	SH
Coshaw, Oliver Perry	2:19	CHW
   	1:380	NH
Coshaw, Mrs. Oliver Perry, see
   Coshaw, Sarah (Cochrane)
Coshaw, Sarah (Cochrane)	1:380	NH
Coshun, R	H	1924:176	WSP
Cosmos, Amor de, see
   De Cosmos, Amor
Cosper, O	F	1910:43	TDL
Cosper, William Ingold	192	AG
Costello, Michael	4:787	BCF
Costelloe, J	T	2:751	LHC
Cott, Mary van, see
   Young, Mary (Van Cott)
Cotterill, George F	56 no.1:7	PN
   	59 no.4:179	PN
   	[92]	RLX
   	unp.	SEA

   	58	SSP
   	1 no.2:12	WN
Cotton, Miles Penner	3:395	BCF
Couch, John H	437	CHO
   	1:210-211	GP
   	19	LDM
   	3:204	LH
   	1:107	LHC
   	1:64	NH
   	1:6	PMO
   	2:332	PMO
Couch, Thomas	523	MI
   	2:1260	SM
   	2:498	SMS
Coudeyre, Augustus J	3:761	LHC
Couffrand, F	159	OB
Coughanour, William Albert	2:815	FH
   	1:138	FSB
   	2:403	HHI
Coughlin, William J	255	GG
Coulcoultlia, see
   Hirom(?), Kettle chief
Coulter, Samuel	400	SHP
Coulthard, George H	3:1050	FH
Countryman, C	W	41	MG
Coupe, George M	186	LDM
Coupe, Thomas	41	LDM
Courcel, Alphonse de	2:463	BCF
Course, Herbert M	165	PSW
Courtney, Caroline	6:436	MC
Couzens, James	54 no.3:111	PN
Covington, Bob	5:front.	UV
Covington, C	C	2:488	SMS
Covington, L	J	348	AG
Covington, Madeline	48 no.4:140	PN
Cowan, George F	202	BR
   	4:156, 170	MC
   	1:361	SMS
Cowan, Mrs. George F	202	BR
   	4:156	MC
Cowan, Winfield S	3:896	SMS
Cowen, Israel B	196	DSW
   	1064-1065	SIH
   	16	SPI
Cowgill, Ralph P	1945-46:45	OO
Cowles, H	D	1910:3	TDL
Cowley, Agnes	30, 31	DTI
Cowley, Arthur	30, 31	DTI
Cowley, Cazenovia	30, 31	DTI
Cowley, Edith	30, 31	DTI
Cowley, Frederick	30, 31	DTI
Cowley, Grace	30, 31	DTI
Cowley, Henry Thomas	front.,31	DTI
   	2:187	HH
Cowley, Mrs. Henry Thomas, see
   Cowley, Lucy Abigail (Peet)
Cowley, Lucy Abigail (Peet)	VIII, IX	DTI
Cowley, Michael M	265	GG

Name	Ref	Code
_____	1:253	HH
	5:142	SH
Cowley, William M	3:993	BHS
Cowling, Cloah C (Sebastian)	3:222	BEA
Cowling, M Otto	3:222	BEA
Cowling, Mrs. M Otto, see		
Cowling, Cloah C (Sebastian)		
Cox, Azubia Deseret, see		
Hardwick, Azubia Deseret (Cox)		
Cox, Charles	32	THI
Cox, Mrs. Charles	31	THI
Cox, Mrs. Daniel, see		
Cox, Lucy (Smith)		
Cox, Edwin	39	LDM
Cox, J B	2:292	PMO
Cox, John	2:113	BCF
Cox, John G	433	LDM
Cox, Lewis B	1:584-585	GP
Cox, Lucy (Smith)	16	GL
Cox, Ross	16	DU
Cox, Susan Depue, see		
Meldrum, Susan Depue (Cox)		
Cox, William	431	LDM
	1:376	PHP
Cox, William Columbus	2:44	PHP
Crabbe, Mrs. Edwin George, see		
Crabbe, Harriette (Palmer)		
Crabbe, Harriette (Palmer)	1:11	D
Craig, David	1895:110	OO
Craig, E J	135	MLO
Craig, James	2:27	SMS
	176	WOY
Craig, John	6:323	MC
Craig, Sistine, see		
Sistine Craig (Umatilla Indian)		
Craig, William	110	BHSI
	fol.705	JO
Craker, Mary Elizabeth, see		
Donaldson, Mary Elizabeth (Craker)		
Johnston		
Cramer, Ben	3:857	SMS
Cramer, Mrs. Ben, see		
Cramer, Clara (Ducharme)		
Cramer, Clara (Ducharme)	3:856	SMS
Crandall, S A	1905-06:[54]	RLW
Crane, George T	1905-06:[56]	RLW
Crane, Thomas	665	IHI
Craner, George	3:481	HHI
Craner, Mrs. George, see		
Craner, Lillian Charlotte (Bicknell)		
Craner, Lillian Charlotte (Bicknell)	3:481	HHI
Crang, Thomas H	317	LDM
Crate, Edward	1:107	LHC
Craven, R M	37	LHN
Craver, Louis H	1943-44:77	OO
Crawford, Edward F	2:714	FH
Crawford, Frank M	3:235	HHT
Crawford, George H	218	E
Crawford, Jack, see		
Crawford, John		
Crawford, James W	1931-32:40	OO
	1945-46:92	OO
Crawford, John	3:315	PH
Crawford, Mary	215	BR
Crawford, Mazie, see		
Crawford, Mary		
Crawford, Ronald C	5:326	SH
Crawford, Samuel Leroy	583	HI
	5:328	SH
Crawford, Thomas H	1:384	GP
Crazy Bear, see		
Fool Bear, Assiniboine chief		
Crease, Edward Albert	fol.pt.1	SHB
Crease, Henry Pering Pellew	2:191	BCF
	fol. title page	SHB
	1897:124,135	YB
	1911:70-71	YB
Crease, Lindley	2:front.1924	BCHA
	1921:83	WSP
Creel, George Rollin	2:191	SMS
Creighton, Mrs. John C	4:81	PNLA
Crichfield, Fred W	2:721	HHI
Cridge, Edward	fol. title page	SHB
	1897:44	YB
Crim, Peter H	250	LDM
Crimont, Raphael J	181	GG
	366	PI
	436	PIW
Crimp, Mrs. E	2:front.1924	BCHA
Crisler, C B	1943:29	ENC
Crisler, Minnie (King)	1943:29	ENC
Crisler, Vera, see		
Rose, Vera (Crisler)		
Critchfield, Jane W (Wilson)	2:613	HHI
Critchfield, Lewis A	2:613	HHI
Critchfield, Mrs. Lewis A , see		
Critchfield, Jane W (Wilson)		
Crites, Donald A	3:1814	SM
Crittenden, Lyman B	6:334-335	MC
Crittenden, Mrs. Lyman B	6:334-335	MC
Crittenden, Mary G , see		
Davidson, Mary G (Crittenden)		
Crocker, Benjamin David	6:40	SH
Crocker, Charles	80	BOO
	204	QT
Crocket, Charlotte, see		
Gough, Charlotte (Crocket)		
Crocket, Daniel	4 no.2:86	BCH
Crockett, Dave	96	LS
Crockett, O Winfred	185	E
Crockett, Walter, Sr.	1:60	NH
Croft, Edmund	[129]	RLX
Crogan, Mrs. Arthur	2:front.1924	BCHA

Crogstad, Andrew N	186	SS	Cruse, Thomas	4:70	MC
Crogstad, Mrs. Andrew N , see				484	PIW
Crogstad, Wilhelmina Augusta (Jensen)				2:981	SM
Crogstad, Wilhelmina Augusta (Jensen) 187 SS			Crutcher, James I	92	IHI
Crogster, Annette	6:74	PNLA	Cruzen, Alonzo R	2:325	HHI
Crompton, Robert Walter	4:263	BCF	Cryderman, W A	89	MLO
Cromwell, John B	1:474	PHP	Cuddy, G L	270	AG
Cronin, E A 60 no. 3:137, 138		PN	Culbertson, Alexander	1:228	CES
Cronin, John T	255	GG		unp.	HOF
Cronin, William B	231	GG		94	LBT
Crook, George	299	VT		3:201	MC
Crooks, Amelia (Warren)	96	WMW		10:4	MC
Crooks, Joseph	80	WMW		1:214	SMS
Crooks, Mrs. Joseph, see			Culbertson, Mrs. Alexander, see		
Crooks, Amelia (Warren)			Culbertson, Natawista Iksana		
Crooks, Ramsay	1:184	CAFT	Culbertson, Natawista Iksana 98		AM
	1:184	FI		10:8	MC
	1:42-43	GP	Culbertson, William Clifton 3:503		LHC
	2:268	LH	Cullen, (Doctor)	2:368-369	EPD
	1:364	SH	Cullen, Caroline (Stokes)	5:306	MC
Crooks, Warren	80	WMW	Cullen, William E	5:306	MC
Cropsey, Mrs. Myron	32 no. 3:14	PNLA		788	MI
Croquet, Adrian	180	OPC	Cullen, Mrs. William E , see		
Crosby, Alfred	47	LDM	Cullen, Caroline (Stokes)		
Crosby, Bing	388	SCH	Cumberland, Duke of, see		
Crosby, Clanrick	123	LDM	Rupert, Prince		
	1:616	NH	Cumming, Alfred	10:42	MC
Crosby, H R	219	E	Cummings, Allen	2:113	BCF
Crosby, Harry W	3:629	BHS	Cummings, Duncan	2:257	BCF
Crosby, L L	21:160 1916	WBP	Cummings, Hamilton	4:100	MC
Crosby, Nat	1:411	LHC	Cummins, Deseret (Severe)	3:1124	FH
Crosby, Thomas	front., 128	CAA	Cummins, F M	3:1124	FH
	1897:44	YB	Cummins, Mrs. F M , see		
Croson, Carl E	1924:129	WSP	Cummins, Deseret (Severe)		
Cross, Osborne	front.	CM	Cunha, Alfred F	1939-40:30	OO
	preceding p. 1	CMG		1941-42:63	OO
Crosson, Joseph Esler	1943:58	ENC	Cunliffe, Benjamin Armitage 3:469		BCF
Crouch, Charles D	104	LHN	Cunningham, Ambrose J	221	GG
Crouch, Lora	22:19	PNLA	Cunningham, C D	20	LT
Crouch, Samuel James	2:273	SMS		1924:97	WSP
Crow, Emma (Russell)	4:205	BHK	Cunningham, Francis Henry	3:249	BCF
Crow, Herman D	255	BHSS	Cunningham, Fred J	1941:149	EN
Crow, James J	1:219	BHK	Cunningham, James Calvin	6:102	SH
	4:205	BHK	Cunningham, J G	37	MG
	2:142	NH	Cunningham, James G	165	GG
Crow, Mrs. James J , see			Cunningham, R G	378	LDM
Crow, Emma (Russell)			Cunningham, Robert	134	KB
Crow, L C	1895-96:65	SSS	Cunningham, Thomas	2:139	BCF
Crow, Mrs. S E	29	MHS		140	KB
Crowe, Luther E	3:641	GP	Curley (Crow Indian)	302-303	HCM
Crowe, Sanford Johnson	3:353	BCF		4:268	MC
Crowfoot, Blackfoot chief	287	GI		1:352	SMS
Crowley, D J	1905-06:[28]	RLW	Curly, see		
Crowley, Daniel Martin	2:1109	SM	Curley (Crow Indian)		
Crowley, William J	260	GG	Ereaux, Lazare		
Cruikshanks, George	2:front. 1924	BCHA	Currey, George B	65:18	OHQ
Crumley, Alonzo Edmond	1941:304	EN	Currie, Arthur William	4:169	BCF
Cruse, Mary A	5:103	MC		50 no. 3:113	PN

Currie, Dan	174	E
Curry, George	182-183	KO
Curry, George Law	447	CHO
	66:136	OHQ
	24	TUR
Curry, Kid, see		
Logan, Harvey		
Curry, Peter B	1936:3	S
	1937:3	S
	unp.	SAA
Curtis, C J	1895:95	OO
Curtis, Charles D	147	LHM
Curtis, David S	3:127	BCF
Curtis, Edward J	274	DL
Curtis, Edward L	22	HIT
Curtis, Emma Zoller	5:196	MC
Curtis, Frank	3:779	BHK
Curtis, Frank E	400	MI
Curtis, Ivol Ira	53	JP
Curtis, John H	461	LHM
Curtis, Thomas Jenifer	42	HIT
Curtiss, D W	409	LHM
Curtiss, Leon W	1895-96:87	SSS
Curtiss, William M	2:531	BHK
	3:889	BHS
Cusack, John F	391	PL
Cushan, Amos (Salish Indian)	208	CAA
Cushing, John H	380	BF
Cushing, Milo M	1:423	LHC
Cushman, Francis W	5:60	SH
	1899:33	SSS
Cusick, Helena (Nye)	3:852	SMS
Cusick, W A	2:123	CHW
Cusick, William Conklin	57:116	OHQ
Cusick, William M	3:852	SMS
Cusick, Mrs. William M	, see	
Cusick, Helena (Nye)		
Custer, George A	311	AM
	110-111	HCM
	304	VT
Custer, Mrs. George A	110-111	HCM
Custer, Tom W	110-111	HCM
Cuthbert, Mrs. Annie C	6:358	MC
Cuthbert, D H	383	LHM
Cutler, Dorothy	18:9	PNLA
Cutler, Edwin	3:1085	FH
Cutler, M F	447	LDM
Cutler, Oscar	1945-46:204	OO
Cutler, Thomas Robinson	245	GL
Cutlip, Stella A	1943-44:77	OO
Cutting, Otis	4:494	PH
Cutting, S H	1924:97	WSP
Cyriaks, Meta, see		
Lohse, Meta (Cyriaks)		
Czizek, Jay A	582	IHI

D

Dagefoerde, Ernst Henry	3:343	BEA
Daggy, Maynard Lee	6:29 1906	WDT
Dahl, A	88	SS
Dahl, S H	2:477	BHK
Dahlgren, Frank	936	SIH
Dailey, Chester A	1943:177	ENC
Daily, John F	3:584	HHI
Daily, Mrs. John F , see		
Daily, Serena (Davis)		
Daily, Serena (Davis)	3:585	HHI
Dakan, Thomas Wilbur	3:245	BEA
Dale, Edna Valeria	3:364	PH
Dale, James McGeorge	3:811	BCF
Dall, William	51	LDM
Dall, William Healey	fol. 207	SHI
Dallam, Frank M	1905-06:[28]	RLW
Dallas, Mrs. Charles	1:917	LHC
Dallas, H	1897:18	YB
Dalley, Edwin	2:front. 1924	BCHA
Dalley, Mrs. Edwin	2:front. 1924	BCHA
Dallimore, Philip	284	GL
Dalrymple, Alexander	1:116	BCF
Dalton, John A	3:813	HHI
Dalvit, Amel	234	FF
Daly, Edgar J	3:301	LHC
Daly, James H	2:1158	SM
Daly, John D	1895:105	OO
Daly, John H	2:452	PMO
Daly, Peter	195	E
Daly, William A	3:151	GP
Daly, William B	2:446	SMS
Dam, Everett S	3:814	BHS
Dam, Milton E	3:815	BHS
Damiani, Joseph	191, 364, 366	PI
	72, 432, 436	PIW
Dammasch, F H	1943-44:77	OO
Dammeier, George H	2:741	LHC
Dammon, J D	1:516	NH
Damon, John F	148	AG
	240	BE
Daniels, (Captain)	79	BET
Daniels, Charles F	unp.	SOU
Daniels, John W	3:382	BHK
Daniels, John William	1:197	FSB
	486	IHI
Daniels, Mansfield A	3:881	SMS
Daniels, Thurston	1899:129	SSS
Daniels, William	May 1907:38	TDL
Danielson, John A	4:725	PH
Danielson, Mrs. John A , see		
Danielson, Louisa J	(Holderman)	
Danielson, Louisa J	(Holderman)	
	4:725	PH
Danner, John H	836	SIH

Danskin, F B	1924:32	WSP
Danz, George J	3:717	BHS
D'Arcy, Peter H	2:37	CHW
D'Arcy, Will	55 no.3:116	PN
Darknell, Arthur A	884	SIH
Darling, Dan A	220	E
Darling, Glen W	1943:227	ENC
Darling, Henry	377	LDM
Darling, J E	May 1907:68	TDL
Darling, John	284	GL
Darling, Lucia, see		
Park, Lucia (Darling)		
Darrow, Clarence	59 no.1:26	PN
Darrow, E E	206	BHSS
Darrow, Permelia, see		
Lott, Permelia (Darrow)		
Dassonville, J	2:front.1924	BCHA
D'Aste, Jerome	fol.512	BUR
_____	56, 364	PI
_____	72, 432	PIW
Daugherty, Nora K , see		
Sherman, Nora K (Daugherty)		
Dauphinee, Thomas T	3:207	BCF
Daut, John	3:918	SMS
Dauth, Gaspard	1:634	BCF
Davenport, George Lewis	3:779	GP
Davenport, Homer C	66:38	OHQ
_____	1:28	PMO
Davenport, T W	323	PL
Davey, Catherine (Arthur)	3:793	SMS
Davey, Frederick	1911:70-71	YB
Davey, John	3:793	SMS
Davey, Mrs. John, see		
Davey, Catherine (Arthur)		
David, Nez Percé chief	1:57	BEA
David (Indian Dave)	1:672	GP
David, J E	1895:100	OO
Davidson, Annie, see		
Wright, Annie (Davidson)		
Davidson, Dorothy	67	MG
Davidson, Edward M	6:330-331	MC
Davidson, Mrs. Edward M , see		
Davidson, Mary G (Crittenden)		
Davidson, George	93	SHE
_____	fol.207	SHI
Davidson, John	329	LDM
Davidson, John B	3:18	PH
_____	1924:41	WSP
_____	1926:20	WSP
Davidson, Joseph J	6:305	MC
Davidson, Mary G (Crittenden)		
_____	6:334-335	MC
Davie, Alexander	4:173	BCF
Davie, Alexander Edmund Batson	2:451	BCF
_____	4:327	BCF
_____	70	JAC
_____	fol.pt.1	SHB
_____	1897:64	YB
_____	1911:70-71	YB
Davie, J C	1897:42	YB
Davie, Theodore	2:653	BCF
_____	90	JAC
_____	160	KB
_____	fol.pt.1	SHB
_____	1897:64,136	YB
_____	1911:70-71	YB
Davies, D Thomas	1914:137	S
Davies, David B	3:282	PH
Davies, David L	66:292	OHQ
_____	67:204	OHQ
Davies, John F	1 no.1:13	WN
Davies, Josiah S	3:119	BH
Davies, Phil	2:front.1924	BCHA
Davis, Allison	2:1295	SM
Davis, Alphonzo Mitchel	276	GL
Davis, Andrew Jackson	206	MI
Davis, Arthur W	108	BHSS
Davis, Mrs. Benjamin, see		
Davis, Catherine (Sluyter)		
Davis, Catherine (Sluyter)	1:488	NH
Davis, Clark	1:unp.1900-01	WDT
Davis, D J	1905-06:[55]	RLW
_____	[124]	RLX
Davis, David R	720-721	SIH
Davis, David William	2:239	HHI
Davis, E C	20:64 1915	WBP
Davis, Edwin Griffith	2:593	FH
Davis, Elisha Hildebrand	94	GL
Davis, Mrs. Elisha Hildebrand, see		
Davis, Mary Ann (Mitchell)		
Davis, Francis Marion	2:712-713	FH
_____	538	IHI
Davis, Mrs. Francis Marion, see		
Davis, Hester A (Cory)		
Davis, Frank L	3:1070	FH
_____	May 1907:38	TDL
Davis, G W H	1:277	HH
_____	May 1907:39	TDL
Davis, George A	2:338	NH
Davis, George L	1905-06:[67]	RLW
Davis, Harold	33:32 1928	WBP
Davis, Henry	3:51	BCF
Davis, Henry C	2:48	PHP
Davis, Hester A (Cory)	2:712-713	FH
Davis, I J , see		
Castleman, I J (Davis) Evans		
Davis, Irwin F	3:828	SMS
Davis, James H	1:566	BH
_____	74-75	GA
_____	unp.	WD
Davis, James S	1:136	NH
Davis, Jefferson C	311	BN
Davis, John	unp.	VU
Davis, John W	26	TUR
Davis, Julia (McCrum)	2:41	HHI
Davis, Levi	3:1409	SM

Davis, Lincoln   1905-06:[46]   RLW
                           [88]   RLX
————
Davis, Mary Ann (Mitchell) 94   GL
Davis, N   A   43 no.1:16-17 PN
Davis, Mrs. Phil   2:front.1924   BCHA
Davis, R   S   11   MLO
Davis, Robert   277   LDM
Davis, Roland E   356   LDM
Davis, Serena, see
    Daily, Serena (Davis)
Davis, T   H   89   MLO
Davis, Thomas J   48   LS
Davis, Thomas Jefferson   2:40   HHI
Davis, Mrs. Thomas Jefferson, see
    Davis, Julia (McCrum)
Davis, Tom   135   DCW
Davis, William Hatch   27:65 1922   WBP
                           31:32 1926   WBP
————
Davis, William L   2:315   HHT
Davis, William Lyle   260   GG
Davisson, Ira S   1 no.4:11   WN
Dawe, Albert James   4:437   BCF
Dawe, Samuel   4:423   BCF
Dawe, William P   3:1057   FH
Dawes, Joseph H   1905-06:[66]   RLW
Dawes, Willard Crockett   2:317   SMS
Dawson, Andrew   unp.   HOF
                           3:201   MC
————   7:61   MC
————   1:153,214   SMS
Dawson, Benjamin Franklin 3:1580   SM
Dawson, Fred   1937-38:62-63 OO
Dawson, Lewis R   813   HI
Dawson, S   A   1895:77   OO
Dawson, Volney J   2:449   GP
Dawson, William   155   GL
Dawson, William Leon   1 no.2:106   WM
Day, Benjamin F   365   HI
Day, Cassius M   121   AI
Day, E   B   1931-32:41   OO
Day, Edward Cason   4:32   MC
                           2:530   SMS
————
Day, Edwin Mahlon   2:549   HWW
                           2:496   PHP
————
Day, Eugene R   3:445   BEA
Day, George A   2:337   HHI
Day, Harry L   3:445   BEA
Day, Henry Herbert   3:623   BH
Day, Henry Lawrence   3:445   BEA
Day, Henry Loren   3:445   BEA
                           1080   SIH
————
Day, Jerome J   3:445   BEA
Day, Jesse N   1:115   HH
Deady, Lucy A   (Henderson) 2:267   GP
Deady, Matthew Paul   2:544a   CGO
                           1:415,641   CHW
————   1:556   GP
————   2:266   GP

————   349   HIO
————   4:340   LH
————   1:519   LHC
————   1:56   NH
————   1:182   PMO
————   70   SHP
————   226   WRE
Deady, Mrs. Matthew Paul, see
    Deady, Lucy A   (Henderson)
Deal, Edson Hart   3:49   BEA
Dean, M   2:front.1924   BCHA
Dean, Mrs. Max   2:front.1924   BCHA
Dean, W   M   221   E
Deans, Albert   4:177   BCF
Dearborn, H   H   5:242   SH
DeArmon, Esther, see
    Taylor, Esther (DeArmon)
DeBeck, Clarence Hunter   4:19   BCF
DeBeck, George Ward   4:403   BCF
DeBerdt, Esther, see
    Reed, Esther (DeBerdt)
DeCamp, R   H   1:189   ACR
Deckebach, F   G   2:455   HH
                           1895-96:121   SSS
Decker, Clara, see
    Young, Clara (Decker)
Decker, Lucy Ann, see
    Young, Lucy Ann (Decker)
De Cosmos, Amor   2:335   BCF
————   8 no.3:189   BCH
————   16   JAC
————   fol.pt.1   SHB
————   96-97   SHL
————   1897:64   YB
————   1911:70-71   YB
de Courcel, Alphonse, see
    Courcel, Alphonse de
Defenbach, Byron   321   BR
————   18:53 1941-42 IH
Deffenbaugh, George L   198, 231   PSW
De Ford, H   B   222   E
Degen, Joseph   3:617   HHI
DeGrange, McQuilken   6:30 1906   WDT
De Haven, John J   228   PL
De Huff, Peter W   125   LDM
Deich, Frank   1937-38:62-63 OO
————   1939-40:30   OO
————   1943-44:77   OO
DeKoven, Reginald   51 no.2:83   PN
Dekum, Frank   202   SHP
De Lacy, Walter Washington 75   LHM
————   2:241   MC
Delamater, John   45   DW
De la Motte, George   181   GG
Delaney, Matilda J   (Sager) front.   DSR
Delaney, Thomas R   59   SSP
De Lap, Perry   1931-32:41   OO
De Lape, George W   1910:11   TDL

De La Perouse, Jean Francois Galaup, see
    Laperouse, Jean Francois de Galaup,
    Comte de

De Lashmutt, Van B   2:318   NH
                      410   SHP

DeLay, Edith Freelove   1:456   GP

De Lin, Gertrude (Meller)   1:14   HHT
                      155   PMT

De Lin, Grace Alice, see
    Richards, Grace Alice (De Lin)

De Lin, Nicholas   1:14   HHT

De Lin, Mrs. Nicholas, see
    De Lin, Gertrude (Meller)

Delle, Lee C   1924:144   WSP

Dellinger, Daniel N   963   LHM

De Lotbiniere, Henri Joli, see
    Lotbiniere, Henri Gustave Joly de

Delsol, Louis   334   BR

Demars, Joseph   3:757   SMS

De Mazenod, Charles J E , see
    Mazenod, Charles J E de

Dement, Ellis S   63:9   OHQ

Dement, Lucy E , see
    Keller, Lucy E (Dement)

De Mers, Elzeor   3:888   SMS

Demers, Modeste   2:605   BCF
                  268   EW
                  3:422   LH
                  2:284   MCC
                  152   MHC
                  232   MHN
                  1:40   NH
                  9   OP
                  front.   OPC
                  1:524   PMO
                  2:164   SH
              fol. title page   SHB
                  1897:44   YB

De Mers, Robert J   3:866   SMS

Demers, Rudolph   243   GG

Deming, A W   1 no.1:11   WN

Deming, E B   1 no.11:15   WN

Dempsey, C C   223   E

Denig, Edwin T   10:110   MC

Denison, J M   128   AG

Denison, John N   165   AG

Denman, A H   2:98   HHT

Dennett, Fred   481   PL

Denney, John C   1:241   HH

Denning, James   3:787   HHI

Dennis, Graham Barclay   2:301   HH
                  6:134   SH

Denny, Arthur Armstrong   1:63   BHK
                  2:19   BHK
                  1:426   BHS
                  18-19   GA
                  1:536   NH
                  2:front.   PHP
                  52 no.2:65   PN
                  3:498   SH

Denny, Mrs. Arthur Armstrong, see
    Denny, Mary Ann (Boren)

Denny, David Thomas   1:67   BHK
                  2:704   BHS
                  2:217   HH
                  1:536   NH

Denny, Mrs. David Thomas, see
    Denny, Louisa (Boren)

Denny, Gertrude (Hall)   103   CW
                  1:52   NH
                  65:258   OHQ
                  1:62   PMO

Denny, John B   2:217   HH

Denny, Louisa (Boren)   1:536   NH

Denny, Louisa C , see
    Frye, Louisa C (Denny)

Denny, Mary Ann (Boren)   2:23   BHK
                  1:536   NH

Denny, Oliver N , see
    Denny, Owen Nickerson

Denny, Owen Nickerson   3:745   GP
                  65:230,258   OHQ
                  1895:86   OO
                  1:22   PMO

Denny, Mrs. Owen Nickerson, see
    Denny, Gertrude (Hall)

Denny, Sarah Louisa, see
    Baker, Sarah Louisa (Denny)

Densmore, H B   50:39 1949   WDT

Dent, Frederick   31   DH

Dent, Hawthorne K   1 no.11:17   WN

Denton, Arthur P   52   PIG

Denver, James W   7:46   MC

DePencier, Adam Urias, see
    Pencier, Adam Urias de

Depew, Edward E   224   E

De Pledge, H G   1:313   HH

Deputee, George T   3:1035   SMS

Derbyshire, Sarah A , see
    Palmer, Sarah A (Derbyshire)

Derrickson, D K   196   E

De Ryckere, Remigius   298,364,366   PI
                  340,432,436   PIW

Deschamps, Gaspard   2:1036   SM

Des Combes, Henry L   2:945   SM

De Siere, Peter   302, 366   PI
                  340, 436   PIW
                  3:1359   SM

De Smet, Peter, see
    Smet, Pierre Jean de

De Smet, Pierre Jean, see
    Smet, Pierre Jean de

DeSoto, Alexander   156   AG

De Spain, Jeremiah   2:242   NH

Deuel, Halbert S   1931-32:41   OO

Deutsch, Cecile Laramie   3:64   D

Deutsch, Mrs. David M   , see
   Deutsch, Cecile Laramie
Deutsch, William   1:501   HH
DeVane, Thomas Jones   1941:295   EN
De Vanter, Van   1905-06:[42]   RLW
Devereaux, Edmund Lincoln   3:39   LHC
Devereaux, William (?)   110   LDM
Devers, J   M   2:645   CHW
Devers, M   J   2:985   HHI
Devin, William F   unp.   SEA
Devine, John Joseph   1941:231   EN
Devine, Oshey, see
   Devine, John Joseph
Devlin, Lawrence K   2:1103   SM
Devlin, Mary A   , see
   Burke, Mary A   (Devlin)
De Voe, Mrs. Emma Smith   2:82   HHT
   1:332   HWW
De Volder, Arthur L   25:5,101,161   PNLA
DeVore, John Fletcher   391   AG
   1:101   BH
   1:560   NH
   3:154   SH
De Vore, Josie, see
   Johnson, Josie (De Vore)
De Waissey, L   L   1935:5   S
   1936:3   S
   1937:3   S
Dewdney, Edgar   2:281   BCF
   fol.pt.1   SHB
   1897:105,124   YB
   1911:70-71   YB
Dewey, Edward Henry   3:97   BEA
Dewey, William H   245   DSW
   3:1189   FH
   2:475   HHI
   20:128 1945-46   IH
   74   IHI
DeWhitesell, Henry, see
   Whitesell, Henry
De Wolf, Samuel J   133   LDM
Dexter, Wheeler O   3:673   SMS
DeYong, Joe   1:189   ACR
D'Herbomez, Louis Joseph   2:328   MCC
   230   MHC
   176   WCS
Dick, Archibald   4:793   BCF
Dick, Mrs. Archibald, see
   Dick, Elizabeth Clara (Westwood)
Dick, Elizabeth Clara (Westwood) 4:793   BCF
Dickens, Joseph   2:921   HHI
Dickens, Julius   1:379   BH
   2:162   HHT
Dickerson, William Walter   360   GL
Dickey, S   A   1905-06:[28]   RLW
Dickie, Charles Herbert   fol.pt.1   SHB
Dickinson, Emma C   (Slack)   840   LHM
Dickinson, George E   3:131   BHK

Dickinson, Robert   168   KB
Dickinson, Mrs. Sarah (Tongas Indian)
   231   JA
Dickinson, W   H   H   840   LHM
Dickinson, Mrs. W   H   H   , see
   Dickinson, Emma C   (Slack)
Dickman, R   L   3:53   BH
Dickson, Ashby C   1935-36:50   OO
   1939-40:15   OO
   1941-42:62   OO
   1945-46:92   OO
Dickson, George E   1905-06:[63]   RLW
   [119]   RLX
Dickson, Jerome   21   DCW
Dickson, John   1943-44:77   OO
   1945-46:85   OO
Dickson, William H   1910:2   TDL
Dickson, William L   1935-36:51   OO
   1937-38:62   OO
   1939-40:15   OO
Dickson, William Stuart   3:699   BCF
Dierdorff, William   188   LDM
Dietrich, Frank Sigel   628   IHI
   1911:132   WSP
Dietrich, Henry V   3:316   BEA
Dietrich, Richard   3:153   MC
Dietz, Carl F   393   BHSS
Dietz, William H   393   BHSS
Diggs, Ellen (Bast)   3:263   HWW
Diggs, Mrs. N   J   , see
   Diggs, Ellen (Bast)
Dildine, Henry   6:415   MC
Dill, Phoebe (Beasley), see
   Chapman, Phoebe (Beasley) Dill
Dillen, Parmelia, see
   Fergus, Pamelia (Dillon)
Diller, Leonard   3:153   BHK
Dilley, Mary, see
   Rockwood, Mary (Dilley)
Dilley, Sebastian C   147   PL
Dillin, Pamelia, see
   Fergus, Pamelia (Dillon)
Dilling, George W   unp.   SEA
   58   SSP
Dillman, L   C   1:187   HH
Dillon, Francis C   207   GG
Dillon, Isaac   456   AG
   154   BE
   8   OS
Dillon, Pamelia, see
   Fergus, Pamelia (Dillon)
Dilworth, John   fol.pt.1   SHB
Dimick, Aphia Lucinda   3:751   GP
Dimier, Augustine   29   JJ
Dimmick, Thomas M   2:454   PMO
Diomedi, Alexander   366   PI
   436   PIW
Dion, Henry   2:1144   SM

Dirstine, P H	430	BHSS		342	SHP
Disbrow, Mrs. A A	1:917	LHC	Dolph, Joseph N	1:519	LHC
Dishno, Silas C	3:1186	SMS	Dolphin, C E	14	SSP
Disney, Harold	3:463	BCF	Dols, John J	307,364,366	PI
Ditty, Sarah Catherine, see				432, 436	PIW
Ingraham, Sarah Catherine (Ditty)			Domitrovich, Frances	67	MG
Dix, Mary Augusta, see			Domroes, Augusta, see		
Gray, Mary Augusta (Dix)			Brose, Augusta (Domroes)		
Dixey, Ralph	363	BF	Donahoe, Francis	1:416	PHP
Dixon, Edward W	363	PL		1895-96:65	SSS
Dixon, Joseph	3:219	BCF	Donahue, James M	211	GG
Dixon, Sarah, see			Donaldson, Gilbert	3:1134-1135	FH
Broadbent, Sarah (Dixon)			Donaldson, Mrs. Gilbert, see		
Dixon, Susan S , see			Donaldson, Mary Elizabeth (Craker)		
Jennings, Susan S (Dixon)			Johnston		
Doane, Basil	393	BHSS	Donaldson, John	2:817	HHI
Doane, Ida May (Freeman)	3:79	LHC	Donaldson, Mary Elizabeth (Craker)		
Doane, Nehemiah	392	AG	Johnston	3:1134-1135	FH
Doane, O D	3:78	LHC	Donaldson, Robert M	6:311	MC
Doane, Mrs. O D , see			Doncaster, Hiram	2:218	NH
Doane, Ida May (Freeman)			Donckt, Cyril Van der	3:1101	FH
Doane, R W	219	BHSS	Doniphan, Alexander W	172	GMM
Doane, W J	98	LDM	Donley, Katie (Simonson)	3:255	BH
Dobbin, Dale Andrew	3:174	BEA	Donley, Samuel Hunter	3:255	BH
Dobbins, D W	355	LDM	Donley, Mrs. Samuel Hunter, see		
Dobie, Gilmore	74-75	GA	Donley, Katie (Simonson)		
	52 no.3:102	PN	Donnelly, John J	481	MI
	1 no.1:18	W	Donohoe, H E	1924:49	WSP
Dobson, Alfred P	1945-46:92	OO	Donohue, Daniel J	3:1627	SM
Dobson, Frank	3:819	HHI	Donovan, Charles	192	JNT
Dobson, John	1:442	PHP	Donovan, James	4:148	MC
	6:16	SH	Donovan, John Joseph	1:481	BHK
Dobson, Thomas	1:487	BHK		2:4	HWW
	3:465	BHK		1:288	PHP
	1905-06:[67]	RLW		5:366	SH
Dockery, Mrs. Eva Hunt	16:69 1937-38	IH		1 no.2:9	WN
Dockrill, Walter R	4:147	BCF	Donworth, Charles T	1924:41	WSP
Dodd, Charles H	424	SHP	Donworth, George	5:72	SH
Dodd, William	4:565	BCF		1923:77	WSP
	fol. title page	SHB	Doran, J F	225	E
Dodge, Grenville Mellen	3, 73	BOO	Doran, William	65	LDM
	front.,23,31,113	DH	Dore, John F	unp.	SEA
	32	QT	Doren, Mrs. Nancy L van, see		
Doering, Charles G	fol.pt.1	SHB	Van Doren, Mrs. Nancy L		
Doggett, Jefferson D	2:652	SMS	Dorr, Charles W	1895-96:65	SSS
Doherty, Charles Edward	3:289	BCF		1910:138	WSP
Doherty, Mary, see			Dorton, Joseph A	361	GL
Kenny, Mary (Doherty)			Dosch, Henry E	1:584-585	GP
Doig, James	3:443	BCF		unp.	VU
Doig, Thomas	187	LDM	Doty, Chauncey Albert	6:52	SH
Dolan, Philip A	16 no.6:727	MWHN	Doubt, Thomas Eaton	1:unp.1900-01	WDT
	June 1891:22 suppl.	PM	Doud, Leslie L	3:657	BH
Doland, C M	37	MG	Dougall, John	3:952	BCF
Dolby, J W	3:14 1925	BCHA	Dougall, Mrs. John, see		
Dole, E P	April 1891:421	PM	Dougall, Rosana (Graham)		
Dolholte, John	88	LDM	Dougall, Rosana (Graham)	3:953	BCF
Dolliver, Mark C	260	GG	Dougan, James Madison	2:441	LHC
Dolph, Cyrus Abda	2:17	GP	Dougherty, William P	1:145	BH

	1:655	LHC
Dougherty, William Thomas	2:625	HHI
Doughty, J A	63	LHN
Doughty, James Winfield	3:125	PH
Douglas, A	431	LDM
Douglas, Alexander	17 no. 1-2:44	BCH
Douglas, Amelia (Connolly)	1897:4	YB
Douglas, Benjamin	3:723	BCF
	144	KB
Douglas, Charles Stanford	4:659	BCF
	fol. pt. 1	SHB
Douglas, David	2:149	BCF
	170	CIR
	125	GBS
Douglas, Mrs. Earl C , see		
Douglas, Leanna (Terry)		
Douglas, J F	1 no. 11:18	WN
Douglas, James	162	AC
	1:510	BCF
	2:277	BCF
	7 no. 2:93	BCH
	front.	DC
	156	DW
	80	GI
	109	HBC
	front.	KB
	10	LCT
	262	MH
	34	MHN
	22, 24	NF
	1:16	NH
	2:56	PMO
	fol. title page	SHB
	83	WTH
	1897:63	YB
	1911:70-71	YB
Douglas, Mrs. James, see		
Douglas, Amelia (Connolly)		
Douglas, Leanna (Terry)	3:72	D
Douglas, Sallie Hume	23:6 1951-52	IHD
Douglas, Thomas	63	GI
	147	MH
Douglass, Samuel S	137	LDM
Douglass, Thomas E	36	PSW
Doust, William J	226	E
	35	SCC
Dove, Samuel E	2:149	SMS
Dovell, W T	1911:front.	WSP
Dow, Alex	317	MI
Dow, E E	3:860	SMS
Dow, Matthew	5:364	SH
Dowell, Benjamin Franklin	1:524	NH
Dowell, Stephen L	3:961	BHS
Dower, John	1 no. 4:8	WN
Dowling, James A	3:675	GP
Downey, William R	1:560	NH
Downing, Charles O	2:253	HH
Downing, Elizabeth, see		
Blakeley, Elizabeth (Downing)		
Downing, Walter O	2:105	SMS
Dowton, Sydney Mark	3:297	BEA
Draham, Mark H	2:58	PHP
Drake, Brian T	2:front. 1924	BCHA
Drake, F E	108	AG
Drake, Francis	171	CIR
	23	GBS
	12	GI
	2	LDM
	1:248	LH
	1:90	SH
Drake, James Francis	3:831	LHC
Drake, James H	3:1020,	SMS
Drake, John M	60:95	OHQ
	65:18	OHQ
Drake, June D	66:313	OHQ
Drake, Montague William Tyrwhitt-, see		
Tyrwhitt-Drake, Montague William		
Drake, W H	398	AG
Drake, W W	48:211 1936	WSGP
Dralle, Fred W	3:1745	SM
Draper, Charles David	4:524	PH
Draper, Charles H	2:66	SMS
Draper, Edgar M	50:23 1949	WDT
Draper, Sutton H	3:1826	SM
Drayton, Charles Robert	3:279	BCF
Dreibelbis, Louis	3:1565	SM
Drennan, Henry T	26:18	PNLA
Drennon, James	321	LDM
Dressel, Baltus W , see		
Driessel, Baltus W		
Dresser, Algeron S	43	PL
	2:448	PMO
Drew, C S	60:94	OHQ
Driessel, Baltus W	261	GG
Driessel, George A	211	GG
Driggs, Don C	2:593	HHI
Drinkwater, Charles	216, 302	GI
Drips, Andrew	1:276	CAFT
Driscoll, John	2:442	PMO
Driscoll, John Lynn	3:front.	BEA
Driscoll, Michael	3:1493	SM
Drissler, John H	3:41	HWW
Drum, Henry	1:61	HH
	14 no. 2:147	MWH
	2:458	NH
	2:96	PHP
	1895-96:131	SSS
Drumheller, Daniel Montgomery	2:55	HH
Drumheller, Joseph	50:21 1949	WDT
Dry, Walter	1945-46:60	OO
Dryer, Thomas J	1:498	GP
	2:342	PMO
	16	TO
	front.	WRE
Drysdale, Gordon	3:183	BCF
Dubois, Fred T	47 no. 4:115	PN
	53 no. 4:140	PN

	56 no.1:24	PN	Duncan, Robert M	1935-36:50	OO
	60 no.4:195	PN	_____	1937-38:62	OO
DuBois, Joseph Bell	2:349	CHW	_____	1939-40:15	OO
Dubuc, Joseph	2:234	MCC	Duncan, S Laus	6:442-443	MC
Ducharme, Baptiste	16	LHM	Duncan, William	front.	HS
Ducharme, Clara, see			_____	front.	WSM
Cramer, Clara (Ducharme)			_____	1897:44	YB
Duchesnay, Albert Edward	fol.pt.2	SHB	Dunham, H W	253	LDM
Duchesnay, Charles E J			Dunham, J F	261	LDM
	fol.pt.1	SHB	Dunham, Slemmons L	6:392	MC
Duck, S	2:337	BCF	Duniway, Abigail (Scott)	1:606	GP
_____	10 no.1:43	BCH	_____	3:53	GP
Duck, William	2:front.1924	BCHA	Duniway, Mrs. Ben C , see		
Dudley, Frederic Merritt	3:210	PH	Duniway, Abigail (Scott)		
Dudley, Rose	26	RO	Duniway, Clyde Augustus	1:402-403	GP
Dudley, William Lincoln	622	SHP	Duniway, Robert E	1943-44:77	OO
Duerst, W B	1935-36:51	OO	_____	1945-46:85	OO
_____	1937-38:62-63	OO	Duniway, Willis S	1895:169	OO
Duff, John R	23	DH	Dunlap, George W	6:164	SH
Duff, Lyman Pease	1911:70-71	YB	Dunlap, J H	92	LHN
Duff-Stuart, James	fol.pt.2	SHB	Dunlevy, Peter Curran	3:717	BCF
Duffy, Irene, see			_____	132	WSE
Bellefleur, Irene (Duffy)			Dunlevy, Stanley Paul	3:779	BCF
DuFraine, Frances	25:34	PNLA	Dunn, Adam Duncan	108,408,453	BHSS
Dufur, Andrew J , Sr.	3:793	GP	Dunn, Alexander	3:685	BCF
Dufur, Enoch Burnham	3:501	GP	Dunn, George W	1895:100	OO
Dufur, William Henry Harrison	3:727	GP	_____	1931-32:40	OO
	2:236	PMO	_____	1935-36:50	OO
Dugas, C A	176	WOY	_____	1937-38:62	OO
Duggan, G H	254	GI	_____	1939-40:15	OO
Duke, John P	19:160	WBP	_____	1941-42:62	OO
_____	21:128	WBP	Dunn, J W McK	23	DH
_____	22:128	WBP	Dunn, James D	2:898	FH
_____	23:112	WBP	Dunn, John C	2:184	SMS
_____	25:32	WBP	Dunn, Joseph W	544	SIH
Duke of York, see			Dunn, Mathew	2:1045	SM
Chetzemoka, Clallam chief			Dunne, Joe E	1931-32:40	OO
Dumont, Gabriel	2:168	MCC	Dunne, T M	1945-46:57	OO
Dunagan, Harriet H , see			Dunnigan, William H	3:1485	SM
Andrewartha, Harriet H			Dunning, Daniel A	2:648	FH
Dunbar, John H	1924:33	WSP	Dunphy, E M	417	LHM
Dunbar, Maggie J	231	JA	Dunphy, Mrs. E M , see		
Dunbar, Ralph Oregon	2:298	NH	Dunphy, Mary A (Small)		
_____	1905-06:[28]	RLW	Dunphy, Mary A (Small)	416	LHM
_____	1895-96:61	SSS	Dunshee, Bertram H	3:1583	SM
_____	1927:front.	WSP	Dunsmuir, James	2:281	BCF
Dunbar, William	1:242	GP	_____	4:53	BCF
Dunbar, William Rice	2:306	NH	_____	134	JAC
Duncan, (Father)	69	BET	_____	fol.pt.1	SHB
Duncan, David	6:416-417	MC	_____	1911:70-71	YB
Duncan, George R	1939-40:30	OO	Dunsmuir, Robert	3:667	BCF
_____	1941-42:65	OO	_____	152	KB
_____	1945-46:92	OO	_____	fol. title page	SHB
Duncan, James A	52 no.3:85	PN	_____	1897:132	YB
_____	55 no.4:155	PN	Dunwell, Dennis W C	144	SIH
Duncan, Leonard	3:153	MC	Durand, Ezra	637	SHP
Duncan, McRae	3:1033	BCF	Durant, Charles	227	E
Duncan, Mel G	27	SCC	Durant, T C	31	DH

Durfee, David M 2:284 SMS
Durham, Nelson W 1:199 HH
Durham, T A 393 BHSS
Durieu, Pierre P 2:352 MCC
Durrie, Archibald 143 PSW
Dussault, Arthur 383 SCH
Dutcher, Eugene S 42 LHN
Dutton, W P 177 PL
Duval, Louis 2:front. 1924 BCHA
Duval, Mrs. Louis 2:front. 1924 BCHA
Dvorak, August 36:26 1935 WDT
Dwyer, Maurice F 247 GG
Dyas, John P 1019 LHM
Dye, Charles Henry 2:291 LHC
Dye, Mrs. Charles Henry, see
    Dye, Eva L (Emery)
Dye, Eva L (Emery) 1:650 GP
    2:291 LHC
_____ 58 no.1:9 PN
Dye, Willoughby G 3:1690 SM
Dyer, Charles Newell front. DT
Dyer, T L 131 AG
Dyer, Theresa, see
    Miller, Minnie Myrtle (Dyer)
Dyer, Trusten P 1905-06:[28] RLW
Dygard, Joe 58 BR
Dyke, George J fol.pt.2 SHB
Dyke, Walter J 292 E
    1905-06:[59] RLW
_____
Dysart, James S 1:648 NH
Dzikenis 113 FT

E

Eads, William G 3:343 PH
Eagle, Nez Percé chief 153 BR
    54 MW
Eagle Heart, see
    Spotted Eagle, Nez Percé chief
Eagle Wing, see
    Joseph, Nez Percé chief
Eagleson, Andrew Hervey 3:365 BEA
    2:539 HHI
Eagleson, Mrs. Andrew Hervey, see
    Eagleson, Martha A (Kerr)
Eagleson, Don H 3:365 BEA
Eagleson, Ernest George 2:295 HHI
Eagleson, John William 3:365 BEA
    2:209 HHI
Eagleson, Martha A (Kerr) 2:539 HHI
Eakin, Stewart B 2:65 CHW
Earhart, Rockey P 1:632 NH
    484 SHP
Earl, J M 1905-06:[44] RLW
Earle, Dan 1924:97 WSP
Earle, Thomas 156 KB

_____ 1897:110 YB
Earley, J A 1935:5 S
_____ 1936:3 S
_____ 1937:3 S
_____ unp. SAA
Early, George D unp. SAA
Early, Jack 287 BHSS
Easterbrook, George Troop 2:145 HH
Easterbrook, Mrs. George Troop, see
    Easterbrook, Hannah Lawton (Coit)
Easterbrook, Hannah Lawton (Coit)
    2:145 HH
Easterday, C M 1895-96:67 SSS
Easterday, Joseph Holt 6:22 SH
Eastman, Benjamin Manson 1:62 FSB
Eastman, Hosea B 2:716 FH
    1:57 FSB
_____ 2:13 HHI
Eastman, Jess O 3:109 HHI
Eastman, Sam 2:front.1924 BCHA
Eaton, Abel E 1:556 NH
Eaton, Curtis Turner 3:505 BEA
Eaton, George O 537 LHM
Eaton, George Penston 6:86 SH
Eaton, Harry Wentworth 3:505 BEA
Eaton, James F 296 NM
Eaton, Lewis T 3:1079 SMS
Eaton, William 908 SIH
Eayrs, George T 1937-38:62 OO
    1939-40:15 OO
Ebbage, Ernest 3:267 BCF
Ebbert, George Wood 1:20 NH
    19:263 OHQ
Eberhard, Colon R 1931-32:40 OO
Eberle, Adam W 267 LDM
Eberle, J Louis 3:476 BEA
Eberman, N A 1:152 NH
Eberschweiler, Frederick Hugo 41 NL
    364 PI
_____ 432 PIW
Ebert, Eloise 26:5, 77 PNLA
Eberts, David McEwen 2:547 BCF
    fol.pt.1 SHB
_____ 1897:104 YB
_____ 1911:6-7,70-71 YB
Ebler, Elizabeth, see
    Widmer, Elizabeth (Ebler)
Ebsen, Chris 3:629 LHC
Ebsen, Mrs. Chris, see
    Ebsen, Jorgine (Johansen)
Ebsen, Jorgine (Johansen) 3:629 LHC
Eckersley, James W 1935-36:51 OO
    1937-38:62-63 OO
Eckerson, Elizabeth (McCabe) 1:82 PMO
Eckerson, Theodore J 1:512 NH
    1:82 PMO
Eckerson, Mrs. Theodore J, see
    Eckerson, Elizabeth (McCabe)

Name	Ref	Code
Eckert, Jacob L	2:464-465	EPD
	552	SIH
Eckert, Mrs. Jacob L	2:464-465	EPD
Eckles, Mary, see		
Burbank, Mary E (Eckles)		
Eckley, Victor	1931-32:41	OO
Eckmann, Ray	176-177	GA
Eckstein, Nathan	1 no. 10:13	WN
Eddings, Nort	60	SHO
Eddy, B L	1931-32:40	OO
	2:430	PMO
Eddy, John W	367	LHM
Eddy, John Whittemore	3:183	PH
Eddy, Thomas V	1895-96:89	SSS
Eden, John C	5:384	SH
Edens, John James	2:468	PHP
Edgar, Henry	3:124	MC
Edgerton, E D	665	LHM
Edgerton, Pauline	5:187	MC
Edgerton, Sidney	189	BHSI
	3:331	MC
Edgington, Grace, see		
Jordan, Grace (Edgington)		
Edmonds, Henry Valentine	3:73	BCF
	162	KB
Edmondson, W Walker	145	PSW
Edmonson, Frank M	1112	SIH
Edmundson, Clarence S	176-177	GA
Edmundson, "Hec", see		
Edmundson, Clarence S		
Edsen, Eduard P	2:259	HH
Edson, O E	2:444	PMO
Edwards, Amanda (Evans)	362	GL
Edwards, Anna D	6:422	MC
Edwards, Byrd H	3:950	SMS
Edwards, Charles	47, 145	LDM
Edwards, David	892	LHM
Edwards, E S	413	LDM
Edwards, Edward William	100	GL
Edwards, Mrs. Edward William, see		
Edwards, Amanda (Evans)		
Edwards, Frank E	unp.	SEA
Edwards, Fred	2:212	HHT
Edwards, George	6:440-441	MC
Edwards, Herbert	4:561	BCF
Edwards, L N	177	PL
Edwards, Mrs. M A	438	AG
Edwards, Mary C , see		
Kellogg, Mary C (Edwards) Morand		
Edwards, Robert O	unp.	SAA
Eells, Cushing	460	BE
	1:134	BS
	135	DE
	197	DS
	94	DTI
	290	EW
	2:24	FI
	3:312	LH
	100	MW
	1:28	NH
	160	NM
	1:469	PMO
	2:124	SH
Eells, Mrs. Cushing, see		
Eells, Myra (Fairbank)		
Eells, Edwin	248-249	DE
Eells, Ida	248-249	DE
Eells, Myra (Fairbank)	135	DE
	41	EI
	1:168	NH
	1:66	PMO
Eells, Walter	248-249	DE
Egan, Howard	3, 289	EP
Egan, Mrs. Howard, see		
Egan, Tamson (Parshley)		
Egan, Howard Ransom	12, 256, 290	EP
Egan, Hyrum William	291	EP
Egan, Ira Ernest	290, 291	EP
Egan, Jack	182-183	KO
Egan, Richard Erastus	214, 290	EP
Egan, Tamson (Parshley)	289	EP
Egan, William A	181	BET
Egan, William M	8, 290	EP
Egbert, Joseph Clemmer	2:671	LHC
Egbert, Richard A	3:289	BEA
Eggan, James	90	SS
Egge, Albert E	219	BHSS
Eggertson, Simon P	226	GL
Ehlert, Adelgunde (Goltz)	872	SIH
Ehlert, William	872	SIH
Ehlert, Mrs. William, see		
Ehlert, Adelgunde (Goltz)		
Ehorn, John P	165	GG
Ehrlich, Frank Oscar	2:501	BHK
Ehrlichman, Ben Bernard	4:23	BHK
Eidemiller, Fred	1905-06:[54]	RLW
	[88]	RLX
Eielson, Carl Ben	60	AL
Eisenbeis, Charles	4:588	PH
Eklund, Hildore C	3:1773	SM
Elder, Janet, see		
Steele, Janet (Elder)		
Eldridge, Alice	154	JNT
Eldridge, Arthur Symons	4:327	BHK
Eldridge, Belle	355	JNT
Eldridge, Delisca J (Bowers)	6:126	SH
Eldridge, Edward	2:41	HWW
	1:232	NH
	1905-06:[28]	RLW
	4:40	SH
Eldridge, Nannie (Steptoe)	272	MCO
Eldridge, William Henry	3:916	FH
Elerath, Arthur F	3:255	GP
Elfers, Henry J	450-451	SIH
Eliot, Charles D	2:570	SMS
Eliot, Henrietta Robins (Mack)	45	WFU
Eliot, Thomas Lamb	43	WFU

Eliot, Mrs. Thomas Lamb, see
    Eliot, Henrietta Robins (Mack)
Eliot, Victor Alexander George
                4:297   BCF
Eliott, E   D   293   E
Elison, Charles G   3:457   HHI
Elison, Mrs. Charles G   , see
    Elison, Mary M   (Worthington)
Elison, Mary M   (Worthington) 3:457   HHI
Elizabeth, Queen of England 1:330   LH
Ella, Fred   2:front.1924   BCHA
Ella, Harry   2:front.1924   BCHA
Ellingson, Oley   228   GL
Ellington, Clarence   1 no.12:20   WN
Ellingwood, Charles William 2:1150   SM
Elliott, Andrew Charles   2:335   BCF
               42   JAC
               fol.pt.1   SHB
               1897:64   YB
               1911:70-71 YB
Elliott, Edwin E   215   BHSS
               1 no.4:266 WM
Elliott, Frank E   unp.   SAA
Elliott, Henry   fol.207   SHI
Elliott, John   4:569   BCF
Elliott, John B   4:1065   BCF
Elliott, John J   fol.274   HIT
Elliott, Nancy (Sconce) 1:248   NH
Elliott, R   J   2:675   BHK
Elliott, Sara, see
    Wolheter, Sara (Elliott) Price
Elliott, Thompson Coit 22   LBT
               44:229   OHQ
Elliott, W   A   83   LDM
Elliott, William   1:248   NH
Elliott, Mrs. William, see
    Elliott, Nancy (Sconce)
Ellis, Anna   206   BHSS
Ellis, Anna M   1943-44:77   OO
               1945-46:85   OO
Ellis, Charles F   6:350   MC
Ellis, Edwin M   6:394,440-441 MC
Ellis, George Dabney 2:704-705 FH
               609   IHI
Ellis, Mrs. George Dabney, see
    Ellis, Telitha J   (Arnett) Stafford
Ellis, Hubert J   2:303   HWW
Ellis, Isaac C   2:358   NH
Ellis, Jennie (Wilhite) 1:13   D
Ellis, Kathleen   25   AT
Ellis, Myron H   1:355   HH
Ellis, Overton Gentry May 1907:39 TDL
               1910:15   TDL
Ellis, Mrs. Overton Gentry, see
    Ellis, Jennie (Wilhite)
Ellis, Rex   1937-38:62   OO
               1939-40:15   OO
               1941-42:62   OO

               1943-44:75   OO
               1945-46:82   OO
Ellis, Telitha J (Arnett) Stafford
               2:704-705   FH
Ellis, Thomas   25   AT
           fol. title page SHB
Ellis, Mrs. Thomas, see
    Ellis, Wilhelmina (Wade)
Ellis, Wilhelmina (Wade) 25   AT
Ellison, Amy Allen (Childs) 4:555   PH
Ellison, John Clemmens 4:555   PH
Ellison, Mrs. John Clemmens, see
    Ellison, Amy Allen (Childs)
Ellison, Price   2:547   BCF
               fol.pt.1   SHB
               1911:6-7,70-71 YB
Ellsworth, Donald M 3:424   BEA
Ellsworth, Edmund, Sr. 3:673   HHI
Ellsworth, Harris   1941-42:63 OO
               1943-44:13   OO
               1945-46:13   OO
Ellsworth, Louis Jerome 3:424   BEA
Ellsworth, Mrs. Louis Jerome, see
    Ellsworth, Rose (Ball)
Ellsworth, Preston   3:241   BEA
Ellsworth, Richard E 3:424   BEA
Ellsworth, Rose (Ball) 3:424   BEA
Ellsworth, Stukely   1:104   NH
Elrod, J   O   2:911   LHC
Else, John Earl   3:679   LHC
Elson, William Henry Quiggan 4:267 BCF
Elton, J   287   BHSS
Elvidge, Ford Q   1924:129   WSP
Elvrum, L   P   137   SS
Elvrum, Mrs. L   P   , see
    Elvrum, Martha (Beck)
Elvrum, Martha (Beck) 137   SS
Embrey, Austin Morgan 3:869   SMS
Emerick, Lucetta (Zachary) 1:236   NH
Emerick, Solomon   1:236   NH
Emerick, Mrs. Solomon, see
    Emerick, Lucetta (Zachary)
Emerson, Mrs. Emma   6:358   MC
Emerson, George H   2:61   HWW
               2:34   NH
Emery, Eva L   , see
    Dye, Eva L   (Emery)
Emery, Fred W   2:903   FH
Emery, Rufus   126   HIT
Emken, H   A   146   LDM
Emmert, Jacob H   3:363   GP
Emmitt, R   A   2:439   PMO
Emmons, Samuel Franklin 135   MMR
Emory, C   D   50:57 1949 WDT
Engdahl, Carl   1935-36:51 OO
               1937-38:62-63 OO
               1939-40:30   OO
               1941-42:65   OO

Name	Reference	Code
	1943-44:77	OO
	1945-46:82	OO
Engen, Richard B	32 no.1:25	PNLA
	34 no.1:33	PNLA
Enger, T T	135	SS
Englehart, Ira Philip	6:70	SH
	1913 front.	WSP
English, Marshall Martin	170	KB
Engquist, Frank	104	SS
Engstrom, Paul	503	BR
Enke, Herman	3:561	LHC
Ennis, E R	228	E
Ennis, Frank	278	E
Enough, Abraham	105	GL
Ensign, Francis Edward	249	IHI
Ensign, Henry F	2:900	FH
Ensley, Robert F	34 no.1:31	PNLA
Enthoven, E James	4:323	BCF
Entz, Catharine, see		
Pugh, Catharine (Entz)		
Eoff, Alfred	2:752	FH
	2:667	HHI
Eoff, Cynthia Ann, see		
Geer, Cynthia Ann (Eoff)		
Epperson, George R	1:372	HHT
Epps, Theodore C Van, see		
Van Epps, Theodore C		
Ereaux, Curley, see		
Ereaux, Lazare		
Ereaux, Lazare	15	NL
	3:936	SMS
Ereaux, Mrs. Lazare, see		
Ereaux, Mary J (Johnson)		
Ereaux, Mary J (Johnson)	3:936	SMS
Erickson, Andrew J	320	SIH
Erickson, Charles J	3:325	BHS
Erickson, E O	[129]	RLX
Erickson, Erick	320	SIH
Erickson, G	1905-06:[65]	RLW
Erickson, H M	1945-46:34	OO
Erickson, John Edward	150	LBT
Erickson, Joseph	3:454	BHK
Ermatinger, Francis	264	BF
	82	BHSI
	2:372	LH
Ermatinger, Mrs. Francis	83	BHSI
Erskine, James	431	LDM
Erskine, Melville C	104	LDM
Ervin, Henry	2:867	FH
	126	HIT
Erwin, Edward K	229	E
Erwin, R Wayne	1937-38:62-63	OO
Erwin, Richard Patton	1931-32:140	IH
Erwin, Walter	3:1053	BCF
Erwin, Warren	1935-36:51	OO
	1941-42:65	OO
	1945-46:85	OO
Esary, David N	4:671	PH

Name	Reference	Code
Esch, Levi	896	SIH
Eshelman, J F	1:289	HH
Eshelman, J T	1905-06:[28]	RLW
	May 1907:38	TDL
Esler, Alfred M	97	MI
	2:939	SM
Esling, William K	1895-96:147	SSS
Espey, Julia A	2:67	HH
Espey, Robert Hamilton	2:61	HH
Espy, Ethel E	207	BHSS
Esselstyn, Elmer E	2:506	SMS
Essner, Joseph	177	PL
Esson, A M	1937-38:62-63	OO
Estby, Marie	207	BHSS
Esterquist, Ralph	18:11	PNLA
Ettershanks, William	121	LDM
Ettinger, U L	266	BHSS
Evans, Abel	241	GL
Evans, Mrs. Abel, see		
Evans, Mary (Jones)		
Evans, Abel John	271	GL
Evans, Abigail, see		
Lott, Abigail (Evans)		
Evans, Amanda, see		
Edwards, Amanda (Evans)		
Evans, Barbara A , see		
Bush, Barbara A (Evans)		
Evans, Barbara Ann (Ewell)	369	GL
Evans, Bessie (Spencer)	3:801	HHI
Evans, Blanche, see		
Jones, Blanche (Evans)		
Evans, C W	318	LDM
Evans, Daniel J	unp.	SE
Evans, David	3:709	BCF
Evans, Mrs. David, see		
Evans, Margaret (McLay)		
Evans, David	32	GL
Evans, Mrs. David, see		
Evans, Barbara Ann (Ewell)		
Evans, Rebecca (Coleman)		
Evans, Margaret Christina (Holm)		
Evans, David, Jr.	374	GL
Evans, Don H	3:371	BHK
Evans, Elwood	1:104	NH
	51 no.3:106	PN
	52 no.1:17	PN
	4:148	SH
Evans, Ernst	311	BHSS
Evans, Mrs. G W , see		
Castleman, I J (Davis) Evans		
Evans, Geneva (Clark)	366	GL
Evans, George W	206, 408	BHSS
Evans, Hannah, see		
Anderson, Hannah (Evans)		
Evans, Israel	167	GL
Evans, Mrs. Israel, see		
Evans, Matilda Ann (Thomas)		
Evans, Israel, Jr.	224	GL

Evans, John C	1945-46:64	OO
Evans, John M	2:607	HHI
Evans, Lewis O	2:5	SMS
Evans, Margaret (McLay)	3:709	BCF
Evans, Margaret Christina (Holm) 393		GL
Evans, Martha, see		
Winn, Martha (Evans)		
Evans, Mary	1:456	GP
Evans, Mary (Jones)	364	GL
Evans, Mary Elizabeth, see		
Flett, Mary Elizabeth (Evans)		
Evans, Matilda Ann (Thomas) 24		GL
Evans, Minnie M (Wright) 272		SIH
Evans, Morgan	224	GL
Evans, Mosiah	287	GL
Evans, Nathan	126	AG
Evans, Nathaniel Powell	3:1161	SMS
Evans, R J	27	PSW
Evans, Rachel, see		
Wing, Rachel (Evans)		
Evans, Rebecca (Coleman)	371	GL
Evans, William C	3:1286	SMS
Evans, William H	3:801	HHI
Evans, Mrs. William H , see		
Evans, Bessie (Spencer)		
Evans, William M	272	SIH
Evans, Mrs. William M , see		
Evans, Minnie M (Wright)		
Evans, William Samuel	305, 306	GL
Evans, Mrs. William Samuel, see		
Evans, Geneva (Clark)		
Eveleigh, Sydney Morgan	3:909	BCF
Evenden, Mrs. Annie	207	BHSS
Everest, H P	50:33 1949	WDT
Everett, B R	1:372	HHT
Everett, Billy	225, 256	LS
Everette, Willis Eugene	12	DA
	159	WOY
Ewald, Mark	1943:184	ENC
Ewell, Barbara Ann, see		
Evans, Barbara Ann (Ewell)		
Ewen, Alexander	176	KB
Ewing, B Gard	1943:206	ENC
Ewing, Harry C	6:416-417	MC
Eyres, Walter	4:714	PH

F

Fabian, Edward	2:127	SMS
Fabre, Joseph	2:256	MCC
Fabry, Frank	3:871	BCF
Fackler, St. Michael	1:44	NH
	1:566	PMO
Fadden, H D	1937:3	S
Fader, E J	3:373	BCF
Fafard, R P	2:180	MCC

Fagg, Mearl L	1941:216	EN
Failing, Elizabeth A	1:210-211	GP
Failing, Henry	447	CHO
————	1:641	CHW
————	1:519	GP
————	2:67	GP
————	1:519	LHC
————	2:19	LHC
————	1:16	PMO
————	2:336	PMO
————	118	SHP
Failing, Joseph	2:348	PMO
Failing, Josiah	1:614-615	GP
————	2:51	GP
————	1:64	NH
————	1:300	PMO
Fair, James G	224	QT
Fairbank, Myra, see		
Eells, Myra (Fairbank)		
Fairbanks, Sarah, see		
King, Sarah (Fairbanks) Olds		
Fairchild, Asher Clarke	394	AG
Fairhurst, Cyril J	261	GG
Fairley, Robert	43	SCC
Fairman, J D (Jack)	63:286	OHQ
Fairweather, H W	2:410	NH
————	1905-06:[28]	RLW
Fairweather, William	40	BV
Falconer, J A	1905-06:[69]	RLW
————	[107]	RLX
Falen, Ernest Albert	3:227	BEA
Fales, William Ellery	4:851	BCF
Falk, Ben	2:1160	SM
Falk, E G	411	AG
Falk, Leo J	2:233	HHI
Falk, Nathan	2:27	HHI
Falknor, Judson F	50:59 1949	WDT
————	1924:64	WSP
Faltermeyer, Lewis C	3:1617	SM
Fancher, John A	1905-06:[56]	RLW
————	[111]	RLX
Fannin, Jack	2:141	BCF
Fansler, Jesse H	272	SIH
Faraud, Henri	1:292	MCC
Far-Away-Cough (Blackfoot Indian) 127		GI
Farley, Daniel	69	LDM
Farmer, Rhoda C , see		
Billups, Rhoda C (Farmer)		
Farnham, Russell	1:42-43	GP
Farnsworth, A C	47	LDM
Farnsworth, Charles E	3:1795	SM
Farnsworth, Clare Edward	6:114	SH
Farquharson, Alexander Scott 3:299		HWW
Farquharson, Mrs. F B , see		
Farquharson, Mary (Nichols)		
Farquharson, Mary (Nichols) 59 no.2:96		PN
Farr, Eli M	2:53	SMS
Farrand, Fountain R	6:416-417	MC

Farrell, John	151	LDM
Farrell, Robert S , Jr.	1939-40:30	OO
_____	1941-42:65	OO
_____	1943-44:17	OO
_____	1945-46:19	OO
Farrell, Sylvester	2:133	GP
Farrell, Theodore	221	GG
Farrer, Erwin	295	LDM
Farris, A T	58	BHSS
Farris, J W DeB	1922:118	WSP
Farrow, Edward Samuel	236	AI
_____	135	BN
_____	front.	BSC
_____	1925-26:27	IH
Farthing, Annie Cragg	139	PJ
Fast Walker (Sioux Indian)	110-111	HCM
Fastabend, John Antone	66:179	OHQ
Father Abraham	149	DE
Fatland, Ernest R	1935-36:51	OO
_____	1937-38:62-63	OO
_____	1939-40:30	OO
_____	1945-46:82	OO
Faucett, "Grandma"	1:715	BHK
Faucett, Nancy H , see		
Stewart, Nancy H (Faucett)		
Faulkner, Walter Edward	3:336	PH
Faunce, Charles E	336	SIH
Faust, John Nelson	4:510	PH
Fawcett, Angelo Vance	2:335	HHT
Fawcett, Annie	2:front.1924	BCHA
Fay, Charles T	1905-06:[28]	RLW
Feagles, Robert S	50	PSW
Featherman, John A	2:980	SM
Featherston, John	3:993	BCF
_____	5:210	MC
Fechter, Oscar A	74-75	GA
_____	unp.	WD
Fee, David F	97	LDM
Fee, James A	2:438	NH
Feely, Alice M (Kemp)	836	SIH
Feely, D W	unp.	SOU
Feely, Thomas N	836	SIH
Feely, Mrs. Thomas N , see		
Feely, Alice M (Kemp)		
Feider, Andrew S	261	GG
Feige, E	151	OB
Feighan, John W	1:163	HH
Felden, Marie Louise	fol.plate 82	IN
Fell, Theron E	2:566	NH
Fellman, Werner H	3:577	LHC
Fellowes, Eugene J	230	E
Fellows, A J	315	LDM
Felton, Charles	102	LDM
Felton, Robert Theodore	3:114	BEA
Fender, George W	unp.	SOU
Fenn, Frank A	1923-24:6	IH
Fenn, Stephen Southmyd	47 no.4:112	PN
Fenner, E B	4 no.14:9	C
Fenner, William D	2:1285	SM
Fenton, Edwin L	2:90	SMS
Fenton, Hicks C	1:192	PMO
Fenton, James Edward	2:193	HH
Fenton, S W	1905-06:[59]	RLW
_____	1895-96:91	SSS
Fenton, William David, Sr.	2:79	LHC
Ferey, George R	431	LDM
Fergus, James	134	LHM
_____	4:83,188	MC
_____	261	MI
_____	1:318	SMS
Fergus, Mrs. James, see		
Fergus, Pamelia (Dillon)		
Fergus, Pamelia (Dillon)	135	LHM
_____	4:188	MC
_____	1:318	SMS
Fergus, William	6:440-441	MC
Ferguson, Angus	3:797	BCF
Ferguson, David	2:328	PHP
Ferguson, Emory Canda	1:67	HH
_____	1:328	NH
_____	2:400	PHP
_____	6:78	SH
Ferguson, Hector Ross McLean	3:941	BCF
Ferguson, Herbert V A	3:968	FH
Ferguson, Myron A	2:343	HH
Fernan, John	864	SIH
Fernandez, J N	1:372	HHT
Fernie, William	fol.title page	SHB
Ferree, Fred C	1935:5	S
_____	1936:3	S
_____	1937:3	S
Ferrell, William F	920	SIH
Ferrera, Josephine, see		
Werner, Josephine Ferrera		
Ferris, Joel E	45 no.3:92	PN
Ferry, Clinton Peyre	2:22	HHT
_____	2:646	NH
_____	1:274	PHP
_____	5:284	SH
Ferry, Elisha Peyre	3:535	BHS
_____	168	BHSS
_____	27, 39	MAG
_____	46	ME
_____	1:320	NH
_____	1:415	PH
_____	1 no.6:193	PM
_____	34 no.4:400-401	PN
_____	52 no.1:19	PN
_____	[55]	RLX
_____	unp.	SE
_____	4:front.	SH
_____	1893-94:front.	SSS
_____	1895-96:38	SSS
Ferry, Eliza, see		
Leary, Eliza (Ferry)		
Fertig, Mrs. Annie M	449	BHSS

Fetzner, Joseph 177 PL
Fidelis, Flathead chief fol.512 BUR
Field, William B 1895-96:67 SSS
Fielding, Mrs. Henry 6:325 MC
Fierens, J T 1:208-209 GP
    210 OPC
Fietz, Walter Fred, Jr. 3:389 BH
Fife, William H 2:26 HHT
    2:214 NH
Finch, D B 76 LDM
Finch, Edward C 2:335 HWW
    1895-96:117 SSS
    2 no.1:5 WN
Findlay, James 3:191 BCF
Finerty, John F 6:129 MC
Finkbonner, C C 153 JNT
Finlayson, Roderick fol.title page SHB
    1897:18 YB
Finn, Paul 58 BR
Finnegan, John J 165 GG
Finnegan, Thomas 243 GG
Finnerty, G E 2:529 CHW
Finnerty, Michael 2:front.1924 BCHA
Finney, Edward 393 BHSS
Finseth, Lief 1943-44:77 OO
Finstad, John S 4:675 PH
First-red-feather-of-the-wing, see
    Ha-wow-no-ilp-ilp (Nez Percé Indian)
Fischer, Frederick T 3:351 BHK
Fischer, George William 3:347 BHK
Fish Hawk, Cayuse chief 1:568-569 GP
    103 JM
Fishback, Thomas 393 BHSS
Fishburn, M S 1895-96:91 SSS
Fisher, A N 456 AG
Fisher, Beryl 67 MG
Fisher, Clara B (Aiken) 3:795 HHI
Fisher, Earl E 1931-32:40 OO
    1939-40:30 OO
    1941-42:62 OO
    1943-44:75 OO
Fisher, Ford 202, 207 BHSS
Fisher, George H 43 no.2:136 PN
Fisher, George Howard 2:575 HHI
Fisher, George McVey 6:423 MC
Fisher, Mrs. George McVey 6:423 MC
Fisher, George R unp. VU
    16:87 1911 WBP
Fisher, H M 96 LS
Fisher, Harry L 2:640 FH
Fisher, Isaac Birch 182 KB
Fisher, Milton (Twana Indian) 191 ET
Fisher, Mrs. Oliver 127 CBC
Fisher, Orin Wallace 4:487 PH
Fisher, S G 135 BN
Fisher, Vardis 59 no.2:70 PN
    25:102 PNLA
Fisher, W E 3:794 HHI

Fisher, Mrs. W E , see
    Fisher, Clara B (Aiken)
Fisher, Walter S 1931-32:41 OO
    1935-36:50 OO
Fisher, William Joseph 3:77 BH
Fisher, Willis 2:228 PMO
Fisk, Daniel W 723 LHM
Fisk, R E 83 LHM
Fisk, Wilbur 26 AC
Fiske, John front. FO
Fitch, Margaret, see
    Kelly, Margaret (Fitch)
Fitzgerald, C B unp. SEA
    58 SSP
Fitzgerald, Clara (Aram) 1:154-155 EPD
FitzGerald, Edgar James 1941:219 EN
FitzGerald, Maurice 351 MS
Fitzpatrick, Howard Baker 3:137 BEA
Fitzpatrick, Thomas 2:702 CAFT
Five Crows, Cayuse chief fol.705 JO
Fjeld, Andrew 254, 305 GL
Fjeld, Mrs. Andrew, see
    Fjeld, Eliza Ann (Broadbent)
Fjeld, Anna (Olson) 376 GL
Fjeld, Carl John Ellevsen 205 GL
Fjeld, Mrs. Carl John Ellevsen, see
    Fjeld, Anna (Olson)
    Fjeld, Maren Eline (Peterson)
Fjeld, Eliza Ann (Broadbent) 378 GL
Fjeld, Maren Eline (Peterson) 114 GL
Flagg, George H 1945-46:49 OO
Flaherty, R T 39 MG
Flamm, Henry J 3:59 HHI
Flanagan, May G unp. HOF
Flanagan, Merritt 2:467 SMS
Flanders, Alvan 24 MAG
    38 ME
    34 no.4:400-401 PN
    [51] RLX
    unp. SE
Flanders, Ford 206 BHSS
Flat Nose George, see
    Curry, George
Flatebo, J E 2:807 BHK
Flavel, George 26 LDM
    3:545 LHC
Flavel, Mrs. George, see
    Flavel, Mary Christiana Lydia (Boelling)
Flavel, Mary Christiana Lydia (Boelling)
    3:544 LHC
Fleetwood, Jennie, see
    Gibson, Jennie (Fleetwood)
Fleischner, Louis 1:614-615 GP
    2:259 GP
    1:306 PMO
    214 SHP
Fleming, Clara, see
    Gossett, Clara (Fleming)

Fleming, Flora, see			
Foster, Flora (Fleming)			
Fleming, H B	200	MCO	
Fleming, Sandford	2:427	BCF	
———————	118	GI	
———————	2	SC	
Flenner, John D	2:front.	FSB	
Fletcher, Alice C	229	BR	
———————	27	THI	
Fletcher, Edgar I	6:415	MC	
Fletcher, Edwin B	3:279	HHI	
Fletcher, F W	215	BHSS	
Fletcher, Francis	134	DO	
———————	1:404	NH	
Fletcher, John D	May 1907:39	TDL	
Fletcher, Robert H	55	BN	
Fletcher, William S	front.	HSP	
Flett, J B	1910:46	TDL	
Flett, John	1:476	NH	
Flett, John William	3:1072,1073	BCF	
Flett, Mrs. John William, see			
Flett, Mary Elizabeth (Evans)			
Flett, Mary Elizabeth (Evans)	3:1073	BCF	
Fliedner, William	2:329	GP	
Flink, John W	1112	SIH	
Flinn, John	176	AG	
———————	3:45	GP	
Flint Necklace, see			
Looking Glass, Sr., Nez Percé chief			
Flood, Beryl	410	BHSS	
Flood, James C	224	QT	
Flood, Pearl	410	BHSS	
Flood, Wilfrid E	260	GG	
Flournoy, A W	213	DL	
Flowerree, Daniel A G	2:951	SM	
Flowerree, William Kemp	2:583	SMS	
Floyd, John	70:334	OHQ	
Fluhart, Selden S	3:225	BHS	
Fluhrer, Alphaeus V	3:1568	SM	
Flumerfelt, Alfred C	fol.pt.2	SHB	
Flynn, Elizabeth Gurley	57 no.3:111	PN	
Fogg, Charles Sumner	5:74	SH	
Fogg, Fred S	1910:3	TDL	
Fogg, James E	3:1181	FH	
Follet, Charles G	366, 378	PI	
———————	436	PIW	
Folsom, D E	4:68	MC	
Folsom, Harriet Amelia, see			
Young, Harriet Amelia (Folsom)			
Folsom, Myron Archer	6:152	SH	
Fool Bear, Assiniboine chief	10:136	MC	
Foote, A F , Jr.	723	LHM	
Foote, Hamilton R	334	LDM	
Foote, Samuel S	2:801	FH	
———————	3:195	HHI	
Forbes, Frederick L	47	PSW	
Forbes, J H	2:778	FH	
Forbes, John	1:372	HHT	

Forbes, Peter Dewar	2:558	NH	
Forbes, W O	185	PSW	
Ford, David	2:430	NH	
Ford, J C	unp.	VU	
Ford, James A	1 no.8:21	WN	
Ford, Robert S	2:954	SM	
———————	2:535	SMS	
Forest, F C	31:48 1926	WBP	
Forney, James Harvey	209	IHI	
Forrest, Robert W	1:139	HH	
Forrest, W T	1895-96:145	SSS	
Forrest, William Rupert	6:98	SH	
Forse, Albert G	10	BSC	
———————	1925-26:32	IH	
Forster, George M	1924:96	WSP	
Forster, Neslen K	255	GG	
Forster, Thomas	fol.pt.1	SHB	
———————	1897:106	YB	
———————	1911:70-71	YB	
Forsyth, Mrs. F	2:19 1924	BCHA	
Forsyth, J	3:14 1925	BCHA	
Fortman, Clemens H	3:1258	SMS	
Fortson, George H	2:325	HH	
Fortune, Alexander Leslie			
	fol.title page	SHB	
Fortune, James Henry	3:857	BCF	
Fortune, William	fol.title page	SHB	
Foss, L C	145	SS	
Foss, Louis	2:360	PHP	
———————	191	SS	
———————	1895-96:67	SSS	
Foss, Phoebe (Purser)	2:771	LHC	
Foss, Mrs. William Webster, see			
Foss, Phoebe (Purser)			
Fosse, Knute O	3:41	BHK	
Foster, Addison G	1899:97	SSS	
Foster, Mrs. Addison G , see			
Foster, Martha Ann (Weatherbee)			
Foster, Charles B	2:276	HHT	
Foster, Earl	390	BHSS	
Foster, Edward Walker	1:568	PHP	
Foster, Emily (Yonge)	803	LHM	
Foster, F G	2:355	HWW	
Foster, Mrs. Flora	1945-46:37	IH	
Foster, Flora (Fleming)	4:500	PH	
Foster, Frank	2:606	FH	
Foster, Fred	3:302	PH	
Foster, George	2:144-145	EPD	
Foster, George E	6:416-417	MC	
Foster, Hillory Adams	4:500	PH	
Foster, Mrs. Hillory Adams, see			
Foster, Flora (Fleming)			
Foster, Homer Redfield	1:unp.1900-01	WDT	
Foster, J E	1895-96:91	SSS	
Foster, John Onesimus	136-137	SRW	
Foster, John W	2:463	BCF	
Foster, Joseph	240	BE	
———————	2:354	NH	

_____	4:500	PH
_____	6:128	SH
Foster, Mrs. Joseph, see		
Foster, Martha J (Steele)		
Foster, Joseph Henry	3:575	BCF
Foster, Martha Ann (Weatherbee)	1:9	D
Foster, Martha J (Steele)	4:500	PH
Foster, Mary Agness	1:456	GP
Foster, William Wasbrough	fol. pt. 2	SHB
Foster, Z D	803	LHM
Foster, Mrs. Z D , see		
Foster, Emily (Yonge)		
Fotheringham, Charlotte (Gentle)	34	GL
Fotheringham, John	34	GL
Fotheringham, Mrs. John, see		
Fotheringham, Charlotte (Gentle)		
Fotheringham, William	37	GL
Fouquet, Leon	2:310	MCC
Four Horns, Piegan chief	170	PI
	204	PIW
Four Rivers, Gros Ventre chief	10:120	MC
Fousek, Albert J	2:588	SMS
Fouts, William H H	2:289	HH
Fowler, Ed F	2:699	FH
Fowler, Enoch S	2:250	NH
Fowler, James	3:881	BHS
	390	LDM
Fowler, Thomas	209	GL
Fox, Dominick	2:600	SMS
Fox, Mrs. Dominick, see		
Fox, Magdalena (Spani)		
Fox, Elmer Wellington	1941:222	EN
Fox, Henry	unp.	SAA
Fox, Isaac W	104	GL
Fox, J H	2:429	BHK
Fox, J M	4:68	MC
Fox, Jacob Edgar	6:72	SH
Fox, L S	172-173	HA
Fox, "Link"	131	JNT
Fox, Magdalena (Spani)	2:600	SMS
Fox, Martha Ann, see		
Taylor, Martha Ann (Fox)		
Fox, Nettie (Hayward)	131	JNT
Fox, Robert Rolston	6:170	SH
	unp.	VU
Foy, John H	3:854	SMS
Frackleton, William S	6:303	MC
Fragmeier, William O	44:338	OHQ
France, C J	46	SA
Frances, pseud., see		
Wright, Fannie V		
Franchère, Gabriel	1:220	CAFT
	1:192	FI
	56	FRA
	2:242	LH
	1:47	LHC
Francis, Carl H	1943-44:77	OO
	1945-46:85	OO
Francis, Edwin H	200	LDM
Francis, Simeon	1:752	LHC
Francis Saxa, see		
Old Ignace (Flathead Indian)		
Franciscovich, F M	1931-32:40	OO
	1935-36:50	OO
	1937-38:62	OO
	1939-40:15	OO
	1941-42:62	OO
Francois (Flathead Indian)	5	JJ
Frank, H L	4:70	MC
Frank, Howard M	283	PSW
Frank, Mrs. Howard M	283	PSW
Frank, Sigmund	2:247	GP
Franklin, John	159	WOY
Franklin, W	2:front. 1924	BCHA
Franklin, W A	1897:124	YB
Franklyn, Fred	2:464-465	EPD
Franks, C W	2:191	BCF
Frary, Thomas Corwin	1:392	PHP
Frase, C W	23:45 1911	WSGP
	24:51 1912	WSGP
	25:56 1913	WSGP
Fraser, Frank D	1:unp. 1900-01	WDT
Fraser, Henry Charles	4:445	BCF
Fraser, Hugh Murray	3:523	BCF
Fraser, John Anderson	fol. pt. 1	SHB
	1911:70-71	YB
Fraser, Robert P	2:620	FH
Fraser, Simon	1:235	BCF
	47, 58	GI
	53	HBC
	53	MHN
	6	NF
	1:232	SH
	fol. title page	SHB
	35	WTH
	1911:70-71	YB
Fratt, Charles D	2:312	PHP
Fratt, David	2:931	SM
Frawley, Edward J	2:723	FH
Frazer, Arthur L	1:470	GP
	2:699	GP
Frazer, Harry	1935-36:51	OO
Frazer, J M	84	LDM
Frazer, Jacob	1:116	NH
Frazier, Georgia	207	BHSS
Frazier, William M	712	SIH
Frederckson, A S	159	WOY
Frederic, John W	896	SIH
Free, Emmeline, see		
Young, Emmeline (Free)		
Freece, James S	1924:176	WSP
Freeland, Ray	May 1907:38	TDL
Freeman, Frank F	2:431	GP
Freeman, Ida May, see		
Doane, Ida May (Freeman)		
Freeman, Legh Miller	2:361	BHK
Freeman, Legh R	2:229	HH

Freeman, Miller, see			
Freeman, Legh Miller			
Freeman, S S	460	AG	
Freer, Lemuel	4:947	BCF	
Freeze, John	712	SIH	
Freidenrich, A	2:154-155	EPD	
Frein, Pierre Joseph	6:31 1906	WDT	
Frémont, John Charles	288	BF	
_____	74	BHI	
_____	223	CIR	
_____	146	DSW	
_____	2:136	FI	
_____	3:360	LH	
French, E L	1 no.8:8	WN	
French, George W	5:191	MC	
French, Giles L	1937-38:62-63	OO	
_____	1939-40:30	OO	
_____	1941-42:65	OO	
_____	1943-44:77	OO	
_____	1945-46:86	OO	
French, Hiram Taylor	1:front.	FH	
French, Permeal Jane	14	SPI	
French, Walter M	3:4	PH	
_____	1926:47	WSP	
Freuchtnicht, Anna	42:32 1930	WSGP	
Freudenberg, W F	[131]	RLX	
Friars, Q E	296	E	
Friberg, William	3:401	GP	
Frick, Laura A (Malm), see			
Svenson, Laura A (Malm) Frick			
Friede, George W	1937-38:62-63	OO	
Friele, Haakon B	3:277	BHK	
Friendly, S H	1:639	CHW	
Fries, Anna Catherine (Fries)			
	186,190,259	FF	
Fries, David Christianson	192, 286	FF	
Fries, Jacob Jorgen	192, 286	FF	
Fries, Signa Cecilia	192, 286	FF	
Fries, Ulrich Englehart	passim	FF	
Fries, Mrs. Ulrich Englehart, see			
Fries, Anna Catherine (Fries)			
Frink, John M	1:661	BHK	
_____	2:83	BHK	
_____	3:45	BHS	
_____	5:246	SH	
_____	1895-96:67	SSS	
Frisbie, R C	1941-42:65	OO	
_____	1943-44:77	OO	
_____	1945-46:86	OO	
Frisch, Erik	88	SS	
Fritchman, Harry K	2:713	FH	
_____	1:182	FSB	
Frith, Henry A	2:1062	SM	
Frobisher, Joseph	114	MH	
Frog, see			
Ollokot, Nez Percé chief			
Fromme, Julius Martin	3:1065	BCF	
Frosig, Mikkel	2:941	HHI	

Frost, E J	219	BHSS	
Frost, John Edgar	1943:142	ENC	
Frostad, K P	1905-06:[62]	RLW	
Froula, Vaclav Karel	1941:252	EN	
Fry, Elmina E	648	SIH	
Fry, George	2:front.1924	BCHA	
Fry, Philip V W	2:881	LHC	
Fry, Richard A	860	SIH	
Fry, Robert Hope	3:97	PH	
Frye, Frank Fremont	4:499	PH	
Frye, George Frederick	1:73	BHK	
_____	2:69	BHK	
_____	2:722	BHS	
Frye, Mrs. George Frederick, see			
Frye, Louisa C (Denny)			
Frye, James M	3:171	BHS	
Frye, Louisa C (Denny)	2:73	BHK	
Frye, Theodore Christian	6:26 1906	WDT	
_____	26:51 1925	WDT	
Fuhrer, Walter	1935-36:51	OO	
_____	1937-38:62-63	OO	
_____	1939-40:30	OO	
Fuld, Leon	3:1056	FH	
Fuller, Almon Homer	1:unp.1900-01	WDT	
_____	6:23 1906	WDT	
Fuller, Andrew J	3:1022	FH	
Fuller, August	3:970	SMS	
Fuller, E N	2:162	HHT	
Fuller, Franklin Ide	3:797	GP	
Fuller, George F	257	LDM	
Fuller, James L	3:1045	FH	
Fuller, Melinda, see			
King, Melinda (Fuller)			
Fuller, Richard Eugene	4:468	PH	
Fuller, Roy H	2:1287	SM	
Fuller, Samuel	3:970	SMS	
Fuller, Thomas P	183	LHM	
Fullerton, Mark A	1922:20	WSP	
Fullerton, Roscoe F	1923:50	WSP	
Fulmer, Elton	219, 418	BHSS	
Fulton, Charles W	475	PL	
_____	2:460	PMO	
Fulton, Frederick John	fol.pt.1	SHB	
Fulton, H C	1905-06:[61]	RLW	
_____	[114]	RLX	
Fulton, John	2:371	CHW	
Fulton, R W	97	DH	
Fulton, Walter Shepard	3:425	BHK	
_____	1924:161	WSP	
Fulton, William M	1941:441	EN	
Fultz, Hollis B	1 no.8:28	WN	
Funnemark, Birgitte Svendson	66:104	OHQ	
Funnemark, Christine	66:104	OHQ	
Furey, Charles H	138	HIT	
Furgueson, John B	2:318	NH	
Furnell, Della (Peek)	204	LHM	
Furnell, M	204	LHM	
Furnell, Mrs. M , see			
Furnell, Della (Peek)			

Furnish, Robert T	3:1440	SM
Fursey, F R	37	MG
Furst, John C	1120	SIH
Furstnow, Albert F	2:1282	SM
Furth, Jacob	1:525	BHK
	2:732	BHS
————	2:568	PHP
————	1905-06:[75]	RLW
————	5:106	SH
————	unp.	VU
————	19:137 1914	WBP
Furuya, Masajiro	1 no.3:193	WM
Fyfer, Julius T	2:342	NH

G

Gabel, Joseph	1905-06:[74]	RLW
Gabica, Miguel	3:295	HHI
Gabie, W Gardner	2:765	BHK
Gabisch, George	243	GG
Gable, George	105	AG
Gaches, Charles E	[136]	RLX
Gaffney, Frank	1096	SIH
Gaffney, John J	1096	SIH
Gafney, Mary, see		
Brosnan, Mary (Gafney)		
Gage, John W	143	LDM
Gage, Julia (Sampson)	304	SIH
Gage, William H	304	SIH
Gage, Mrs. William H , see		
Gage, Julia (Sampson)		
Gagnier, J B	1:20	NH
Gaillac, Emille	unp.	SAA
Gaines, John P	22	TUR
Galbraith, A A	265	JNT
Galbraith, Mrs. A A 267		JNT
Galbraith, Elbert P	28	SCC
Galbraith, Robert Leslie Thomas		
	fol.pt.1	SHB
Galbraith, Will A	1943:68	ENC
Galbraith, William J	4:110	MC
	1:428	SMS
Galbreaith, Walter S	3:941	FH
Gale, John P	1:358	PHP
Gale, Joseph	5	TUR
Galen, Albert John	1941:254	EN
Galen, Hugh F	2:990	SM
Galen, Mrs. Hugh F , see		
Galen, Matilda (Gillogly)		
Galen, Matilda (Gillogly)	402-403	PI
	472	PIW
Galeno, Fred	3:317	BHK
Galer, Roger C	4:887	BCF
Gallagher, D Wayne	43 no.2:137	PN
Gallagher, G	1:566	BH
Gallagher, Sarah Jane, see		
Russell, Sarah Jane (Gallagher)		

Gallagher, William Henry	4:1011	BCF
Gallaway, Thomas B	544	SIH
Galloway, Charles V	1945-46:56	OO
Galloway, Emma (Baker)	unp.	SOU
Galloway, Thomas C	114	IHI
Galloway, Mrs. William, see		
Galloway, Emma (Baker)		
Gallup, Martha, see		
Griggs, Martha (Gallup)		
Gallup, Philo W	48	LS
Gallwey, Harry A	2:542	SMS
Galt, Alexander T	109	GI
Galt, John	78	GI
Galvani, W H	44:338	OHQ
Gambell, V C	252	PSW
Gamble, Thomas D	32	SCC
Gamble, Thomas L	2:418	NH
Gamelin, Emmelie (Tavernier), see		
Gamelin, Mother		
Gamelin, Mrs. Jean Baptiste, see		
Gamelin, Mother		
Gamelin, Mother	12	MG
Gamer, Frederick	113	MI
	2:1007	SM
Ganahl, Frank	151	GG
Ganahl, Richard	151	GG
Gandy, J E	1895-96:93	SSS
Gannon, Michael	165	GG
Gans, Edward M	3:1231	SMS
Gantenbein, Calvin U	2:101	GP
	59:299	OHQ
Garcia-Prada, Carlos	36:26 1935	WDT
Gardiner, William Frederick	4:377	BCF
Gardner, Alan	168	MV
Gardner, Edward M	6:323	MC
Gardner, Hamilton	305	GL
Gardner, James Hamilton	255	GL
Gardner, Mrs. James Hamilton, see		
Gardner, Rhoda Priscilla (Huffaker)		
Gardner, Mina M , see		
Irwin, Mina M (Gardner)		
Gardner, Rhoda Priscilla (Huffaker)		
	383	GL
Gardner, W T	1:470	GP
Garfield, James Rudolph	465	PL
Garfielde, Selucius	4:184	SH
Garignano, Brother	376	PIW
Garland, M Neelin	4:293	BCF
Garnett, Robert Selden	46 no.2:48	PN
Garretson, Hiram F	2:168	PHP
Garrett, Clarence B	194	MI
Garrett, Harvey W	6:350	MC
Garrett, Pat	300	SW
Garrett, Robert Max	26:7 1925	WDT
Garrigus, Lewis C	2:323	GP
Garry, Joseph Richard	3:17	BEA
Garry, Nellie	52	LC
Garry, Nicholas	166	MH

Garry, Spokane, see
    Spokane Garry, Spokan chief
Garry, Thomas (Spokan Indian) 58   LC
Gary, George   1:410   PMO
Gass, Patrick   1:60   GP
Gaston, Giles, see
    Miller, Joaquin
Gaston, Joseph   1:front.   GP
    2:286   NH
Gaston, William   104   MCO
Gatch, Thomas Milton   18-19   GA
    32   OS
Gates, Cassius Emerson   3:739   BHS
    3:119   PH
Gates, Charles Marvin   54 no. 2:50   PN
Gates, John   101   LDM
    1:468   NH
Gatley, John   4:411   BCF
Gatter, Frank W   166   LDM
Gatzert, Bailey   unp.   SEA
Gaucher, Peter, see
    Left Handed Peter (Flathead Indian)
Gaudette, Edmund L   2:325   HWW
Gauld, James G   3:619   GP
Gault, F B   2:56   HHT
Gauvreau, Narcisse Belleau   4:151   BCF
Gay, Charles   96   LS
Gay, George K   1:92   NH
Gay, William H   4:673   BCF
Gay, Wilson Riley   3:237   BHS
    96   LS
Gazzoli, Gregory   fol. 512   BUR
    182   PI
Gearin, Walter J   1943-44:77   OO
Geary, John J   247   GG
Geddings, Ab   60   SHO
Geddings, Hank   60   SHO
Geddis, S R   1:528   NH
Geer, Cynthia Ann (Eoff)   1:534   PMO
Geer, Heman J   1:534   PMO
Geer, Mrs. Heman J , see
    Geer, Cynthia Ann (Eoff)
Geer, Irwin S   2:437   PMO
Geer, Theodore T   1:681   CHW
    60:281, 282   OHQ
    330   PL
    1:12   PMO
    unp.   SOU
    54   TUR
Geese-lighting, see
    Yi-yi-wa-som-way (Nez Percé Indian)
Gehres, Aloysius J   235   GG
Gehres, Francis B   261   GG
Geiger, William E   172-173, 213   HA
    404   WOY
Geiger, William F   3:367   HHT
Geisness, Thomas   1924:113   WSP
Gekeler, David   3:11   HHI
Genoway, Charles V   2:613   FH

Gentle, Charlotte, see
    Fotheringham, Charlotte (Gentle)
George III, King of Great Britain and
    Ireland   166   MV
George, Agnes, see
    Agnes George (Umatilla Indian)
George, Hugh N   2:16   NH
George, J W   2:16   NH
George, Mahala (Nickerson)   2:16   NH
George, Melvin Clarke   2:16   NH
    1:82   PMO
George, Presley   2:16   NH
George, Mrs. Presley, see
    George, Mahala (Nickerson)
George, S Alexander   167   PSW
George, Wade H   3:800   SMS
Geraghty, James M   45   MG
Gerlach, Miriam   448   BHSS
Gerow, G   2:front. 1924   BCHA
Gerry, Robert   1895-96:91   SSS
Gershevsky, Ruth (Hale)   6:74   PNLA
    8:127   PNLA
    18:9   PNLA
Gerstle, Lewis   31   KI
Gesner, Alonzo   1895:78   OO
Gesner, Van   340   PL
Getchell, Delroy   1941:109   EN
Getchell, L W   1:259   HH
Ghent, J A   80   DA
Ghormley, David O   181   PSW
Gibb, David   3:275   BCF
Gibb, John L   101   GL
Gibbon, John   31   DH
    7:97   MC
    1:348   SMS
Gibbon, Mrs. John   31   DH
Gibbon, John, Jr.   31   DH
Gibbon, Katie   31   DH
Gibbon, William D   2:785   BHK
Gibbs, A L   89, 134, 139   MLO
Gibbs, Addison C   1:572-573   GP
    2:157   GP
    4:304   LH
    31   TUR
Gibbs, Josiah Francis   front.   GLS
Gibney, Ezra P   6:416-417   MC
Giboney, G William   89   PSW
Gibson, Angus   1939-40:30   OO
    1941-42:65   OO
    1943-44:75   OO
    1945-46:82   OO
Gibson, C E   1895-96:93   SSS
Gibson, Esther   252   PSW
Gibson, J A   172-173   HA
Gibson, James   2:472   SMS
Gibson, Mrs. James, see
    Gibson, Jennie (Fleetwood)
Gibson, James S   3:703   BHS
Gibson, Jennie (Fleetwood)   2:473   SMS

Gibson, Paris	4:89	MC
_____	418	MI
	3:659	SMS
Gibson, Richard	3:409	BCF
Gibson, Samuel	2:41	HBT
Gibson, William Wallace	8 no.2:96	BCH
Giddings, Mrs. J	48	LS
Gifford, Benjamin Arthur	66:317	OHQ
Gifford, John	45	SCC
Gifford, Thomas	1911:70-71	YB
Gilbert, Emery P	[112]	RLX
Gilbert, Frances Olive, see		
Hammer, Frances Olive (Gilbert)		
Gilbert, Harold B	1924:145	WSP
Gilbert, Helen	29:5	PNLA
Gilbert, Horace E	712	SIH
Gilbert, J B	[110]	RLX
Gilbert, Mahlon Norris	6:459	MC
Gilbert, W H	1895-96:69	SSS
Gilbert, Warren J	1924:65	WSP
Gilbertson, John M	43no.2:136-137	PN
Gilbreath, James	387	LDM
Gilchrist, George K	6:416-417	MC
Gilchrist, Hugh W	123	PSW
Gilcrest, Evelyn	63:321	OHQ
Gilcrest, John, Jr.	63:308,321	OHQ
Gilcrest, Mary	63,308,321	OHQ
Gile, Robert C	1941-42:65	OO
	1943-44:77	OO
	1945-46:86	OO
Gilkey, Charles	3:130-131	PH
Gilkey, Daniel Emerson	3:517	BH
Gilkey, Frank	3:130-131	PH
Gilkey, William E	3:129	PH
Gill, Clyde	287	BHSS
Gill, Hiram C	53	PIG
	59 no.4:182	PN
_____	unp.	SEA
	58	SSP
Gill, Joseph K	506	SHP
Gill, Ralph C	3:931	BHS
Gill, Ray W	1931-32:41	OO
Gill, Samuel F	250	LDM
Gillahan, Mrs. Martin, see		
Spencer, Sarah A (Tindle) Gillahan		
Gillahan, Sarah A (Tindle), see		
Spencer, Sarah A (Tindle) Gillahan		
Gillespie, H J	336	LDM
Gillette, Charles H	64:324	OHQ
Gillette, Preston Wilson	3:111	GP
Gillette, Warren	231	GG
Gillette, Warren C	2:884	SM
Gilley, James Rogers	3:131	BCF
Gilley, Walter R	3:115	BCF
Gilliam, Mitchell	1926:20	WSP
Gilliam, William A	252	LDM
Gillies, B D	fol.pt.2	SHB
Gillis, M C	1:372	HHT

Gillis, Malcolm	3:1425	SM
Gillis, Wallace David	1941:77	EN
Gillogly, Matilda, see		
Galen, Matilda (Gillogly)		
Gilman, James M	1244-1245	HIO
_____	37	LDM
	2:658	NH
Gilman, Mrs. James M , see		
Gilman, Laura F (Graves)		
Gilman, Laura F (Graves)	1245	HIO
Gilman, Luthene Clairmont	3:205	PH
Gilmore, David	2:155	BHK
Gilmore, Lorraine	67	MG
Gilpatrick, L S	39	MG
Gilsdorf, Andrew John	2:1204-1205	SM
Gilsdorf, Mrs. Andrew John, see		
Gilsdorf, Olavea (Olson)		
Gilsdorf, Olavea (Olson)	2:1204-1205	SM
Gilstrap, William H	122	AC
_____	12, 48	PC
_____	2:272	PHP
_____	[78]	RLX
Giorda, Joseph	fol.512	BUR
_____	47	GG
_____	50	PI
_____	308	PIW
Gipson, Albert E	1:176	FSB
Gipson, J H	48 no.3:103	PN
Gird, William	68:144	OHQ
Gist, Duke	3:1170	SMS
Gittlesen, Lionel	311	BHSS
Giustin, George	177	PL
Givens, J A	14:132 1909	WBP
Glase, Robert L	2:721	FH
Glasgow, Alexander	231	E
Glasgow, Joseph M	1924:97	WSP
_____	3:1142	BHS
Glasgow, Samuel	232	E
Glasgow, William Adams	3:261	BHS
Glass, David G	1931-32:41	OO
Glass, Joseph C	43 no.1:16-17	PN
Glass, R C	120	AG
Glasscock, B B	1905-06:[28]	RLW
Glavis, Louis Russell	55 no.2:72	PN
Gleason, A B	1:428	NH
Gleason, Charles S	1905-06:[55]	RLW
Gleason, James P	1895-96:135	SSS
Gleason, M James	1941-42:65	OO
	1945-46:86	OO
Glen, Irving	26:51 1925	WDT
Glen, James J	[128]	RLX
Glen, R J	1895-96:93	SSS
Glenk, J Wesley	306	AC
Glenn, Edwin F	fol.207	SHI
Glenn, Mitchell Willard	3:307	BHK
Glenn, Thomas L	3:986	FH
Glide, Harry	46	LDM
Glisan, R B	1:536	GP

Glisan, Rodney	1:536	GP
	2:206	GP
_____	1:632	NH
_____	1:366	PMO
_____	286	SHP
Glorieux, Alphonsus Joseph	2:692	FH
	132	IHI
Gloster, Richard Ignatus	2 no. 6:10	W
Glougie, Clyde A	2:373	HHI
Glover, George	276	GL
Glover, James Nettle	3:224	FI
	5:176	SH
Gloyd, F H	1:566	BH
Gnagey, U D	1924:129	WSP
Goates, Martha, see		
Wing, Martha (Goates)		
Goates, Rebecca (Pilgrim)	110	GL
Goates, William	62	GL
Goates, Mrs. William, see		
Goates, Rebecca (Pilgrim)		
Goble, Fannie (Smith)	1:13	D
Goble, Mrs. George H , see		
Goble, Fannie (Smith)		
Goble, Sarah C , see		
Rein, Sarah C (Goble) Shuler		
Goddard, A J	1895-96:93	SSS
Goddard, O Fletcher	1941:395	EN
	599	MI
	2:211	SMS
Godfrey, Eva S	38:36	G
Godfrey, Frank S	3:657	LHC
Godfrey, Harry R	3:481	BCF
Godman, M M	1905-06:[28]	RLW
	[115]	RLX
Goepel, Mrs. William	2:front. 1924	BCHA
Goerig, A C	3:829	BHK
Goetz, Herman	2:285	BHK
Goetz, Jacob	233	E
Gohn, Anna (Zweifell)	771	LHM
Gohn, George	771	LHM
	235	MI
Gohn, Mrs. George, see		
Gohn, Anna (Zweifell)		
Going, James W	2:201	GP
Goldsmith, J S	unp.	VU
Goldsmith, Margaret (Hall)	191	SIH
Goldsmith, Martin L	191	SIH
Goldsmith, Mrs. Martin L , see		
Goldsmith, Margaret (Hall)		
Goldstone, Samuel	528	SIH
Goldsworthy, H E	290	BHSS
Golighley, Joseph W	3:1317	FH
Goller, Herman Joseph	207	GG
	10	SCH
Goltz, Adelgunde, see		
Ehlert, Adelgunde (Goltz)		
Good, Charles	1897:124	YB
Good, Henry	1943:111	ENC

	3:847	SMS
Good, Thomas	3:1106	SMS
Goodacre, L	2:293	BCF
Goodale, Charles W	3:1307	SM
Goodall, James P	1:278	NH
Goode, Henry Walton, Jr.	2:9	LHC
Goode, Henry Walton, Sr.	2:91	GP
	2:4	LHC
Goodell, Henry	217	JNT
Goodell, Melancthon Z	1:628	NH
Goodeve, A S	1911:70-71	YB
Gooding, E E	2:228	PMO
Gooding, Frank Robert	1:145	FSB
Gooding, Fred W	3:1035	FH
Goodman, Alfred Edwin	4:347	BCF
Goodman, Anna E , see		
McCormick, Anna E (Goodman)		
Goodrich, Forest J	50:63 1949	WDT
Goodrich, L J	21:160 1916	WBP
Goodrich, Luke L	135	MLO
	36:64 1931	WBP
Goodsell, C H	202, 408	BHSS
Goodspeed, G E	50:48 1949	WDT
Goodwin, Betsy (Smith)	109	GL
Goodwin, Ervin Shirley	3:689	BHK
	6:196	SH
Goodwin, Francis M	25	SCC
Goodwin, George	191	JNT
Goodwin, George W	1:396	NH
Goodwin, Isaac	166	GL
Goodwin, Isaac H	387	GL
Goodwin, Mrs. Isaac H , see		
Goodwin, Betsy (Smith)		
Goodwin, Phillip Charles	2:519	SMS
Goodwin, William Isaac	3:967	BCF
Goody, Arthur	3:575	HHI
Gordon, Burgess L , Jr.	260	GG
Gordon, George	3:642	BCF
Gordon, Mrs. George, see		
Gordon, Isabella (Grant)		
Gordon, George Robertson	3:front.	BCF
Gordon, Herbert	1931-32:41	OO
Gordon, Isabella (Grant)	3:643	BCF
Gordon, John B	31	SSP
Gordon, John Kidd	3:677	BH
Gordon, Merritt J	2:587	HHT
	1895-96:61	SSS
Gordon, Thomas W	511	HI
Gordon, William Alexander	3:61	GP
Gore, Charles	319	LDM
Gore, George	319	LDM
Gore, John C	236	LDM
Gore, Vera	66	MG
Goreczky, Anton	2:616	FH
Gorham, Helen	36:16 1935	WDT
Gorin, Henry Jerome	3:911	BHS
Gorman, Daniel M	2:196	HHI
Gorman, Katherine, see		
Robinson, Katherine (Gorman)		

Gorman, Thomas J	6:84	SH	
Gorp, Leopold van, see			
Van Gorp, Leopold			
Gortemuller, Adolph	6:404-405	MC	
Gorton, George W	640	IHI	
Gose, C C	1909:front.	WSP	
	1910:107	WSP	
Gose, Mack F	1 no.6:1	TF	
	1915:front.	WSP	
	1924:48	WSP	
Gosnell, John C	3:571	BHS	
Goss, E Lyle	36:32 1935	WDT	
Goss, John D	1935-36:50	OO	
Gosse, John F	4:1107	BCF	
Gosset, William Driscoll	15no.1-2:107	BCH	
	56	DC	
	92	RA	
Gossett, Charles Clinton	3:33	BEA	
Gossett, Mrs. Charles Clinton, see			
Gossett, Clara (Fleming)			
Gossett, Clara (Fleming)	3:33	BEA	
Goudie, John M	6:350	MC	
Gough, Charlotte (Crocket)	389	GL	
Gough, James	388	GL	
Gough, Mrs. James, see			
Gough, Charlotte (Crocket)			
Goul, Sarah Louisa, see			
Pethtel, Sarah Louisa (Goul)			
Gould, Augustus Warren	3:681	BHS	
	6:100	SH	
Gould, J L	252	PSW	
Gould, James Edward	6:26 1906	WDT	
Gouley, Romeo	1931-32:41	OO	
	1935-36:51	OO	
Govan, David	[125]	RLX	
Gove, A B	62	LDM	
Gove, Mrs. David A , see			
Gove, Eva (Wead)			
Gove, Eva (Wead)	1:12	D	
Gove, George W	132	JNT	
	261	LDM	
Gove, Herbert H	1:602	PHP	
Gove, I W	41	LDM	
Gove, Jesse Augustus	front.	GU	
Gove, Royal Amenzo	6:188	SH	
Gove, Warren	3:357	HHT	
	1:560	NH	
Gove, William	129	LDM	
Gow, Alexander	3:759	BHK	
Gowan, A W	1895:79	OO	
Gowen, Charles	10 no.1:43	BCH	
Gowen, Gus	2:front. 1924	BCHA	
Gowen, Herbert H	26:52 1925	WDT	
	1 no.10:12	WN	
Gowey, John F	1905-06:[28]	RLW	
Gowrie, Peter	3:768	SMS	
Grabow, William	2:1209	SM	
Grace (Flathead Indian)	14	JJ	

Grace, Emma, see			
Austin, Emma (Grace)			
Grace, Hannah, see			
Webb, Hannah (Grace)			
Grace, Harriet, see			
Webb, Harriet (Grace)			
Grace, William E	2:437	PMO	
Grady, Frank M	2:1297	SM	
Grady, Michael J	3:274	PH	
Graeter, Augustus F	5:323	MC	
	2:876-877	SM	
Graeter, Mrs. Augustus F , see			
Graeter, Mary J (Taylor)			
Graeter, Margaret French	5:191	MC	
Graeter, Mary J (Taylor)	2:876-877	SM	
Grafton, A E	May 1907:68	TDL	
Graham, A E	1924:129	WSP	
Graham, Donald	1897:106	YB	
Graham, George Edgar	4:599	BCF	
Graham, James Edward	3:332	BEA	
Graham, John S	3:1101	BHS	
Graham, Leonard E	3:235	BEA	
Graham, Richard	3:734	SMS	
Graham, Robert John	3:228	PH	
Graham, Rosana, see			
Dougall, Rosana (Graham)			
Graham, Susie (Mercer)	1:89	BHK	
Graham, Thomas P	1937-38:62	OO	
Graham, William L	1935-36:51	OO	
Grahame, Harry McAdoo	4:917	BCF	
	fol.pt.2	SHB	
Grahame, James Allan	3:821	BCF	
	232	MHN	
	fol. title page	SHB	
	1897:18	YB	
Grahs, Edward J	3:611	GP	
Gram, C H	2:423	CHW	
	1931-32:8	OO	
	1935-36:34	OO	
	1937-38:7	OO	
	1939-40:7	OO	
	1941-42:13	OO	
Gram, Gregers	2:463	BCF	
Gramkow, William	2:693	FH	
Gramling, Ferne Amy	3:1338-1339	SM	
Gramling, Nicholas Howard	3:1338-1339	SM	
Grammer, Elijah Sherman	4:439	PH	
Grandin, Vital J	1:286	MCC	
Grandy, Benjamin W	1:300	NH	
Granger, Clarence A	263	GL	
Granger, Walter Norton	5:254	SH	
Grannis, George W	unp.	SOU	
Grant, (Captain)	433	LDM	
Grant, A S	1937-38:62-63	OO	
	1939-40:30	OO	
Grant, Henry I	2:290	SMS	
Grant, Isabella, see			
Gordon, Isabella (Grant)			

Grant, Jedediah Morgan   112-113(xxxv) PR
Grant, John   188   KB
Grant, John M   48   LS
Grant, Ulysses Simpson   31   DH
_____   4:214   LH
Grass, Robert   1924:48   WSP
Grauer, Jacob   4:911   BCF
Graveley, Walter E   4:637   BCF
Graves, Andrew C   3:1483   SM
Graves, Carroll B   3:127   BHS
                          5:280   SH
_____   1926:20   WSP
Graves, Dorsett V   176-177   GA
Graves, Edward Oziel   5:204   SH
Graves, Frank H   461   HI
                          5:278   SH
Graves, Frank Pierrepont 18-19   GA
_____   1:front.1900-01 WDT
Graves, Highland C   3:1157   FH
Graves, Mrs. Highland C   , see
    Graves, Matilda K (Parker)
Graves, Jay P   5:278   SH
Graves, Laura F   , see
    Gilman, Laura F (Graves)
Graves, Matilda K (Parker) 3:1157 FH
Graves, Melvin MacPike   3:40   BEA
Graves, Orth C   3:761   BHS
Graves, "Tubby", see
    Graves, Dorsett V
Graves, Victor R   43 no.2:136-137   PN
Graves, W   B   1926:20   WSP
Graves, Will G   1905-06:[45]   RLW
_____   [91]   RLX
_____   5:280   SH
Gray, A   W   199   LDM
Gray, Arthur Harville   3:791   BHS
Gray, Caroline Augusta, see
    Kamm, Caroline Augusta (Gray)
Gray, Edith (Elison)   2:935   HHI
Gray, George Edward   3:976   FH
Gray, Isabel, see
    Powers, Isabel (Gray)
Gray, James Taylor   2:59   LHC
Gray, John H   D   82   LDM
                          1:124   PMO
Gray, John Hamilton   3:933   BCF
                          1911:70-71   YB
Gray, John Hamilton, Jr. 3:987   BCF
Gray, John J   2:89   HHI
Gray, Mary Augusta (Dix) 134   DE
                          2:51   LHC
                          1:132   NH
                          .:66   PMO
Gray, Robert   1:160   BCF
_____   1:83, 85   BS
_____   252   CIR
_____   1:76   D
_____   1:30   FI

_____   16   FW
_____   76   GBS
_____   1:28-29   GP
_____   64   LCR
_____   64-65   LCRH
_____   9   LDM
_____   1:26   LHC
_____   22:257   OHQ
_____   1:592   PMO
Gray, Sarah F   , see
    Abernethy, Sarah F (Gray)
Gray, W   B   1905-06:[28]   RLW
Gray, William Henry   134   DE
_____   55   DO
_____   232   DW
_____   58   EW
_____   1:596   GP
_____   front.   GUG
_____   3:276   LH
_____   1:287   LHC
_____   2:51   LHC
_____   1:132   NH
_____   1:6   PMO
_____   233   PSW
Gray, Mrs. William Henry, see
    Gray, Mary Augusta (Dix)
Gray, William Polk   2:319   HH
_____   258   LDM
_____   2:55   LHC
Gray, William Price   3:67   PH
Gray, William R   2:934   HHI
Gray, Wilmoth, see
    Jones, Wilmoth (Gray)
Graybill, T   48   LS
Greaves, Joseph Blackburn 2:293   BCF
_____   4:881   BCF
_____   fol.title page SHB
Greeley, William B   1 no.7:14   WN
Green, A   de Y   May 1907:38   TDL
Green, Alice, see
    Whitman, Alice (Green)
Green, Alphonzo A   872   SIH
Green, Charles W   184   SIH
Green, Mrs. Charles W   , see
    Green, Eva (Taylor)
Green, E   M   3:567   GP
Green, Eva (Taylor)   184   SIH
Green, Henry D   250   SHP
Green, James   3:803   SMS
Green, John   115   DL
_____   2:587   FH
Green, Joshua   1 no.11:18   WN
Green, O   M   19:64 1914   WBP
_____   22:32 1917   WBP
_____   23:front.1918 WBP
Green, R   J   1945-46:93   OO
Green, Robert Francis   4:125   BCF
Greene, A   R   87   PL

Greene, David	3:24	HM
Greene, J H	3:1083	FH
Greene, P B	41	MG
Greene, R A	39	MG
Greene, Raymond William	3:114	PH
	1924:144	WSP
Greene, Roger Sherman	1:599	BHK
	2:728	BHS
Greenfield, John S	70:207, 209	OHQ
Greenhow, Thomas	fol. title page	SHB
Greenough, Thomas	4:68	MC
Greenwood, J S	1939-40:30	OO
	1941-42:65	OO
	1943-44:77	OO
	1945-46:86	OO
Greenwood, Marcellus B	6:440-441	MC
Greer, John	1096	SIH
Gregg, A S	112	AG
Gregg, Alexander H	234	E
	[113]	RLX
Gregg, David M	124	MCO
Gregg, J T	1:553	CHW
Gregory, Charles	1:154-155	EPD
Gregory, Edwin	3:199	BH
Gregory, W A	338	LDM
Greig, Richard	3:963	SMS
Grennan, Lawrence	5:128	SH
Grenville, William Wyndham	64	MV
Grey, Albert Henry George, fourth Earl		
	1911:6-7	YB
Grieve, M	41	MG
Grieve, M Irene	41	MG
Grieve, W E	37	MG
Griffin, E H	1:400	GP
Griffin, Jim	115	DL
Griffin, John Smith	55	DO
	197	DS
	1:28	NH
Griffin, L N	1905-06:[62]	RLW
Griffin, Louisa M , see		
Hailey, Louisa M (Griffin)		
Griffith, Charles Roger	3:747	LHC
Griffith, Lewis E	1945-46:42	OO
Griffith, Luther H	6:118	SH
Griffith, Mabel C	1 no. 1:24	WM
Griffith, Sarelia, see		
Miller, Sarelia (Griffith)		
Griffiths, Austin E	59	SSP
Griffiths, James	118	LDM
Griffits, Thomas C	1905-06:[28]	RLW
Grigg, Thomas A	3:1498	SM
	2:393	SMS
Griggs, Chauncey Wright	1:169	HH
	3:11	HHT
	1:310	PHP
	5:158	SH
Griggs, Mrs. Chauncey Wright, see		
Griggs, Martha (Gallup)		

Griggs, Edward Howard	1:148	FSB
Griggs, Everett G	1910:2	TDL
Griggs, George Albert	2:1232	SM
Griggs, Martha (Gallup)	1:11	D
Grim, Mrs. Alta M	6:74	PNLA
	25:34	PNLA
	30:102	PNLA
Grimes, George	218	BHSS
Grimes, L R	1895-96:59	SSS
Grimes, Mary Eliza, see		
Stanley, Mary Eliza (Grimes)		
Grimm, Warren O	13	LT
Grimmer, John M	41	SCC
Grimmett, Samuel H	2:781	FH
Grinnell, Charles H	2:407	HHT
Grinwald, Charles H	260	LDM
Griswold, Sylvia (Zoll)	3:69	D
Groce, Oliver J	3:105	GP
Groefsema, John H	3:44	BEA
Groefsema, Mrs. John H , see		
Groefsema, Olive De Ette (Jenson)		
Groefsema, Olive De Ette (Jenson) 3:44		BEA
	1945-46:37	IH
Groeneveld, Eiko J	6:382-383	MC
Groeneveld, Mrs. Eiko J , see		
Groeneveld, Mrs. Loretta V		
Groeneveld, Mrs. Loretta V	6:382-383	MC
Groff, Guy B	1924:64	WSP
Groom, F H	1910:43	TDL
Gross, Abraham	1:145	HH
Gross, David	1:145	HH
Gross, Ellis H	1:145	HH
Gross, Morris	1:145	HH
Gross, William H	200	OPC
	176	SG
Grosscup, B S	1912:front.	WSP
Grosse-tête (Carrier Indian)	23	MHN
Ground, Franklin Pierce	2:299	CHW
Grounds, Brazil	21	LDM
Grover, Cuvier	1:416	NH
Grover, Edward P	3:690	HHI
Grover, Mrs. Edward P , see		
Grover, Fannie (Clawson)		
Grover, Fannie (Clawson)	3:691	HHI
Grover, La Fayette	301	HIO
	4:306	LH
	1:723	LHC
	1:416	NH
	67:258	OHQ
	1:182	PMO
	60 no. 3:140	PN
	37	TUR
	82	WRE
Groves, H T	321	LDM
Grubbs, F H	86	AC
Grubbs, Mrs. F H	86	AC
Grube, C Howard	6:413	MC
Gruening, Ernest	406-407	HU

Gubbins, Francis   491   SCH
Gudmunsen, Scott   3:425   HHI
Guffey, John H   3:329   PH
Guffey, S   M   , see
     Burt, S   M   (Guffey)
Guichon, Joseph   fol.title page   SHB
Guidi, Joseph   364, 368   PI
                                432   PIW
_____
Guie, E   H   1899:161   SSS
Guild, George G   3:849   LHC
Guild, Henry Grant   1895:91   OO
Guillod, Harry   19 no.3-4:187   BCH
Guindon, J   M   71   LDM
Guinean, Thomas   2:74   NH
Guise, Julius   404   WOY
Guleke, Harry   430   BR
                                1:90-91   EPD
_____   2:48-49,144-145   EPD
Gunderson, Charles S   289   LDM
Gunderson, Martha, see
     Rekdahl, Martha (Gunderson)
Gunn, Arthur   1905-06:[79]   RLW
                                [95]   RLX
_____
Gunn, John S   2:423   HWW
Gunn, Thomas M   180, 231   PSW
Gunn, W   Chalmers   37   PSW
Gunnison, Royal Arch   1943:40   ENC
Gunston, Malcolm E   May 1907:68   TDL
Gunther, Erna   36:26 1935   WDT
                                50:50 1949   WDT
_____
Gurdane, J   S   1895:112   OO
Gurney, William   210   GL
Gurske, Paul E   1945-46:38   OO
Gussenhoven, Joseph   3:779   SMS
Gussenhoven, Mrs. Joseph, see
     Gussenhoven, Susan (Munger)
Gussenhoven, Susan (Munger) 3:779   SMS
Gustafsen,   (Little Gussie)
                                2:464-465   EPD
Guthard, Charles H   2:201   SMS
Guthrie, Edwin R   50:58 1949   WDT
Guthrie, William P   3:1012   FH
Gwaltney, Z   Sanford   2:979   HHI
Gwin, William P   2:1016   SM
Gwinn, Gardner J   3:709   BHK
Gwinn, J   A   2:253   CHW
Gwinn, Mrs. J   A   , see
     Gwinn, Rose Emma (Simon)
Gwinn, Montie B   2:59   HHI
                                1923-24:6   IH
_____   14:90 1909   WBP
Gwinn, Rose Emma (Simon) 2:253   CHW
Gyde, James Ellsworth, Sr. 1941:250   EN
Gzowski, Casimir Stanislaus, Jr.
                                fol.pt.2   SHB

                                H

Haag, J   J   15   SSP
Hackett, F   447   LDM
Hackett, H   A   1:917   LHC
Hackett, Mellie Albertus   3:393   GP
Hackney, Annie, see
     Krug, Annie (Hackney) Ketchen
Hackney, John S   7:83   MC
Hackney, William H   7:83   MC
Hadfield, William   390   GL
Hadley, Alonzo M   3:243   HWW
Hadley, Hiram Elwood   3:645   BHS
Hadley, James   45   DW
Hadlock, Samuel   1:440   NH
Hadorn, John   560   SIH
Hafenbrack, Gus   135   MLO
Haffey, James   1895-96:115   SSS
Haga, Oliver O   2:696   FH
                                2:116   FSB
_____   2:173   HHI
Hagberg, Charles E   2:525   HHT
Hagelie, Helmer   2:354   SMS
Hagenbarth, Mrs., see
     Wood, Katherine (Veit) Hagenbarth
     Murphy
Hager, John   896   SIH
Haggard, Charles Lafayette 2:837   BHK
Haggett, Arthur Sewell   6:24 1906   WDT
Hagie, F   O   1 no.8:29   WN
Hagler, Ronald   31:50   PNLA
Hague, Arnold   264   CIR
Hahn, C   H   186   E
Hahn, John   2:435   PMO
Hahn, Nicholas Philip   2:511   HHI
Hahn, Robert Ernest   3:231   BHS
Haight, C   P   1935-36:51   OO
Haight, Charles L   3:385   HHI
Haight, Hector C   2:891   FH
Hailey, Jesse C   1945-46:28   IH
Hailey, John   249   DSW
                                1:224   FSB
_____   2:113   HHI
_____   1921-22:33   IH
_____   1949-50:32   IHD
_____
Hailey, Mrs. John, see
     Hailey, Louisa M   (Griffin)
Hailey, Louisa M   (Griffin) 2:113   HHI
Hailstone, William   2:431   BCF
Haines, Ancil F   1 no.6:26   WN
                                1 no.12:15   WN
_____
Haines, E   8 no.2:107   BCH
Haines, Ernest   2:front. 1924   BCHA
Haines, J   C   2:660   NH
                                3 no.8:423   PM

Haines, John Michener	2:590	FH	Hallalhotsoot, see			
	1:106	FSB	Lawyer, Nez Percé chief			
Haldon, John Pattinson	4:513	BCF	Hallam, Bertha B	21:31	PNLA	
Hale, Charles E	1:277	HH	————	31:241	PNLA	
Hale, Heber Quincy	3:964	FH	Hallauer, Josephine (Pardee)	30:102	PNLA	
	2:104	FSB	Hallberg, P A	80	SS	
Hale, Robert S	200	MI	Haller, Granville Owen	1:687	BHK	
Hale, Ruth, see			————	2:135	BHK	
Gershevsky, Ruth (Hale)			————	2:744	BHS	
Halferty, Peter F	3:461	HWW	————	1:31	HH	
Hal-hal-tlos-sot, Nez Percé chief			————	254	HI	
	3:154	LH	————	1:200	NH	
	294	WCS	————	3 no. 4:277	PM	
Hall, Alice, see			————	3:334	SH	
Jackson, Alice (Hall)			Hallock, Charles	154	DT	
Hall, Charles	1931-32:40	OO	Hallock, Leavitt	152	DT	
Hall, Charles W	1924:40	WSP	Halloran, Patrick M	2:304	SMS	
Hall, Edgar Moore	2:1030	SM	Halm, Joe	290	BHSS	
Hall, Edwin J	2:591	LHC	Hals, John I	164	SS	
Hall, George W	unp.	SEA	Halsey, Elmer E	1924:40	WSP	
Hall, Gertrude, see			Halteman, William A	[138]	RLX	
Denny, Gertrude (Hall)			————	1895-96:95	SSS	
Hall, Gilbert Minor	1941:221	EN	Halverson, Emma	12	SS	
Hall, Grant	386	GI	Halverson, Petra	12	SS	
Hall, Granville B	1:929	LHC	Halvorson, Halvor	3:1661	SM	
Hall, Harvey D	2:1213	SM	Ham, David T	1:373	HH	
Hall, Henry	152	BF	Ham, George H	247	GI	
	80	BHSI	Ham, William H	1895-96:95	SSS	
Hall, Henry Knox	5:208	SH	Hambelton, Melvina, see			
Hall, Horace M	3 no. 4:285	PM	Black, Melvina (Hambelton)			
Hall, James Z	3:89	BCF	Hambidge, Richard	3:143	HWW	
Hall, John	2:front. 1924	BCHA	Hamblen, R N	37	MG	
Hall, John A	fol. pt. 2	SHB	Hamilton, Mrs. Alexander B , see			
Hall, John H	3:505	HHI	Hamilton, Anna (Balch) Stump Morrell			
	359	PL	Hamilton, Anna (Balch) Stump Morrell			
Hall, John Hubert	1939-40:30	OO		2:766	GP	
————	1943-44:77	OO	Hamilton, Boyd	202	BHSS	
————	1945-46:86	OO		14:5 1909	WBP	
————	91	TUR	Hamilton, Edward S	197	E	
Hall, Joseph E	1923:51	WSP	————	2:248	PHP	
Hall, Mrs. Joseph E	6:408-409	MC	Hamilton, G Wire	[138]	RLX	
Hall, Mrs. Laura E	48	LS	Hamilton, Hugh	2:front. 1924	BCHA	
Hall, Lewis	3:455	BCF	Hamilton, J W	306	AC	
Hall, Margaret, see			Hamilton, James H	fol. pt. 2	SHB	
Goldsmith, Margaret (Hall)			Hamilton, John S	6:430	MC	
Hall, Oliver	168	BHSS	Hamilton, Leslie H	2:1104	SM	
Hall, P S	10 no. 1:43	BCH	Hamilton, Marcus de Lafayette	21	PIG	
Hall, Phil J	2:front. 1924	BCHA	Hamilton, Moore	1935-36:51	OO	
Hall, Rebecca, see			Hamilton, Ralph S	1931-32:41	OO	
Hopkins, Rebecca (Hall)			————	1945-46:93	OO	
Hall, Temperance Statira, see			Hamilton, S	1:641	CHW	
Bown, Temperance Statira (Hall)			Hamilton, Thomas	1905-06:[66]	RLW	
Hall, W A	2:278	SMS	Hamilton, Thomas C	245	LHM	
Hall, W H H	40	LDM	Hamilton, W J	2:434	NH	
Hall, Will A	206	BHSS	Hamilton, William Thomas	front.	HMS	
Hall, William	2:113	BCF	————	3:33	MC	
Hall, William Kendall	3:1039	BCF	Hamlen, Freeman	158	DT	
Hallakallakeen, see			Hamlet, Wesley Sylvester	3:46	BEA	
Joseph, Nez Percé chief			Hamley, Wymond Ogilvy	2:191	BCF	

	1897:124, 135	YB
Hammer, A M	2:637	CHW
Hammer, Mrs. A M , see		
Hammer, Frances Olive (Gilbert)		
Hammer, A W	83	LHN
Hammer, Anne Christine (Orego)	392	GL
Hammer, Emerson	1905-06:[41]	RLW
Hammer, Frances Olive (Gilbert)	2:637	CHW
Hammer, Hans	195	GL
Hammer, Mrs. Hans, see		
Hammer, Anne Christine (Orego)		
Hammond, A B	84	PL
Hammond, C R	89	MLO
Hammond, Edward	1096	SIH
Hammond, George John	3:23	BCF
	fol.pt.2	SHB
Hammond, Milton M	3:1075	FH
Hammond, T W	May 1907:39	TDL
Hammond, William	193	LDM
Hanan, Archimedes	1:204	NH
Hanauer, Milton S	1924:176	WSP
Hanawa, Y	1 no.2:31	WN
Hand, William M	1:929	LHC
Handel, Fred W	2:464	SMS
Handschy, F F	23:112 1918	WBP
	24:64 1919	WBP
	25:128 1920	WBP
Haney, Ella, see		
Boyer, Ella (Haney)		
Hanford, Cornelius Holgate	1:481	BHK
	2:458	NH
	20	PC
	5:front.	SH
	1924:112	WSP
	1926:20	WSP
Hanford, Edward	1:71	BHK
	3:104	SH
Hanford, Frank	1895-96:95	SSS
Hankey, Gerald Cramer Alers, see		
Alers-Hankey, Gerald Cramer		
Hankin, Philip J	96-97	SHL
	1897:43,124	YB
Hanlein, W S	365	AG
Hanley, Richard	393	BHSS
Hanlon, John H	3:1439	SM
Hanlon, Thomas O	352	SIH
Hanna, Herbert K	1945-46:92	OO
Hanna, John W	845	HI
Hanna, Joseph A	front.	HD
Hanna, Lyman E	6:398	MC
Hanna, William	2:118	SMS
Hannah, Dolphus Brice	1:372	HHT
	1:500	NH
Hannah, George	4:102	MC
Hannah, V D	2:691	HHI
Hannay, N B	19:32 1914	WBP
	24:128 1919	WBP
Hanns, P J	2:369	CHW
Hannum, Clarence S	17	DA
Hanratty, Mrs. Margaret Louisa	402	PI
	472	PIW
Hansbrough, G F	3:1087	FH
Hansee, Martha Lois	1:unp. 1900-01	WDT
Hansen, Hans	84	SS
Hansen, John C	3:173	HWW
Hansen, John F	3:971	FH
Hansen, John H	1112	SIH
Hansen, Khalil V	3:286	BEA
Hansen, Lawrence	3:1002	FH
Hanson, A J	402	AG
Hanson, Axel G	2:371	BHK
Hanson, C L	423	AG
Hanson, Charles	1:118	HHT
	6:10	SH
Hanson, Frank G	2:449	BHK
Hanson, Havelock H	3:1319	SM
Hanson, Howard A	48 no.1:6	PN
	[132]	RLX
Hanson, L G	180	SS
Hanson, Mrs. L G	180	SS
Hanson, Mrs. Mary L	6:420-421	MC
Hanson, Mrs. Nellie S	443	AG
Hanson, Ole	52 no.3:94	PN
	unp.	SEA
	58	SSP
Hanson, Philena W , see		
Thorp, Philena W (Hanson)		
Hanson, Philo C	3:1594	SM
Hanson, Wilbur F	6:420-421	MC
Hanson, William Henry	2:26	HHT
	6:14	SH
Happy, Cyrus	5:272	SH
	1924:80	WSP
Harbaugh, Ignatius	2:58	HHT
Harber, Nora E	unp.	HOF
Hardan, John, Jr.	135	JNT
Hardan, John, Sr.	135	JNT
Hardin, John O	3:597	GP
Harding, Benjamin F	82	WRE
Harding, Frank S	3:1216	FH
	unp.	SOU
Harding, John W	50:23 1949	WDT
Harding, S , see		
Langille, S (Harding)		
Harding, Warren G	67:243,244	OHQ
Hardwick, Azubia Deseret (Cox)	21	GL
Hardwicke, 3rd Earl of, see		
Yorke, Philip		
Hardy, George	290	BHSS
Hardy, R M	34:20 1929	WBP
	35:front.1930	WBP
Hare, David Henry	80	PSW
Hare, W D	2:651	LHC
Hare, W H	285	E
	1905-06:[70]	RLW
Harford, John	1:348	NH

62

Harkins, Harry	278	LDM		Harris, M C	2:477	HWW
Harkness, Henry O	3:983	FH		Harris, Margaret, see		
Harkness, P D	191	JNT		McKee, Margaret (Harris)		
Harlin, Robert H	unp.	SEA		Harris, Michael	3:721	GP
Harlow, John	1:584	PMO		Harris, Rex	2:144-145	EPD
Harlow, Neal	30 no.4:cover	PNLA		Harris, Richard T	xiii	DEA
Harlow, Samuel A	6:339	MC		Harris, Samuel	147	PSW
Harman, Rose	66	MG		Harris, Thomas Ewing	10 no.3:182	F
Harmon, Daniel W	34	MHN		Harris, William E	1:198	PMO
Harmon, Fremont Smith	3:295	BH		Harris, Wyatt	unp.	SOU
_____	2:483	HHT		Harrison, E S	43	DA
Harmon, U E	1924:41	WSP		Harrison, Eli	3:580	BCF
Harney, William S	31	DH		Harrison, Mrs. Eli, see		
Harold, Alex	2:183	CHW		Harrison, Elizabeth (Warburton)		
Harold, Mrs. Alex, see				Harrison, Elizabeth, see		
Harold, Anna (Olson)				Brown, Elizabeth (Harrison)		
Harold, Anna (Olson)	2:183	CHW		Harrison, Elizabeth (Warburton)	3:581	BCF
Harold, Thomas	431	LDM		Harrison, Florence	430	BHSS
Harper, Andrew Miller	3:451	BCF		Harrison, Frank	206	BHSS
Harper, Arthur	159	WOY		Harrison, Fred E	1935-36:52	OO
Harper, F C	1895-96:71	SSS		_____	1937-38:62-63	OO
Harper, Robert J C	32 no. 4:27	PNLA		Harrison, George Stevenson	3:81	BCF
_____	33 no. 1:27	PNLA		Harrison, James Madison	3:101	PH
Harper, William Wilson	2:1202	SM		Harrison, Joseph B	48 no.3:72	PN
Harpole, Elizabeth, see				Harrison, Norman B	277	PSW
Bayley, Elizabeth (Harpole)				Harrison, Sarah Mabel, see		
Harrell, Louis	3:351	HHI		Rose, Sarah Mabel (Harrison)		
Harriman, Edward Henry	206	BOO		Harrison, Victor B	2:19 1924	BCHA
_____	1:302	GP		Hart, Eliza (Paynton)	2:125	HHI
_____	400	QT		Hart, Fred A	2:411	LHC
_____	fol. 207	SHI		Hart, James	3:183	HWW
Harrington, J V	2:609	SMS		Hart, James Hinmond	2:125	HHI
Harrington, Mrs. J V , see				Hart, Mrs. James Hinmond, see		
Harrington, Nellie (Richards) Hathaway				Hart, Eliza (Paynton)		
Harrington, Lief	305	BR		Hart, John	232	JAC
Harrington, Mark Walrod	18-19	GA		Hart, John W	2:33	HHI
Harrington, Nellie (Richards) Hathaway				Hart, Louis Folwell	53	MAG
	2:610	SMS		_____	34 no.4:400-401	PN
Harrington, William S	456	AG		_____	unp.	SE
_____	65	OS		_____	136-137	SRW
Harrington, Mrs. William S	443	AG		Hart, Ray M	1941:290	EN
Harris, Abner	284	GL		Hart, William S	1:216	ACR
Harris, Al	233	LDM		Hartin, David	41	MG
Harris, B M	3:1128	SMS		Hartley, Roland Hill	2:173	HWW
Harris, Benjamin	244	LDM		_____	55	MAG
Harris, Bill	182-183	KO		_____	34 no.4:400-401	PN
Harris, Charles	447	LDM		_____	unp.	SE
Harris, Mrs. Dennis	2:front. 1924	BCHA		_____	1 no.8:8	WN
Harris, Frank	254	IHI		_____	2 no.1:9	WN
Harris, Frankie	63:321	OHQ		Hartman, Charles D	2:433	PMO
Harris, Henry E	3:685	LHC		Hartman, George B	873	LHM
Harris, Jack	63:321	OHQ		Hartman, J L	14:94 1909	WBP
Harris, John	2:908	SM		Hartman, John Peter	1:481	BHK
_____	404	WOY		_____	2:219	BHK
Harris, John S	441	LHM		_____	3:239	PH
Harris, Lawrence Thomas	2:440	PMO		_____	5:356	SH
_____	2:47	CHW		_____	unp.	VU
Harris, M , see				_____	1924:80	WSP
Weatherford, M (Harris)						

Hartman, Newton	262	LDM	Haverfield, Orville Snell	3:1032	SMS
Hart-McHarg, William	4:105	BCF	Havird, Cary C	3:409	HHI
Hartness, Candace M (Boyle)	3:341	GP	Hawes, Ed M	2 no. 6:15	W
Hartness, George	3:340	GP	Hawkes, John B	400	PI
Hartness, Mrs. George, see			Hawkins, Edwin K	1895-96:134	SSS
Hartness, Candace M (Boyle)			Hawkins, George L	2:432	PMO
Hartsuck, Ben	290	BHSS	Hawkins, John	1:244	LH
Hartung, Charles	3:360	BEA	Hawkins, Lester Leander	2:359	GP
Hartvigsen, Heber H	3:1168	FH	Hawkins, Martin W	1945-46:92	OO
Hartwig, William J	2:1086	SM	Hawkins, Mary Elizabeth, see		
Harvey, Augustus H	2:733	HHI	Lyman, Mary Elizabeth (Hawkins)		
Harvey, E H	6:404-405	MC	Hawkins, Mrs. Ora B	1941-42:10	IH
Harvey, F	44	MG	Hawley, H W	6:218	SH
Harvey, George	2:front. 1924	BCHA	Hawley, James H	314	BR
Harvey, J N	3:1714	SM		342	DSW
Harvey, Joseph E	1943-44:77	OO		2:585	FH
	1945-46:86	OO		1:189	FSB
Harwood, James	70	GL		1:front.	HHI
Harwood, Stanley William	3:389	BEA		1921-22:front.	IH
Hasbrouck, H C	311	BN		1923-24:6	IH
Haseltine, James E	2:151	GP		1929-30:112	IH
Haskell, Dan	419	LDM		205	IHI
Haskett, Edwin W	168	AN		58 no. 1:25	PN
Haskins, Charles Darwin	271	HA	Hawley, Jess	2:70	FSB
Haskins, Mrs. Frank, see			Hawley, N M	728	SIH
Haskins, Jennie (Beam)			Hawley, Willard P	2:139	LHC
Haskins, Jennie (Beam)	128	CBC	Hawley, Willard P , Jr.	2:219	LHC
Hasselblad, G V	10, 15	SSP	Haworth, Arthur	30	THI
Hastie, Addison W	38:18	G	Ha-wow-no-ilp-ilp (Nez Percé Indian)		
Hastie, John	1 no. 3:29	WN		1:525	HHI
Hastie, Thomas Peers	2:448	PHP	Hawthorne, Adam	876	SIH
Hastings, Fred W	1924:64	WSP	Hawthorne, James C	2:119	GP
Hastings, H H A	1923:129	WSP		461	HIO
Hastings, Loren B	53	LDM		46:292	OHQ
	1:228	NH		1:416	PMO
Hastings, Loren Bingham	3:360	PH		2:335	PMO
Hastings, Mrs. O	2:front. 1924	BCHA		274	SHP
Haswell, Robert	2:84	LH	Hawthorne, Joseph Brierley	6:32	SH
Hatch, Abram	40	GL		May 1907:38	TDL
Hatch, Lorenzo H	160	GL	Hawthorne, Mary A (Jones) Phelps		
Hatch, Z J	230	LDM		3:219	BHS
Hatfield, Job	24	LDM	Hawthorne, Mrs. Willard C , see		
Hatfield, John A	262	LDM	Hawthorne, Mary A (Jones) Phelps		
Hatfield, Mark O	105	TUR	Hawthornthwaite, James Hurst		
Hathaway, J G	39	MG		1911:70-71	YB
Hathaway, M R	1:404	NH	Hay, Arthur D	1943-44:21	OO
Hauck, Gus	2:front. 1924	BCHA		1945-46:33	OO
Haug, Nicholas	2:670	FH	Hay, Mae Marguerite (Pettit)	3:65	D
	3:441	HHI	Hay, Marion E	168	BHSS
Hauger, Marjorie	2:464-465	EPD		49	MAG
Hauser, Samuel T	32	LHM		104	ME
	4:106	MC		34 no. 4:400-401	PN
	126	MI		59 no. 3:130	PN
	13 no. 5:531	MWH		unp.	SE
	2:880	SM		June 1909:13	TDL
	1:410	SMS		1910:1	TDL
Hausmann, Clemens	2:513	HWW	Hayden, Benjamin	1:545	CHW
Hauswirth, Simon	3:831	SMS		66:150	OHQ
Hautier, Alphonse	2:front. 1924	BCHA	Hayden, Gay	2:202	NH

Hayden, Mrs. Gay, see			
Hayden, Mary J (Bean)			
Hayden, John C , Sr.	2:439	BHK	
	3:903	BHS	
Hayden, Mary J (Bean)	2:202	NH	
Hayden, Obadiah Bennett	3:135	BH	
Hayden, William O	153	LDM	
Haydon, Ambrose P	6:413	MC	
Haydon, John M	unp.	SAA	
Hayes, Ambrose M , see			
Hays, Ambrose M			
Hayes, Mrs. Anna Hansen	1941-42:68	IH	
Hayes, C Willard	fol.207	SHI	
Hayes, H A	301	E	
Hayes, Jack A	1945-46:214	OO	
Hayes, James (Nez Percé Indian)	212	BR	
	268	DSW	
	127	DTI	
Hayes, Katherine, see			
Means, Katherine (Hayes)			
Hayes, Leonard F	261	GG	
Hayes, Margaret Stewart (Mick)	3:143	BHK	
Hayes, Patrick C	3:142	BHK	
	6:175	SH	
Hayes, Mrs. Patrick C , see			
Hayes, Margaret Stewart (Mick)			
Hayes, Phoebe	32 no.1:25	PNLA	
Hayes, R M	26	PSW	
Hayes, Robert J	2:203	HHI	
Hayes, Mrs. Rutherford B	438	AG	
Hayman, Herbert Harry	3:328-329	BEA	
Haynes, C E	86	LHN	
Haynes, Harry	367	BR	
Haynes, James B	3:203	HWW	
Haynes, John Carmichael	14 no.1-2:63	BCH	
	100	HEH	
Haynes, William	2:113	BCF	
Hays, Ambrose M	255	GG	
Hays, Anna F	206	BHSS	
Hays, Charles Marshall	549	IHI	
Hays, George M	4:148	MC	
Hays, George S	134	MLO	
Hays, Gilmore	313	MP	
Hays, J R	177	PL	
Hays, Jessie	207	BHSS	
Hays, Samuel Hubbard	3:1257	FH	
	3:769	HHI	
Hays, Walter	6:388	MC	
Hayton, Thomas	1905-06:[28]	RLW	
Hayward, Harry C	235	E	
Hayward, R S	1924:129	WSP	
Hayward, William Henry	1911:70-71	YB	
Haywood, William Dudley	59 no.1:26	PN	
Hazelbaker, Frank A	3:1591	SM	
Hazen, Mary A (Moats)	3:247	LHC	
Hazen, Matthew F	3:247	LHC	
Hazen, Mrs. Matthew F , see			
Hazen, Mary A (Moats)			

Hazlett, James H	1935-36:50	OO	
Hazlitt, Henry	2:48-49	EPD	
H'co-a-h'co-a-h'cotes-min, see			
No-Horns-On-His-Head			
Headington, Mrs. Mattie	648	SIH	
Headington, William M	656	SIH	
Heagney, H	151	OB	
Heagy, Edgar B	2:1118	SM	
Heald, Perley Chandler	3:733	GP	
Heale, Mrs. Harry	2:front.1924	BCHA	
Healey, J Earl, see			
Healy, J Earl			
Healey, John P , see			
Healy, John P			
Healey, Timothy E	3:1491	SM	
Healy, Agnes, see			
Anderson, Agnes (Healy)			
Healy, Ellen, see			
Nagle, Ellen (Healy)			
Healy, George H	6:404-405	MC	
Healy, J Earl	235	GG	
Healy, John P	235	GG	
Healy, Joseph M	3:9	GP	
Healy, Michael A	95	BET	
Healy, Nicholas C	3:437	BHS	
	5:262	SH	
Heaps, Edward Hewetson	4:83	BCF	
Heard, William E	612	IHI	
Hearns, Henry	2:front.1924	BCHA	
Hearst, George	224	QT	
Heater, George	439	LDM	
Heath, A H	May 1907:68	TDL	
Heath, Albert	2:715	HHI	
Heath, Frederick	6:148	SH	
Heath, George	116	CBC	
Heath, Herbert L	unp.	SOU	
Heath, Sidney Moor	2:233	HWW	
	1895-96:95	SSS	
Heathcote, Lesley	18:9	PNLA	
	30 no.4:cover	PNLA	
	31:49	PNLA	
	34 no.4:28	PNLA	
Hebard, Grace Raymond	58 no.1:4	PN	
Hebb, Frank M	3:1095	SMS	
Hebgen, Max	3:1446	SM	
Hechtner, Howard D	3:321	BEA	
Heckman, James W	3:277	BEA	
Heckman, Martin	2:464-465	EPD	
Hector, James	111	GI	
Hedden, Edward	2:703	HHI	
Hedgecock, Ruhannah, see			
Allison, Ruhannah (Hedgecock)			
Hedges, Cornelius	115	LHM	
	4:32	MC	
	5:371	MC	
	6:305,350	MC	
	7:181	MC	
	62	MI	

_____	2:924	SM		1911:6-7, 70-71	YB
_____	1:495	SMS	Helmick, Sarah	26:444	OHQ
Hedges, E L	14	SSP	Helsing, John O	2:116	SMS
Hedges, Gilbert	2:438	PMO	Hembree, Walter L	unp.	SOU
Hedges, Judd P	3:1011	SMS	He-mene-Ilppilp, see		
Hedges, Samuel Hamilton	6:18	SH	Red Wolf, Nez Percé chief		
Hedges, Wyllys A	3:1354	SM	He-mene-Mox-mox, see		
_____	2:81	SMS	Yellow Wolf, Nez Percé chief		
Hedlund, Leroy E	3:161	BEA	Hemenway, James	2:438	PMO
Hedlund, William H	1941-42:65	OO	Hemphill, Wylie	1 no. 2:16	WN
Hee-oh-'ks-te-kin, see			_____	1 no. 10:25	WN
Rabbit-Skin-Leggins (Nez Percé Indian)			Hempstead, Walter	1939-40:30	OO
Heermans, Harry Clay	2:11	HWW	Hemrich, Andrew	4:33	BHK
_____	3:134	PH	_____	1905-06:[44]	RLW
Hefferlin, Charles S	2:1206	SM	_____	6:130	SH
Heffernan, John Timothy	4:front.	BHK	_____	unp.	VU
_____	74-75	GA	Hendee, Denny H	1:366	PMO
_____	5:390	SH	Hendershott, George W	3:1789	SM
_____	unp.	WD	_____	unp.	SOU
Heggie, George	fol. pt. 2	SHB	Henderson, David E	1943:213	ENC
Heidecke, J A	167	PL	Henderson, E R	1905-06:[64]	RLW
Heidelman, John Henry	2:406	SMS	_____	[116]	RLX
Heidenreich, Charles J	236	E	Henderson, Enoch Pratt	56:331	OHQ
Heigho, Edgar Maurice	2:592	FH	Henderson, George A	fol. pt. 2	SHB
_____	1:160	FSB	Henderson, J W	134	MLO
Heileman, W H	215	BHSS	Henderson, James H D	2:681	LHC
Heilman, Robert B	50:40 1949	WDT	Henderson, Mrs. James H D		
Heim, Joseph G	1:368	PHP	_____	2:681	LHC
Heinly, W G	1924:176	WSP	Henderson, John Calvin	3:637	BCF
Hein-mot-Hi-hi, see			Henderson, Louis F	57:116	OHQ
Yellow Wolf, Nez Percé chief			Henderson, Lucy A, see		
Heisler, Donald E	1941-42:65	OO	Deady, Lucy A (Henderson)		
_____	1943-44:77	OO	Henderson, Milton Fillmore	2:321	LHC
_____	1945-46:86	OO	Henderson, Richard Arthur	3:607	BCF
Heist, Harlan D	2:878	FH	Henderson, Robert D (Bob)	114	BET
Heitkemper, Frank A	2:447	PMO	Henderson, W G	unp.	SOU
Heitman, Charles L	1:126	FSB	Henderson, William	176	LDM
Heldt, F George	2:941	SM	Hendley, Harry B	2:345	HHT
Hellberg, Fred A	1943-44:77	OO	Hendricks, Paul R	1945-46:86	OO
_____	1945-46:86	OO	Hendricks, Thomas G	1:641	CHW
Hellberg, G A	1931-32:41	OO	_____	2:243	CHW
Heller, Eliza (Roth)	1120	SIH	Hendrickson, Catherine, see		
Helliwell, John Frederick	fol. pt. 2	SHB	Tefft, Catherine (Hendrickson)		
Helm, Charles I	1895-96:69	SSS	Hendrickson, Erick	320	SIH
Helm, Elizabeth (Sager)	134	CW	Hendron, Carroll	1895-96:119	SSS
Helm, McKinley	1951-52:6	IHD	Hendry, John	4:721	BCF
Helmcken, Harry Dallas	fol. pt. 1	SHB	_____	202	KB
_____	1897:106	YB	_____	fol. pt. 1	SHB
Helmcken, Mrs. J D			Henehan, Martin J	3:273	BHS
_____	2:front. 1924	BCHA	Heney, Francis J	front., 177, 218	PL
Helmcken, John Sebastian	1:542	BCF	Henley, Joseph	4:211	BCF
_____	2:293	BCF	Henley, Neil	2:338-339	BCF
_____	3:1133	BCF	_____	226	LDM
_____	194	KB	Hennessy, Daniel J	694	MI
_____	front.	LCT	_____	484	PIW
_____	fol. title page	SHB	Henning, Leonora, see		
_____	96-97	SHL	Huckins, Leonora (Henning)		
_____	1897:43, 103	YB	Henningsen, Anker Paulsen	2:511	LHC

Henrichsen, Lars C   588   SHP
Henricks, Jacob A   88   SS
Henry, Francis   1905-06:[28]   RLW
Henry, Frank   2:1255   SM
Henry, Horace Chapin   3:19   BHK
_____   3:front   BHS
                            5:102   SH
                            unp.   WD
_____
Henry, Langdon Chapin   3:27   BHK
Henry, Margaret, see
    Stocking, Margaret (Henry)
Henry, Mrs. Olivette Webb   18:68 1941-42   IH
Henry, Paul Mandell   3:31   BHK
Henry, Robert   2:597   BHK
Henry, Samuel E   960   SIH
Henry, Walker A   1905-06:[43]   RLW
Henry, Will   222   HA
Henry, William E   26:42, 52 1925   WDT
Hensler, Gus   2:490   PHP
Henter, Leo A   2:145   SMS
Henton, S C   228   HA
Hepburn, Walter   3:937   BCF
Hepp, Joseph   432   AG
Heppner, Henry   2:90   NH
Herbert, George F   1:584   NH
Herbst, Gottfried   311   BHSS
Herendeen, George   105   NL
Heritage, J A   4 no.2:86   BCH
Herman, Fred   1939-40:30   OO
Hermann, Binger   62, 386   PL
Herndon, Charles, see
    Herndon, John Charles
Herndon, James A   430   BR
Herndon, John Charles   3:511   BEA
Herndon, Joseph Warren   3:293   BEA
Heron, David   2:755   FH
Heron, Mrs. David, see
    Heron, F A (Canfield)
Heron, F A (Canfield)   2:755   FH
Herr, Willis B   3:593   BHS
                            1924:113   WSP
_____
Herrall, George   1:144   NH
Herren, L R   177   PL
Herrick, Elmar S   2:1274   SM
Herrick, Jeanette, see
    Smith, Jeanette (Herrick)
Herring, Mrs. Arthur, see
    Herring, Frances Elizabeth
Herring, Frances Elizabeth 4:233   BCF
Herrman, Arthur P   50:29 1949   WDT
Herron, Joseph   fol.207   SHI
Herron, Paul   41   MG
Herron, W J   1:553   CHW
Herron, William C   284   GL
Hess, Fred   134   MLO
Hess, Henry L   1935-36:50   OO
Hesse, Fred   3:713   LHC
Hesse, H T   1939-40:30   OO

_____   1941-42:65   OO
_____   1943-44:77   OO
                            1945-46:86   OO
Hesse, William H   328   HA
Heuel, Peter   151   OB
Heussy, Carl Rumsey   3:368   PH
Heussy, William Charles   3:368   PH
Heuston, Benjamin Franklin 3:193   HHT
Hevly, E A   161   SS
Hewen, H W B   1924:176   WSP
Hewitt, C C   313   MP
Hewitt, Charles E   3:569   HWW
Hewitt, D A   39   MG
Hewitt, E Arlita, see
    Adams, E Arlita (Hewitt)
Hewitt, Elizabeth (Matheny) 1:168   NH
Hewitt, Harry B   2:387   HHT
                            [123]   RLX
_____
Hewitt, Henry   1:168   NH
Hewitt, Mrs. Henry, see
    Hewitt, Elizabeth (Matheny)
Hewitt, Henry, Jr.   2:31   HH
                            3:31   HHT
_____
                            1:298   PHP
_____
                            5:166   SH
Hewitt, James T   3 no.4:227   BCH
Hewitt, John D   6:301   MC
Hewitt, Joseph   3:889   HHI
Hewitt, Louis P   1945-46:92   OO
Hewitt, R Floyd   3:24   BEA
Heyburn, Weldon B   58 no.1:29   PN
                            60 no.4:196   PN
_____
Hezekiah, see
    Five Crows, Cayuse chief
Hibbard, Charles L   3:267   BHS
Hibben, T N   2:front. 1924   BCHA
Hibben, Thomas Napier   3:695   BCF
Hibbs, Frank W   unp.   SOU
Hible, Samuel   4:445   BHK
Hickerson, Walter   1:154-155   EPD
Hickey, J Frank   2:447   HHT
                            1 no.1:8   WN
_____
Hickman, Richard Owen   432   MI
Hickman, William A   front.   HB
Hickok, James Butler (Wild Bill)
                            234   SW
Hicks, Gwin   1905-06:[28]   RLW
Hicks, Robert   143   LDM
Hidden, Lowell M   2:353   GP
Hidden, Mrs. M L T   1:603   GP
Hiddin, Jackson   3:783   GP
Hieber, John G F   1943:81   ENC
Higday, Hamilton   46   SA
Higgins, C P   65   LHM
Higgins, David William   fol.pt.1   SHB
                            1897:105   YB
_____
                            1911:70-71   YB
Higgins, Inez Eileen   2:24   CPD

Higgins, Jonas   295   LHM

Higgins, Kate, see
    McCormick, Kate (Higgins)

Higgins, Mrs. W   2:front. 1924   BCHA

Higgins, Zenna (Cochran)   2:24   CPD

Higginson, Ella (Rhoads)   1:239   PMO
                            1:603   GP

Higginson, Mrs. Russell Carden, see
    Higginson, Ella (Rhoads)

Higgs, Alexander Ayer   2:517   HHI

Higgs, Archie K   1937-38:62-63   OO

Higham, John O   2:21   SMS

Highley, Lee   2:809   FH

Hildreth, Lulu Dean (Scudder) 3:970   FH

Hildreth, William H   3:970   FH

Hildreth, Mrs. William H   , see
    Hildreth, Lulu Dean (Scudder)

Hileman, Margaret   32 no.1:25   PNLA

Hilger, David   2:1003   SM

Hill, Belinda (Reed)   1:620   NH

Hill, C   E   237   E

Hill, Carl C   1941-42:65   OO
                       1943-44:77   OO
                       1945-46:86   OO

Hill, Charles E   1:560   PHP

Hill, David H   372   LDM

Hill, Earl H   1931-32:41   OO
                       1935-36:51   OO
                       1939-40:30   OO
                       1943-44:77   OO
                       1945-46:86   OO

Hill, Edmund E   365   HA

Hill, Flemming R   1:620   NH

Hill, Mrs. Flemming R   , see
    Hill, Belinda (Reed)

Hill, Frank Albert   6:136   SH

Hill, Gale S   2:481   CHW

Hill, George A   525   HI

Hill, George B   322   IHI

Hill, George Leslie   3:521   BHS

Hill, George W   137   BHI

Hill, Helen, see
    Charles, Helen (Hill)

Hill, James   208   LDM

Hill, James Jerome   unp.   AYP
                            170   BOO
                            177   GI
                            1:301   GP
                            front.   KS
                            400   QT
                            5:290   SH
                            1 no.3:150 WM
                            2 no.1:13   WN

Hill, John M   1:481   HH

Hill, Joseph A   3:211   LHC

Hill, Laban   66:51   OHQ

Hill, Louis   69:293   OHQ

Hill, M   M   1935-36:51   OO

Hill, Mary B   6:386   MC

Hill, Minnie   339   LDM

Hill, Robert Corbet   3:673   BHS
                            1:448   NH

Hill, Robert W   179   PSW

Hill, Samuel   1:481   BHK
                            2:115   BHK
                            66:250   OHQ

Hill, Sylvester   3:319   HHI

Hill, Thomas B   1 no.1:44   WN
                            1 no.6:27   WN
                            1 no.8:29   WN

Hill, William Lair   1:556   GP
                            621   HI
                            14 no.6:664 MWH
                            2:286   NH

Hillebrand, Anthony   2:801   LHC

Hiller, James A   3:479   LHC

Hillman, Ada B   1910:52   TDL

Hills, Elizabeth M   , see
    McGilvra, Elizabeth M   (Hills)

Hills, George   60 no.4:200   PN
                       fol. title page SHB
                            1897:44   YB

Hill-Tout, Charles   4:1195   BCF

Hillyer, Munson C   168   AN

Hilton, A   A   1910:2   TDL

Hilton, Charles   3:471   GP

Hilton, Frank H   1939-40:30   OO
                       1945-46:82   OO

Himelwright, Fred   1943-44:79   OO
                       1945-46:86   OO

Himes, George Henry   1:596   GP
                            2:139   GP
                            458   MP
                            41:front. OHQ
                            70:207,209 OHQ
                            1:130   PMO

Himrod, Charles   2:672   FH

Hinckley, Francis   48   LS

Hinckley, Timothy Duane   1:261   BHK
                            2:788   BHS
                            5:396   SH

Hinden, H   44   MG

Hines, Gustavus   220   AC
                            55   DO
                            3:192   LH
                            1:32   NH
                            1:410   PMO
                            52 no.1:20 PN

Hines, Harvey K   220   AC
                            456   AG
                            1:596   GP
                            1:188   PMO

Hines, J   C   172-173   HA

Hines, Jack   377   HA

Hines, James (Nez Percé Indian) 212   BR
                            127   DTI
                            199   PSW

Hinkle, C   P   31   THI

Hinkle, Mrs. C P 31 THI
Hinkle, James M 3:1586 SM
Hinkly, F L 305 BR
Hin-mah-too-yah-lat-kekht, see
    Joseph, Nez Percé chief
Hin-mah-tute-ke-kaikt, see
    James, Nez Percé chief
Hinman, Alanson 1:424 NH
Hinman, Jersey, see
    Hinman, Josiah
Hinman, Josiah 7:43 MC
Hinricks, Eliza 1:917 LHC
Hinsdale, Sylvester 45 LDM
Hinton, George Clifford 3:331 BCF
Hinton, Martha, see
    Burnett, Martha (Hinton)
Hirom (?), Kettle chief fol.512 BUR
Hirsch, Edward 1:545 CHW
    1:292 NH
Hirsch, Solomon 2:145 GP
    2:69 LHC
    1:22 PMO
    166 SHP
Hirschberg, Max R 237 HA
Hirst, John D 2:276 SMS
Hitchcock, C L 50:48 1949 WDT
Hitchcock, Ethan Allen 453 PL
Hitchcock, Susan E , see
    Rouse, Susan E (Hitchcock)
Hitchcock, W 20-21 RA
Hitchcock, W A 97 PSW
Hite, Glenn Butler 3:719 LHC
Hi-youts-to-han, see
    Rabbit-Skin-Leggins (Nez Perce Indian)
Hoban, Leo James 3:466-467 BEA
Hobensack, Isaac Morris 2:84 SMS
Hobkirk, Peter 3:83 GP
Hobson, John 1:540 NH
Hobson, Richard 147 LDM
Hobson, Simeon S 2:567 SMS
Hobson, W H 1895:77 OO
Hoch, Basil 4 no.2:86 BCH
Hoch, Daniel 1905-06:[60] RLW
Hockett, C T 1935-36:51 OO
    1937-38:62-63 OO
    1939-40:30 OO
    1941-42:65 OO
Hodge, David Smith 6:350 MC
Hodge, Robert Tait 3:981 BHS
Hodge, Walter H 1924:144 WSP
Hodges, Henry C 87 WCS
Hodges, James 54 JP
Hodgin, Shadrach L 2:630 FH
Hodgskiss, William 3:999 SMS
Hodgson, B H 110-111 HCM
Hodgson, George T 3:864 SMS
Hodgson, Richard Charles 3:365 BCF
Hodson, Alvin 3:722 SMS

Hodson, Orlando Orville unp. SOU
Hoecken, Adrian fol.512 BUR
Hofer, E 1895:90 OO
Hoffman, Alfred F 48 LS
Hoffman, Charles Wheeler 5:314 MC
    354 MI
    2:1010 SM
Hoffman, Conrad R 3:1516 SM
Hoffman, D V unp. SOU
Hoffman, G Albert 4:595 PH
Hoffman, H E 2:19 1924 BCHA
Hoffman, Mrs. Henry, see
    Coble, Jane (Bell)
Hoffman, Ida 26 RO
Hoffman, Jane (Bell), see
    Coble, Jane (Bell)
Hofius, W D 3:609 BHK
Hofrichter, Cassius H 2:725 BHK
Hogan, Aloysius P 235 GG
Hogan, Francis Pierce 1:247 HH
Hogan, John P 195 GG
Hogan, John W , Jr. 247 GG
Hogan, Russell 1937-38:62-63 OO
Hogan, T S 4:72 MC
Hoge, James D unp. VU
    19:96 1914 WBP
    20:112 1915 WBP
Hoge, R G 1924:112 WSP
Hoge, Walter 3:1249 FH
Hogeboom, L V 71 LDM
Hogeland, Abraham 3:1203 SMS
Hoggan, David L 3:869 LHC
Hoggan, George D 3:327 HHI
Hogue, Charles P 2:583 GP
Holbrook, Amory 1:356 NH
Holbrook, Callie Augusta, see
    Carlyle, Callie Augusta (Holbrook)
Holbrook, E D 144 DL
Holbrook, Fred P 2:1125 SM
Holbrook, Henry 2:191 BCF
    1897:43, 124, 135 YB
Holbrook, Mrs. Mary L 1:470 GP
Holbrook, Paul 1895-96:119 SSS
Holbrook, Wellman 1943:167 ENC
Holcomb, Curtis 3:769 LHC
Holcomb, George W 2:439 PMO
Holcomb, O R 1924:17 WSP
Holden, William 4:1165 BCF
    fol.pt.2 SHB
Holden, William Burroughs 1943:116 ENC
Holderman, Louisa J , see
    Danielson, Louisa J (Holderman)
Holderness, earl of, see
    Rupert, Prince
Holladay, Ben 128 BOO
    689 CHO
    1:288-289 GP

———————	297	HOM
———————	152	LDM
———————	353	QT
Holland, Ernest O	108, 414	BHSS
———————	22	LW
———————	50 no.3:104	PN
Holland, John J	194	LDM
Holland, O E	1 no.10:17	WN
Hollenbeck, Horace O	200	BE
Holliday, George T	216	SIH
Holliday, Mary	6:408-409	MC
Hollis, W H	1:566	BH
Hollister, Harry L	3:1307	FH
Hol-Lol-Sote-Tote, see		
Lawyer, Nez Percé chief		
Holloway, Charles P	3:703	GP
———————	unp.	SOU
Hollreigh, Mollie	20:80	PNLA
Holly, James F	34 no.2:22	PNLA
Holm, Jens Neilson	117	GL
Holm, Margaret Christina, see		
Evans, Margaret Christina (Holm)		
Holman, Frederick Van Voorhies	1149	HIO
———————	2:352	PMO
Holman, George Phelps	1:254	PMO
Holman, Herbert	2:401	LHC
Holman, James Duval	1:534	PMO
———————	142	SHP
Holman, Mrs. James Duval, see		
Holman, Mrs. Rachael Hixson		
Holman, Joseph	1:92	NH
Holman, Mabel M (Bird)	2:282	PMO
Holman, Mrs. Rachael Hixson	1:534	PMO
Holman, Rufus C	66:250	OHQ
———————	1931-32:8	OO
———————	1935-36:34	OO
———————	1937-38:7	OO
———————	1943-44:13	OO
Holman, Walter J	2:282	PMO
Holman, Mrs. Walter J , see		
Holman, Mabel M (Bird)		
Holmes, Alexander M	2:469	CHW
Holmes, Byron Zebriski	2:779	GP
Holmes, Gertrude	1:242	PMO
Holmes, H E	1 no.7:20	WN
Holmes, John Robert	1943:263	ENC
———————	3:139	PH
Holmes, Mrs. M D	1:104	HWW
Holmes, Robert D	102	TUR
Holmes, Samuel Judd	front.	SRW
Holmes, Thomas J	366	SHP
Holmes, W H	1:368	NH
Holmes, William	277	LDM
Holt, Herbert S	250	GI
Holt, Samuel H	1895:87	OO
Holt, William Stull	50:42 1949	WDT
Holter, Anton M	107	LHM
———————	497	MI

———————	14 no.3:266	MWH
———————	2:903	SM
———————	2:517	SMS
Holter, Mrs. Anton M , see		
Holter, Mary Pauline (Loberg)		
Holter, Mary Pauline (Loberg)	106	LHM
Holter, Norman B	5:307	MC
Holtzheimer, Ed	229	JNT
Holznagel, Fred C	2:561	LHC
Homan, L W	20:48 1915	WBP
Homer, J A R	2:191	BCF
Homer, Walter	1897:135	YB
Homfray, Walter Unet	fol.pt.2	SHB
Honeyman, Jessie M	23 no.2:138	CR
———————	1:480	GP
Honeyman, Nanny Wood	1935-36:51	OO
Honeyman, Walter James	3:241	GP
Honeyman, Mrs. Walter James, see		
Honeyman, Jessie M		
Hood, Caroline, see		
Ralston, Caroline (Hood)		
Hood, Charles	2:388	PHP
Hood, Mrs. Emma	2:front. 1924	BCHA
Hood, James A	2:459	HWW
Hood, John W	131	PSW
Hood, Percy	20:48 1915	WBP
Hood, Samuel	108	MV
Hooker, Harley J	2:457	HHI
Hooker, W F	1:372	NH
Hoole, W E	96	LS
Hoomissen, Joseph van, see		
Van Hoomissen, Joseph		
Hooper, Arthur	287, 408	BHSS
Hoover, E V	1:480	PMO
Hoover, Edgar M	2:594	FH
Hoover, Jake	1:43	ACR
Hoover, Stewart W	366	BHSI
Hope, Alice M , see		
O'Leary, Alice M (Hope)		
Hope, I W	1895:92	OO
Hopkins, Frances, see		
Bray, Frances (Hopkins)		
Hopkins, Frank Frederick	4:367	BHK
———————	4:506	PH
Hopkins, James F	2:464	PHP
Hopkins, Mabel (McKinlay)	1:14	D
Hopkins, Mark	80	BOO
———————	204	QT
Hopkins, Paul	6:30 1906	WDT
Hopkins, Rebecca (Hall)	55	CW
———————	1:62	PMO
Hopkins, W C	4:102	MC
Hopp, John	fol.pt.2	SHB
Hopping, William P	3:743	BH
———————	3:407	HHT
Horgan, D J	172-173	HA
Horgan, Edward Eugene	6:75	SH
Horn, Charles	908	SIH

Horn, Tom   182-183   KO
Hornberger, L   P   [113]   RLX
Horne, Adam   37   WSE
Horne, James Welton   208   KB
                                            fol. pt. 1   SHB
Horne, Presley F   2:269   HHI
Horns Worn Out, see
    No-Horns-On-His-Head (Nez Percé Indian)
Horr, Christopher W   136-137   SRW
Horr, J   C   1895-96:69   SSS
Horsfall, Charles G   376   HA
Horst, Elias E   1120   SIH
Horton, Alonzo E   321   QT
Horton, Dexter   1:85   BHK
                                            2:59   BHK
                                            1:426   BHS
                                            2:564   PHP
                                            3:128   SH
Horton, G   P   50:23 1949   WDT
Horton, George Monroe   2:209   BHK
Horton, John H   704   SIH
Horton, Julius   6:222   SH
Horton, William N   56   LDM
Hosch, J   F   1935-36:51   OO
                                            1937-38:62-63   OO
                                            1939-40:31   OO
                                            1941-42:65   OO
Hose, Walter   7 no. 1:7   BCH
Hoseason, Cecil DeCourcy Sinclair   4:121   BCF
Hosford, A   A   238   E
Hosford, Chancey Osborn   171   AG
Hoska, Conrad L   3:183   HHT
Hosmer, Hezekiah L   3:288   MC
                                            4:102   MC
Hosmer, Theodore   1:198   HHT
                                            2:26   HHT
Hosmer, Mrs. Theodore   1:198   HHT
Hoss, Hal E   1931-32:8   OO
Hoss, Jennie M   38:42   G
Ho-sus-pa-ow-yun (Nez Percé Indian)
                                            1:529   HHI
Hotchkin, James H   26   DS
Hotchkiss, Clarence Roland   2:841   LHC
Hote, John (Puyallup Indian)   1:16   HHT
                                            1:496   HWW
Hote, Mrs. John (Puyallup Indian)   1:16   HHT
                                            1:496   HWW
Hough, F   F   172-173   HA
Houghton, Alice (Ide)   2:139   HH
Houghton, Mrs. Horace E   , see
    Houghton, Alice (Ide)
Houghton, Leonard Frank   3:425   BCF
Houlgate, Robert Kerr   3:15   BCF
                                            fol. pt. 2   SHB
Hoult, Enoch   1:104   NH
House, Mrs. Helen Chapman   32   THI
Houser, George   1924:160   WSP
Houser, Paul W   1924:64   WSP

Houston, Charles E   1905-06:[70]   RLW
Houston, Henry F   225   LDM
Houten, Walter John Van, see
    Van Houten, Walter John
Hovenden, Alfred   3:210   GP
                                            1:584   NH
Hovenden, Mrs. Alfred, see
    Hovenden, Sarah Ann (Soden)
Hovenden, Sarah Ann (Soden)   3:211   GP
Hovey, A   G   1:200   NH
Hovey, Chester R   1921:front.   WSP
                                            1926:20   WSP
Hovey, Joseph C   1924:161   WSP
Howard, Annie   126   BHSS
Howard, C   A   1931-32:8   OO
                                            1935-36:34   OO
                                            1937-38:7   OO
                                            1945-46:75   OO
Howard, Charles J   2:551   BHK
Howard, Clinton W   1910:front.   WSP
                                            1911:86   WSP
Howard, Edward   112   LDM
Howard, Emil W   2:207   CHW
Howard, Emmett   1931-32:41   OO
Howard, Loa   1945-46:50   OO
Howard, Mart A   50 no. 2:54   PN
Howard, Mrs. Minnie   366   BF
Howard, Oliver Otis   127   AI
                                            208   BHSI
                                            fol. 705   JO
                                            1:68   NH
                                            70:101   OHQ
Howard, Percy Sewell   4:241   BCF
Howard, W   F   366   BF
Howay, Frederic William   2:front., 113   BCF
                                            8 no. 1:1   BCH
                                            1:front. 1923   BCHA
Howe, Alma L   (Lawrence)   1:917   LHC
                                            2:311   LHC
Howe, H   L   1:917   LHC
Howe, Mrs. H   L   1:917   LHC
Howe, Herman   1924:144   WSP
Howe, J   B   1926:20   WSP
Howe, J   Howard   232   BR
Howe, M   J   , see
    Wyrouck, M   J   (Howe)
Howe, Richard   192   MV
Howe, Samuel Lyness   fol. pt. 2   SHB
Howe, Mrs. Samuel T   , see
    Howe, Alma L   (Lawrence)
Howe, W   A   2:456   PMO
Howell, Elizabeth B   , see
    McCorkle, Elizabeth B   (Howell)
Howell, I   M   1:566   BH
                                            2:337   HH
Howell, James   146   PSW
Howell, Jefferson D   2:338-339   BCF
                                            223   LDM

Howell, John J	190	LDM
Howell, Mary E , see		
Jaggar, Mary E (Howell)		
Howell, Thomas	57:108	OHQ
Howell, William Henry	2:619	HHI
Howes, Edward J	1910:2	TDL
Howes, Eliza Maria, see		
Trane, Eliza Maria (Howes)		
Howes, R E	369	LDM
Howey, Laura E (Spencer)	6:24A	MC
Howey, Robert H	347	LHM
Howey, Mrs. Robert H , see		
Howey, Laura E (Spencer)		
Howie, Neil	4:100	MC
	5:210	MC
Howie, W C	2:851	FH
Howlett, Luther S	5:296	SH
Howorth, Samuel	unp.	SOU
Hoxsey, T E	39	MG
Hoxsie, Charlie E	172-173	HA
	404	WOY
Hoy, M T	1945-46:28	OO
Hoyt, Elwell H	2:461	HHT
Hoyt, F S	24	OS
Hoyt, George W	40	LDM
	1:480	PMO
Hoyt, Henry L	1:210-211	GP
	1:480	PMO
Hoyt, John P	2:286	NH
	1905-06:[28]	RLW
	1895-96:61	SSS
	6:31 1906	WDT
Hoyt, Ralph Warren	2:16	PMO
Hoyt, Richard, Jr.	136	LDM
Hoyt, Richard, Sr.	23	LDM
Hoyt, Samuel A	347	LDM
Hubbard, Charles F	1905-06:[68]	RLW
Hubbard, Clarence G	28	SCC
Hubbard, Dale	16	LT
Hubbard, Eddie	45 no.2:41	PN
Hubbard, Forrest L	1945-46:93	OO
Hubbard, Francis Barton	5:354	SH
Hubbard, Frank Marion	542	IHI
Hubbard, Mrs. T C	2:front. 1924	BCHA
Hubbard, Mrs. Thomas	2:front. 1924	BCHA
Hubbard, Thomas J	134	DO
Hubbell, Norman S	2:733	FH
Huber, J Richard	50:44 1949	WDT
Huckins, Charles F	3:930	SMS
Huckins, Mrs. Charles F , see		
Huckins, Leonora (Henning)		
Huckins, Leonora (Henning)	3:930	SMS
Huddart, James	20 no.1-2:46	BCH
Hudson, Isaac	4:135	BCF
Hudson, John Stauffer	4:255	BHK
Hudson, Maurice	1945-46:25	OO
Hudson, R G	1926:20	WSP
Hudson, Robert M	3:769	GP

Hudson, Sarah A , see		
Rea, Sarah A (Hudson)		
Hudson, Vianna Frances, see		
Willburn, Vianna Frances (Hudson)		
Huetter, Bernard R	260	GG
Huetter, Theodore	243	GG
Huff, George Albert	1897:106	YB
Huffaker, Rhoda Priscilla, see		
Gardner, Rhoda Priscilla (Huffaker)		
Huggin, Janet Tait, see		
Lang, Janet Tait (Huggin)		
Huggins, Edward	162	AC
	1:17, 566	BH
	1:115	HH
	550	MP
	1:476	NH
	3:50	SH
	47	WCS
Huggins, George C	1941-42:63	OO
Hughes, E C	unp.	VU
Hughes, Ellis	59:101	OHQ
Hughes, Ellis G	2:495	GP
Hughes, Ellwood Clarke	3 no.8:421	PM
	5:58	SH
Hughes, George R	1895:172	OO
Hughes, Glenn	36:26 1935	WDT
	50:28 1949	WDT
Hughes, Harry Marshall	2:611	FH
Hughes, J C	2:337	BCF
Hughes, J L	2:293	BCF
Hughes, J M	111	PSW
Hughes, J W	1935-36:51	OO
	1937-38:62-63	OO
Hughes, P D	187	E
Hughes, William H	1905-06:[61]	RLW
Hulbert, Edward	3:335	HWW
Hulbert, J H	108	BHSS
Hulbert, Robert Ansel	3:475	BHS
	3:165	PH
Hulbush, William A	3:1436	SM
Hull, Clair Burton	3:47	BEA
Hull, Frank W	3:337	BHK
Hull, J J	4:100	MC
Hull, John A T	7:81	MC
Hull, John Roper	fol.pt.1	SHB
Hull, Joseph F	1:655	LHC
Hull, Mary Ann (Chadwick)	215	DSW
Hultberg, Nels Olson	220	HA
Humason, Orlando	3:509	GP
Humber, Robert Hart	172-173, 277	HA
Humble, Bernard Maynard	4:805	BCF
Humble, John L	1941:137	EN
	881	LHM
Humble, Mrs. John L , see		
Humble, M Caroline (Wilkerson)		
Humble, M Caroline (Wilkerson)		
	881	LHM
Hume, C B	fol.pt.2	SHB

Hume, John Frederick   1897:107   YB
Hume, Robert Alexander   3:379   GP
Hume, Robert D   2:431   PMO
                              50 no.4:127 PN
Humes, Thomas J   3 no. 8:422 PM
                              unp.   SEA
                              58   SSP
Humishuma, see
    Mourning Dove (Okanogan Indian)
Humphrey, J   G   172-173   HA
Humphrey, Omar J   352   LDM
Humphreys, Thomas   1897:124   YB
Humphries, James T   3:1080   FH
Humphries, Mrs. T   B   2:front. 1924 BCHA
Hungate, James   1905-06:[28] RLW
Hunger, Laura, see
    Muehler, Laura (Hunger)
Hunsaker, Emily (Collins)   1:620   NH
Hunsaker, J   T   1:620   NH
Hunsaker, Mrs. J   T   , see
    Hunsaker, Emily (Collins)
Hunt, Frank W   2:149   HHI
Hunt, George W   2:547   GP
Hunt, Herbert   2:431   HHT
                              3:443   HWW
Hunt, J   Frank   2:128   FSB
Hunt, James E   2:450   PMO
Hunt, John H   3:1647   SM
Hunt, Louis C   31   DH
Hunt, Ralph Stephen   2:155   HHI
Hunt, Thomas D   2:685   BHK
Hunt, Warren P   334   BR
                              376   SIH
Hunt, William H   4:115   MC
                              102   PL
Hunt, Wilson Price   74   BHI
                              60   BHSI
                              1:108   BS
                              1:136   CAFT
                              2:448a   CGO
                              65   DSW
                              1:184   FI
                              1:42-43   GP
Hunter, Dad, see
    Hunter, H   P
Hunter, Frederick   1945-46:68 OO
Hunter, Gordon   2:653   BCF
                              fol.pt.1   SHB
                              1911:70-71 YB
Hunter, H   P   292   PL
Hunter, Joseph   fol.pt.1   SHB
                              1897:107   YB
Hunter, T   A   1905-06:[41] RLW
                              [90]   RLX
Hunter, William   278-279   HU
                              1911:70-71 YB
Huntington, Collis P   80   BOO
                              204   QT

Huntington, Eunice, see
    Winsor, Eunice (Huntington)
Huntington, Henry Edwards 261   QT
Huntington, J   B   1895:171   OO
Huntington, S   A   1910:4   TDL
Huntington, Thomas   62   LDM
Huntington, Zina Diantha, see
    Young, Zina Diantha (Huntington)
Huntley, S   S   709   LHM
Hurd, F   H   38:28   G
Hurley, C   C   3:1614   SM
Hurley, Mary A   (McCarver) 3:649   GP
Hurley, Richard Hillard   3:648   GP
Hurley, Mrs. Richard Hillard, see
    Hurley, Mary A   (McCarver)
Hurley, Webb   1905-06:[79] RLW
Hurn, Reba   1924:48   WSP
Hurshman, Henry   [136]   RLX
Hurst, C   N   107   LHN
Hurst, Carrie, see
    Patterson, Carrie (Hurst)
Huse, J   Ward   3:1478   SM
Huson, H   S   2:157   HH
Hustler, J   G   25, 47   LDM
Huston, Joseph Waldo   213   DL
                           29   IHI
Huston, S   B   1895:81   OO
Huston, Simeon Arthur   40   JP
Huston, Thad   May 1907:39 TDL
Hutchings, William L   180   GL
Hutchinson, Joseph H   1:152   FSB
Hutchinson, R   H   1:331   HH
Hutchinson, Richard Ashton [110]   RLX
                           6:42   SH
                           1895-96:69   SSS
Hutchison, A   L   64   PSW
Hutchison, James   664   SIH
Hutchison, John H   664   SIH
Huth, Anton   3:247   BH
                           2:218   PHP
Hutson, Charles T   1905-06:[45] RLW
                           [98]   RLX
Hutton. Mrs. Leyi, see
    Hutton, May (Arkwright)
Hutton, May (Arkwright)
                           57 no.2:cover, 53 PN
Huxtable, A   2:front. 1924 BCHA
Huxtable, Jesse   1905-06:[64] RLW
                           [109]   RLX
Huycke, A   H   2:711   LHC
Hyatt, Glen Carroll   3:371   HWW
Hyde, Charles Henry   3:69   BH
                           1941:170   EN
                           6:80   SH
Hyde, Clarence F   1935-36:51   OO
                           1937-38:62-63 OO
Hyde, Edward C   1924:128   WSP
Hyde, George T   3:1116   FH

Hyde, Orson 187 BU
Hyland, Peter Edward 19 JP
Hymer, Elbert 2:62 SMS
Hynd, Robert Forbes 2:551 LHC
Hynes, Edward O'Dea 151, 159 OB
Hynson, George W 4:100 MC

I

Ide, Alice, see
   Houghton, Alice (Ide)
Ide, Clarence W 1895-96:71 SSS
Iffland, John 2:223 HWW
Ifft, George Nicholas, II 3:9 BEA
   1941:264 EN
Ignace, Old, see
   Old Ignace (Flathead Indian)
Ignace, Young, see
   Young Ignace (Flathead Indian)
Ignace La Mousse, see
   Old Ignace (Flathead Indian)
Iksana, Natawista (Blood Indian), see
   Culbertson, Natawista Iksana
Iliff, T C 10 LHN
Illsley, Mrs. F F , see
   Illsley, Minnie (Warren)
Illsley, Minnie (Warren) 128 WMW
Imlay, James B 3:145 LHC
Imoda, Camillus 364 PI
   432 PIW
Imus, Alvah Herman 3:156 PH
Imus, Hite 3:157 PH
Ind-a-yanek, Chilkat chief 7 WOY
Indian Jim, see
   Squa-ha-lish Jim Yelo-kan-um
Ingalls, H A 172-173 HA
Ingalls, James 1:917 LHC
Ingalls, Mrs. James 1:917 LHC
Ingalls, Merrell Whittier 394 GL
Ingalls, N B 43 LDM
Inghram, John F 240-241 SIH
Inghram, Robert L 240-241 SIH
Ingraham, Albert J 3:972 SMS
Ingraham, Mrs. Albert J , see
   Ingraham, Sarah Catherine (Ditty)
Ingraham, Edward Sturgis 200 BE
   108 BHSS
   150 MMR
Ingraham, Sarah Catherine (Ditty)
   3:972 SMS
Ingram, Nick 1:442-443 EPD
Ingram, W H 2:444 PMO
Inman, Robert D 2:455 PMO
Innis, James Henry 214 KB

Inouye, Orio 206 PSW
Insley, Asbury 94 LDM
Insula, Flathead chief fol. 512 BUR
   273 SO
Ipnasalatalc (Nez Percé Indian) 54 MW
Ipnats Olatalkt, see
   Minthorn, Sarah
Ireland, Joseph N 3:1311 FH
Ireland, Willard 18:9 PNLA
   20:11 PNLA
   21:31 PNLA
Irvin, George W 263 LHM
   7:175 MC
   2:888 SM
Irvin, William Edward 3:125 BEA
Irvine, B F 4 LSJ
Irvine, Caleb E 6:475 MC
Irvine, Jackson P unp. SOU
Irvine, Mrs. Jennie unp. SOU
Irvine, Thomas Howard 2:965 SM
Irvine, William M 3:859 SMS
Irving, John 4:1077 BCF
   2:front. 1924 BCHA
   29 DA
   220 KB
   303 LDM
   1897:107 YB
Irving, Joseph 1905-06:[65] RLW
Irving, Mrs. P Ae 2:front. 1924 BCHA
Irving, Thomas 1895-96:113 SSS
Irving, Washington 2:248 LH
Irving, William 4:1059 BCF
   3:119 GP
   24 LDM
   2:335 PMO
Irwin, Carl D 3:308 BEA
Irwin, Mrs. Carl D , see
   Irwin, Mina M (Gardner)
Irwin, George M 1895:67 OO
Irwin, Isaac M 544 SIH
Irwin, Mina M (Gardner) 3:308 BEA
Irwin, Nancy, see
   Morrison, Nancy (Irwin)
Isaac, Mary, see
   Blackstock, Mary (Isaac)
Isaachsen, Daniel Otto Christian
   3:347 PH
Isaacs, Walter F 50:30 1949 WDT
Isaacson, John 4:477 PH
Isaman, Samuel G 352 SIH
Isch, John 3:844 SMS
Israel, George C 2:144 PHP
Ives, Helen 67 MG
Ives, Jesse F 3:497 BHK
Iworrigan (Eskimo) 278-279 HU
Izer, George W 58:50 OHQ

J

Jack, Arthur Canby Brydon   3:167   BCF
Jack, Captain, see
    Kintpuash, Modoc chief
Jack, William Disbrow Brydone, see
    Brydone-Jack, William Disbrow
Jack, William M   6:311   MC
Jackman, P   2:front. 1924 BCHA
Jackman, Philip   2:113   BCF
Jackobson, Victor   447   LDM
Jacks, Benjamin F   264   SIH
Jackson, Alice (Hall)   3:94   BH
Jackson, Charles Samuel   2   LSJ
_____   57:314   OHQ
_____   66:250   OHQ
_____   16   TO
Jackson, Commodore   3:1267   FH
Jackson, Daniel Bachelder 2:762   BHS
                           281   LDM
Jackson, Florence Germaine 3:95   BH
Jackson, Frank C   1 no. 9:10   WN
Jackson, George J   96   KT
Jackson, H   F   [133]   RLX
Jackson, Harriet (Prentiss) 81   DW
Jackson, Henry D   3:953   FH
Jackson, James   3:94   BH
                           311   BN
_____   2:481   GP
Jackson, Mrs. James, see
    Jackson, Alice (Hall)
Jackson, Mrs. John, see
    Jackson, Harriet (Prentiss)
    Jackson, Mary (Joynson)
Jackson, John H   30   LDM
Jackson, John Robert   1911:70-71   YB
Jackson, L   G   198   E
Jackson, Mary (Joynson)   395   GL
Jackson, Robert J   1 no.3:178   WM
Jackson, Rose T   3:95   BH
Jackson, S   M   17:141 1912   WBP
                           18:160 1913   WBP
_____   19:144 1914   WBP
                           26:32 1921   WBP
_____   27:front. 1922 WBP
Jackson, Sam, see
    Jackson, Charles Samuel
Jackson, Samuel   118   LDM
Jackson, Samuel Morley   1 no.4:18   WN
Jackson, Scott F   2:521   CHW
Jackson, Sheldon   front.   JA
_____   6:298, 303   MC
_____   10   PJ
_____   54 no.2:68   PN
_____   250, 259   PSW

                           93   SHE
Jacobs, Alma S   21:31   PNLA
                           22:19   PNLA
_____   27:75   PNLA
Jacobs, B   F   1924:40   WSP
Jacobs, Edgar E   3:988   FH
Jacobs, Mrs. Johannah   91   GL
Jacobs, John   8   GL
Jacobs, John P , Jr.   unp.   SAA
Jacobs, Nancy A (Osborne) 55   CW
_____   1:62   PMO
Jacobs, Orange   179   HI
_____   1:164   NH
_____   2:570   PHP
_____   3 no.8:424   PM
_____   unp.   SEA
_____   1926:20   WSP
Jacobs, R   542   SHP
Jacobsen, Theodor Siegumfeldt
                           36:26 1935   WDT
_____   50:41 1949   WDT
Jacobson, Oscar   311   BHSS
Jaeger, Gottlieb J   3:343   BH
Jaeger, Mrs. Gottlieb J , see
    Jaeger, Sophia D (Appelhagen)
Jaeger, Sophia D (Appelhagen)
                           3:343   BH
Jagers, John F   311   LDM
Jaggar, Ann W (Rigley)   2:741   GP
Jaggar, Benjamin   2:741   GP
Jaggar, Mrs. Benjamin, see
    Jaggar, Ann W (Rigley)
Jaggar, Louis   3:142   GP
Jaggar, Mrs. Louis, see
    Jaggar, Mary E (Howell)
Jaggar, Mary E (Howell)   3:143   GP
Jahnke, Robert   26:64 1921   WBP
James, Nez Perce chief   fol.705   JO
James II, king of England, Scotland and
    Ireland   19   MH
James, Edwin Evens   3:797   SMS
James, Henry   59 no.4:187   PN
James, John R   1924:161   WSP
James, L   L   12   DA
James, Orson   2:48-49   EPD
James, Tom, see
    Whyuctan Swalamesett
James, Will   1:216   ACR
Jamieson, Annie B   6:166   PNLA
Jamieson, Edward Herbert   6:50   SH
Jamieson, Jesse M   41   SCC
Jamieson, Mrs. Laura E   6:151   PNLA
Jamieson, Robert   3:187   BCF
                           2:front. 1924 BCHA
_____   1897:44   YB
Jamieson, William   6:392   MC
Jamison, Neil C   2:405   HWW
Jamison, Robert   1905-06:[28]   RLW

Jane (Nez Percé Indian)	225	DD	Jennings, C W E	1937-38:62-63	OO
Janes, Thomas John	4:987	BCF	Jennings, Charles H	206	LDM
Jannsen, Alfred M	1931-32:41	OO	Jennings, E S	37	MG
Jans, Carl	430	AG	Jennings, Mary Ann, see		
Janson, Eliiv	68	SS	McCarver, Mary Ann (Jennings)		
Janson, Ivar	6	SS	Jennings, Susan S (Dixon)	3:556	HHI
Jaquette, Walter P	3:981	SMS	Jennings, Thomas W	3:556	HHI
Jaquith, Gail B	3:328-329	BEA	Jennings, Mrs. Thomas W , see		
Jardine, John	4:45	BCF	Jennings, Susan S (Dixon)		
_____	6:416-417	MC	Jensen, August Edham	3:1657	SM
_____	1911:70-71	YB	Jensen, Martin	2:860	HHI
Jardine, Simon Graham	fol.pt.2	SHB	Jensen, Mrs. Martin, see		
Jarrett, Mark V	544	SIH	Jensen, Mattie (Orr)		
Jarrett, Mrs. Mark V , see			Jensen, Mattie (Orr)	2:861	HHI
Jarrett, Rebecca A (Mann)			Jensen, Soren H	3:314	BEA
Jarrett, Rebecca A (Mann)	544	SIH	Jensen, Wilhelmina Augusta, see		
Jason (Nez Percé Indian)	158	DTI	Crogstad, Wilhelmina Augusta (Jensen)		
Jay, George	2:front. 1924	BCHA	Jenson, Olive De Ette, see		
Jayne, Stephen	287	BHSS	Groefsema, Olive De Ette (Jenson)		
Jeannet, Fred D	1937-38:62-63	OO	Jerauld, F N C	172-173	HA
Jeffcott, J E	276	LDM	Jerome, George	64	LDM
Jeffcott, P A	341	JNT	Jervis, John	202	MV
Jeffcott, P R	front.	JNT	Jesson, Edward R	47 no.3:69	PN
Jeffcott, Rebecca E (Tarte)	345	JNT	Jewell, Edward S	2:833	FH
Jeffers, Clyde G	3:47	PH	Jewell, Mrs. Edward S , see		
Jeffers, Joseph	2:42	NH	Jewell, Mary (Markham)		
Jeffers, Mrs. Joseph, see			Jewell, Mary (Markham)	2:833	FH
Jeffers, Mrs. Sarah H			Jewell, Robert Markham	3:386	BEA
Jeffers, Mrs. Sarah H	2:42	NH	Jewett, George Frederick	3:34	BEA
Jefferson, Thomas	65	BHI	Jewett, Mrs. Harriet M Kimball	102	CW
_____	1:96	BS	_____	1:52	NH
_____	16	FW	_____	2:60	PMO
_____	1:146	GP	Jewitt, John R	4 no.3:143	BCH
_____	2:108	LH	Jim, California, see		
_____	1:239	SH	California Jim		
Jeffery, Edward James	3:741	LHC	Jim, Captain, see		
_____	490	SHP	Captain Jim		
Jeffery, G A	172-173	HA	Jim, Long, see		
Jeffrey, Christopher C	3:1553	SM	Long Jim, Chelan chief		
Jeffreys, Solomon M	44	IHI	Jim, Loop Loop, see		
Jeffreys, Thomas M	229	IHI	Loop Loop Jim (Okanogan Indian)		
Jeffries, Garry Jackson	3:820	SMS	Jim, Split Lip, see		
Jeffs, Richard	1:456	NH	Split Lip Jim		
_____	1905-06:[28]	RLW	Jim Indian	2:141	BCF
Jeffs, Thomas W	fol.pt.1	SHB	Jimmy-the-Bear	34-35	MCK
Jellum, Lloyd	34 no.1:28	PNLA	Joab, Albert Emerson	1:277	HH
Jemmett, (Captain)	2:139	BCF	_____	May 1907:39	TDL
Jenkins, David P	1:73	HH	Joe or Alquema, see		
_____	5:184	SH	Alquema, Santiam chief		
Jenkins, Ray L	1941-42:65	OO	Johansen, Jorgine, see		
Jenkins, Warren M	43 no.1:17	PN	Ebsen, Jorgine (Johansen)		
Jenkins, William G , Jr.	2:897	HHI	Johanson, Nils A	3:287	BHK
Jenks, Cecil Evart	2:511	BHK	John, Bruno P	3:863	LHC
Jenne, Eldon	476	BHSS	Johnesse, Frank E	2:766	FH
Jenner, Charles K	2:145	HH	_____	2:947	HHI
_____	3 no.8:425	PM	Johnny-Behind-the Rock, see		
Jennings, Berryman	29	LDM	McKeown, John		
_____	1:667	LHC	Johns, Bennett Willson	2:386	HWW

	2:128	PHP
Johns, Mrs. Bennett Willson, see		
Johns, Mary J (Vertrees)		
Johns, Edwin	2:front. 1924	BCHA
Johns, Loeta	31:48	PNLA
Johns, Mary J (Vertrees)	2:387	HWW
Johns, Minnie Jane, see		
Linderman, Minnie Jane (Johns)		
Johnson, A H	562	SHP
Johnson, A J	1895:84	OO
Johnson, Ada L , see		
McCleary, Ada L (Johnson)		
Johnson, Agnes	42:32 1930	WSGP
Johnson, Albert	2:162	HHT
	1 no. 9:22	WN
Johnson, Andrew William	3:465	HHI
Johnson, Mrs. Andrew William, see		
Johnson, Louisa Catharine (Bruncell)		
Johnson, Anna (Anderson)	212	GL
Johnson, Anna (Moen)	3:453	LHC
Johnson, Arthur D	3:1489	SM
Johnson, Arthur H	849	HIO
Johnson, Arthur Livingstone	3:661	BCF
Johnson, B W	1931-32:40	OO
Johnson, Brian Clair	3:269	BEA
Johnson, Byron Ingemar	244	JAC
Johnson, C D	unp.	SOU
Johnson, C L	172-173	HA
Johnson, Casper	680	SIH
Johnson, Charles	1905-06:[56]	RLW
	36:21 1935	WDT
Johnson, Charles F	358	LDM
Johnson, Charles Gardiner	4:517	BCF
Johnson, Charles J	2:593	CHW
Johnson, Charles Nelson	3:553	LHC
Johnson, Charles Sumner	172-173, 330	HA
Johnson, Charles W	6:28 1906	WDT
	26:53 1925	WDT
	1924:80	WSP
Johnson, Dallas D	1943:103	ENC
Johnson, Daniel	1:548	NH
Johnson, Mrs. Daniel, see		
Johnson, Elsina (Perkins)		
Johnson, E C	430, 483	BHSS
Johnson, E G	2:397	HHI
Johnson, Edwin F	112	BOO
Johnson, Elsina (Perkins)	1:548	NH
Johnson, Emily Pauline (Mohawk Indian)		
	front.	JV
Johnson, Eric	177	LDM
Johnson, Ervin W	704	IHI
Johnson, Frank Fisk	2:71	HHI
	14:108 1909	WBP
Johnson, Gertrude	27	US
Johnson, Gus	1943:33	ENC
Johnson, Harvey L	May 1907:39	TDL
Johnson, Hattie (Long)	160	SIH
Johnson, Henry Z	2:82	FSB
Johnson, Hiram Frederick	3:1529	SM
Johnson, Mrs. I	2:front. 1924	BCHA
Johnson, Iver	159	SS
Johnson, J C	21:128 1916	WBP
	22:128 1917	WBP
Johnson, J O	1945-46:86	OO
Johnson, James	1:548	NH
Johnson, Mrs. James, see		
Johnson, Juliet (Perkins)		
Johnson, John	212	GL
	97	SS
	102	SS
	302	HA
Johnson, Mrs. John, see		
Johnson, Anna (Anderson)		
Johnson, John W	1:643	CHW
Johnson, Jonathan	1:441	HH
Johnson, Josie (De Vore)	2:292	PMO
Johnson, Juliet (Perkins)	1:548	NH
Johnson, Lee A	1905-06:[56]	RLW
	[119]	RLX
Johnson, Lelia	67	MG
Johnson, Liver-eating	166	KY
Johnson, Louis	3:1405	SM
Johnson, Louisa Catharine (Bruncell)		
	3:465	HHI
Johnson, Mark J	1931-32:41	OO
Johnson, Mary J , see		
Ereaux, Mary J (Johnson)		
Johnson, Mathilde, see		
Olson, Mathilde (Johnson)		
Johnson, N D	3:452	LHC
Johnson, Mrs. N D , see		
Johnson, Anna (Moen)		
Johnson, Nancie (King)	2:863	FH
Johnson, O B	18-19	GA
Johnson, Ofell	1924:81	WSP
Johnson, Orville Payne	3:1005	FH
Johnson, Otis	May 1907:68	TDL
Johnson, Patrick Louis	278-279	KO
Johnson, Pete	3:715	SMS
Johnson, Philip	32	LDM
Johnson, Richard E	3:1445	SMS
Johnson, Richard Z	front.	IHI
Johnson, Swede, see		
Johnson, Patrick Louis		
Johnson, W A	1935-36:51	OO
	1937-38:62	OO
Johnson, Mrs. W C , see		
Johnson, Josie (De Vore)		
Johnson, W Lon	1924:25	WSP
Johnson, William	239	LDM
Johnson, William, Jr.	1935-36:51	OO
Johnson, William Calvin	2:863	FH
Johnson, Mrs. William Calvin, see		
Johnson, Nancie (King)		
Johnson, William F	160	SIH

Johnson, Mrs. William F , see		
Johnson, Hattie (Long)		
Johnson, William H	2:775	FH
Johnson, William Lawrence	4:587	BCF
Johnson, William T	1945-46:86	OO
Johnson, Zephaniah A	224	SIH
Johnson brothers	222	DSW
	1:199	FH
Johnsone, C W	20:48 1915	WBP
	21:128 1916	WBP
	22:128 1917	WBP
Johnston, A P	2:412	SMS
Johnston, Albert Sidney	393	GU
Johnston, Charles C	3:1445	SMS
Johnston, David S	1:528	PHP
Johnston, David William	3:653	BCF
Johnston, Elias W	261	HA
	6:186	SH
Johnston, George William	3:117	LHC
Johnston, Mrs. Harvey, see		
Johnston, Lena Tacoma (Baker)		
Johnston, Lena Tacoma (Baker)	1:126	HHT
Johnston, Ronald Campbell Campbell-,see		
Campbell-Johnston, Ronald Campbell		
Johnston, Roy H	3:1446	SMS
Johnston, Thomas A	3:960	FH
Johnston, Thomas Conrad	4:591	BCF
Johnston, Thomas Huston	2:459	PMO
Johnston, Thomas L	3:1136	FH
	138	HIT
Johnston, Mrs. Thomas L , see		
Donaldson, Mary Elizabeth (Craker)		
Johnston		
Johnston, W S	1895-96:97	SSS
Joiner, Truman	3:274	BEA
Jones, Arthur William	fol.pt.1	SHB
Jones, Benjamin J	648	SIH
Jones, Blanche (Evans)	2:223	CHW
Jones, C E	202	HIT
Jones, Mrs. C W	438	AG
Jones, Cecil C	1:634	BCF
Jones, Charles Hebard	3:36	BH
	3:41	HHT
	78	LDM
	5:170	SH
Jones, Mrs. Charles Hebard, see		
Jones, Franke M (Tobey)		
Jones, Charles Henry	4:225	BCF
Jones, Daniel	1:181	HH
Jones, David Lloyd	fol.pt.2	SHB
Jones, Mrs. Eliza Jane	291	MP
Jones, Ellen (Williams)	397	GL
Jones, Ernest M	50:61 1949	WDT
Jones, Evan	unp.	HOF
Jones, Everett O	3:547	BHK
Jones, Francis Bedford	408	LDM
	3:705	LHC
Jones, Franke M (Tobey)	3:37	BH

Jones, Frederick Steele	3:317	BCF
Jones, George H	1905-06:[28]	RLW
Jones, H R	1941-42:66	OO
	1943-44:79	OO
	1945-46:86	OO
Jones, Hannah (Christensen)	409	GL
Jones, Harry	fol.pt.1	SHB
	20:80 1915	WBP
Jones, Mrs. Harvey H , see		
Jones, Mrs. Eliza Jane		
Jones, Henry	3:1043	FH
Jones, Mrs. Henry, see		
Jones, Wilmoth (Gray)		
Jones, Henry E	376	SHP
Jones, Hugh W	6:404-405	MC
Jones, J M	22:128 1917	WBP
	23:112 1918	WBP
	24:64 1919	WBP
Jones, J N	1941-42:62	OO
	1943-44:75	OO
	1945-46:82	OO
Jones, Jesse S	[86]	RLX
Jones, John H	287, 390	BHSS
Jones, Mrs. John J , see		
Jones, Hannah (Christensen)		
Jones, John James	3:145	BCF
Jones, John P	244	QT
Jones, L F	252	PSW
Jones, Linn E	1931-32:40	OO
Jones, M G	172-173	HA
Jones, Martha Pane, see		
Thomas, Martha Pane (Jones)		
Jones, Mary, see		
Evans, Mary (Jones)		
Jones, Mary A , see		
Hawthorne, Mary A (Jones) Phelps		
Jones, Missouri C , see		
Shelton, Missouri C (Jones)		
Jones, Nellie V	410	BHSS
Jones, Otto M	2:487	HHI
Jones, Owen	183	PSW
Jones, Philo Everett	3:183	LHC
Jones, Richard Saxe	1924:145	WSP
Jones, Robert Rubie	4:367	BCF
Jones, Ronald E	1935-36:51	OO
	1937-38:62-63	OO
	1939-40:15	OO
	1941-42:62	OO
Jones, S Paul	2:223	CHW
Jones, Mrs. S Paul, see		
Jones, Blanche (Evans)		
Jones, Stephen	4:655	BCF
Jones, T J	39	IHI
Jones, Thomas A	3:243	BHS
Jones, Thomas Elwood	6:94	SH
Jones, Thomas R	145	GL

Jones, Mrs. Thomas R   , see
    Jones, Ellen (Williams)
Jones, Mrs. Thora Stranahan 32   THI
Jones, W   A1   2:153   CHW
Jones, W   C   2:199   HH
     1895-96:59   SSS
Jones, Walter W   3:72   PH
Jones, Wesley L   42 no.2:112   PN
     1899:65   SSS
     1 no.4:253   WM
Jones, Willard N   29   PL
Jones, William   5:191   MC
Jones, William H   50:56 1949   WDT
Jones, William P   3:23   GP
Jones, Wilmoth (Gray)   3:1043   FH
Jonez, Hinton D   3:103   BH
     3:591   HHT
Joplin, Ferdinand   3:553   GP
Jordan, F   W   273   LDM
Jordan, Grace (Edgington)   3:37   BEA
Jordan, Ida I   , see
    Riggin, Ida I   (Jordan)
Jordan, J   Eugene   4 no.2:41   PM
     1895-96:156   SSS
Jordan, J   T   unp.   SEA
Jordan, Leonard Beck   3:37   BEA
     1949-50:2   IHD
Jordan, Mrs. Leonard Beck, see
    Jordan, Grace (Edgington)
Jordan, Thomas   67:325   OHQ
Jordan, Walter M   5:325   MC
Jordison, John   285   LDM
Jory, J   W   177   PL
Josenhans, Timotheus   3:637   BHS
Joseph, Nez Percé chief   front., 109,127   AI
     325   AM
     253   BHI
     214   BHSI
     front.   BN
     122, 157, 166, 229   BR
     345   CIR
     223   DCW
     254   DSW
     126   DTI
     1:49   FH
     1:72   FI
     3:36   FI
     1:568-569   GP
     1:521   HHI
     1935-36:36   IH
     102   JM
     fol.705   JO
     192   KY
     134   LBT
     230   LCR
     352-353   LCRH
     4:238   LH
     4:156   MC
     176   MCO
     370   MS
     2:4   NH
     61   NL
     1:122   PMO
     45 no.1:cover   PN
     49 no.4:133   PN
     70   SIH
     303   SK
     308   SKA
     1:361, 368   SMS
     6, 40   SPI
     27   THI
     614   USCI
     363   VT
Joseph, Emile C   2:325   CHW
Joseph, Old, Nez Percé chief, see
    Tuekakas, Nez Percé chief
Joseph, S   E   2:453   PMO
Joseph, Young, see
    Joseph, Nez Percé chief
Joseph of the Sacred Heart, Mother   14 MG
Josepha, Mother   336   PIW
Josephi, Simeon Edward   2:286   NH
     27:96, 109   OHQ
     46:292   OHQ
Joset, Joseph   fol.512   BUR
     35   CCA
     47   GG
     17   JJ
     152   MCO
     10   SCH
Joshua, Walla Walla chief   1:123   PMO
Joshua, Mrs. (Snoqualmie Indian)
     4 no.1:fol.83   UV
Joslyn, A   J   220   AC
     401   AG
Joslyn, Howard   3:747   BHS
Jossey, B   B   1895-96:130   SSS
Jourden, J   D   172-173   HA
Joy, George C   1 no.4:29   WN
Joy, Oliver H   1905-06:[28]   RLW
Joyce, Thomas M   3:927   LHC
Joynson, Mary, see
    Jackson, Mary (Joynson)
Judah, Theodore D   80   BOO
     204   QT
Judd, Isabell (Norton)   97   GL
Judd, Riley   130   GL
Judge, Father   44   AL
Judson, Helen C   , see
    McClane, Helen C   (Judson)
Judson, Henry H   43 no.2:136   PN
Judson, Peter   1:12   HHT
     155   PMT
Judson, Mrs. Peter   1:12   HHT
Judson, Phoebe   125   JNT
Judson, Stephen   1:90   HHT

Judson, Mrs. Stephen	1:90	HHT
Judy, Martin	242	AG
Julia, Sister	336	PIW
Julian (Carrier Indian)	23	MHN
Juneau, Joseph	347	CIR
	xiii	DEA
Junkin, Mrs. Eliza	6:410-411	MC
Junkin, William F	6:410-411	MC
Just, Emma (Bennett)	59	CBC
	6	MHS
Just, Nels A	9	MHS
Just, Mrs. Nels A , see		
Just, Emma (Bennett)		
Jutte, Peter	304	SIH

K

Kadashan, Tlingit chief	30	CT
	31	CTL
Kae-kae-shee, Flathead chief	8	JJ
Kaelin, Martin	3:271	BH
Kaesemeyer, T J	239	E
Kahn, B I	41	MG
Kain, Francess Ann	3:1368	SM
Kain, Thomas	3:1368	SM
Kain, Mrs. Thomas, see		
Kain, Francess Ann		
Kaiser, John Boynton	3:347	HHT
	24:272	PNLA
Kaiser, Louisa (Wagner)	570	LHM
Kaiser, M	570	LHM
Kaiser, Mrs. M , see		
Kaiser, Louisa (Wagner)		
Kakisimla, see		
Angeline, Princess		
Ka-koop-et (Seshaht Indian)	81	CI
Kalland, O A	3:457	BH
Kamaiakan, Yakima chief	fol.705	JO
	4:196	LH
	14	SK
	16	SKA
	179	WCS
Ka-mi-akin, see		
Kamaiakan		
Kamm, Caroline Augusta (Gray)	2:127	GP
	2:40	LHC
	2:8	PMO
Kamm, Charles Tilton	259	LDM
	2:47	LHC
Kamm, Jacob	1:258	GP
	2:126	GP
	31	LDM
	1:287	LHC
	2:41	LHC
	2:8, 337	PMO
	528	SHP

Kamm, Mrs. Jacob, see		
Kamm, Caroline Augusta (Gray)		
Kandle, George B	1:566	BH
	2:224	PHP
Kane, Cap (Nez Percé Indian)	226	BR
Kane, Thomas Franklin	18-19	GA
	1905-06:[39]	RLW
	6:20 1906	WDT
Kane, Thomas L	84	GMM
Kanim, Pat, see		
Patkanim, Snoqualmie chief		
Kanipe, Daniel A	4:277	MC
Kanosh	186	EP
Kanzler, Jacob	3:811	LHC
Kappleman, F G	172-173	HA
Karapo, Mrs. Luke (Umatilla Indian)		
	212	AI
Karr, Abigail Boutwell (Walker)		
	202, 240, 248	DE
	2:83	HWW
Karr, Eunice Viola	248-249	DE
Karr, James Anderson	2:82	HWW
Karr, Mrs. James Anderson, see		
Karr, Abigail Boutwell (Walker)		
Karr, Ruth, see		
McKee, Ruth (Karr)		
Karren, John	398	GL
Karren, Mrs. John, see		
Karren, Maria (Lawrence)		
Karren, Maria (Lawrence)	398	GL
Karshner, Warner M	3:111	HWW
	3:91	PH
Karstad, Bertha	12	SS
Ka-sh-ak, Chilkat chief	7	WOY
Kasper, William	4:580	PH
Kauffman, H R	1941-42:62	OO
	1943-44:75	OO
Kauffman, John Jacob	1941:373	EN
Kauffman, Percival Coover	1910:35	TDL
	8:72 1903	WBP
	13:28 1908	WBP
	19:119 1914	WBP
Kaufman, M	1:372	HHT
Kautz, August Valentine	31	DH
	73	MMR
	48 no.4:136	PN
Kay, John Mathew	3:772	SMS
Kean, Thomas	2:1113	SM
Kearns, R J	41	MG
Kearns, Thomas	483	GLS
Keary, Mrs. James	2:113	BCF
Keary, William Holland	2:113	BCF
	fol.pt.1	SHB
Keasey, Dorr E	1931-32:41	OO
Keate, Stuart	23:136	PNLA
Keator, Frederic William	3:163	HHT
	34	JP

Keats, Harry L	2:347	GP	Kellogg, Jay A	2:612	NH	
Kee, Hong	3:871	HHI	————	1895-96:73	SSS	
Keefer, William W	3:367	HHI	Kellogg, John A	1905-06:[66]	RLW	
Keen, George W	unp.	SOU	Kellogg, Joseph	1037	HIO	

Keen, James W   , see
   Keene, James W

	23	LDM	
Keene, Henry	2:436	PMO	1:661	LHC

Keats, Harry L — 2:347 — GP
Kee, Hong — 3:871 — HHI
Keefer, William W — 3:367 — HHI
Keen, George W — unp. — SOU
Keen, James W   , see
  Keene, James W
Keene, Henry — 2:436 — PMO
Keene, James W — 3:967 — BHS
———— — 83 — LDM
Keeney, D — 366 — BF
Keeney, Elijah N — 184 — SIH
Keeney, Mrs. Elijah N   , see
  Keeney, Eugenia (Allen)
Keeney, Eugenia (Allen) — 184 — SIH
Keeney, James Maynard — 2:571 — LHC
Kegg, Nicholas E — unp. — SOU
Kegley, C   B — 21:18 1909 — WSGP
———— — 23:27 1911 — WSGP
———— — 24:29 1912 — WSGP
———— — 25:31 1913 — WSGP
Kegley, R   K — 1895-96:97 — SSS
Keith, Adelphus Bartlett — 190 — MI
Keith, Mrs. J — 2:front. 1924 — BCHA
Keith, James Cooper — fol.pt.1 — SHB
Keith, John Charles Malcolm — 3:567 — BCF
Kellar, Alice M   , see
  Streeter, Alice M   (Kellar)
Kelleher, Daniel — 2:381 — BHK
Kelleher, Francis J — 275 — PI
Keller, Albert W — 77 — LDM
Keller, Christian G — 3:1067 — FH
Keller, F   L — 3:401 — HHI
Keller, Mrs. F   L   , see
  Keller, Lucy E   (Dement)
Keller, Joseph P — 3:51 — PH
Keller, Lucy E   (Dement) — 3:401 — HHI
Kelley, A   Eugene — 4:562 — PH
Kelley, E   L — 3:966 — SMS
Kelley, Hall Jackson — 81 — BF
———— — 1:150 — GP
———— — 18:1 — OHQ
Kelley, Joseph — front. — KT
Kelley, Oliver H — 25:148 1913 — WSGP
Kelley, W   B — 1:566 — BH
Kellie, James M — 1897:107 — YB
Kelling, Detrick — 1:288 — NH
Kelling, Henry — 2:169 — HH
Kellog, C   L   F — 3 no.8:428 — PM
Kellog, J   C — 1905-06:[28] — RLW
Kellogg Albert S — 6:415 — MC
Kellogg, Charles H — 1:452 — NH
———— — 1:198 — PMO
Kellogg, Estella A   (Bushnell) — 1:452 — NH
———— — 1:72 — PMO
Kellogg, Fannie E   , see
  Young, Fannie E   (Kellogg)
Kellogg, George — 1:120 — NH
Kellogg, Mrs. George, see
  Kellogg, Mary C   (Edwards) Morand

Kellogg, Jay A — 2:612 — NH
———— — 1895-96:73 — SSS
Kellogg, John A — 1905-06:[66] — RLW
Kellogg, Joseph — 1037 — HIO
———— — 23 — LDM
———— — 1:661 — LHC
———— — 1:452 — NH
———— — 1:72 — PMO
———— — 2:338 — PMO
Kellogg, Mrs. Joseph, see
  Kellogg, Estella A   (Bushnell)
Kellogg, Margaret (Miller) — 1:452 — NH
———— — 1:72 — PMO
Kellogg, Martha A   , see
  Ross, Martha A   (Kellogg)
Kellogg, Mary C   (Edwards) Morand
———— — 1:120 — NH
Kellogg, Noah S — 1:400 — NH
Kellogg, Orrin, Jr. — 1:452 — NH
———— — 1:198 — PMO
Kellogg, Orrin, Sr. — 1:452 — NH
———— — 1:72 — PMO
Kellogg, Mrs. Orrin, Sr., see
  Kellogg, Margaret (Miller)
Kellogg, Orson M — 2:243 — HWW
Kelly, Clinton — 2:219 — GP
———— — 1:248 — NH
Kelly, David — 1:unp. 1900-01 — WDT
Kelly, Edward J — 398 — BR
———— — 21, 151, 159, 167 — OB
Kelly, Elizabeth C   (Clark) — 1:312 — PMO
Kelly, Elliott — 2:547 — HHT
Kelly, Guy E — 3:175 — BH
Kelly, Hampton — 3:270 — GP
———— — 1:248 — PMO
Kelly, Mrs. Hampton, see
  Kelly, Margaret (Fitch)
Kelly, J   H — 172-173 — HA
Kelly, James K — 1:556 — GP
———— — 1:929 — LHC
———— — 1:64 — NH
———— — 66:136 — OHQ
———— — 2:172 — PMO
———— — 178 — SHP
Kelly, John — 1:144 — NH
Kelly, Loren B — 1 no.1:10 — WN
Kelly, Luther Sage — 265 — BHI
———— — 107 — FM
———— — 110-111 — HCM
———— — passim — KY
Kelly, Margaret (Fitch) — 3:271 — GP
———— — 1:248 — PMO
Kelly, Milton — 196 — DL
———— — 224 — IHI
Kelly, Penumbra — 65:280 — OHQ
Kelly, Percy R — 1931-32:8 — OO
———— — 1935-36:34 — OO
———— — 1937-38:7 — OO
———— — 1939-40:7 — OO

	1941-42:14	OO	Kennelly, James A	251	GG
	1943-44:21	OO		175	SCH
	1945-46:33	OO	Kennett, Ferd	6:305, 392	MC
	2:451	PMO	Kenney, F M	20:80 1915	WBP
Kelly, Peter J	2:437	SMS		21:128 1916	WBP
Kelly, Plympton	2:661	GP	Kenney, Michael	192	MCO
	1:312	PMO	Kennicott, Robert	fol. 207	SHI
Kelly, Mrs. Plympton, see				82	WOY
Kelly, Elizabeth C (Clark)			Kennison, E A , see		
Kelly, Richmond	1:428	PMO	Metlen, E A (Kennison)		
Kelly, S L	10 no. 1:43	BCH	Kenny, Mary (Doherty)	69:135	OHQ
Kelly, Thomas	195	GG	Kenny, Michael	69:135	OHQ
Kelly, William	60:94	OHQ	Kenny, Mrs. Michael, see		
Kelly, William A	252, 259	PSW	Kenny, Mary (Doherty)		
Kelly, Yellowstone, see			Kenoyer, G C	1905-06:[61]	RLW
Kelly, Luther Sage			Kent, Harry W	3:739	BHK
Kelsey, F D	6:386	MC		3:1077	BHS
Kelsey, Frank T	3:1343	SMS		3:306	PH
Kelsey, Samuel W	3:1370	SM	Kent, Herbert	2:front. 1924	BCHA
Kemp, Alice M , see			Kent, J H	4:70	MC
Feely, Alice M (Kemp)			Kent, Mrs. James Marshall, see		
Kemp, Erwin E	3:1771	SM	Kent, Leslie (Swigart)		
Kemp, Mrs. Florence Clemens	3:70	D	Kent, John	2:609	FH
Kemp, Mrs. Frederick G B , see			Kent, Leslie (Swigart)	2:303	CHW
Kemp, Mrs. Florence Clemens			Kenyon, William R	231	MI
Kemp, G Ward	1924:112	WSP	Keppler, Joseph Carl	2:932	SM
Kemp, Harry	1:917	LHC	Ker, Julia Waldrip	3:322	PH
Kemper, S V	443	MI	Ker-leng-ner, Eskimo princess	106	HEG
Kempster, Arthur L	3:313	BHS	Kermode, Francis	4:487	BCF
Kenck, Albert F	157	GG	Kern, Emma, see		
Kenck, Charles	3:153	MC	Marquam, Emma (Kern)		
Kenck, Oscar M	151	GG	Kern, Mrs. J W	438	AG
Kendall, Benjamin F	63:223	OHQ	Kern, Peter E	18	DA
Kendig, (Captain)	1:185	BH	Kern, Alexander S	6:442-443	MC
Kenedy, Eliza J (Cash) Abernathy			Kerr, Frank Lawrence	3:489	BCF
	896	SIH	Kerr, Harry J	4:448	PH
Kenedy, James H	896	SIH		19:160 1914	WBP
Kenedy, Mrs. James H , see				25:64 1920	WBP
Kenedy, Eliza J (Cash) Abernathy			Kerr, James Alexander	4:1047	BCF
Kenin, Harry M	1939-40:15	OO	Kerr, James B	44:338	OHQ
	1941-42:62	OO	Kerr, Martha A , see		
Kennaly, John, Sr.	2:848	FH	Eagleson, Martha A (Kerr)		
Kennedy, Arthur Edward	1:510	BCF	Kerr, William Jasper	2:665	CHW
	2:277	BCF	Kerr, William John	3:259	BCF
	14 no. 1-2:62	BCH	Kerrigan, J F	384	PL
	fol. title page	SHB	Kerrigan, Jack, see		
	1897:63	YB	Kerrigan, J F		
	1911:70-71	YB	Kerry, A S	unp.	VU
Kennedy, Charles D	3:89	LHC	Kessler, Charles N	2:899	SM
Kennedy, David	328	LDM	Kessler, Harry Clay	1:616	SM
Kennedy, G W	1:917	LHC		1:645	SMS
Kennedy, Mrs. G W	1:917	LHC	Kessler, Harry Stuart	3:259	BEA
Kennedy, George A	1905-06:[50]	RLW		2:645	FH
Kennedy, Hugh	2:464-465	EPD	Kessler, Nicholas	423	LHM
Kennedy, James Buckham	1897:107	YB		269	MI
Kennedy, John F	557	SCH	Ketchum, Delaney Paulin	2:781	LHC
Kennedy, John W	3:1573	SM	Ketchum, Frank E	fol. 207	SHI
Kennedy, Thomas J L	1924:49	WSP		86	WOY
Kennedy, Thomas L	4:131	BCF			

Ketner, R A	1:566	BH	
Kettenbach, Otto	305	BR	
Kettenbach, William F , Jr.	112	IHI	
Kettenbach, William F , Sr.	3:1144	FH	
	111	IHI	
Keyes, Stillman James	3:473	HHI	
Keyt, D L	1895:107	OO	
Kickbush, Frederick Charles	3:621	BCF	
Kicking Bear (Sioux Indian)	238	KY	
Kidd, Thomas	4:31	BCF	
	1897:107	YB	
Kiddle, Clyde L	1937-38:62	OO	
Kiddle, Fred E	1931-32:40	OO	
Kidson, William	172-173	HA	
Kientpoos, see			
Kintpuash, Modoc chief			
Kiest, J S	172-173	HA	
Kilbourne, Edward Corliss	2:766	BHS	
	1:181	HH	
Kilcup, John	360	JNT	
Kildow, George Oliver	3:21	BEA	
Kilkenny, John Sheridan	69:101	OHQ	
Killam, Frank William	3:1121	BCF	
Killin, Benton	566	SHP	
Kilpatrick, Ben	86-87, 278-279	KO	
Kilpatrick, Thomas	fol. pt. 2	SHB	
Kilton, Thomas	157	LDM	
Kimball, Byron S	102	CW	
Kimball, Dave	137	EP	
Kimball, Mrs. Dave	137	EP	
Kimball, Frank A	321	QT	
Kimball, Heber C	106	EP	
	112-113 (xxxv)	PR	
Kimball, Horace	240	E	
Kimball, Mima, see			
Negler, Mima (Kimball)			
Kimball, Mrs. Nathan S , see			
Jewett, Mrs. Harriet M Kimball			
Kimball, Ray C	2:655	HHI	
Kimball, Sarah, see			
Munson, Sarah (Kimball)			
Kimball, Solomon F	16	EP	
Kimball, Susan M , see			
Wirt, Susan M (Kimball)			
Kimberling, E W	1937-38:62-63	OO	
	1939-40:31	OO	
	1941-42:66	OO	
	1943-44:79	OO	
	1945-46:86	OO	
Kimble, Louise (McCoy)	2:24	CPD	
Kimble, Mrs. Virgil, see			
Kimble, Louise (McCoy)			
Kimbrough, Herbert	311, 430	BHSS	
Kimmel, Edward	202, 239	BHSS	
Kimple, Clara (Maxey)	2:349	HHI	
Kimple, W W	2:349	HHI	
Kimple, Mrs. W W , see			
Kimple, Clara (Maxey)			

Kimsey, W E	1943-44:17	OO	
	1945-46:29	OO	
Kincaid, Abraham Edmund	fol. pt. 2	SHB	
Kincaid, Harrison Rittenhouse	2:318	NH	
	1895:65	OO	
	16	TO	
Kincaid, John Francis	1:133	BH	
	2:178	NH	
Kincaid, John S	2:368-369	EPD	
Kincaid, Robert	2:138	PHP	
Kincaid, Ruth, see			
McCarty, Ruth (Kincaid)			
Kincaid, Susan, see			
Thompson, Susan (Kincaid)			
Kincaid, Trevor Charles Digby	3:615	BHS	
	46 no.3:66	PN	
	1:unp. 1900-01	WDT	
	6:25 1906	WDT	
	26:53 1925	WDT	
Kincaid, William M	1:133	BH	
Kindred, B C	22	LDM	
	2:46	NH	
Kindred, Mrs. B C , see			
Kindred, Rachel (Mylar)			
Kindred, Lizzie (Brown)	2:415	HH	
Kindred, Rachel (Mylar)	2:46	NH	
Kindred, W S	2:415	HH	
Kindred, Mrs. W S , see			
Kindred, Lizzie (Brown)			
Kineth, John	1:640	NH	
King, Amos N	1:248	NH	
	1:360	PMO	
	2:332	PMO	
King, Mrs. Amos N , see			
King, Melinda (Fuller)			
King, C B	241	E	
	1:415	HH	
King, C E	1:372	HHT	
King, Charles Willard	3:233	GP	
	2:350	PMO	
King, Mrs. Cynthia D	6:436	MC	
King, Dal M	1945-46:92	OO	
King, Edward Beaumont	3:571	HHT	
King, Ervin E	48:211 1936	WSGP	
King, F W	242	E	
King, Fred C	3:775	LHC	
King, Homer B	243	E	
King, Horace P	305	HA	
King, James	2:1180	SM	
King, James Horace	fol. pt. 1	SHB	
King, John I	291	MP	
King, L W	3:723	HHI	
King, Lewis	3:1091	BCF	
King, Melinda (Fuller)	1:248	NH	
King, Minnie, see			
Crisler, Minnie (King)			
King, Nahum Amos	2:381	LHC	

King, Nancie, see
   Johnson, Nancie (King)
King, Peter   512   SIH
King, Peter Leo   4:453   BCF
King, R   W   unp.   SOU
King, Samuel Willard   1:614-615   GP
King, Mrs. Samuel Willard, see
   King, Sarah (Fairbanks) Olds
King, Sarah (Fairbanks) Olds 1:356   NH
                                    2:350   PMO
King, Thomas J   3:1047   BHS
King, Will R   1895:80   OO
King, William Rufus DeVane   358   CIR
                                    36   FEE
King-Price, Mrs. M   J   6:397   MC
Kingsbury, F   D   84   LHN
Kingsbury, Selden Bingham   294   IHI
Kingsley, J   S   2:287   PMO
Kinkead, John H   168   AN
                                    93   BET
Kinley, George T   354   JNT
Kinman, Evert L   3:241   BCF
Kinnear, George   2:714   BHS
Kinnear, John R   2:804   BHS
                                    1905-06:[28]   RLW
Kinnear, Ritchey M   1905-06:[41]   RLW
Kinney, Frank W   2:1224   SM
Kinney, Robert C   3:415   GP
                                    2:99   LHC
                                    1:524   NH
Kinney, Samuel   1:524   NH
Kinney, William Sylvester   2:236   PMO
Kinsolving, Charles Johnson 3:264   BEA
Kintpuash, Modoc chief   331   CIR
                                    2:4   NH
Kip, Lawrence   2:216   FI
                                    248   MCO
Kipp, Blanche (Nez Percé Indian) 372   BR
Kipp, Henry   2:139   BCF
Kipp, Isaac   3:1021   BCF
Kipp, Mrs. Isaac, see
   Kipp, Mary Ann (Nelems)
Kipp, James   94   LBT
Kipp, Mary, see
   Knight, Mary (Kipp)
Kipp, Mary Ann (Nelems)   3:1021   BCF
Kirby, Homer   2 no.6:12   W
Kirby, Letitia Sarah, see
   Baker, Letitia Sarah (Kirby)
Kircher, Albert   3:1593   SM
Kirk, J   W   252   PSW
Kirk, Thomas J   2:446   PMO
Kirkbride, William   305   BR
Kirkendall, Lester   34 no.1:33   PNLA
Kirkham, George William   172   GL
Kirkham, Mrs. George William, see
   Kirkham, Mary (Astington)
Kirkham, Mary (Astington)   399   GL

Kirkhope, William   192   PSW
Kirkman, Oscar   2:144-145   EPD
Kirkpatrick, E   W   1935-36:51   OO
                             1939-40:31   OO
Kirkpatrick, Minor P   2:344   PHP
Kirkpatrick, Thomas   3:327   BCF
Kitching, Albert C   2:879   HHI
Kittilsen, A   N   52   HA
Kittinger, George B   1895-96:115   SSS
Kittrell, Sarah Texanna (Cochran)
                                    2:24   CPD
Kittson, Norman W   176   GI
Kittson, Robert Edward   4:953   BCF
Kjelsberg, Magnus   116, 172-173   HA
Klaue, Louisa, see
   Proctor, Louisa (Klaue)
Kleeb, John W   2:115   HWW
Klein, Marcus M   2:1093   SM
Kleinschmidt, Albert   813   MI
Kleinschmidt, Reinhold Henry 673   MI
Kleinschmidt, Theodore H   389   LHM
                                    224   MI
Klenze, Henry Gysbert   3:1385   SM
Klickitat Peter   44 no.2:65   PN
Kline, Robert L   1:481   BHK
                                    2:514   PHP
                                    [90]   RLX
Klippel, Adam   432   AG
Klippel, Henry   1:156   NH
Klockstead, Henrietta   12   SS
Klosterman, John   572   SHP
Klovberg, N   [128]   RLX
Kluss, Theodor   664   SIH
Knabel, Rudolf   3:511   HHT
Knaggs, George H   60   LDM
                                    1:191   LHC
Knapp, Daniel   3:1332   SMS
Knapp, Louis L   1931-32:41   OO
Knapp, Ralph R   1924:40   WSP
Knatvold, H   E   112   SS
Kneeland, William Henry   1:448   PHP
                                    6:6   SH
Knepper, Florence   410   BHSS
Knepper, George E   2:301   HHI
Knickerbocher, I   B   [92]   RLX
Knievel, Anton J   3:1548   SM
Knight, Albert B   2:1018   SM
Knight, Bertha Ethel, see
   Landes, Bertha Ethel (Knight)
Knight, Charles Cair   3:161   BCF
Knight, Edward Christman   3:335   BCF
Knight, Edward Wones   699   LHM
                                    78   MI
                             14 no.6:631   MWH
Knight, Henry G   1:unp. 1900-01   WDT
Knight, John   262   MV
Knight, Mary (Kipp)   4:893   BCF

Knight, N B	1:292	NH	
Knight, P S	1:585	CHW	
Knight, William	4:893	BCF	
Knight, Mrs. William, see			
Knight, Mary (Kipp)			
Knight, William W	1935-36:51	OO	
Knoff, Alfred Emerson	3:481	BHS	
Knoff, John J	48	LS	
Knollin, Albert Jason	2:47	HHI	
Knott, Andrew J	103	LDM	
Knott, Herbert Thomas	4:621	BCF	
Knowles, Ella L	85	MI	
Knowles, Hiram	67	LHM	
_____	69	MI	
	14 no. 3:243	MWH	
Knowles, Robert Earle	4:553	BCF	
Knowlton, E Bruce	1943:100	ENC	
Knowlton, Edmond Shorey	fol. pt. 2	SHB	
Knox, Jim	1:236	HHT	
Knox, Mary A	1:456	GP	
Knox, R C	927	LHM	
Knudsen, Krist	23	PIG	
Knudsen, Thorsten	400	GL	
Knudsen, William P	2:377	SMS	
Knudson, Knud	149	SS	
Koch, Edwin	3:1195	SMS	
Koch, Henry F	3:213	BEA	
Koch, Mrs. Peter	6:438-439	MC	
Kockteech, Tlingit chief	278-279	HU	
Koelsch, Charles F	2:683	FH	
Koerner, William H	222	LDM	
Koezi (Carrier Indian)	86	MHN	
Kohl, William	156	LDM	
Kohlhepp, Catherine, see			
Lemp, Catherine (Kohlhepp)			
Kohrs, Conrad	1941:18	EN	
_____	557	LHM	
Kokrine, Gregory	159	WOY	
Kokuf, Albert	41:154	OHQ	
Kolash, F J	172-173	HA	
Kolstad, A S	1:917	LHC	
Kommers, W J	43 no. 1:16	PN	
Koonce, M Egbert	282	PSW	
Koons, H L	97	DH	
Koontz, Frank L	48:211, 296 1936	WSGP	
Koontz, James H	2:28	NH	
Koppe, Emil	2:265	CHW	
Koquilton, Slugamus	120	AC	
	1:96	HWW	
_____	32, 40, 48	PC	
Krader, Ruth	24:147	PNLA	
Kraft, Charles F	44	LDM	
Krall, John	657	IHI	
Kramer, Louis C	3:341	LHC	
Kranz, Mathias	2:576	SMS	
Kreager, Frank O	298	BHSS	
Kreider, E G	1926:20	WSP	
Krengel, Charles Hartwell	3:83	BEA	
Krettek, Germaine	32 no. 3:34	PNLA	
Kribs, Frederick A	45	PL	
Krieger, Otto F	111	LHN	
Krieger, Mrs. Otto F	111	LHN	
Krier, Roscoe	1935-36:51	OO	
Kristoferson, Alfred	3:279	BHS	
Kroetch, Edmund L	260	GG	
Kroeze, Barend H	213	PSW	
Kroll, Morton	20:168	PNLA	
Kruegel, W C	390	BHSS	
Krug, Annie (Hackney) Ketchen	2:1138-1139	SM	
Krug, Charles	2:1138-1139	SM	
Krug, Mrs. Charles, see			
Krug, Annie (Hackney) Ketchen			
Krull, Emma, see			
Mahncke, Emma (Krull)			
Kruse, John L	2:429	PMO	
Krutz, Harry	3:91	BHK	
Kucher, Charles W	3:719	BHK	
Kuck, Henry L	1931-32:40	OO	
Kümmel, Julius	44 no. 4:150	PN	
Kuhn, Mrs. Albert H , see			
Kuhn, Ida (Soule)			
Kuhn, Ida (Soule)	1:12	D	
Kuhn, Joseph A	2:146	NH	
Kuiltkuiltlouis, see			
Hirom (?), Kettle chief			
Kulp, Myron	1941:326	EN	
Kultus Jim, see			
Captain Jim			
Kulzer, Albert I	215	GG	
Kummer, A	48	LS	
Kuner, Albert	96	RA	
Kuner, Max	1941:274	EN	
Kunigk, Willibald A	66:117	OHQ	
Kuoni, Christine Anna, see			
Bigham, Christine Anna (Kuoni)			
Kuppens, Francis X	278	PI	
Kuratli, H A	1941-42:66	OO	
_____	1943-44:79	OO	
Kuster, J P	3:449	HHI	
Kuykendall, Elgin Victor	3:9	PH	
Kuykendall, George Benson	1:472	NH	
Kuykendall, William	2:193	CHW	
_____	2:459	PMO	
Kyle, Daniel Cardwell	3:992	SMS	

L

LaBarge, Joseph	1:front., 1	CES	

LaBarge, Mike, see
   LeBarge, Michael
Lacaff, Joseph   869   LHM
Lacey, Michael   2:493   HHT
Lacey, Walter W   de, see
   De Lacey, Walter Washington
Lack-um-tin (Umatilla Indian) 83   JM
Laclede Liguest, Pierre de 54   GE
Lacombe, Albert   1:348   MCC
Lacy, Dan M   33 no.4:36   PNLA
Ladd, J   Wesley   2:241   GP
Ladd, John R   2:262   NH
Ladd, William Sargent   447   CHO
          1:519   GP
          395   HIO
          1:423   LHC
          1:416   NH
          1:16   PMO
          2:337   PMO
          46   SHP
Ladner, Thomas Ellis   3:171   BCF
Ladner, William Henry   2:139   BCF
          4:1119   BCF
LaDue, Joseph   159   WOY
La Farge, John   159   WOY
Lafitte, Jean   80   SW
Laflèche, Louis Francois Richer   1:184   MCC
LaFond, John Thomas   3:30   BEA
Lage, E   Riddell   1941-42:66   OO
          1943-44:79   OO
          1945-46:86   OO
Lage, Hans   1:917   LHC
          2:481   LHC
Lagoni, Peter   2:603   SMS
Lah-Tis, Princess, see
   Kipp, Blanche (Nez Percé Indian)
Laidlaw, James   3:183   HHI
Laidlaw, James Anderson   2:257   BCF
          228   KB
Laing, Andrew D   227   LDM
Laing, I   B   1895-96:97   SSS
Laing, Robert   42   LDM
Laird, Charles   60   SHO
Laird, James   2:191   HHI
Laird, Ralph P   1937-38:62-63   OO
Lajeunesse,   (Father)   3:240   SH
Lake, Josephine, see
   Nelson, Josephine (Lake)
Lamb, Frank H   1 no.1:14   WN
          1 no.5:23   WN
Lamb, Mrs. Frank H   1 no.6:23   WN
Lamb, Harriet Laura, see
   Zimmerman, Harriet Laura (Lamb)
Lamb, Harry E   3:958   FH
Lamb, James   82   GL
Lamb, Mrs. James J   , see
   Lamb, Sarah E   (Ross)
Lamb, John   64   LT

Lamb, John M   42   HIT
Lamb, Sarah E   (Ross)   401   GL
Lambaere, A   H   302-303, 366   PI
          436   PIW
Lamberson, Joseph   63:299   OHQ
Lambert, Ed   110-111   HCM
          50   KY
Lambert, Joseph Hamilton   1:242   GP
          3:575   GP
Lambert, Lawrence Taylor   3:376   BEA
Lambert, Russ S   1905-06:[58]   RLW
          [137]   RLX
Lambert, S   E   41   MG
Lame Bull, Blackfoot chief   10:98   MC
Lamme, A   5:314   MC
Lamont, Hugh   6:388   MC
Lamoureux, Edward   3:863   SMS
Lamoureux, Fred   96   LS
Lamping, Evart   3:869   BHK
Lampman, Henry   138   LDM
Lamport, Frederick S   1943-44:75   OO
          1945-46:82   OO
Lamport, George T   2:1192   SM
Lamport, Warren D   unp.   SAA
Lamson, Edward F   2:445   PMO
Lancaster, Columbia   1:56   NH
          3:222   SH
Lancaster, Samuel Christopher
          66:250, 252   OHQ
Lancaster, William S   880   SIH
Land, Paul   48   LS
Land, Sarah, see
   Bower, Sarah (Land)
Landen, George A   264   AG
Lander, Edward   1:56   NH
          49 no.2:68   PN
          52 no.1:22   PN
          3:488   SH
Landes, Bertha Ethel (Knight)   4:749   PH
          unp.   SEA
          1 no.7:11   WN
Landes, Henry   120-121   GA
          194   MMR
          4:749   PH
          1:unp. 1900-01   WDT
          6:22 1906   WDT
          26:54 1925   WDT
          36:21 1935   WDT
Landes, Mrs. Henry, see
   Landes, Bertha Ethel (Knight)
Landes, Henry, 1843-   1:436   NH
Landon, Daniel   1924:48   WSP
Landon, Max M   1943-44:79   OO
          1945-46:86   OO
Landreth, George Robert   3:262   PH
Landvatter, Ernest   3:254   BEA
Lane, Charles D   5   HA
          351   WOY

Name	Reference	Source	Name	Reference	Source
Lane, Elizabeth Agnes (Whitesell)	3:429	HHT	Langille, S (Harding)	3:817	GP
Lane, F F	131	JNT	Langland, S S	72	SS
Lane, Franklin Knight	1:397	HH	Langley, W H	2:front. 1924	BCHA
	2:162	HHT	Langley, William Wallace	1943:178	ENC
	4 no.6:158	PM	Langlie, Arthur B	59	MAG
Lane, Harry	457	PL		34 no.4:400-401	PN
Lane, Harry L	261	GG		unp.	SE
Lane, James E	3:1510	SM		unp.	SEA
Lane, John	314	BR		50:20 1949	WDT
Lane, Joseph	2:512a	CGO	Langlois, Thomas Talton	fol. pt. 2	SHB
	1:403	CHW	Lanning, Frank	3:669	GP
	2:176	FI	Lansing, Peter	567	LHM
	3:437	GP	Lant, David	182-183	KO
	4:100	LH	Laperouse, Jean Francois de Galaup,		
	1:721	LHC	Comte de	4	LDM
	1:36	NH	Largent, John	739	LHM
	1:12	PMO	Largent, Joseph L	739	LHM
	44 no.3:111	PN	Largey, Edward Creighton	3:1395	SM
	58 no.2:66	PN	Largey, Patrick A	2:972	SM
	3:66	SH	Larimore, Leon A	378	HA
	17	TUR	Larios, J W	172-173	HA
	50	WRE	Larkin, Thomas B	247	GG
Lane, L L	172-173	HA	Larkin, Wallace S	1941-42:66	OO
Lane, Nat H , Jr.	206	LDM	Larkins, James	97	DH
Lane, Nat H , Sr.	117	LDM	Larkins, William E	318	LDM
Lane, Tom T	246	HA	Larrabee, Charles Xavier	2:21	HWW
Lane, William	3:428	HHT	Larsen, John	319	LDM
	40, 48	PC	Larsen, Lars Douglas	3:159	BEA
Lane, Mrs. William, see			Larsen, Lars K	3:159	BEA
Lane, Elizabeth Agnes (Whitesell)			Larsen, Lars P	3:159	BEA
Lang, Frank Silas	172-173, 312	HA	Larsen, Nephi	2:885	HHI
	3:375	PH	Larson, A E	4:542	PH
Lang, Gregor	3:1044	SMS	Larson, John	864	SIH
Lang, Mrs. Gregor, see			Larson, Mrs. John, see		
Lang, Janet Tait (Huggin)			Larson, Matilda (Anderburg)		
Lang, Janet Tait (Huggin)	3:1044	SMS	Larson, L F	3:107	LHC
Lang, John	2:606	SMS	Larson, Lars Victor	402	GL
Lang, Mrs. John, see			Larson, Matilda (Anderburg)	864	SIH
Lang, Margaret (Stone)			Larson, Ole E	3:115	HHI
Lang, Julius C	3:61	BHK	Larson, Oscar	648	SIH
Lang, Louis M	59	SSP	Larson, Zack	1:242	ACR
Lang, Margaret (Stone)	2:606	SMS	Laselle, Beach Adonijah	3:313	BCF
Lang, William Arthur	fol. pt. 2	SHB	Lasher, William	287	BHSS
Lang, William G	3:1043	SMS	Lashmutt, Van B De, see		
Lang, William H	206	HA	De Lashmutt, Van B		
Langdon, A	393	BHSS	Laswell, Annie (Pope)	2:292	PMO
Langevin, Adelard	2:272	MCC	Laswell, William B	2:292	PMO
Langford, Edward Edwards	17 no.1-2:16	BCH	Laswell, Mrs. William B , see		
Langford, George	2:277	GP	Laswell, Annie (Pope)		
Langford, Nathaniel P	5:349	MC	Latcham, Frank A	May 1907:38	TDL
	1:244	SMS	Latham, Mrs. E H , see		
Langhorne, Maurice A	1923:128	WSP	Latham, Mary (Archer)		
Langhorne, Samuel W	333	LHM	Latham, John	1:566	BH
	5:315	MC		3:481	HHT
Langhorne, W W	1924:160	WSP	Latham, Mary (Archer)	2:73	HH
Langille, Mrs. James E , see			Latham, Peter	2:139	BCF
Langille, S (Harding)			Lathrop, Austin Eugene	1941:310	EN
			Lathrow, James	2:435	HH

Latimer, Norval H	2:800	BHS
	9:front. 1904	WBP
Latimer, W G	200	BE
Latourette, Earl C	1945-46:93	OO
Latourette, Howard	1935-36:51	OO
Laubach, A	163	AG
Laue, John M A	3:559	GP
Lauer, Edward H	36:front. 1935	WDT
	50:26 1949	WDT
Laughlin, James Thomas	2:257	HHI
Laughlin, Lee	unp.	SOU
Laurence, Sydney	406-407	HU
Laurgaard, Olaf	3:293	LHC
Laurie, James A	95	PSW
Laurie, James A , Jr.	87	PSW
Lauterbach, Maxmilian	2:1289	SM
Lauzier, Geoffrey A	3:1301	SM
Lavelle, James Patrick	2:31	SMS
La Verendrye, Pierre Gaultier de Varennes		
	24	GI
	30	LBT
LaViolette, F A	306	AC
Law, Benjamin B	3:1603	SM
Law, Henry	1:210-211	GP
Law, William	151	LDM
La Wall, Frank	199	E
Lawler, George	2:552	PHP
	5:404	SH
	1910:38, 81	TDL
Lawler, Isaac Joseph	3:813	GP
Lawler, James T	1924:80	WSP
Lawler, John	3:1380	SM
Lawlor, Dennis	173	LDM
Lawrence, Alma L , see		
Howe, Alma L (Lawrence)		
Lawrence, Araminta, see		
Ashton, Araminta (Lawrence)		
Lawrence, Arthur W	1931-32:41	OO
Lawrence, E J	39	MG
Lawrence, Maria, see		
Karren, Maria (Lawrence)		
Lawrence, W H	287	BHSS
	1910:49	TDL
Lawrence, William McRae	fol. pt. 2	SHB
Lawson, George D	1:372	HHT
Lawyer, Nez Percé chief	46	AI
	153	BR
	158	DTI
	2:224	FI
	fol. 705 (no. 3)	JO
	367	MS
	1:76	NH
	27	SPI
Lawyer, Archie (Nez Percé Indian)	212	BR
	127	DTI
	199	PSW
Lawyer, Corbett B	3:219	BEA
Lay, Edith Freelove de, see		
DeLay, Edith Freelove		
Lay, Ellsworth	182-183	KO
Lay, Elza, see		
Lay, Ellsworth		
Lay, Fred	1941:469	EN
Lazenby, A L	3:585	BCF
Leach, Charles H	1935-36:51	OO
	1937-38:62-63	OO
Leachman, E A	30	THI
Leard, Willard H	6:416-417	MC
Leary, Eliza (Ferry)	1:8	D
Leary, John	1:581	BHK
	2:724	BHS
	2 no.1:front.	PM
	unp.	SEA
	4:332	SH
Leary, Mrs. John, see		
Leary, Eliza (Ferry)		
Leary, John P	557	SCH
Leask, David	362	WSM
Leasure, John C	2:446	NH
	1:86	PMO
Leavitt, E D	614	MI
Leavitt, John Pennell	3:303	BH
Le Ballister, A E	3:937	BHS
LeBarge, Michael	fol. 207 (no. 11)	SHI
	86	WOY
Le Crone, S M	1905-06:[43]	RLW
Ledingham, George W	4:381	BCF
Lee, Anna Maria (Pittman)	86	AC
	106	FW
Lee, Daniel	86	AC
Lee, Mrs. Daniel	86	AC
Lee, Dorothy McCullough	1931-32:41	OO
	1935-36:50	OO
	1939-40:15	OO
	1941-42:62	OO
	1943-44:75	OO
Lee, George A	379	LDM
Lee, Harold Foster	3:696	SMS
Lee, J D	16	KT
Lee, J H	172-173	HA
Lee, Jason	front.	AC
	123	BF
	92	BHSI
	front.	BJ
	1:134	BS
	front.	CPP
	48	FW
	1:208-209	GP
	34	GR
	134	HO
Lee, Mrs. Jason, see		
Lee, Anna Maria (Pittman)		
Lee, Jason W	1:157	HH
Lee, John Andrew	3:7	BCF
	fol. pt. 2	SHB
Lee, John Doyle	491	GLS
	front.	LMM
Lee, Joseph Daniel	2:383	GP

_____	2:660	NH	
	1:86	PMO	
Lee, Lewis A	2:367	HHI	
Lee, Lloyd A	2:221	CHW	
Lee, Wallace Howe	86	AC	
	48	PSW	
Leech, W H	134	AG	
Leede, Carl Stockbridge	3:255	BHK	
	3:711	BHS	
Leeds, Josiah B	185	LDM	
Leedy, John D	172-173, 208	HA	
Leeper, Charles A	257	SIH	
Lefevre, John Matthew	3:737	BCF	
	fol. pt. 1	SHB	
Left Handed Peter (Flathead Indian) 22		PI	
Legaic, Paul, Tsimshian chief 167		HS	
	40	WSM	
Lehman, Isaac	4:539	BCF	
LeHuquet, John	848	SIH	
Leigh, Richard	94, 95	BHI	
	120, 122	CBC	
Leighton, Francis L	fol. pt. 2	SHB	
Leighton, George V	3:1141	FH	
Leighton, Ira Albert	3:1461	SM	
Leitch, Archibald	fol. title page	SHB	
Leitch, George A	fol. pt. 2	SHB	
Leland, Alonzo	250	HIT	
	51 no.3:118	PN	
Leland, Mrs. Alonzo	1:210-211	GP	
Leland, Charles F	250	HIT	
LeMert, Marie	66	MG	
Lemmens, John Nicholas	2:370	MCC	
	222	MHC	
Lemon, Joseph James	4:763	BCF	
Lemon, Thomas J	872	SIH	
Lemp, Catherine (Kohlhepp)	2:596-597	FH	
	2:21	HHI	
Lemp, Herbert Frederick	2:597	FH	
	2:215	HHI	
Lemp, John	2:596-597	FH	
	2:168	FSB	
	2:20	HHI	
	499	IHI	
Lemp, Mrs. John, see			
Lemp, Catherine (Kohlhepp)			
Lenihan, Mathias L	488	PIW	
Lennen, J E	142	LDM	
Lennie, Robert Scott	3:349	BCF	
	fol. pt. 2	SHB	
Leolo, Baptiste, see			
Lolo, Jean Baptiste (Shuswap Indian)			
Leonard, Abiel	212	TMP	
Leonard, Alton W	2:491	BHK	
	3:563	BHS	
Leonard, Edward C	3:1626	SM	
Leonard, H C	2:455	GP	
Leonard, James	1104	SIH	

Leonard, N R	6:382-383	MC	
Leque, N P	141	SS	
Leschi, Nisqualli chief	203	MP	
	349	MS	
	55 no.3:cover	PN	
Leslie, David	88	AC	
	41	EI	
	1:32	NH	
	2	OS	
	1:410	PMO	
	50 no.3:96	PN	
Leslie, Preston Hopkins	4:98	MC	
	7:203	MC	
LeSourd, Charles L	43 no.1:16	PN	
LeSourd, D G	397	AG	
Lessard, Dellmore	1935-36:50	OO	
	1937-38:62	OO	
Lester, C F	1895:90	OO	
Letterman, E H	58	BHSS	
Leupold, Frederick	3:733	LHC	
Levalley, Ben	3:1460	SM	
Levalley, Dan	2:1015	SM	
LeValley, Frances Ellen, see			
Pethtel, Frances Ellen (LeValley)			
Levander, John O	3:944	FH	
Levin, David	1905-06:[54]	RLW	
Levy, H E	10 no.1:43	BCH	
Lewelling, L G	1945-46:93	OO	
Lewelling, Seth	68:196	OHQ	
Lewelling, Mrs. Seth, see			
Lewelling, Sophronia (Vaughn) Olson			
Lewelling, Sophronia (Vaughn) Olson			
	68:199	OHQ	
Lewin, Walter	4 no.2:86	BCH	
Lewis, A W	93	DA	
	unp.	VU	
Lewis, Andrew T	168	AN	
Lewis, Anna Mary, see			
Mann, Anna Mary (Lewis)			
Lewis, Charles L	2:103	HWW	
Lewis, Charles R	1924:160	WSP	
Lewis, Cicero H	447	CHO	
	1:614-615	GP	
	2:107	GP	
	1:433	LHC	
	1:16	PMO	
	2:338	PMO	
Lewis, Clancy M	1 no.1:23	WN	
Lewis, Cougar Dave, see			
Lewis, Dave			
Lewis, D H	39	MG	
Lewis, Dave	1:26-27	EPD	
Lewis, Mrs. David, see			
Lewis, Mrs. Rebecca			
Lewis, Frank Pardee	1895-96:73	SSS	
Lewis, Fred W	23:59 1911	WSGP	
	24:55 1912	WSGP	
	25:68 1913	WSGP	

Lewis, Freeborn S — 48:210 1936 WSGP
Lewis, Freeborn S — 2:495 HWW
Lewis, Haman C — 1:584 NH
Lewis, Henry — 256 GL
Lewis, Herbert G — 46 LDM
Lewis, Isaac I — 261 LHM
Lewis, James Hamilton — 3 no.8:425 PM
——— — 1895-96:126 SSS
——— — 1:unp. 1900-01 WDT
Lewis, John — 1:231 ACR
Lewis, John Alexander — 3:825 BCF
Lewis, John H — 1931-32:41 OO
Lewis, Joseph R — 5:156 SH
Lewis, Meriwether — 26 AC
——— — 64 AM
——— — 33 BF
——— — 64 BHI
——— — 41 BHSI
——— — 17, 403 BR
——— — 1:96 BS
——— — 1:288a CGO
——— — 171 CHO
——— — 380 CIR
——— — 1:34 CP
——— — 1:92 D
——— — 42 DSW
——— — 1:112 FI
——— — 16 FW
——— — 105, 107 GBS
——— — front. GE
——— — 1:54-55 GP
——— — 160 LBT
——— — 64-65 LCRH
——— — 2:142 LH
——— — 1:44 LHC
——— — 69:4 OHQ
——— — 1:261 SH
——— — 1:31, 59 WT
Lewis, Mrs. Rebecca — 1:288-289 GP
Lewis, Robert E — 43 no.2:136-137 PN
Lewis, Swan — 3:255 BHS
Lewis, William — 319 LDM
Lewis, William Fisher — 50 JP
Lewthwaite, William Atkinson — 4:373 BCF
Ley, Ronald — 23:7, 85, 127 PNLA
——— — 24:272 PNLA
Libby, Charles W — 308 LDM
Libby, Daniel B — 202 HA
——— — 85 WOY
Libby, George — 86 RO
Libby, J — 1167 LHM
Liddiard, Sarah Ann, see
    Smith, Sarah Ann (Liddiard)
Lieberman, Irving — 20:81 PNLA
——— — 24:7, 117, 177, 225, 272 PNLA
——— — 30:102 PNLA
Lien, Arthur E — 37 MG
Lienemann, Louis A — 215 GG

Lieuallen, C L — 1943-44:79 OO
——— — 1945-46:87 OO
Light, Barnet E — 126 HIT
Lightfoot, R M — 5:316 MC
Liguest, Pierre Laclede de, see
    Laclede Liguest, Pierre de
Lilley, George — 483 BHSS
Lillie, John — 1895-96:97 SSS
Lilligren, J M — 290 BHSS
Lillis, Henry M — 1:397 HH
——— — 1905-06:[28] RLW
Linck, John W — May 1907:39 TDL
——— — June 1909:62 TDL
Lincoln, Mrs. W L — 23 NL
Lincoln, W S — 43 SA
Lind, Carl E — 2:829 HHI
Lind, Carl O — 2:391 BHK
Lind, Carol (Conklin) — 30:102 PNLA
Lind, William — 3:301 GP
Lindberg, Art W — 1945-46:87 OO
Lindberg, Gustaf — 3:245 HHT
——— — 122 SS
Lindblom, Erik O — 20 HA
Lindeberg, Jafet — 12 HA
——— — 354 WOY
Linden, James — 492 SCH
Linderman, Frank Bird — 11 no.1:front. F
——— — 19 no.3:front. FA
——— — 54-55 LI
Linderman, Mrs. Frank Bird, see
    Linderman, Minnie Jane (Johns)
Linderman, Minnie Jane (Johns) — 54-55 LI
Lindesmith, E W J — 364, 373 PI
——— — 432 PIW
Lindley, Hervey — 1 no.10:9 WN
Lindley, Thomas — 1:545 HHI
Lindsay, J W — 1924:40 WSP
Lindsay, Lav — 144 DL
Lindsay, Mary — 67 MG
Lindsay, William — 2:1237 SM
Lindsey, A A — 1905-06:[28] RLW
Lindsey, Ed — 55 no.3:122 PN
Lindsey, Edwin J — 6:432-433 MC
Lindsey, Mrs. Edwin J — 6:432-433 MC
Lindsley, Aaron Ladner — 1:443 GP
Lindsley, Joseph B — 1905-06:[62] RLW
Lindsley, Peter (Nez Percé Indian) — 212 BR
——— — 127 DTI
Lindstadt, Mabel, see
    Campbell, Mabel (Lindstadt)
Linfield, Frances Eleanor (Ross) — 2:567 CHW
Linfield, George Fisher — 2:566 CHW
Linfield, Mrs. George Fisher, see
    Linfield, Frances Eleanor (Ross)
Linklater, W A — 1 no.8:6 WN
Linn, Lewis Field — 3:182 LH
——— — 1:477 PMO
——— — 2:208 SH

Linn, Ole H 1112 SIH
Linnemann, Catharina Elizabeth (Von Falde)
    3:685 GP
Linnemann, Mrs. John G D , see
    Linnemann, Catharina Elizabeth
    (Von Falde)
Linsley, Nelson E 1905-06:[58] RLW
Lipsett, W J 1905-06:[68] RLW
Lisa, Manuel 73 BHI
    62 DSW
Lisle, Berneita 32 no.1:25 PNLA
Lister, Alfred 3:327 BH
Lister, David 1:600 NH
Lister, Ernest 374 BHSS
    51 MAG
    110 ME
    34 no.4:400-401 PN
    50 no.3:104 PN
    unp. SE
    6:28 SH
Lister, Samuel G 1:512 PHP
Litfin, Ben R 2:431 LHC
Litherland, Alexander 144 PSW
Little, Andrew 1943:91 ENC
Little, Charles B 3:489 HHI
Little, Gilbert F 1:349 HH
Little, Job H 75 LHN
    4:32 MC
Little, Nathaniel S 6:392 MC
Little, S D 2:927 HHI
Little Bear, Cree chief 393 VT
Little Dog, Piegan chief 170 PI
    204 PIW
Little Ignace, see
    Young Ignace (Flathead Indian)
Little Plume, Piegan chief 170 PI
    204 PIW
    153 VT
Littlefield, Horace R 2:569 GP
Littlehale, Amy Gertrude, see
    Walker, Amy Gertrude (Littlehale)
Littlejohn, Julia Ann (Turner) 3:91 HWW
Littlejohn, William 3:91 HWW
Littlejohn, Mrs. William, see
    Littlejohn, Julia Ann (Turner)
Livesley, Mary (Taylor) 4:337 BHK
Livesley, Thomas A 2:343 CHW
    1937-38:62-63 OO
Livesley, William Lamb 4:337 BHK
Livesley, Mrs. William Lamb, see
    Livesley, Mary (Taylor)
Livingston, Sarah, see
    Stirling, Sarah (Livingston)
Llewellyn, William H 2:223 HH
    909 HI
Lloyd, Clyde D 151 PL
Lloyd, Harold 1:228 ACR
Lloyd, John Eynon 767 MI

    2:1052 SM
Lloyd, Windsor James 3:118 BEA
LLwyd, J P D 188 E
Loader, Mrs. Mariah 112 GL
Loaiza, Katharyn 1945-46:64 OO
Loat, Christopher J 4:255 BCF
Lobaugh, Claude 287 BHSS
Loberg, Mary Pauline, see
    Holter, Mary Pauline (Loberg)
Lochrie, Arthur J 3:1785 SM
Locke, C E 447 LDM
Locke, D W 1924:49 WSP
Locke, James K 1:428 PMO
Locke, L P 365 LDM
Lockett, Dorothy 66 MG
Lockett, George Vernon fol. pt. 2 SHB
Lockey, Richard 433 LHM
    773 MI
    2:1032 SM
    2:526 SMS
Lockley, Fred 1:front. LHC
    2:179 LHC
    25 LSJ
Lockwood, Alfred 136-137 SRW
Lockwood, C M 1895-175 OO
Lockwood, Henry Greenshields 3:369 BCF
Lockwood, Myron M 7:122 MC
Lockwood, Watkins P 3:659 BHS
Lodge Pole, Flathead chief
    fol. 512 (no. 26) BUR
    front. SO
Loeber, Fred 939 LHM
Loeding, Charles 3:471 LHC
Loeffler, Katherine, see
    Miller, Katherine (Loeffler)
Loeser, August F 151, 167 OB
Lofqvist, Abr. 96 DA
Logan, Andrew 2:1083 SM
Logan, Arthur C 2:1155 SM
Logan, David 1:551 GP
Logan, George front., 44 LHN
Logan, Harvey 86-87, 278-279 KO
Logan, W H unp. SOU
Lohse, Henry, Jr. 2:589 BHK
    1941:299 EN
    3:232-233 PH
    1 no.3:29 WN
Lohse, Henry D , Sr. 2:909 BHK
    3:232-233 PH
Lohse, Mrs. Henry D , see
    Lohse, Meta (Cyriaks)
Lohse, Meta (Cyriaks) 3:232-233 PH
Lolo, Jean Baptiste (Shuswap Indian)
    3 no.2:115 BCH
Lombard, Charles 2:front. 1924 BCHA
Lomen, Gudbrand J 348 HA
London, Charles E 3:927 BCF
Lonergan, Frank J 1931-32:41 OO

	1939-40:31	OO
	1941-42:66	OO
Lonergan, Pat	1945-46:87	OO
Long, Donald E	1945-46:92	OO
Long, Edward	2:74	NH
Long, Fred	202	BHSS
Long, George S	1910:21	TDL
Long, Hattie, see		
Johnson, Hattie (Long)		
Long, J M	1895:106	OO
Long, Logan L	1924:97	WSP
Long, Robert Alexander	vi, 11, 87, 139	MLO
Long, W O	1905-06:[60]	RLW
	[115]	RLX
Long Jim, Chelan chief	322	FF
Longabaugh, Harry	86-87	KO
Longaker, Francis A	1941:120	EN
Longanecker, Mary E (Morris), see		
Bibb, Mary E (Morris) Longanecker		
Longfellow, Henry Wadsworth	2:19	DN
Longmire, Charles	55 no.3:126	PN
Longworth, Mrs. Ruth	34 no.1:47	PNLA
Loo Sing	2:19	DN
Looking-Glass, Nez Percé chief	125	AI
	391	CIR
Looking Glass, Sr., Nez Percé chief		
	fol. 705 (no. 8)	JO
Loomis, Edwin G	1:91	HH
Loomis, Floyd LeRoy	3:237	BEA
Loomis, L A	1:97	HH
	232	LDM
	1:520	NH
Loomis, Lee B	1941:276	EN
Loomis, Ray	393	BHSS
Looney, Norris H	2:455	PMO
Loop Loop Jim (Okanogan Indian)	331	FF
Loose, Ursinus K	2:432	PHP
Lootens, Louis	1897:44	YB
Lopp, William Thomas	54 no.4:170	PN
Lorain, Lorenzo	69:243	OHQ
Lord, Mrs. B B	24:1 1912	WSGP
Lord, C J	8:front. 1903	WBP
	24:80 1919	WBP
	1 no.8:17	WN
Lord, Harry	193	LDM
Lord, Harry Cobb	2:792	BHS
Lord, William Paine	1:556	GP
	1:368	NH
	1895:front.	OO
	51	TUR
Lorenz, E	439	LDM
Lorenz, Moses	159	WOY
Loretto, Sister	292	PI
Lorne, Marquis of	223	GI
Losee, Abraham	30	GL
Losee, Mrs. Abraham, see		
Losee, Mary Elizabeth (Lott)		
Losee, Mary Elizabeth (Lott)	403	GL

Lot, Spokan chief	70:161	OHQ
Lotan, James	1197	HIO
	570	SHP
Lotbiniere, Henri Gustave Joly de		
	2:281	BCF
	fol. pt. 1	SHB
	1911:70-71	YB
Lott, Abigail (Evans)	41	GL
Lott, Alzina Lucinda, see		
Willes, Alzina Lucinda (Lott)		
Lott, Mrs. Benjamin Smith, see		
Lott, Abigail (Evans)		
Lott, Mrs. Cornelius P , see		
Lott, Permelia (Darrow)		
Lott, John S	57	GL
Lott, Malissa, see		
Willes, Melissa (Lott) Smith		
Lott, Mary Elizabeth, see		
Losee, Mary Elizabeth (Lott)		
Lott, Melissa, see		
Willes, Melissa (Lott) Smith		
Lott, Mortimer H	2:934	SM
Lott, Permelia (Darrow)	31	GL
Loucks, Roger Brown	50:45 1949	WDT
Loud, Charles H	3:1423	SM
Louder, Thomas	36	CBC
Lough, Thomas Warner	1:unp. 1900-01	WDT
Loughborough, 1st baron, see		
Wedderburn, Alexander		
Lounsbury, Andrew	2:896	FH
Loury, Robert L	3:223	HWW
Love, Fred H	184	LDM
Lovejoy, Amos Lawrence	168	EW
	1:206-207	GP
	3:324	LH
	1:416	NH
	1:6	PMO
	2:329	PMO
Lovejoy, Bartlett	2 no.6:26, 30	W
Lovejoy, Frank Edward	3:392	PH
Lovejoy, George Albert	3:42	PH
Lovejoy, I R	373	AG
Lovell, Don G	1895-96:119	SSS
Lovell, Philip	5:323	MC
Lovell, Walt	[7]	HN
Loveridge, Alexander	66	GL
Lovsted, Carl Martin	3:879	BHK
Low, Charles	244	LDM
Low Horn, Piegan chief	10:66	MC
Lowden, Frank	202	BHSS
Lowe, James Jesse	3:192	BEA
Lowe, John O	3:936	FH
Lowe, William	2:892	SM
Lowenberg, Julius	1:519	GP
Lower, R A	39	MG
Lowery, Robert W	3:1055	SMS
Lowery, Woodbury	front.	LDL
Lowney, Kathryn	67	MG

Lowney, Teresa   67   MG

Name	Reference	Code
Lowney, Teresa	67	MG
Lownsdale, Daniel H	437	CHO
————	1:206-207	GP
————	1:292	NH
————	2:330	PMO
————	34	SHP
Lownsdale, J P O	226	SHP
Lowrey, Robert L	3:1518	SM
Lowry, Robert J	14:160 1909	WBP
Lowry, Thomas J	525	LHM
Lowry, Thomas Melvin	1941:186	EN
Lowther, Granville	136-137	SRW
Lucas, Alexander	1911:70-71	YB
Lucas, F G T	1923:14	WSP
Lucas, H C	19:16 1914	WBP
————	20:front. 1915	WBP
————	24:80 1919	WBP
Lucas, Howard	43 no. 1:16-17	PN
Lucas, John Baptiste Charles	1:42-43	GP
Luce, F H	1895-96:4	SSS
————	19:64 1914	WBP
————	20:48 1915	WBP
Luce, Henry Buckle	2:229	LHC
Luce, Sarah A (Seaman)	2:503	SMS
Luce, Thompson W	2:503	SMS
Luce, Mrs. Thompson W , see Luce, Sarah A (Seaman)		
Ludington, Flora B	18:9	PNLA
Ludlow, J P	296	LDM
Lueders, Henry W	Feb. 1906:27	TDL
Luelling, Alfred	68:159	OHQ
Luelling, Henderson	789	CHO
————	1:351	GP
————	68:154	OHQ
Luelling, Seth, see Lewelling, Seth		
Lugenbeel, Pinkney	39	DL
Luger, G	44	MG
Luhn, Henry B	244	E
————	42	MG
Luhn, William L	245	E
Luke, Mrs. Emma Smith	18:68 1941-42	IH
Lum, Irma, see Schumann, Irma (Lum)		
Lummis, Charles	1:228	ACR
Lump On The Nose, Crow chief	216	PI
————	248	PIW
Lumsden, Alexander	2:721	GP
Lund, Emil Gunnar	1941:73	EN
Lund, Thomas	286	E
Lundberg, A	74	SS
Lundberg, George A	50:43 1949	WDT
Lundblad, P A	3:127	HHI
Lundin, Alfred H	50	PIG
Lundvick, Cyril V	3:127	BH
Luney, M G	202	HIT
Lung, Henry W	[134]	RLX
Lurie, David E	1905-06:[28]	RLW
Lusby, C Erwin	43 no. 1:17	PN
Lusk, Hall S	1939-40:7	OO
————	1941-42:14	OO
————	1943-44:21	OO
————	1945-46:33	OO
Lutz, Sam	17	LHN
Lutz, Mrs. Sam	17	LHN
Lychywek, Peter J	3:727	LHC
Lyford, Charles Albert	4:165	BHK
Lyle, A R	1895:103	OO
Lyle, J T S	3:735	BH
Lyle, Roy	54 no. 3:97	PN
Lyman, Cornelius	1895-96:99	SSS
Lyman, Francis M	306	GLS
Lyman, Horace	437	CHO
————	1:208-209, 596	GP
————	1:433	LHC
Lyman, Horace Sumner	6:105	OHQ
————	1:254	PMO
Lyman, Mrs. Lorenzo Branch, see Lyman, Mary Elizabeth (Hawkins)		
Lyman, Mary Elizabeth (Hawkins)	4:192	MC
Lynch, J J	1943-44:75	OO
Lynch, J W	37	MG
Lynch, Jack, see Lynch, J J		
Lynch, James H	6:123	MC
Lynch, Paul	1935-36:51	OO
Lynden Jim	327	AG
Lynn, Arethusa E , see Smith, Arethusa E (Lynn)		
Lynn, Clarence O	3:621	HHT
————	1910:73	TDL
Lynn, John F	6:413	MC
Lyon, C L	41	MG
Lyon, Caleb	232	DL
Lyon, Dorsey Alfred	1:unp. 1900-01	WDT
Lyon, Hylan B	216	MCO
Lyon, Ivan D	568	SIH
Lyon, John H	2:757	GP
Lyon, William H	908	SIH
Lyons, James H	2:755	BHK
Lyons, Joseph	1905-06:[63]	RLW
Lyons, William	884	SIH
Lysons, J Will	[85]	RLX
Lytle, Elmer Elm	3:201	GP
Lytle, Robert F	2:71	HWW

M

Name	Reference	Code
Maaske, Roben J	1945-46:74	OO
McAleer, John	3:319	BH
McAlevy, George	May 1907:38	TDL
McAllen, Daniel	1:584-585	GP
McAllister, D A	2:66	NH
————	1895:87	OO

	2:431	PMO
McAllister, Lee	1931-32:41	OO
McAllister, Ward	168	AN
McAllister, William M	1937-38:62-63	OO
_____	1939-40:31	OO
_____	1941-42:66	OO
_____	1943-44:79	OO
McArdle, William	1895-96:101	SSS
McArthur, L L	1:641	CHW
McArthur, Lewis Ankeny	56:5	OHQ
McArthur, William Pope	16:246	OHQ
Macartney, R H	24:64 1919	WBP
_____	25:128 1920	WBP
_____	26:128 1921	WBP
_____	27:17 1922	WBP
_____	28:front. 1923	WBP
McAtee, M	1:372	HHT
Macaulay, Alexander Malcolm	1941:402	EN
Macaulay, William James	234	KB
Macauley, C D	176	WOY
McAuley, Thomas P	1895-96:103	SSS
McBane, Gillis J	680	SIH
McBeth, Kate	218	BR
McBeth, Sue L	197	PSW
Macbeth, William Charles	3:339	BCF
McBride, Angus	172-173, 350	HA
McBride, Arthur H	244	KB
McBride, C H	172-173	HA
McBride, George Wickliffe	3:709	GP
_____	1895:61	OO
_____	318	PL
_____	1:28	PMO
McBride, Henry	45	MAG
_____	91	ME
_____	34 no. 4:400-401	PN
_____	[69]	RLX
_____	unp.	SE
McBride, J S	3:755	BHS
McBride, James	2:658	NH
_____	1:248	PMO
McBride, Mrs. James, see		
McBride, Mahala (Miller)		
McBride, John R	239	HI
McBride, Mahala (Miller)	1:312	PMO
MacBride, Philip	36:19 1935	WDT
McBride, Richard	2:113, 547	BCF
_____	4:front.	BCF
_____	16 no. 3-4:134	BCH
_____	154	JAC
_____	fol. pt. 1	SHB
_____	1911:6-7, 70-71	YB
McBride, Thomas A	2:11	CHW
McCabe, C C	63	OS
McCabe, Elizabeth, see		
Eckerson, Elizabeth (McCabe)		
McCabe, Harry J	211	GG
McCabe, J F	172-173	HA
McCain, Mrs. M	222	FF

McCall, John Marshall	1:156	NH
_____	60:90	OHQ
McCall, Thomas L	67:204	OHQ
McCallum, Alexander	4:607	BCF
MacCallum, Charles A	2:308	SMS
McCallum, Joseph Wilson	3:263	BCF
McCallum, Walter L	248	E
McCann, Francis William	1941:480	EN
McCarter, William M	904	SIH
McCarthy, Charles Penderghast	2:134	FSB
McCarthy, Eugene	3:996	SMS
McCarthy, Frank W	3:1739	SM
McCarthy, James Frederick	3:466-467	BEA
McCarthy, James Frederick, Jr.		
	3:466-467	BEA
McCarthy, Joseph	1922:front.	WSP
McCarthy, Joseph Langton	3:466-467	BEA
McCarthy, Omie (Cochran)	2:24	CPD
McCarthy, W J R	172-173	HA
McCartney, Fannie, see		
Porter, Fannie (McCartney)		
McCarty, Henry	294	SW
McCarty, John	13	JP
_____	1:44	NH
_____	1:566	PMO
McCarty, Jonathan W	1:129	BH
_____	1:572	NH
McCarty, Mrs. Jonathan W , see		
McCarty, Ruth (Kincaid)		
McCarty, Ruth (Kincaid)	1:129	BH
McCarty, Tom	86-87	KO
McCarty, William, Jr.	86-87	KO
McCarver, Julia Ann (McCoy) Buckalew		
	1:476	NH
_____	121-122	PMT
McCarver, Mary A , see		
Hurley, Mary A (McCarver)		
McCarver, Mary Ann (Jennings)	1:104	HHT
McCarver, Morton Matthew	3:653	GP
_____	1:104	HHT
_____	1:476	NH
_____	1:322	PH
_____	front.	PMT
_____	4:226	SH
_____	Feb. 1906:94	TDL
McCarver, Mrs. Morton Matthew, see		
McCarver, Julia Ann (McCoy) Buckalew		
McCarver, Mary Ann (Jennings)		
McCaskill, Alex	2:143	HWW
McCaslin, David S	6:311	MC
McCauley, James W	1895-96:157	SSS
McClain, Alice	31:5, 133	PNLA
McClane, Helen C (Judson)	1:428	NH
McClane, John Birch	1:428	NH
McClane, Mrs. John Birch, see		
McClane, Helen C (Judson)		
McCleary, Ada L (Johnson)	1:10, 13	D

Entry	Reference	Source
McCleary, Mrs. Henry, see		
McCleary, Ada L (Johnson)		
McCleery, Fitzgerald	4:981	BCF
McCleery, Mrs. Fitzgerald, see		
McCleery, Mary (Wood)		
McCleery, Mary (Wood)	4:981	BCF
McClellan, George B	143	WCS
McClelland, J M	89	MLO
McClelland, Samuel B	6:413	MC
McClintock, J F	293	LHM
McCloskey, J H	1935-36:51	OO
	1937-38:62-63	OO
_____	1939-40:31	OO
	1941-42:66	OO
McCloy, William M	3:755	BCF
McClung, Donald	67:200	OHQ
McClure, Edgar	183	MMR
McClure, Patricia	50:22 1949	WDT
McClure, Royal A	2:715	BHK
McClure, Walter	1924:49	WSP
McClure, William	234	LDM
McColl, Angus John	2:653	BCF
_____	fol. pt. 1	SHB
	1911:70-71	YB
McColl, William	2:267	BCF
McCollum, Elvira (Stokes)	3:41	HHI
McCollum, J R	3:41	HHI
McCollum, Mrs. J R , see		
McCollum, Elvira (Stokes)		
McCollum, Robert M	3:1061	FH
McComb, Charles	364	JNT
McConachie, A	48	LS
McCone, George	2:1222	SM
McConkey, William A	3:801	BCF
McConnell, Henry	18	GL
McConnell, Newton W	275	MI
McConnell, Odell W	3:659	SMS
McConnell, Samuel	2:1162	SM
McConnell, William John	304	DSW
_____	10:front. 1925-26	IH
	2:346	NH
McConville, Edward	311	DSW
_____	15:61 1935-36	IH
	79	IHI
McCool, Hugh	249	E
McCord, Evan S	3:81	BHK
McCorkle, Elizabeth B (Howell)	2:278	PMO
McCorkle, George F	2:278	PMO
McCorkle, Mrs. George F , see		
McCorkle, Elizabeth B (Howell)		
McCormick, Anna E (Goodman)	3:18	BH
McCormick, E L	1910:2	TDL
McCormick, Kate (Higgins)	849	LHM
McCormick, Paul	6:84	MC
	575	MI
McCormick, Robert Laird	122	AC
_____	3:19	BH
	3:153	HHT
_____	68	PC
_____	[77]	RLX
_____	5:186	SH
_____	June 1909:36	TDL
_____	1910:63	TDL
McCormick, Mrs. Robert Laird, see		
McCormick, Anna E (Goodman)		
McCormick, W H	2:2	SMS
McCormick, Washington J	849	LHM
McCormick, Mrs. Washington J , see		
McCormick, Kate (Higgins)		
McCormick, William L	3:27	BH
McCornack, Elwin A	1931-32:41	OO
	1935-36:50	OO
_____	1937-38:62	OO
McCornack, J K	13:222 1908	WBP
	26:128 1921	WBP
_____	27:97 1922	WBP
McCoskrie, Edward	454	LDM
McCourt, John B	1931-32:41	OO
	1939-40:31	OO
_____	1941-42:66	OO
McCoy, A C	2:24	CPD
McCoy, Mrs. A C , see		
McCoy, Edna (Cochran)		
McCoy, Edna (Cochran)	2:24	CPD
McCoy, George	1905-06:[60]	RLW
McCoy, J A	201	LDM
McCoy, Julia Ann, see		
McCarver, Julia Ann (McCoy) Buckalew		
McCoy, Louise, see		
Kimble, Louise (McCoy)		
McCoy, Patrick	3:357	PH
McCracken, Harold	passim	MCK
McCraken, John	2:436	PMO
McCready, Norman Sylvester	2:240	PHP
McCreight, John Foster	2:335, 337	BCF
_____	8 no. 3:189	BCH
_____	2	JAC
_____	fol. pt. 1	SHB
_____	1897:64, 136	YB
_____	1911:70-71	YB
McCroskey, J P T		
	1905-06:[28]	RLW
McCroskey, Lucyle	206	BHSS
McCroskey, Milton	202, 287	BHSS
McCroskey, R C	452	BHSS
McCroskey, R L	1924:145	WSP
McCroskey, Sam	2:24	CPD
McCrossan, George E	fol. pt. 2	SHB
McCrum, Julia, see		
Davis, Julia (McCrum)		
McCulloch, Bert O	3:287	HHI
McCulloch, William	97	LDM
McCullough, George T	3:1468	SM
McCullough, Robert	2:475	HHT
McCully, Alfred	388	LDM
McCully, Asa A	58	LDM

McCully, David   58   LDM
McCumber, M   D   172-173   HA
McCune, William Asa   unp.   SOU
McCurdy, James Darwin   160   IHI
McCush, William   3:101   HWW
McCutcheon, Otis Eddy   2:245   HHI
McDaniel, Ford   4:537   PH
McDaniel, Myron   3:944   SMS
McDermoth, Charles   303   AG
McDermoth, Mrs. Cora A   438   AG
McDermott, Mrs. Alice   unp.   WD
McDermott, D   A   198   LDM
McDermott, Edith F   241   BHSS
McDermott, Frank   413   LDM
McDermott, Jeffrey   233   HA
MacDonald, Alexander   4:275   BCF
McDonald, Alexander   202   LDM
McDonald, Angus   1:228   FI
McDonald, Archibald   1:224   FI
                                        12   NF
_____   fol. pt. 1   SHB
_____   1911:70-71   YB
McDonald, Betsey M   (Sampson) 1:212 NH
McDonald, Donald A   1924:112   WSP
Macdonald, Donald Alexander fol. pt. 2 SHB
Macdonald, Duncan   499   LHM
McDonald, Harley   1:210-211   GP
                                        1:212   NH
McDonald, Mrs. Harley, see
   McDonald, Betsey M   (Sampson)
McDonald, Henry   2:817   BHK
McDonald, Hugh   3:343   BCF
McDonald, J   H   1895-96:130 SSS
McDonald, J   R   48   LS
McDonald, J   T   1905-06:[28] RLW
Macdonald, James Alexander fol. pt. 1 SHB
                                        1911:70-71   YB
McDonald, James R   429   HI
McDonald, James W   3:665   LHC
McDonald, Jessie   207   BHSS
Macdonald, John A   passim   GI
                                        front.   SC
McDonald, John Allan   1941:267   EN
McDonald, John D   2:572   SMS
Macdonald, John Wesley   3:563   BCF
McDonald, Magdalen, see
   McGillivray, Magdalen (McDonald)
McDonald, Mordo   [116]   RLX
MacDonald, Ranald   48 no. 1:15 PN
McDonald, W   D   unp.   SOU
McDonald, W   L   200   E
McDonald, W   R   3:11   LHC
Macdonald, William John   2:293   BCF
                                        1897:109   YB
_____   1911:70-71   YB
McDonald, William S   4:1017   BCF
Macdonell, A   J   fol. pt. 2   SHB
MacDonell, Alexander   fol. title page SHB

Macdonell, James Alexander fol. pt. 2 SHB
McDonnell, Emma Pearl   6:30 1906   WDT
McDonnell, John W   1895-96:101 SSS
McDonnell, Robert E   front.   BM
McDonnell, Robert H   front.   BM
McDonough, Joseph A   3:685   SMS
McDonough, Roger H   32 no. 3:33 PNLA
McDougal, W   D   431   LDM
McDougall, Alexander   fol. pt. 2   SHB
McDougall, T   M   110-111   HCM
McDougall, Mrs. T   M   110-111   HCM
MacDougall, Violet   66   MG
McDowell, George M   44:338   OHQ
McDowell, Walter F   3:223   BH
Mace, Charles P   2:823   HHI
McEldowney, W   H   3:331   LHC
McElfresh, Arthur   15   LT
McElhanney, William Gordon 3:867   BCF
McElmon, B   K   92   PSW
McElroy, E   B   1:332   NH
McElroy, M   J   1905-06:[28] RLW
McElroy, Thornton Fleming 51 no. 4:172 PN
                           54 no. 2:57 PN
McEneany, Edward   96   LDM
McEvers, Edward   119   AG
McFadden, Obadiah B   66:26   OHQ
                            4:8   SH
McFadden, S   Willis   91   PSW
McFarland, A   J   3:649   HHI
McFarland, Mrs. A   R   145, 231   JA
                            252, 254   PSW
McFarland, J   F   252   PSW
McFarland, Joseph Walter   3:43   BCF
McFarland, William B   231   GG
Macfarlane, Duncan M   4:351   BCF
MacFarlane, John Fraser   3:547   BH
Macfarlane, John Walter   3:107   BCF
McFarlane, Walter R   302   E
MacFarlane, William Daniel 3:761   SMS
McFee, John Gordon   3:463   BHS
McFee, Malcolm   3:375   BHS
McGee, James   177   LDM
McGeer, James   4:1125   BCF
McGettigan, Anthony   311   HA
McGill, Frank   1:372   HHT
McGill, Jeremiah   191   LDM
McGillivray, Ally   1112   SIH
McGillivray, Donald E   3:220   PH
McGillivray, Magdalen (McDonald) 114   MH
McGillivray, William   front.   CML
                            114   MH
McGillivray, Mrs. William, see
   McGillivray, Magdalen (McDonald)
McGilvery, Napoleon   1:404   NH
McGilvra, Caroline E   , see
   Burke, Caroline E   (McGilvra)
McGilvra, Elizabeth M   (Hills) 2:39 BHK

McGilvra, John Jay 2:740 BHS
——— 2:103 HH
——— 284 HI
——— 3 no. 8:420 PM
——— 4:232 SH
——— 1:581 BHK
——— 2:33 BHK
McGilvra, Mrs. John Jay, see
   McGilvra, Elizabeth M (Hills)
McGinley, Hugh S 3:676 SMS
McGinn, Henry E 2:811 LHC
McGinn, John L 172-173, 345 HA
McGinnis, Robert Henry 1941:113 EN
McGinnis, William H , see
   Lay, Ellsworth
McGivern, James 384 SCH
McGlinchey, John 2:282 HHI
McGlinchey, Mrs. John, see
   McGlinchey, May (Noggle) Alvord
McGlinchey, May (Noggle) Alvord 2:283 HHI
McGlinn, John 2:154 NH
McGovern, E B 2:617 BHK
McGovern, J F 2:617 BHK
MacGowan, Alexander Henry Boswell
   fol. pt. 1 SHB
——— 1911:70-71 YB
McGowan, Edward 15 no. 1-2:106 BCH
——— 56 HEH
McGowan, Henry S [100] RLX
McGowan, Ned, see
   McGowan, Edward
McGowan, Patrick J 2:283 HH
McGown, James 4 no. 2:86 BCH
McGrane, James B 30 THI
McGrath, John E fol. 207 (no. 28) SHI
McGrath, Joseph Francis
   16, 151, 159, 167 OB
McGrath, Luke 439 LDM
McGrath, P H 172-173 HA
McGrath, T S 2:419 GP
McGrath, Thomas P 2:297 SMS
McGrath, William H 3:195 BHK
McGraw, H E 1931-32:41 OO
McGraw, John Harte 3:401 BHK
——— 168 BHSS
——— 41 MAG
——— 78 ME
——— 34 no. 4:400-401 PN
——— [65] RLX
——— unp. SE
——— 5:46 SH
——— 1895-96:front. SSS
——— unp. VU
——— 2 no. 1:2 WM
McGreer, Thomas H 1895:94 OO
——— 2:440 PMO
McGregor, Daniel May 1907:68 TDL

MacGregor, Gordon Angus 3:7 BEA
McGregor, Harry Joseph 3:1802 SM
McGregor, Herbert B 195 AT
McGregor, James 1897:107 YB
McGregor, James H 2:213 CHW
McGregor, Peter 266 BHSS
——— 2:361 HH
——— 1905-06:[64] RLW
——— [98] RLX
McGuckin, J M 328 MHN
McGuffin, Eugene Joseph 3:101 BEA
McGuire, Francis 2:354 NH
McGuire, George Albert 4:999 BCF
——— 1911:70-71 YB
McGuire, Hollister D 1:30 PMO
McGuire, Robert 3:255 HHI
McGuire, Samuel M 4:583 BCF
MacGuire, Thomas 193 PSW
McHarg, William Hart, see
   Hart-McHarg, William
McHenry, Thomas 250 E
McHugh, Patrick J 3:445 BHK
McInerney, James 55 LT
McInnes, Thomas Robert 2:281 BCF
——— 250 KB
——— fol. pt. 1 SHB
——— 1897:109 YB
McInnes, William Wallace Burns
   1897:110 YB
McInness, James Loftus 3:603 BCF
McIntosh, Donald 110-111 HCM
McIntosh, Mrs. Donald 110-111 HCM
McIntosh, Ira K 3:457 BEA
Macintyre, A D 39 MG
McIntyre, D G 1 no. 9:12 WN
——— 1 no. 12:13 WN
McIntyre, Duncan 199 GI
McIntyre, James 165 LDM
McIntyre, S S 1 no. 12:12 WN
McIver, Andrew C 139 PSW
McIver, James 389 LDM
Mack, Henrietta Robins, see
   Eliot, Henrietta Robins (Mack)
Mack, Lucy, see
   Smith, Lucy (Mack)
McKaig, Ray 56 no. 1:19 PN
McKay, Charles 1:196 HWW
Mackay, D N 1945-46:93 OO
McKay, David Rodrig 4:62 BHK
McKay, Mrs. David Rodrig, see
   McKay, Matilde P (Meyfarth)
   Rothweiler
MacKay, Donald 3:335 BEA
McKay, Donald 4:112 LH
McKay, Donald Edward 4:415 BCF
McKay, Douglas 1935-36:50 OO

Name	Reference	Source
_____	1937-38:62	OO
_____	1939-40:15	OO
_____	1941-42:62	OO
_____	93	TUR
McKay, Elizabeth	298	BHSS
McKay, George	1:unp. 1900-01	WDT
McKay, Hugh	425	LDM
Mackay, J W	1:542	BCF
	front.	LCT
_____		
MacKay, John	4:139	BCF
MacKay, John James	3:237	BCF
MacKay, John W	224	QT
McKay, Joseph R	1941:259	EN
McKay, Joseph William	1897:103	YB
McKay, Matilde P (Meyfarth) Rothweiler		
	4:63	BHK
Mackay, Michael	167	OB
Mackay, Neil Franklin	1911:70-71	YB
McKay, Philip (Tsimshian Indian)	159	JA
	252	PSW
_____		
McKay, William Cameron	2:696	CP
	1:48	NH
_____		
McKay, William Moore	4:117	BCF
	fol. pt. 2	SHB
_____		
McKay, William Osborne	3:400	PH
McKechnie, Robert Edward	4:975	BCF
	fol. pt. 1	SHB
_____		
McKechnie, William Cecil	4:869	BCF
McKee, David Alexander	4:203	BCF
McKee, John	4:419	BCF
McKee, John, Sr.	3:1046	BCF
McKee, Mrs. John, Sr., see		
McKee, Margaret (Harris)		
McKee, Margaret (Harris)	3:1046	BCF
McKee, Ruth (Karr)	248-249	DE
	74-75	GA
	unp.	WD
_____		
MacKelvie, John Armstrong	fol. pt. 1	SHB
McKenley, Edward D	48	LS
McKenna, Coe A	1939-40:31	OO
	1941-42:62	OO
_____		
	1943-44:75	OO
	1945-46:82	OO
_____		
McKenna, Francis I	2:407	GP
McKenna, Joseph I	195	GG
McKenzie, Alex	2:front. 1924	BCHA
Mackenzie, Alexander	2:149	BCF
	405	CIR
_____	40, 278	GI
_____	1:322	LH
_____	114	MH
_____	34	MHN
_____	1:228	SH
_____	fol. title page	SHB
_____	27	WTH
_____	1911:70-71	YB
_____	1897:17	YB
McKenzie, Alexander	345	WOY
McKenzie, Angus	688	SIH
McKenzie, Archibald M	3:371	GP
McKenzie, D S	3:411	BH
McKenzie, Donald	56	BHSI
_____	185	DU
Mackenzie, Francis James A		
	1911:70-71	YB
McKenzie, Kenneth	2:564	CAFT
	2:front.	CES
_____	94	LBT
MacKenzie, Kenneth A J		
	27:110	OHQ
	616	SHP
McKenzie, R	287	BHSS
McKenzie, Robert T	6:151	PNLA
Mackenzie, S F	fol. pt. 2	SHB
Mackenzie, William	fol. pt. 2	SHB
Mackenzie, William Russell	3:479	GP
McKeon, J B	172-173	HA
McKeown, John	20:42 1945-46	IH
McKercher, Finlay	3:457	GP
McKever, Lucy E , see		
Watters, Lucy E (McKever)		
McKevitt, Francis J	261	GG
McKey, Alys	3 no. 4:238	BCH
Mackie, Peter	38	LDM
McKiel, R E	439	LDM
McKiernan, Raphael	221	GG
Mackin, Charles	117	GG
McKinlay, George W	3:71	HHI
McKinlay, Mabel, see		
Hopkins, Mabel (McKinlay)		
McKinley, Archibald	1:184	NH
_____	2:300	SH
McKinley, Charles	1:154-155	EPD
McKinley, Charles R	426	FF
_____	4:414	PH
McKinley, Horace G	49	PL
McKinley, Mrs. Horace G , see		
McKinley, Marie (Ware)		
McKinley, Marie (Ware)	231	PL
McKinley, William	386	AG
McKinnell, Henry	1:536	GP
_____	2:425	GP
McKinnon, Alexander Balone	1:384	PHP
McKinnon, Angus	3:1027	BCF
McKinnon, Donald Alexander	1941:180	EN
MacKinnon, John McLellan	3:357	BCF
McKinnon, Lockie	16 no. 3-4:134	BCH
MacKinnon, Malcolm Campbell	3:1107	FH
MacKinnon, Thomas Hugh-Campbell		
	1943:198	ENC
Mackintosh, Angus	3:23	BHS
_____	557	HI
_____	12:188	MWH
_____	5:174	SH
Mackintosh, Kenneth	1922:24	WSP

McKinzie, W   S   1051   LHM
McKnight, James C   L   1924:144   WSP
McKnight, Roy E   2:545   SMS
McKown, John L   2:391   HHI
McKy, John R   2:55   CHW
MacLachlan, James A   2:289   HH
McLagan, John Campbell   4:1189   BCF
McLain, Mathew   3:766   SMS
McLaren, Mrs. F   M   2:front. 1924   BCHA
McLaren, George S   unp.   VU
McLaren, Kenneth   16 no. 3-4:134   BCH
McLaughlin, Angus L   2:188   SMS
McLaughlin, J   O   2:285   CHW
McLaughlin, Raymond D   294   E
McLaughlin, W   S   48   LS
McLaughlin, William E   34 no. 4:54 . PNLA
McLay, Margaret, see
     Evans, Margaret (McLay)
McLean, Alex   427   LDM
McLean, Allen F   266   PSW
McLean, Cecil Gower   3:229   BCF
McLean, Charles A   14:88 1909   WBP
_____   16:front. 1911   WBP
_____   17:23 1912   WBP
_____   24:80 1919   WBP
McLean, Clark N   280   E
McLean, Daniel   427   LDM
McLean, Daniel J   3:949   BHS
McLean, Donald   3:849   BCF
MacLean, Ewen Wainwright   4:709   BCF
_____   fol. pt. 2   SHB
McLean, George   6:442-443   MC
McLean, John   69   NT
MacLean, John Duncan   198   JAC
Maclean, John Norman   6:311   MC
McLean, Laughlin   431   LDM
MacLean, Malcolm Alexander   3:323   BCF
McLean, W   J   298   BHSS
McLeary, James H   4:110   MC
                                1:428   SMS
Macleay, Donald   1:594   GP
                                3:front.   GP
_____   436   SHP
Macleay, Lachlan   1910:62   TDL
McLellan, Francis Xavier   3:577   BHK
McLeod, Alfred W   3:571   BCF
McLeod, Colin   2:991   HHI
McLeod, John   439   LDM
                                377   MP
_____
McLeod, Malcolm   4:245   BCF
McLeod, Murdock   63   PSW
McLeod, P   B   374   HA
McLeod, W   Edward   119   PSW
MacLeod, William   3:485   BCF
McLoughlin, David   232   DSW
                                796   SIH
_____
McLoughlin, John   162   AC
                                63   BF

                                63   BHSI
                                1:125   BS
                                2:510   CAFT
                                263, 867   CHO
                                1:155   CHW
                                406   CIR
                                1:206   CP
                                156   DW
                                286   EW
                                1:208   FI
                                61   GI
                                1:186   GP
                                77   HBC
                                4:front.   HBR
                                88   HI
                                102   HIO
                                2:354   LH
                                1:367   LHC
                                115   MH
                                1:16   NH
                                248   NM
                                37:291   OHQ
                                59   OP
                                6   OPC
                                1:79   PH
                                1:2   PMO
                                2:front.   SH
                                1   TUR
                                246   WCS
                                1 no. 6:8   WN
Maclure, John   4:1063   BCF
McMahon, J   H   80   KT
MacMahon, Thomas   3:381   BH
McManus, John E   2:376   PHP
                                1895-96:75   SSS
McMaster, John   3:619   BHK
MacMaster, William   1:612   GP
McMaster, William C   [131]   RLX
McMicken, Maurice   3:75   BHS
                                5:56   SH
                                1924:49   WSP
McMicken, William   4:344   SH
McMicking, Mrs.   2:front. 1924   BCHA
McMicking, R   B   2:293   BCF
McMillan, Archibald   1:303   BH
McMillan, Charles   3:203   BCF
McMillan, Duncan J   6:386   MC
MacMillan, Hugh Allan   2:322   SMS
McMillan, John   2:601   FH
                                1:80   FSB
                                36   PSW
MacMillan, Lydia, see
     Reed, Lydia (MacMillan)
McMillan, Thomas   2:427   HHI
McMillen, James H   1:440   NH
McMillen, Mrs. James H   , see
     McMillen, Tirzah (Barton)

McMillen, Tirzah (Barton)	1:440	NH
McMillin, C K	17:42 1912	WBP
	27:33 1922	WBP
McMillin, John Stafford	6:26	SH
McMillin, W B	336	AG
McMorran, A W	[109]	RLX
McMorris, Daniel Webster	3:899	BHK
	3:695	BHS
McMullin, Fayette	15	MAG
	10	ME
_____	34 no. 4:400-401	PN
_____	[41]	RLX
_____	unp.	SE
McMurray, John	3:326	BEA
McMurray, John L	2:24	PHP
	May 1907:39	TDL
McMurray, John Odell	3:326	BEA
McMurry, F G	59:293	OHQ
McMurry, R B	59:293	OHQ
MacNab, Allan	108	GI
McNair, Benedict P	2:539	SMS
McNair, James A	fol. pt. 2	SHB
McNamara, William J	246	MI
McNamee, Frances C , see		
Northrup, Frances C (McNamee)		
McNary, Charles Linza	66:364	OHQ
	68:126	OHQ
	1943-44:13	OO
McNary, John H	68:129	OHQ
McNaught, James	14 no. 6:659	MWH
McNaughton, Archibald	4:333	BCF
McNaughton, Mrs. Archibald, see		
Manson, Margaret (Peebles) McNaughton		
McNaughton, James	45	DW
McNeeley, Edwin J	3:61	HHT
McNeely, Thomas	4:49	BCF
McNeil, William	230	LDM
McNeill, William	3:675	BCF
	fol. pt. 2	SHB
McNicol, N B	1905-06:[59]	RLW
McNicoll, David	352	GI
McNulty, John	93	LDM
McParland, James A	59 no. 1:26	PN
McPhaden, Donald	4:75	BCF
MacPhail, H W	2:273	HWW
	27:97 1922	WBP
McPhee, D D	251	E
McPhee, W H	172-173	HA
	404	WOY
McPherson, Alexander	3:1000	FH
McPherson, G E	May 1907:68	TDL
MacPherson, Harry A	2:333	SMS
Macpherson, Hector	1931-32:41	OO
	1939-40:31	OO
McPherson, Jack	4 no. 2:86	BCH
McPherson, John U	2:614	FH
Macpherson, Robert	1897:107	YB
McPhillips, Albert Edward	2:547	BCF

_____	fol. pt. 1	SHB
_____	1911:6-7, 70-71	YB
McPhillips, Arthur	1931-32:41	OO
_____	unp.	SOU
McPhillips, Francis Xavier	4:1137	BCF
McQuade, Andrew	2:719	FH
McQuade, John	2:313	BHK
McQuaid, Hugh	5:275	MC
McQueen, Ivan	2:431	PMO
McQuesten, Jack, see		
McQuesten, Leroy Napoleon		
McQuesten, Leroy Napoleon	160	AN
_____	278-279	HU
_____	110	WOY
McRae, Alexander	fol. pt. 2	SHB
McRae, Daniel Carrus	3:150	BEA
McRae, J A	3:471	BH
McRae, James E	36:32 1935	WDT
McRae, R D	[109]	RLX
McRae, Robert James	3:150-151	BEA
MacRae, Will G	197	PL
MacRae, William Alexander	3:4	LHC
MacReady, John	1:534	HHT
McReavey, John	1905-06:[28]	RLW
McSpadden, George	4:829	BCF
McStay, Brother	3:240	SH
McTague, Thomas	322	MI
McTavish, Donald Neil	3:361	BCF
McTavish, Dugald	1897:18	YB
Macuina, see		
Maquinna, Nootka chief		
McVicar, D J	215	LDM
MacWatters, David C	3:1100	FH
MacWhinnie, Arthur Morgan	3:1095	BHS
Macy, William Tecumseh	unp.	SOU
Madden, James	31	THI
Madden, Mrs. James	31	THI
Madden, Thomas A	32	THI
Maddocks, M R	unp.	SEA
Maden, S S	7:122	MC
Madigan, Benjamin	111	LDM
Madigan, Francis E	1:391	HH
Madill, James Cross	4:733	BCF
Madsen, Charlie	34-35 (no. 12)	MCK
Madsen, Mrs. Charlie	34-35 (no. 13)	MCK
Madson, Peter J	2:735	BHK
Magee, George W	2:478	SMS
Magee, Lewis J	2:343	HHI
Magel, Benjamin Franklin	3:396	BEA
Maginn, Edward F	3:1708	SM
Maginness, Martin, see		
Maginnis, Martin		
Maginnis, Martin	99	LHM
	8:front.	MC
_____	2:986	SM
Magnusson, Carl Edward	120-121	GA
_____	6:30 1906	WDT

	26:54 1925	WDT
Magnusson, Charles Edward, see		
Magnusson, Carl Edward		
Magraw, Henry Stephen	2:520	SMS
Magruder, Grace Kent	1935-36:51	OO
	1937-38:62-63	OO
Maguire, Roderick H	261	GG
Mahaffay, Robert E	3:651	HHT
Mahan, John W	1941:209	EN
Mahncke, Emma (Krull)	3:629	BH
Mahncke, Franz	3:629	BH
Mahncke, Mrs. Franz, see		
Mahncke, Emma (Krull)		
Mahon, Charles Edwin	4:109	BCF
Mahon, Marietta (Carr)	1:98	HHT
Mahon, Mrs. William, see		
Mahon, Marietta (Carr)		
Mahoney, J T	1937-38:62-63	OO
Mahoney, Thomas R	1939-40:15	OO
	1941-42:62	OO
	1943-44:75	OO
	1945-46:82	OO
Mah-tot-wap-tus, see		
Three Feathers, Nez Percé chief		
Maier, Christian	701	HI
Maillet, Herbert A	3:1222	SMS
Maillet, Louis R	4:197	MC
Main, David	3:703	BCF
Main, John Fleming	3:34	PH
	4:front.	PH
	6:29 1906	WDT
	1923:17	WSP
Mainland, Donald	3:61	HWW
Mains, William Lee	2:1091	SM
Maitland, George A	1152	SIH
Major, Charles George	2:139	BCF
	3:157	BCF
	fol. title page	SHB
Major, William Alexander	3:69	BHS
	189	E
	103	PSW
Makay, Moses	6:432-433	MC
Malaspina, Alexandro	1:166	BCF
Mallandaine, Edward	fol. title page	SHB
Mallandaine, Edward, Jr.	fol. pt. 2	SHB
Mallory, Rufus	2:front.	GP
	1:184	NH
	2:172	PMO
	388	SHP
Malloy, Joseph	31	THI
Malm, Laura A , see		
Svenson, Laura A (Malm) Frick		
Malmo, Charles	3:669	BHK
Malmoe, Martin B	232	SIH
Malmsten, August	1941:147	EN
Malone, Francis M	2:1246	SM
Maloney, H S	unp.	SOU
Maloney, John	2:649	HHI
Maloney, Martin J	1905-06:[65]	RLW
Maloney, William H	2:397	SMS
Malony, Thomas	48	LS
	May 1907:38	TDL
Malott, Charlotte N	219	BHSS
Malott, Conner	43 no. 1:16-17	PN
Manley, John E	2:330	SMS
Manley, S H	1905-06:[28]	RLW
Mann, Alexander Robert	3:39	BCF
Mann, Alfred Ernest	3:727	BCF
Mann, Amanda	212	SG
Mann, Anna Mary (Lewis)	1:461	GP
Mann, Champion B	1:397	HH
Mann, Donald D	fol. pt. 2	SHB
Mann, John G	261	GG
Mann, L L	1931-32:40	OO
Mann, Peter John	2:469	GP
Mann, Mrs. Peter John, see		
Mann, Anna Mary (Lewis)		
Mann, Rebecca A , see		
Jarrett, Rebecca A (Mann)		
Mann, Thomas	2:361	LHC
Manning, Charles	297	E
Manning, John	1931-32:41	OO
Manning, L R	1910:3	TDL
Mannion, Joseph	fol. title page	SHB
Mannix, Thomas	3:411	LHC
Mansell, Jane, see		
Andrews, Jane (Mansell)		
Manson, Margaret (Peebles) McNaughton		
	4:332	BCF
Manson, Michael	1911:70-71	YB
Manson, William	1911:70-71	YB
Manson, William J	1911:70-71	YB
Mantle, Lee	5:81	MC
	6:23	MC
	343	MI
	2:860	SM
Manville, George	1:245	BH
	1:94	HHT
Manwaring, Orson Elwood	3:280	BEA
Maple, John Wesley	154	BE
Maquilla, see		
Maquinna, Nootka chief		
Maquinna, Nootka chief	1:128, 182	BCF
	101	CHO
Maquinna, Napoleon, see		
Napoleon Maquinna, Nootka chief		
Mara, John Andrew	fol. pt. 1	SHB
	1911:70-71	YB
March, Hiram	413	JNT
March, Mrs. Hiram	413	JNT
Marchand, R P	2:180	MCC
Marchant, George	165	LDM
Marchesseau, Sophronius	2:964	SM
Marckworth, Gordon D	50:53 1949	WDT
Margraf, Henry	246	E

Marineau, William Thomas	3:498	BEA	
	65	RSA	
Marion, Joseph E	280	MI	
Markham, Edwin	1:364	PMO	
Markham, Francis M	908	SIH	
Markham, Lyman F	868	SIH	
Markham, Mary, see			
Jewell, Mary (Markham)			
Markle, George B	630	SHP	
Marks, T E	1:421	HH	
Marks, Willard L	1931-32:40	OO	
	1945-46:36	OO	
Marlborough, 1st duke of, see			
Churchill, John			
Marlow, Thomas A	1941:140	EN	
Marmaduke, J C	unp.	VU	
Marmaseena	130-131 (no. 24)	MCK	
Marpole, Clarence Mawson	4:595	BCF	
Marpole, Richard	3:745	BCF	
	fol. pt. 1	SHB	
Marquam, Emma (Kern)	1:320	NH	
Marquam, Philip A	1:320	NH	
	190	SHP	
Marquam, Mrs. Philip A , see			
Marquam, Emma (Kern)			
Marquam, Philip A , Jr.	2:341	GP	
Mars, James	4:113	BCF	
Marsden, Edward	252	PSW	
Marsh, Arthur C	2:891	LHC	
Marsh, Arthur L	60 no. 3:129	PN	
Marsh, Benjamin F	413	LHM	
Marsh, David	1:592	NH	
Marsh, Edson	2:760	FH	
Marsh, Eugene E	1939-40:31	OO	
	1941-42:66	OO	
	1943-44:79	OO	
	1945-46:85	OO	
Marsh, Grant	110-111	HCM	
Marsh, Horatio Richmond	287	PSW	
Marsh, Mrs. Horatio Richmond	287	PSW	
Marsh, Joseph Walker	front.	FR	
Marsh, Mrs. M E	2:270	NH	
Marsh, S P	2:270	NH	
Marsh, Sidney Harper	1:433	LHC	
Marshall, Charles Joseph	3:182	BEA	
Marshall, Frank Newcomb	3:239	LHC	
Marshall, George	1:360	PMO	
Marshall, Mrs. George, see			
Marshall, Mrs. Margaretta			
Marshall, Hugh J	151	OB	
Marshall, John	57	LDM	
Marshall, John S	2:1263	SM	
Marshall, Joseph Phillip	3:180	BEA	
Marshall, Joseph Walden	3:303	BEA	
Marshall, Mrs. Margaretta	1:360	PMO	
Marshall, O P	40 no. 2:86	BCH	
Marshall, Thomas Corbet	410	MI	
Marshall, William	380	BF	

Marshall, William H	252	LDM	
Marsilliot, M G	209	LDM	
Marsters, A C	2:458	PMO	
Marston, O B	172-173	HA	
Marston, William J R	3:1350	SMS	
Martens, Herman G	322	HA	
Martin, (Captain)	431	LDM	
Martin, A W	50:48 1949	WDT	
Martin, Albert B	6:386	MC	
Martin, Alex, Jr.	14:106 1909	WBP	
Martin, Arthur Chalmers	3:689	BHS	
Martin, August, Lummi chief	32	JNT	
Martin, Charles E	50:43 1949	WDT	
Martin, Charles H	1935-36:34	OO	
	1937-38:7	OO	
	82	TUR	
Martin, Clarence Daniel	57	MAG	
	4:444	PH	
	34 no. 4:400-401	PN	
	unp.	SE	
Martin, Don	1:front.	EPD	
Martin, Frank	18:3 1941-42	IH	
Martin, Frank J	1 no. 1:38	WN	
Martin, Fred W	279	E	
Martin, George Bohun	2:front. 1924	BCHA	
	1897:104	YB	
Martin, Hannah	1935-36:51	OO	
	1937-38:62-63	OO	
	1939-40:31	OO	
Martin, Howard H	50:42 1949	WDT	
Martin, Joel D	191	SIH	
Martin, John A	69	LHN	
Martin, Joseph	2:451	BCF	
	118	JAC	
	fol. pt. 1	SHB	
	1911:70-71	YB	
Martin, Josephine (Rider) Adams Wright			
	117	CBC	
Martin, Kenneth S	1941-42:66	OO	
	1943-44:79	OO	
Martin, Margaret Belle	26:42 1925	WDT	
Martin, Martha Lydia, see			
Wilson, Martha Lydia (Martin)			
Martin, Mrs. Mary E	6:325	MC	
Martin, N L	2:222	SMS	
Martin, Reinhard	247	E	
Martin, Samuel	232	BR	
Martin, Thomas B	2:152	FSB	
Martin, W H	17:67 1912	WBP	
	22:96 1917	WBP	
	24:80 1919	WBP	
	27:81 1922	WBP	
Martin, Walter V	2:806	FH	
Martin, William	3:579	BHS	
	1:84	NH	
Martin, William B	191	SIH	
Martineau, James H	97	DH	

Marty Sam, see
    Martin, Samuel
Marvin, Edward Benjamin   240   KB
    _____   fol. title page SHB
Mary (Haida Indian)   1897:171   YB
Mary, Princess   30:377   OHQ
Mary Edward, Sister   123   PI
Mary Julian, Mother   364   PIW
Mary Ligouri, Sister   352   PI
Mary Magdalene   149   DE
Mary of the Infant Jesus, Sister 122   PI
Mary Rose, Mother   24   SG
Mary Xavier, Sister   350   PI
Masalon (Kalispel Indian) 47 no. 2:49   PN
Mashburn, Ed   206   BHSS
Mashburn, John   206   BHSS
Mashburn, Sandy   287   BHSS
Mashburn, W E   408   BHSS
Mason, A   48   LS
Mason, Allen C   2:26   HHT
    2:214   NH
Mason, Archie   3:349   GP
Mason, Charles H   277   MP
    1:257   PHP
    _____   3:378   SH
Mason, Claude D   2:634   FH
Mason, Dwight N   2:456   SMS
Mason, George   15 no. 1-2:47   BCH
Mason, Joseph T   10, 14   SSP
Mason, Leo Joseph   3:61   BEA
Mason, Mary   31:47   PNLA
Mason, W S   589   HIO
Massayou (Eskimo)   278-279   HU
Massey, Henry Louis   4:875   BCF
Massey, Thomas Joy   404   AG
Mastin, W H   1:624   NH
Matheny, Elizabeth, see
    Hewitt, Elizabeth (Matheny)
Mather, John Douglas   4:285   BCF
Mathers, James B   fol. pt. 2   SHB
Matheson, Alexander McLean 2:345   HWW
Matheson, John   6:430   MC
Mathews, John W   1:355   HH
Mathews, M A   190   E
Mathews, M J   172-173   HA
Mathews, Thomas J   3:1443   SMS
Mathewson, Johnnie   1:104   ACR
Mathias, Ephraim S   2:781   HHI
Mathieu, George E   1924:161   WSP
Matson, John Samuel H   fol. pt. 2   SHB
Matthaei, Henry   3:661   HHT
Matthes, Francois Emile   201   MMR
Matthews, Alexander G   2:91   HH
Matthews, Charles   1:94   HHT
Matthews, Charles A   3:835   SMS
Matthews, G Frazier   3:233   HWW
Matthews, H A   239   LDM
Matthews, Mark Allison 56 no. 1:cover, 8 PN

    _____   45   PSW
Matthies, Adolf   unp.   SOU
Matthieu, Francois Xavier   1:143   BS
    _____   2:458   CP
    _____   134   DO
    _____   1:112, 154   GP
    _____   3:246   LH
Mattice, George W   2:164   HHT
Mattison, R R   33:16 1928   WBP
    34:front. 1929   WBP
Mattoon, Albert R   2:434   PMO
Mauldin, James   278   LHM
Mauldin, William T   3:1325   SM
Maury, R F   60:94   OHQ
Maxey, Clara, see
    Kimple, Clara (Maxey)
Maxey, Edward E   2:831   FH
Maxon, J O   305   BR
Maxson, Frank T   3:623   BHS
Maxwell, C L   278-279   KO
Maxwell, David C   3:1410   SM
Maxwell, G R   1897:110   YB
Maxwell, Gunplay, see
    Maxwell, C L
Maxwell, J W   1895:80   OO
    14:64 1909   WBP
    _____   1 no. 8:17   WN
May, Charles C   50:23 1949   WDT
May, William N   3:143   BH
Mayer, Jacob   3:493   GP
Mayers, Joseph   3:305   BCF
Mayger, William   349   MI
Maynard, A H   2:front. 1924   BCHA
Maynard, Charles Warren   2:215   HWW
Maynard, David S   1:59   BHK
    2:828   BHS
Maynard, Max   6:151   PNLA
Mayo, Al   159   WOY
Mayo, J E   unp.   SOU
Mayor, John C   715   LHM
Mays, Franklin Pierce   26   PL
    2:459   PMO
Mazenod, Charles J E de 1:230 MCC
Meacham, Ida Olivia, see
    Richardson, Ida Olivia (Meacham)
Meacham, William Milo   3:1109   BHS
Mead, Albert Edward   46   MAG
    _____   94   ME
    _____   36, 40   PC
    _____   34 no. 4:400-401   PN
    _____   1905-06:[31]   RLW
    _____   [71]   RLX
    _____   unp.   SE
Mead, George   4:195   BCF
Mead, Mary, see
    Russell, Mary (Mead)
Meads, John F   May 1907:38   TDL

Meagher, Elizabeth M   J   (Townsend)
 6:141 MC
Meagher, George W 48 LS
Meagher, Maurice A 255 GG
Meagher, Thomas Francis 6:137 MC
 1:466 SMS
Meagher, Mrs. Thomas Francis, see
 Meagher, Elizabeth M   J   (Townsend)
Means, Katherine (Hayes) 2:884 FH
Means, Marcus A 2:884 FH
Means, Mrs. Marcus A   , see
 Means, Katherine (Hayes)
Meany, Edmond Stephen 120-121 GA
 46 no. 3:66 PN
 51 no. 1:81 PN
 51 no. 4:162 PN
 unp. VU
 2 no. 1:cover W
 2 no. 8:front. W
 26 no. 3:front. WAS
 1:unp. 1900-01 WDT
 6:23 1906 WDT
 26:55 1925 WDT
Meares, John 63 GBS
 4 LDM
 1:270 LH
 1897:17 YB
 1911:70-71 YB
Mears, Frederick 1941:91 EN
Mears, Samuel M 2:721 LHC
Mears, W   A 3:1029 BHS
Mec-ur-gra, Weit-spek chief 18 BD
Medcalf, Mrs. M   A 2:390 NH
Medcalf, William 2:390 NH
Mee, Robert 3:1009 BCF
Meek, Courtney W 320 SIH
Meek, Joseph L 272 BF
 1:145 BS
 375 CHO
 1:379 CHW
 front. DO
 140 DW
 2:56 FI
 1:127 GP
 3:66 LH
 1:20 NH
 2:20 PMO
 2:22 SH
 168 SIH
 front., 1 TM
Meek, William 68:159 OHQ
Meeker, Ezra 235, 240, 244, 365, 366 BF
 1:159, 393 BH
 1:687 BHK
 1:52 BHS
 334 BR
 84 CPP
 1:94 GP

 1:166 HWW
 front., 86, 170 MP
 front., 19, 313 MS
 2:214 NH
Meeker, Oliver 19 MS
Megaw, W   R fol. pt. 1 SHB
Megazzini, Pascal 284 PI
Megler, J   G 55 no. 1:23 PN
 1905-06:[53] RLW
 [108] RLX
 1895-96:75 SSS
Mehargue, John W 2:758 FH
Mehlhorn, August 6:172 SH
Meier, Aaron 1:614-615 GP
 2:235 GP
Meier, Julius L 66:250 OHQ
 1931-32:8 OO
 79 TUR
Meigs, Carlos O 3:919 FH
Meigs, George Ansor 6:front. SH
Meikle, Stephen Mack, Jr. 3:514 BEA
Meikle, Mrs. Stephen Mack, Sr., see
 Meikle, Vashti Larkin (Price)
Meikle, Vashti Larkin (Price) 3:514 BEA
Meisner, Albert 2:48-49 EPD
Meiway, see
 Looking Glass, Sr., Nez Percé chief
Melcher, A   S 1905-06:[54] RLW
Melcher, Fred L 3:1365 SM
Meldrum, J 2:front. 1924 BCHA
Meldrum, Mrs. J 2:front. 1924 BCHA
Meldrum, John 1:584 PMO
Meldrum, Mrs. John, see
 Meldrum, Susan Depue (Cox)
Meldrum, John W 3:287 GP
Meldrum, Robert unp. HOF
 3:201 MC
 1:214 SMS
Meldrum, Susan Depue (Cox) 1:584 PMO
Meletus, Constantine 327 HA
Meller, Gertrude, see
 De Lin, Gertrude (Meller)
Mellinger, Charles Clement 1943:86 ENC
Mellinger, Clarence M 3:699 HHI
Mellish, Arthur James Benjamin 3:1115 BCF
Mellon, Henry Augustus 3:759 BCF
Mellon, Mrs. Henry Augustus, see
 Mellon, Susanna Gertrude (Clarke)
Mellon, Susanna Gertrude (Clarke)
 3:765 BCF
Melville, J   I 1924:113 WSP
Melvin, Frank L 3:523 GP
Menager, F 159 OB
Mendenhall, Edward 1:372 PMO
Mendenhall, J   W 5:315 MC
Mendenhall, John S 153 LHM
Mendenhall, Walter C
 fol. 207 (no. 38) SHI

Menetrey, Joseph   fol. 512 (no. 11)   BUR
                          364   PI
                          432   PIW
Mengarini, Gregory   fol. 512 (no. 12)   BUR
                          31   PI
Menhinick, Stanley   4 no. 2:86   BCH
Menzies, Archibald   294   MV
Mercer, Alice, see
    Bagley, Alice (Mercer)
Mercer, Asa Shinn   1:195   BHK
                          1:140   BHS
                          423   CIR
                          18-19   GA
                          1:208   HWW
                          44 no. 2:62   PN
Mercer, Effie, see
    Tarr, Effie (Mercer)
Mercer, Mae B   3:52   BEA
                          3:745   HHI
Mercer, Susie, see
    Graham, Susie (Mercer)
Mercer, Thomas   1:87   BHK
                          2:701   BHS
                          2:97   HH
                          589   HI
                          1:240   NH
Mercer, Willis Alfred   1943:131   ENC
Merchant, Joseph   1895-96:99   SSS
Merchant, William   unp.   SOU
Mercier, Charles   10:194   MC
Mercier, Moses   159   WOY
Mercy, Frederick   4:584   PH
Meredith, W   L   59   SSP
Merkle, George Wallace   3:1550   SM
                          3:708   SMS
Merow, Moses   6:432-433   MC
Merrell, Edmond M   3:966   FH
Merriam, Cyrus K   493   HI
                          2:374   NH
Merriam, Howard S   1935-36:51   OO
Merrick, Frank L   unp.   VU
Merrill, Franklin T   3:706   SMS
Merrill, Norman   2:435   PMO
Merrill, Richard Dwight   4:743   PH
Merrill, Thomas Gale   52   MI
Merriman, Homer Eddy   2:361   HH
Merritt, H   D   1926:20   WSP
Merritt, H   L   21:128 1916   WBP
                          22:128 1917   WBP
                          23:112 1918   WBP
Merritt, LeRoy Charles   31:50   PNLA
                          34 no. 4:25   PNLA
Mert, Marie Le, see
    LeMert, Marie
Mervish, Olga   66   MG
Mesplie, Toussaint   61   DL
                          1:825   HHI
Messegee, George D   132   JNT

                          200   LDM
Metcalf, Harry K   2:437   CHW
Metcalf, Ralph   3:151   BH
                          1941:27   EN
                          1:403   HH
                          2:325   HHT
                          3:front.   PH
                          4:472   PH
                          [87]   RLX
                          6:216   SH
Metcalf, William   217   PSW
Metcalfe, James B   3:121   BHS
                          1:79   HH
                          301   HI
                          3 no. 8:420   PM
Metlen, D   E   483   LHM
Metlen, Mrs. D   E   , see
    Metlen, E   A   (Kennison)
Metlen, E   A   (Kennison) 483   LHM
Metschan, Philip   1895:69   OO
Metsker, Glen R   3:443   LHC
Metson, William H   68   HA
Metzger, D   M   unp.   SOU
Meyendorff, Michael A   745   LHM
                          449   PL
Meyer, Arthur   2:804   FH
Meyer, F   C   172-173   HA
Meyer, Henry A   2:1187   SM
Meyer, Herman J   3:1637   SM
Meyer, John Mathew   3:851   BHS
Meyers, A   W   1941-42:66   OO
                          1943-44:79   OO
                          1945-46:87   OO
Meyers, F   L   14:98 1909   WBP
Meyers, George T   1895:106   OO
Meyers, Herbert W   1924:176   WSP
Meyers, William   305   LDM
Meyfarth, Matilde P   , see
    McKay, Matilde P   (Meyfarth)
    Rothweiler
Michael Insula, Flathead chief, see
    Insula, Flathead chief
Michaels, Louis C   136   PSW
Michel, see
    Insula, Flathead chief
    Plenty Grizzly Bears, Pend d'Oreille
    chief
Michel Pete (Kutenai Indian) 2:53   BCF
Michener, W   H   86   AG
Mick, Margaret Stewart, see
    Hayes, Margaret Stewart (Mick)
Mignerey, Henri Jules   4:666   PH
Milburn, F   W   39   MG
Milburn, George R   4:112   MC
Miles, Arthur W   2:1211   SM
                          2:260   SMS
Miles, George M   6:401   MC

```
                              2:1060              SM
Miles, Mrs. George M        , see
   Miles, Helen (Strevell)
Miles, Helen (Strevell)       6:401              MC
Miles, M    W                 1895-96:99         SSS
Miles, Nelson A               332                AM
_____                       302-303            HCM
_____                       162, 176           KY
_____                       fol. 207 (no. 20)  SHI
_____                       362                VT
Miles, Z    C                 2:382              NH
Milheim, Fred A               3:51               HWW
Millar, Edna (Sorensen)       3:25               BEA
Millar, Zenith Reed           3:25               BEA
Millar, Mrs. Zenith Reed, see
   Millar, Edna (Sorensen)
Millard, Eva Margaret         1 no. 3:216        WM
Millard, William J            3:1                PH
_____                       1922:50            WSP
_____                       1923:64            WSP
Miller, Albert Searle         61:153             OHQ
Miller, Alexander             1943:17            ENC
_____                       3:77               PH
_____                       6:34               SH
Miller, Alice H      , see
   Berry, Alice H       (Miller)
Miller, Allen J               1:303              BH
Miller, Mrs. Allen J          1:303              BH
Miller, B    F                172-173            HA
Miller, C    K                290                BHSS
Miller, Carl J                2:709              HHI
Miller, Charles Southard      2:401              BHK
Miller, Cincinnatus Heine, see
   Miller, Joaquin
Miller, Cora A       , see
   Beardsley, Cora A      (Miller)
Miller, D    B                1895-96:121        SSS
Miller, E    Harvey           1941-42:66         OO
Miller, Ed W                  1931-32:40         OO
Miller, Edwin C               1895-96:99         SSS
Miller, Ernest                fol. pt. 1         SHB
                              1911:70-71         YB
_____ Floyd C               unp.               SEA
Miller, Frank                 202                HIT
Miller, Franklin A            2:673              HHI
Miller, Fred Charles          1:307              HH
_____                       3:521              HHT
_____                       1:544              PHP
Miller, Fritz                 16 no. 3-4:134     BCH
Miller, George                2:445              PMO
Miller, George H              1905-06:[60]       RLW
                              [122]              RLX
_____ George Melvin         2:381              CHW
Miller, George W              3:671              BH
Miller, Helen M               26:110             PNLA
                              32 no. 1:25        PNLA
_____ Henry A               3:747              SMS
Miller, Henry B               3:67               LHC

Miller, Herbert C             1:400              GP
_____                       3:825              LHC
Miller, Howard Lloyd          4:518              PH
Miller, J    B                172-173            HA
Miller, James D               28                 LDM
Miller, Joaquin               235                DSW
_____                       4:282              LH
_____                       1 no. 4:8          PM
_____                       1:200              PMO
Miller, Mrs. Joaquin, see
   Miller, Minnie Myrtle (Dyer)
Miller, John Anthony          3:515              GP
Miller, John C                672-673            SIH
Miller, Mrs. John C      , see
   Miller, Katherine (Loeffler)
Miller, John F                unp.               SEA
                              58                 SSP
Miller, John P                2:653              GP
Miller, John Wesley           67                 AG
                              2:416              SMS
Miller, John William          294                AG
Miller, Josiah E              2:463              HHI
Miller, Katherine (Loeffler)  672-673            SIH
Miller, Leslie F              3:1146             SMS
Miller, Lewis Elmer           unp.               SOU
Miller, Lucretia, see
   Worden, Lucretia (Miller)
Miller, Mahala, see
   McBride, Mahala (Miller)
Miller, Margaret, see
   Kellogg, Margaret (Miller)
   Schmidt, Margaret (Miller)
Miller, Mary, see
   Blain, Mary (Miller)
Miller, Minnie Myrtle (Dyer)  1:204              PMO
Miller, Rachel, see
   Paulsen, Rachel (Miller)
Miller, Mrs. Robert A      , see
   Miller, Sarelia (Griffith)
Miller, Sarelia (Griffith)    1:138              PMO
Miller, Sebastian             45                 LDM
Miller, Sylvia A              1924:41            WSP
Miller, Theodor               32                 THI
Miller, Thomas Burchinal      3:763              SMS
Miller, W    A                21:160 1916        WBP
Miller, W    H                1937-38:62-63      OO
                              1939-40:31         OO
Miller, W    O                1924:113           WSP
Miller, William C             3:593              BH
                              3:671              HHT
Miller, William Winlock       3:398              SH
Miller, Winlock W             74-75              GA
_____                       unp.               WD
_____                       36:19 1935         WDT
Miller, Winlock W        , Jr.
                              46 no. 3:77        PN
Milligan, Miles W             1941:127           EN
Millikin, Earl                unp.               SEA
```

Milliner, Charles M	2:867	HHI
Million, Elmer C	2:361	HH
	1:488	PHP
Mills, A J	1895-96:101	SSS
Mills, A U	1:372	HHT
Mills, Charles F	unp.	SOU
Mills, Darius O	244	QT
Mills, James	20 no. 1-2:46	BCH
Mills, James Hamilton	153	LHM
	5:265	MC
	139	MI
Mills, John	1910:50	TDL
Mills, Roy H	1945-46:24	OO
Milne, George Lawson	4:311	BCF
	fol. pt. 1	SHB
Milne, William	4 no. 2:86	BCH
Milroy, R B	1924:65	WSP
Milroy, Robert Houston	2:74	PHP
	50 no. 4:140	PN
Mimms, Maxine	34 no. 1:33	PNLA
Minard, E L	1905-06:[54]	RLW
Miner, E P	439	LDM
Miner, Walter B	6:440-441	MC
Miner, William	290	BHSS
Minette, Charles Henry	1941:410	EN
Minkler, B D	[95]	RLX
Minor, Thomas Taylor	12:84	MWH
	1905-06:[28]	RLW
	unp.	SEA
Minsinger, C	3:293	GP
Minthorn, Sarah	416	DW
Mintie, F L	1895:103	OO
Minto, John	1:545	CHW
	1:598	GP
	1:608	NH
Minto, Mrs. M A	1:608	NH
Minugh, "Daddy"	88	NL
Mires, Austin	1905-06:[28]	RLW
	1924:41	WSP
	1926:20	WSP
Misener, Roy B	4:502	PH
Mitchell, A	172-173	HA
Mitchell, Andrew Henry	3:1097	BCF
Mitchell, Armistead Hughes	4:242	MC
	437	MI
	2:962	SM
Mitchell, Arthur Percival	1941:235	EN
Mitchell, C A	172-173	HA
Mitchell, George M	1924:97	WSP
Mitchell, Joe T	1895-96:79	SSS
Mitchell, John H	1:559	GP
	1:260	NH
	68:211	OHQ
	1895:57	OO
	221	PL
	2:460	PMO
	262	SHP
Mitchell, John H , Jr.	2:331	HH

Mitchell, John Richard	1941:103	EN
	1924:24	WSP
Mitchell, Mary Ann, see		
Davis, Mary Ann (Mitchell)		
Mitchell, Nathaniel	3:493	BCF
Mitchell, "Posey"	456	BR
Mitchell, Mrs. Rebecca	2:775	HHI
	18:48 1941-42	IH
	front.	MHS
Mitchell, S C	179	LDM
Mitchell, S T	2:front. 1924	BCHA
Mitchell, Sidney Zollicoffer	5:350	SH
Mitchell, William	247	LDM
Mitchelmore, Hugh T	66	PSW
Mitchener, J H	2:645	BHK
Mittelstadt, Ernest Edward	4:497	PH
Mixsell, F H	188	PSW
Mizner, J K	23	DH
Mo, Elmer J	2:163	SMS
Moats, Mary A , see		
Hazen, Mary A (Moats)		
Moberly, Walter	2:191, 425	BCF
	134	GI
	fol. title page	SHB
	1897:135	YB
Moceri, Peter E	3:859	BHK
Moceri, Samuel A	3:839	BHK
Mock, Fred G	2:587	HHI
Mock, John	2:675	GP
Mockler, Thomas M	232	SIH
Moeller, Wigbert	3:183	BHS
Moen, Anna, see		
Johnson, Anna (Moen)		
Moench, Carl Richard	1:unp. 1900-01	WDT
Moffat, David F	32	QT
Moffett, Tabitha, see		
Brown, Tabitha (Moffett)		
Moffett, Mrs. Walter, see		
Cartwright, Charlotte (Terwilliger)		
Moffett		
Mohn, Mathis	2:625	SMS
Mohr, Charles W	41	SCC
Mohr, Paul F	2:526	NH
Mohun, Edward	2:293	BCF
Moldstad, N J	1905-06:[62]	RLW
	193	SS
Molen, Frank	176	GL
Molen, Mrs. Frank	176	GL
Molen, Wesley	126	GL
Molt, Rudolph F W	1941:15	EN
	3:1350	SM
Monaghan, James	265	GG
	2:79	HH
	5:144	SH
Monaghan, John Robert	177	GG
	10	SCH
	5:146	SH

Mondloch J   Peter   3:1419   SM
Monohon, Lee   1:481   BHK
_____   2:867   BHK
_____   1941:177   EN
_____   3:407   PH
Monro, Alexander Stewart   3:947   BCF
_____   fol. pt. 2   SHB
Monroe, Henry   256   MI
Monroe, Mrs. N   A   1:917   LHC
Monroe, Robert Duane   24:147   PNLA
Monroe, William Newton   172-173, 205   HA
Montague, Charles B   2:446   PMO
Montague, Effie Ruth (Cochran) 2:24   CPD
Montague, Grover   2:24   CPD
Montague, Mrs. Grover, see
    Montague, Effie Ruth (Cochran)
Montague, Robert B   161   PL
Montakuli (Eskimo)   278-279   HU
Monteith, Moses (Nez Percé Indian) 212   BR
_____   127   DTI
Montgomery, Buck   60   SHO
Montgomery, Donnell R   139   PSW
Montgomery, James Boyce   2:661   LHC
_____   448   SHP
Montgomery, Maurice   6:430   MC
Montgomery, Robert   36:19 1935   WDT
Montgomery, Zachariah   912   SIH
Moody, C   S   2:361   HH
Moody, E   J   209   LDM
Moody, J   D   298   E
Moody, Malcolm A   1:28   PMO
Moody, Ralph E   1895:170   OO
Moody, Richard Clement   15 no. 1-2:90   BCH
_____   102   GI
_____   fol. title page SHB
_____   1897:63   YB
_____   1911:70-71   YB
_____   18:96 1913   WBP
_____   19:9 1914   WBP
_____   24:80 1919   WBP
Moody, Robert
Moody, William Hovey   2:421   LHC
Moody, Zenas Ferry   1:632   NH
_____   45   TUR
Mooney, Harry L   18:3 1941-42   IH
Moore, Alfred S   332   HA
Moore, Arthur H   292   HA
Moore, Charles C   2:545   HHI
_____   9:front. 1923-24 IH
Moore, Christopher Wilkinson   361   DL
_____   3:1030   FH
_____   243   IHI
Moore, Clara   48 no. 4:143   PN
Moore, Floyd   202   BHSS
Moore, I   H   19   DA
Moore, Mrs. J   2:front. 1924   BCHA
Moore, J   W   217   LDM
Moore, James A   unp.   VU
Moore, James Z   1905-06:[28]   RLW

Moore, John   2:front. 1924   BCHA
Moore, Katherine, see
    Armstrong, Katherine (Moore)
Moore, Marshall F   23   MAG
_____   34   ME
_____   34 no. 4:400-401 PN
_____   [49]   RLX
_____   unp.   SE
Moore, Miles Conway   35   MAG
_____   70   ME
_____   1:320   NH
_____   34 no. 4:400-401 PN
_____   [63]   RLX
_____   unp.   SE
_____   5:150   SH
_____   19:176 1914   WBP
Moore, R   S   1905-06:[28]   RLW
Moore, Ralph T   1943-44:79   OO
_____   1945-46:87   OO
Moore, Samuel Alfred   4:181   BCF
Moore, Samuel F   6:440-441   MC
Moore, Thomas Verner   6:339   MC
Moore, Mrs. Thomas Verner   6:339   MC
Moore, William   82   LDM
Moore, William, Crow chief   216   PI
_____   248   PIW
Moore, William H   415   LDM
Moore, William Hickman   128   E
_____   1905-06:[47]   RLW
_____   unp.   SEA
_____   58   SSP
_____   unp.   VU
Moore, William Whiteford   4:1041   BCF
Moorehead, Ann, see
    Thomas, Ann (Moorehead)
Moorehead, Elizabeth (Thomas), see
    White, Elizabeth (Thomas)
Moorehead, Mrs. James Madison, see
    White, Elizabeth (Thomas)
Moorehead, Preston   35   GL
Moores, Charles B   1895:88   OO
_____   1:306   PMO
Moores, John H   1:92   NH
Moores, Merwin M   27:5   PNLA
_____   34 no. 1:28   PNLA
Moorhead, Steele L   1895:101   OO
Moorhouse, Lee, see
    Moorhouse, Thomas Leander
Moorhouse, Thomas Leander   2:582   NH
_____   66:321   OHQ
_____   437   SK
_____   443   SKA
Moran, James   1:unp. 1900-01 WDT
Moran, Patrick   58   LDM
Moran, Robert   2:660   NH
_____   unp.   SEA
_____   1 no. 9:17   WN
Moran, Sherman   4:105   BHK

Morand, Mary C (Edwards), see
  Kellogg, Mary C (Edwards) Morand
More, Charles Church 6:31 1906 WDT
                     26:55 1925 WDT
More, Marion 144 DL
More, Robert S 1:149 BH
More, Mrs. Robert S 1:149 BH
Morehouse, Lee, see
  Moorhouse, Thomas Leander
Moreland, J C N 2:292 PMO
               334 SHP
Morey, Parker Farnsworth 554 SHP
Morey, T 2:141 BCF
Morgan, Benjamin H 1905-06:[59] RLW
Morgan, David 400 LDM
Morgan, David Bruce 3:front. BHK
Morgan, George L 3:1092 FH
Morgan, Hiram D 2:20 NH
Morgan, J W 1895-96:113 SSS
Morgan, James 278 LDM
Morgan, John T 2:463 BCF
              87 IHI
Morgan, Michael R 256 MCO
Morgan, Sadie 182-183 KO
Morgan, W H H 3:179 GP
Morgan, William McKendree 2:24 FSB
Morgans, Morgan 1905-06:[28] RLW
Moriarty, James T 260 GG
Moriarty, W D 26:56 1925 WDT
Morice, Adrien Gabriel front., 32,
              104, 208 FT
              1:front. MCC
              1:front. ML
Morison, C K 6:74 PNLA
Moritz, Robert Edouard 6:28 1906 WDT
              26:56 1925 WDT
Morrell, Mrs. Eli, see
  Hamilton, Anna (Balch) Stump Morrell
Morrell, James F 69:294 OHQ
Morrill, Charles William 3:417 HHT
Morrill, M M 1905-06:[63] RLW
Morris, Albert Alton 1941:394 EN
              2:1276 SM
Morris, Mrs. Benjamin, see
  Morris, Jennie M (Chilton) Pearce
Morris, Benjamin Wistar 1:438 GP
              21 JP
Morris, Clyde L 3:431 BHS
              278 HA
Morris, E E 113 AG
Morris, George C 134 MLO
Morris, J , see
  Rucker, J (Morris)
Morris, Jennie M (Chilton) Pearce
              3:1029 SMS
Morris, Mary Ann, see
  Thomas, Mary Ann (Morris)
Morris, Mary E , see
  Bibb, Mary E (Morris) Longanecker

Morris, O M 347 BHSS
Morris, Osborne fol. pt. 2 SHB
Morris, Richard E 211 GG
Morris, S M 11, 23, 134 MLO
Morris, Thomas B 97 DH
Morris, Will H 6:56 SH
Morris, William J 261 GG
Morrison, (Justice) 1923:15 WSP
Morrison, Alexander 3:211 BCF
Morrison, Aulay 1897:110 YB
Morrison, Daniel 189 LDM
Morrison, Ellis 1895-96:81 SSS
Morrison, Esther 66 MG
Morrison, J R 6 PIG
Morrison, James W 30 SCC
Morrison, Kenneth John 3:413 BCF
Morrison, Nancy (Irwin) 1:608 NH
Morrison, Robert Wilson 1:608 NH
Morrison, Mrs. Robert Wilson, see
  Morrison, Nancy (Irwin)
Morrow, Alan Thomas 3:391 BCF
Morrow, Bertha 42:32 1930 WSGP
Morrow, David 1011 LHM
Morrow, Mrs. David, see
  Morrow, S E (Travers)
Morrow, James W 2:450 PMO
Morrow, John L 1:220 NH
Morrow, S E (Travers) 1011 LHM
Morse, Cecil A 3:327 PH
Morse, Davis W 16 LS
Morse, Edmund 3 no. 10:469 PM
Morse, F W 2:533 BCF
Morse, George W 696 LHM
              2:878 SM
              2:280 SMS
Morse, H G 242 LDM
Morse, Olney N 2:602 NH
Morse, Raymond C 3:465 BH
Morse, Robert I 2:531 HWW
              3:325 PH
Morse, Roger 63:9 OHQ
Morse, Roy F 23 MLO
Morse, Wayne 1945-46:13 OO
Morse, William B 1941-42:66 OO
              1945-46:87 OO
Morthland, D V 1924:40 WSP
Morton, Edmund 557 SCH
Morton, John 2:431 BCF
Morton, Marcus R 1924:40 WSP
Mo-see-ma-ma-mos (Cree Indian) 391 VT
Moseley, Samuel Friend 4:377 BHK
Moser, George 48 LS
Moser, Gus C 1931-32:40 OO
Moser, William 3:1512 SM
Moser, William A 1945-46:83 OO
Moses, Sinkiuse chief 126 DTI
              3:52 FI
              2:4 NH
              70 no. 2:cover OHQ

Name	Ref	Code
————	70:156	OHQ
————	334	SK
	339	SKA
Moses, Agnes	1:368-369	EPD
Mosher, Anna, see		
Mounce, Anna (Mosher)		
Mosher, LaFayette	3:531	GP
	1:120	NH
Mosier, Jefferson N	2:461	LHC
Moss, Albert Bartlett	1:142	FSB
	2:385	HHI
Moss, D H	19:64 1914	WBP
————	24:16 1919	WBP
	25:front. 1920	WBP
Moss, Harvey Jasper	1941:66	EN
Moss, Mattie (Woodson)	1941:95	EN
Moss, Norman	473	BHSS
Moss, Preston Boyd	1941:93	EN
	2:218	SMS
Moss, Robert	473	BHSS
Moss, Sidney W	1:278	NH
Mossman, Isaac V	2:299	PMO
Mott, Elijah	133	LDM
Mott, James W	1931-32:41	OO
	1943-44:13	OO
————	1945-46:13	OO
Motte, George de la, see		
De la Motte, George		
Mottman, George A	1:432	PHP
Mouatt, William	21	LDM
Moulton, M M	1924:40	WSP
Moulton, Ralph W	50:47 1949	WDT
Moultry, William	193	JNT
Mounce, Anna (Mosher)	3:591	BCF
Mounce, J Smith	152-153	SIH
Mounce, Mrs. J Smith, see		
Mounce, Mollie (Smith)		
Mounce, Mollie (Smith)	152-153	SIH
Mounce, Richard G	3:591	BCF
Mounce, Mrs. Richard G , see		
Mounce, Anna (Mosher)		
Mounsey, James W	39	MG
Mount Stephen, George, see		
Stephen, George		
Mountain, Thomas	20	LDM
	72	PC
Mountain Chief (Blackfoot Indian)	118	LBT
Mourning Dove (Okanogan Indian)	front.	HCS
Movius, Arthur J	2:193	SMS
Mowery, C R	41	MG
Moxley, Jessie	31	THI
Moxley, Thomas C	334	BR
Moyer, Charles	59 no. 1:26	PN
Moylan, Myles	110-111	HCM
Moylan, Mrs. Myles	110-111	HCM
Moyle, John R	2:421	SMS
Mudge, Zachary	226	MV
Mudgett, George	30	SCC
Muehlenbruch, Charles T	2:453	HHT
Muehler, Carl F	3:697	BH
Muehler, Mrs. Carl F , see		
Muehler, Laura (Hunger)		
Muehler, Laura (Hunger)	3:697	BH
Muehler, Otto F	3:665	BH
Mueller, Henry	3:1303	SM
Mueller, Joseph W	3:1590	SM
Mueller, R A	3:579	BH
Muench, Louis	1 no. 8:19	WN
Muir, John, 1838-	fol. 207 (no. 18)	SHI
Muir, John	1897:132	YB
Muir, Samuel Alexander	3:1139	BCF
Muir, Thomas	1:29 1923	BCHA
Muirhead, J McL	2:front. 1924	BCHA
Mulhall, Emmet L	247	GG
Mulkey, Benjamin F	2:453	PMO
Mulkey, Fred W	2:177	GP
	99	PL
Mulkey, Portia E (Butler)	2:259	CHW
Mulkey, W J	2:259	CHW
Mulkey, Mrs. W J , see		
Mulkey, Portia E (Butler)		
Mullan, John	123	BHSI
	3:148	FI
————	160	MCO
Mulligan, William G	247	GG
Mulliner, Joseph S	3:763	HHI
Mulliner, Samuel	149	GL
Mullins, Patrick	4:719	PH
Mult-no-mah (Molalla Indian)	1:526	PMO
Mulvaney, William Joseph	1941:212	EN
Mumby, Samuel C	3:279	PH
Mumm, Hans	206, 408	BHSS
Munday, Charles F	3 no. 8:426	PM
	1923:65	WSP
Munger, Susan, see		
Gussenhoven, Susan (Munger		
Munks, William	1:85	HH
	1:280	NH
Munly, Michael G	3:165	GP
	2:149	LHC
Munro, Alex	2:front. 1924	BCHA
Munro, George	3:459	BCF
Munro, Hugh	10:20	MC
Munro, Kathleen	24:147	PNLA
Munroe, Christina (Stanger)	2:691	LHC
	1937-38:62-63	OO
————	1939-40:31	OO
Munroe, W F	132	JNT
	219	LDM
Munroe, Mrs. William, see		
Munroe, Christina (Stanger)		
Munsie, William	428	LDM
Munson, Charles J	712	SIH
Munson, J D	162	LDM
Munson, Jasper Paul	3:472	BEA
Munson, Lyman E	5:200, 229	MC
Munson, Samuel Fred	4:397	BCF

Munson, Sarah (Kimball)	87	CW
Munyan, T W	1935-36:51	OO
Murane, Cornelius D	344	HA
Murdock, John R	157	GL
Murdock, Orrace	51	GL
Murdoff, M L	fol. pt. 2	SHB
Murieta, Joaquin	104	SW
Murn, William P	3:1449	SM
Murphey, Alonzo M	2:205	HH
Murphy, Charles Francis	2:267	SMS
Murphy, Chester J	3:1369	SM
Murphy, Claude	1945-46:51	OO
Murphy, Daniel Timothy	3:751	HHI
Murphy, Mrs. Frank, see		
Wood, Katherine (Veit) Hagenbarth Murphy		
Murphy, George	60	HA
Murphy, J Harold	6:415	MC
Murphy, James Hennesy	3:691	GP
Murphy, Jesse F	1895-96:133	SSS
Murphy, John P	151	GG
Murphy, John P , Jr.	255	GG
Murphy, Mrs. Mary	2:front. 1924	BCHA
Murphy, Patrick Charles	front.	MB
	175	MSG
Murphy, W. J	1924:97	WSP
Murphy, William Larkin	1941:32	EN
Murray, A P	21:160 1916	WBP
Murray, Alexander Hunter	266	MH
Murray, Alexander Sinclair	33	LDM
Murray, Barnard W	1019	LHM
Murray, Charles Arthur	2:567	HHT
	6:66	SH
Murray, David	2:150	NH
Murray, George	fol. title page	SHB
Murray, Hazen T	128	PSW
Murray, John Edward	2:910	SM
Murray, John L	1895-96:101	SSS
Murray, Walter C	1:634	BCF
Murray, William	2:front. 1924	BCHA
Murtha, James	151	OB
Murtha, M	151	OB
Muscek, Louis J	3:551	HHT
Musgrave, Anthony	1:510	BCF
	2:277	BCF
	fol. title page	SHB
	96-97	SHL
	1897:63	YB
	1911:70-71	YB
Musket, H J S	2:19 1924	BCHA
Mutter, James Mitchell	1897:108	YB
Myers, Adolphus D	2:109	SMS
Myers, Alexander	43 no. 1:16-17	PN
Myers, Barbara	124	DD
Myers, Harold Bunce	1941:342	EN
Myers, Ira	758	MI
Myers, Jefferson D	70:224	OHQ
Myers, Sam	456	BR
Myers, William H	1168	SIH
Myers, William Henry Harrison	1:570	GP
Myhre, Anna	12	SS
Mylar, Rachel, see		
Kindred, Rachel (Mylar)		
Myrick, Josiah	3:449	GP

N

Nadeau, I A	4 no. 6:172	PM
	May 1907:37	TDL
	1 no. 2:60	WM
	1 no. 5:352	WM
	unp.	VU
Nadeau, Joseph A	2:1080	SM
Nadstanek, Valentine	2:233	CHW
Naftzger, Ernest Carter	3:190	BEA
Nagle, Ellen (Healy)	402-403	PI
	472	PIW
Nagle, Mrs. George, see		
Nagle, Ellen (Healy)		
Nagle, John C	137	GL
Nailor, C Elmer	4:635	PH
Nalder, F F	539	BHSS
Nanamkin, George	48 no. 4:143	PN
Nanamkin, Mrs. Nancy	67:348	OHQ
Napoleon Maquinna, Nootka chief		
	2:19 1924	BCHA
Nash, Herbert O	6:398	MC
Nash, L D	1931-32:41	OO
	1939-40:31	OO
Natawista Iksana (Blood Indian), see		
Culbertson, Natawista Iksana		
Nathan, Henry	1897:42	YB
Nathoy, Polly, see		
Bemis, Polly (Nathoy)		
Natsape, Nootka chief	54 no. 4:151	PN
Naubert, C A E	2:397	HHT
Naughten, James	1 no. 10:11	WN
Navarro, Jose	3:335	HHI
Naylor, Nelle	207	BHSS
Neace, Lewis	1905-06:[28]	RLW
Neal, C H	unp.	SOU
Neal, Frank C	1924:65	WSP
Neal, George S	44:338	OHQ
Neal, Horace E	447	IHI
Neal, James R	1924:80	WSP
Neal, William B	2:97	CHW
Neale, Harry Burrard	2:149	BCF
	188	MV
Needham, Harry L	32	SCC
Needham, Joseph	2:653	BCF
	fol. pt. 1	SHB
	1911:70-71	YB
Neely, David A	2:142	NH
Neely, David F	2:887	BHK

Neff, Nelson B	3:298	PH
Negler, Mima (Kimball)	135	CW
Neher, John A	2:336	PHP
Neil, James N	3:681	HHT
Neill, John Selby Martin	2:1257	SM
Neill, Thomas	58	BHSS
	3:270	PH
Nelems, Mary Ann, see		
Kipp, Mary Ann (Nelems)		
Nelsen, Herman	48:296 1936	WSGP
Nelsen, Lloyd Lawrence	3:399	BEA
Nelson, A	431	LDM
Nelson, A M	2:139	BCF
Nelson, Aaron H	187	MI
Nelson, Abraham	788	HIO
Nelson, Andrew K	2:337	CHW
Nelson, Mrs. Andrew K , see		
Nelson, Christina (Olson)		
Nelson, Charles P	unp.	SOU
Nelson, Christina (Olson)	2:337	CHW
Nelson, E G	3:147	HHI
Nelson, Mrs. E G , see		
Nelson, Josephine (Lake)		
Nelson, Edward W fol. 207 (no. 21)		SHI
Nelson, Edwin	3:318	BEA
Nelson, Emil J	3:185	BHK
Nelson, George	3:101	BHK
Nelson, Hugh	2:281	BCF
	36	KB
	fol. pt. 1	SHB
	1897:63	YB
	1911:70-71	YB
Nelson, Jack	396, 407	BHSS
Nelson, John Holt	unp.	SOU
Nelson, Josephine (Lake)	3:147	HHI
Nelson, Milton N	1945-46:182	OO
Nelson, N B	63	SS
Nelson, Nels	3:111	BCF
Nelson, Nels B	2:293	BHK
Nelson, S B	215, 529	BHSS
Nelson, Sallie, see		
Whitcomb, Sallie (Nelson)		
Nelson, Sarah Ann, see		
Peterson, Sarah Ann (Nelson)		
Nelson, Sofus B	1905-06:[51]	RLW
Nelson, Soren	2:486	SMS
Nelson, Thomas	2:835	FH
Nelson, Victor J	1935-36:51	OO
Nerny, T J	3:1731	SM
Nesbitt, John Franklin	2:685	HHI
Nesbitt, Mrs. John Franklin, see		
Nesbitt, Mary J (Stuart)		
Nesbitt, Mary J (Stuart)	2:685	HHI
Nesbitt, Milton S	2:763	HHI
Nesdale, Seraphin	151	OB
Nesmith, James W	641	CHO
	1:415	CHW
	3:332	LH
	1:64	NH
	1:182	PMO
	55 no. 4:172	PN
	2:244	SH
	82	WRE
Ne-sou-a-Quoit, Fox chief	99	GBS
Nester, Patrick Henry	2:731	LHC
Nettles, James A	29	DA
Nettleton, Stiles R	1895-96:103	SSS
Neuberger, Richard L	1941-42:66	OO
	55 no. 2:58, 61	PN
Neubert, John	3:662	SMS
Neufelder, A E	1905-06:[68]	RLW
Neuhausen, Thomas Brues	2:305	GP
	68:129	OHQ
	34	PL
Neuner, George	1945-46:29	OO
Nevin, Charles P	2:386	SMS
Nevins, George F	44:338	OHQ
Nevius, Charles F	1910:52	TDL
Nevius, Reuben Denton	26	JP
Newbegin, Edward	2:821	LHC
Newbry, Earl T	1939-40:31	OO
	1941-42:66	OO
	1943-44:75	OO
	1945-46:83	OO
Newburn, Harry K	1945-46:69	OO
Newcombe, Charles Frederick	2:19 1924	BCHA
Newell, Bernice E	2:80	HHT
	1910:33	TDL
Newell, John H	2:151	SMS
Newell, Robert	111	BHSI
	158	DTI
	1:20	NH
Newell, William Augustus	29	MAG
	52	ME
	34 no. 4:400-401	PN
	[57]	RLX
	unp.	SE
Newhall, Frank H	315	LDM
Newhouse, Dean	36:24 1935	WDT
	50:24 1949	WDT
Newland, Annie F , see		
Benson, Annie F (Newland)		
Newman, Andrew Jackson	3:1037	FH
Newman, Charles H	2:894-895	SM
Newman, Jack	50	AL
Newman, Mrs. Jack	50	AL
Newman, Orson N	2:894-895	SM
Newman, Oscar Palmer	3:23	BEA
Newman, Thomas G	176	E
Newman, W B D	2:390	NH
Newman, W E	39	MG
Newman, W M	37	MG
Newsome, Edward B	3:90	BEA
Newton, Emmeline Jane (Tod)		
	18 no. 3-4:145	BCH
Newton, W L	1905-06:[28]	RLW

Newton, William	front.	NT
Newton, Mrs. William H , see		
Newton, Emmeline Jane (Tod)		
Nibbe, John H	360	LDM
Nichol, Walter Cameron	2:19 1924	BCHA
	3:14 1925	BCHA
_____		
Nicholls, Andy	193	PL
Nichols, Ammi Sibley	2:213	GP
Nichols, B F	1931-32:41	OO
Nichols, Edward	172	LDM
Nichols, Mary, see		
Farquharson, Mary (Nichols)		
Nichols, Melville	374	LDM
Nichols, Mid	182-183	KO
Nichols, R J	2:432	PMO
Nichols, Ralph D	[93]	RLX
Nichols, Samuel H	2:112	PHP
	6:214	SH
_____		
Nicholson, Anna, see		
Bridger, Anna (Nicholson)		
Nicholson, Carl A	43 no. 2:136-137	PN
Nicholson, J A	2:270	LHC
Nicholson, Mrs. J A , see		
Nicholson, Marcia Maie (Rust)		
Nicholson, Joseph	4:1183	BCF
Nicholson, Marcia Maie (Rust)	2:271	LHC
Nicholson, Mike	182-183	KO
Nicholson, N J	172-173	HA
Nicholson, Niles Henry	4:483	PH
Nichter, Matt	3:311	HHI
Nickell, Charles	2:600	NH
Nickerson, Mahala, see		
George, Mahala (Nickerson)		
Nicklas, Joseph	4:245	BHK
Nicklason, G	174	SS
Nicolai, Louis	3:315	GP
Nicolle, J J	2:83	CHW
Niendorff, Fred	114	BCN
Nienhuis, Annie (Van Lente)	3:353	PH
Nienhuis, Charles E	3:353	PH
Nienhuis, Mrs. Charles E , see		
Nienhuis, Annie (Van Lente)		
Niesz, U R	3:291	BHS
Night-Gypsy (Blood Indian)	127	GI
Nightingale, William	85	LDM
Nims, L B	1895-96:103	SSS
Ninnevoo, Ira	387	BF
Nirk, Durell Irwin	3:166	BEA
Niskanen, William	1943-44:79	OO
	1945-46:87	OO
_____		
Nissen, Jerry	290	BHSS
Nissler, Chris	311	MI
Nixon, Edmund E	4:633	BCF
Nixon, Oliver Woodson	front.	NW
Nixon, P Thomas	234	HA
Nixon, T L	1:372	HHT
Noble, Clymer Marlay	3:495	LHC
Noble, D W	24:128 1919	WBP
Noble, Osee W	1924:97	WSP
Noble, Robert	2:789	FH
	2:77	HHI
_____	530	IHI
Noble, Robert Baxter	1941:143	EN
Noble, T A	42 no. 2:112	PN
Noggle, May, see		
McGlinchey, May (Noggle) Alvord		
Nogleberg, John	82	SS
Nohle, Andrew F	3:988	SMS
No-Horns-On-His-Head (Nez Percé Indian)		
	20	AC
_____	250	BR
_____	2:124-125	CN
_____	94-95	DGC
_____	82	DS
_____	38	FW
_____	314	NM
_____	1:121	PHP
Nolan, Barney	234	FF
Nolan, Cornelius B	4:72	MC
	3:1353	SM
_____		
Nolan, S M	1:534	HHT
Noland, Pleasant Calvin	1:596	NH
Nolte, G C	1924:81	WSP
Noon, William C	586	SHP
Noonan, William	499	LHM
Nooy, Otto	151, 159, 167	OB
Norblad, Albin W	77	TUR
Norblad, Walter	1935-36:51	OO
	1937-38:62-63	OO
_____		
Nordby, Herman	32	THI
Nordby, Mrs. Herman	31	THI
Nordquist, John H	1072	SIH
Nordtome, Robert	3:841	SMS
Norman, J Arthur	2:901	LHC
Norris, Alexander	7:83	MC
Norris, Leonard	fol. pt. 1	SHB
Norrise, Charlotte, see		
Brown, Charlotte (Norrise)		
North, Austin	3:1137	SMS
North, George	3:134	HHI
North, Mrs. George, see		
North, Peronne Hall (Church)		
North, J A	2:94	SMS
North, Peronne Hall (Church)	3:135	HHI
Northcutt, Edward J	176	SIH
Northrup, E R	37	MG
Northrup, Edward James	2:8, 339	PMO
	354	SHP
_____		
Northrup, Mrs. Edward James, see		
Northrup, Frances C (McNamee)		
Northrup, Frances C (McNamee)	2:8	PMO
Northup, Henry H	498	SHP
Norton, Arthur D	3:1041	FH
Norton, Caroline, see		
Norton, Caroline (Norton)		

Norton, Caroline (Norton) 2:496 NH
Norton, Delbert A 1935-36:51 OO
     1937-38:62-63 OO
_____
Norton, Isabell, see
     Judd, Isabell (Norton)
Norton, J E 1931-32:41 OO
Norton, John C 3:141 BHS
Norton, Mrs. John C , see
     Norton, M A (Widger)
Norton, John W 3:77 HHI
Norton, M A (Widger) 3:140 BHS
Norton, Z C 2:658 NH
Norton, Mrs. Z C , see
     Norton, Caroline (Norton)
Norval, John W 1:184 NH
Nostrand, Howard Lee 50:38 1949 WDT
Notbohm, L R 252 E
Notestein, Frank N 6:386 MC
Nottingham, C W 2:441 PMO
Nourse, Robert L 385 IHI
Noyes, Allen 199 LDM
Noyes, Arthur H 172-173 HA
     340 WOY
_____
Noyes, John 163 LHM
Noyes, T C 172-173 HA
Nozer, Mrs. Joe (Spokan Indian) 79 DS
Nugent, James 3:205 BHK
Numbers, Joseph R 458 IHI
Nunamaker, James R 2:791 LHC
Nutting, Lucius Allison 2:257 SMS
Nutting, W B 2:50 SMS
Nuzum, N E 253 E
Nye, Helena, see
     Cusick, Helena (Nye)
Nylund, Ander Victor 53 no. 4:153 PN

O

Oakes, Prescott 3:769 BHS
Oakes, Walter 5:408 SH
Oakland, August 908 SIH
Oakley, Charles H 3:715 HHI
Oakley, Frank D 3:615 BH
Oatman, Harrison B 2:42 NH
     60:95 OHQ
_____
     460 SHP
Oatman, Mrs. Harrison B , see
     Oatman, Lucena K (Ross)
Oatman, Lucena K (Ross) 2:42 NH
Oben, Phillip 3:957 BCF
Ober, Caroline Haven 1:unp. 1900-01 WDT
     6:24 1906 WDT
Oberholtzer, Clarence M 2:415 HHI
Obermeyer, Henry 3:209 HHI
Oboler, Eli M 20:79 PNLA
     21:31 PNLA
     32 no. 1:24 PNLA
O'Boyle, James 3:976 SMS
O'Brien, Charles Edward 1895-96:149 SSS
O'Brien, Charles Maurice 1943:72 ENC
O'Brien, Harry G 9, 15 SSP
O'Brien, James P 2:45 GP
O'Brien, John A 324 LDM
O'Brien, John J 928 SIH
O'Brien, John T 254 E
O'Brien, Laurence 1895-96:135 SSS
O'Brien, Michael T 2:541 SMS
O'Brien, R G 1895-96:42 SSS
O'Brien, William S 224 QT
O'Connell, Michael J 2:434 SMS
O'Connell, William H 3:1323 SMS
O'Connor, Dominic 159 OB
O'Connor, James 346 PI
O'Connor, John A 167 OB
O'Connor, Louise 66 MG
O'Connor, Margaret, see
     Russell, Margaret (O'Connor)
O'Connor, Thomas Arthur 3:713 BCF
O'Connor, Thomas F 2:549 SMS
O'Day, Thomas 129, 167 PL
O'Dea, Edward John 2:419 BHK
     3:331 BHS
_____
     7 GG
_____
     182 SG
_____
     5:190 SH
Odegaard, Charles E 120-121 GA
     24:147, 272 PNLA
_____
Odel, Isaac 158 LDM
Odell, J M 1945-46:62 OO
Odermatt, Adelhelm 70:331 OHQ
Odin, Frank 233 LDM
Odin, George 208 LDM
Odle, V A 41 MG
Odlum, Edward 4:337 BCF
     fol. pt. 1 SHB
_____
O'Donnell, Charles 2:311 SMS
O'Donnell, J R 1905-06:[43] RLW
Oechsli, George R 3:1398 SM
Oelbaum, Henry 239 HA
O'Farrell, J P 255 E
O'Farrell, John Andrew 2:662-663 FH
     716 IHI
_____
O'Farrell, Mrs. John Andrew, see
     O'Farrell, Mary Ann (Chapman)
O'Farrell, Mary Ann (Chapman) 2:662-663 FH
Offner, W S 219 PSW
Ogden, George R 156 PL
Ogden, I G 234 GI
Ogden, Peter Skene 17 no. 3-4:161 BCH
     67 BF
_____
     67 BHSI
_____
     2:626 CAFT

_____	458	CIR
_____	286	EW
_____	2:40	FI
_____	167	MHN
_____	35:93	OHQ
_____	51 no. 1:18	PN
_____	2:334	SH
_____	259	WCS
Ogden, Raymond Davis	3:382	PH
Ogle, Van	1:203	BH
Ogriz, John	1943:190	ENC
O'Hagan, James A	167	OB
O'Hanlon, Thomas	157	GG
O'Hara, Bernard	2:751	GP
O'Hara, Charles	282	LDM
O'Hare, John	3:697	GP
O'Keefe, Cornelius	fol. title page	SHB
Olander, O E	409	AG
Olatalkt, Ipnats, see		
Minthorn, Sarah		
Olcott, Ben W	57:314	OHQ
	69	TUR
Old Ignace (Flathead Indian)	20	PI
Old Jake (Klikitat Indian), see		
Tonetex, Hunt (Klikitat Indian)		
Old Johnny Price, see		
Price, Johnny		
Old Joseph, see		
Tuekakas, Nez Percé chief		
Old Peter (Aleut)	12	BET
Old Solomon	149	DE
Old Whitehead, see		
Ogden, Peter Skene		
Oldham, Mary (Smith)	3:484-485	BEA
Oldham, Mrs. Volney Lee, see		
Oldham, Mary (Smith)		
Olds, F T	1:534	HHT
Olds, Fred W	4:660	PH
Olds, Mrs. George, see		
King, Sarah (Fairbanks) Olds		
Olds, William Parker	2:401	GP
	2:350	PMO
O'Leary, (Captain)	439	LDM
O'Leary, Alice M (Hope)	3:1625	SM
O'Leary, John J	3:1625	SM
O'Leary, Mrs. John J , see		
O'Leary, Alice M (Hope)		
Oleen, O Henry	1935-36:51	OO
	1937-38:62-63	OO
Oleson, Frank	3:541	BHS
	88	SS
Olinger, Amanda C , see		
Patterson, Amanda C (Olinger)		
Oliphant, U S	168	BHSS
Oliver, J L	173	LDM
Oliver, John	4:959	BCF
	186	JAC
Ollokot, Nez Percé chief		
	fol. 705 (no. 19)	JO
Olmstead, Mrs. Hannah J	1:128	NH
Olmstead, Roy	54 no. 3:90, 100	PN
Olmsted, R W	11, 15	SSP
Olmsted, Thomas D	3:1608	SM
Olney, Cyrus	64:308	OHQ
Olney, Hiram J	359	LDM
Olney, Kane	253	LDM
Olney, Nathan	64:308	OHQ
O'Loughlin, James	2:162	NH
Olsen, Andrew P	3:525	BH
Olson, Andrew	1905-06:[64]	RLW
	[119]	RLX
Olson, Anna, see		
Fjeld, Anna (Olson)		
Harold, Anna (Olson)		
Olson, Christina, see		
Nelson, Christina (Olson)		
Olson, Henry	[73]	HN
Olson, Mathilde (Johnson)	3:267	BHK
Olson, Olaf	3:266	BHK
Olson, Mrs. Olaf, see		
Olson, Mathilde (Johnson)		
Olson, Olavea, see		
Gilsdorf, Olavea (Olson)		
Olson, Raymond	1945-46:12, 210	OO
Olson, S B	172-173	HA
O'Malley, Henry	4:453	PH
O'Meara, Arthur Eugene	58 no. 2:93	PN
Onderdonk, Andrew	185	GI
	49 no. 4:147	PN
Onderdonk, James L	22	HIT
Oneal, Oren	1 no. 6:fol. 524	WM
O'Neil, Daniel	29	LDM
	1:473	PMO
O'Neil, David	256	E
O'Neil, Desmond J	231	GG
O'Neil, Ernest C	6:424-425	MC
O'Neil, William N	fol. pt. 2	SHB
O'Neill, Daniel, see		
O'Neil, Daniel		
O'Neill, Edward J	3:1462	SM
O'Neill, F W	37	MG
O'Neill, James	1:211	HH
O'Neill, John J	3:1688	SM
O'Neill, Michael	319	LDM
Onken, Al	257	E
Onstad, Albert H	1943:186	ENC
Oppenheimer, David	258	KB
Oppenheimer, S S	37	MG
O-push-y-e-cut, see		
Looking Glass, Sr., Nez Percé chief		
Orchard, Ernest Albert	3:877	BCF
Orchard, Harry	59 no. 1:26	PN
Ordway, Eliot	1:254	PMO
Ordway, June MacMillan	1:603	GP
Ordway, Lizzie W	200	BE
Orego, Anne Christine, see		
Hammer, Anne Christine (Orego)		
O'Reilly, Arthur John	fol. pt. 1	SHB
O'Reilly, Charles Joseph	4	OB

Name	Reference	Source
	182	SG
O'Reilly, Drake C	3:715	GP
O'Reilly, Francis Joseph	fol. pt. 1	SHB
O'Reilly, Peter	2:191	BCF
	fol. title page	SHB
	1897:43, 135	YB
Orme, Samuel W	2:959	HHI
Ormsby, Salmon B	143	PL
Ormsby, Sophie	410	BHSS
Orndorff, Clarence A	260	GG
Orndorff, William R	151	GG
O'Rourke, Dennis	151	GG
O'Rourke, John K	3:1541	SM
	2:443	SMS
O'Rourke, Patrick Joseph	151, 167	OB
Orr, Edward S	1895-96:155	SSS
Orr, James	1897:42	YB
Orr, Jane, see		
Cochran, Jane (Orr)		
Orr, Lewis David	3:689	BCF
Orr, Mattie, see		
Jensen, Mattie (Orr)		
Orr, Sample	6:468	MC
Orr, William C	2:1042	SM
Orsdel, William Wesley van, see		
Van Orsdel, William Wesley		
Orton, Charles Wait	3:651	BH
	1 no. 2:26	WN
Orton, George M	2:434	PMO
Orton, Ira D	172-173, 334	HA
Osborn, Burr	14:355	OHQ
Osborn, Caroline, see		
Campbell, Caroline (Osborn)		
Osborn, Frederick Arthur	6:25 1906	WDT
Osborn, G	172-173	HA
Osborn, Richard	2:325	HH
	781	HI
Osborn, William T	1:392	NH
Osborne, Nancy A , see		
Jacobs, Nancy A (Osborne)		
Osborne, W R	1935-36:51	OO
	1939-40:31	OO
Osenbrug, Jacob	2:1128	SM
	2:451	SMS
Osgood, Frank Hines	1:515	BHK
	2:812	BHS
	5:332	SH
O'Shea, John Henry	37	MG
	195	GG
O'Shea, Richard J	157	GG
O'Shea, William H	231	GG
Osmond, Jonathan	36	PSW
Osseward, Cornelius	3:337	BHS
Ostner, Charles Leopold	1:169	HHI
	3:165	HHI
Ostrander, Benjamin R	26	SCC
Ostrander, Ernest J	3:930	FH
O'Sullivan, John	fol. pt. 2	SHB
Ott, Emma, see		
Ray, Emma (Ott) Corbett		
Ott, Lawrence	512	SIH
Otten, Elise (Ranges)	2:121	SMS
Otten, Herman	2:120	SMS
Otten, Mrs. Herman, see		
Otten, Elise (Ranges)		
Ottley, Montague Robert	4:899	BCF
Outman, W D	408	BHSS
Ovall, John	409	AG
Ovens, Thomas	4:647	BCF
Overholser, Joel F	unp.	HOF
Overman, Alice (Watson)	1:154-155	EPD
Overman, Mrs. Cyrus, see		
Overman, Alice (Watson)		
Overton, Eugene E	4:600	PH
Owen, Edwin Stanton	2:727	HHI
Owens, Berthina Angelina, see		
Adair, Berthina Angelina (Owens)		
Owens, James W F	2:426	NH
Owens, Jim	176-177	GA
Owens, Sank	144	DL
Owens, Mrs. Sarah	2:426	NH
Owens, Thomas	2:426	NH
Owens, Warren S	34 no. 1:45	PNLA
Ow-hi, Yakima chief	fol. 705 (no. 13)	JO
	115	SK
	116	SKA
	52	WCS
Owings, Frank C	1924:49	WSP
Owkwowin (Eskimo)	278-279	HU
Owl, Frell MacDonald (Cherokee Indian)	19	BEA
Owsley, Barney, see		
Owsley, T W		
Owsley, T W	92	BR
Oxman, C H	1931-32:41	OO
Ozment, G W	1:488	NH

P

Name	Reference	Source
Pacha, see		
Red Plume, Flathead chief		
Packenham, Bethel	23:6 1951-52	IHD
Packwood, W H	287	E
Padden, Stanley J	231	GG
Paddock, John Adams	1:352	HHT
	25	JP
Padelford, Frederick Morgan	120-121	GA
	26:57 1925	WDT
	36:23 1935	WDT
Paduano, Joe	3:849	BHK
Page, E M	1945-46:92	OO
Page, J Henry	2:317	GP
Page, James M	2:984	SM

Pahkatos Qoh Qoh, see
   Five Crows, Cayuse chief

Paige, H B	1 no. 2:21	WN
Paine, Karl	1:76	FSB
Painter, J R	2:144-145	EPD

Painter, Margaretta, see
   Schnebly, Margaretta (Painter)

Palchina, Flathead chief

	fol. 512 (no. 19)	BUR
Palladino, Lawrence Benedict	141	GG
_____	xxii-xxiii, 364, 366	PI
	x-xi, 432, 436	PIW
Palliser, John	110	GI
Palmer, Alfred Lee	3:57	BHS
	5:292	SH
Palmer, Algernon Judson	4:463	BCF
Palmer, Allen Barnes	3:725	SMS

Palmer, Mrs. Allen Barnes, see
   Palmer, Wealthy (Titus)

Palmer, C H	505	MI
Palmer, D A	41	MG
Palmer, Edward B	1905-06:[42]	RLW
	1924:48	WSP
Palmer, Grace	42:32 1930	WSGP

Palmer, Harriette, see
   Crabbe, Harriette (Palmer)

Palmer, Hartwell W	3:611	HHT
	1910:13	TDL
Palmer, J F	172-173	HA
Palmer, Joel	3:398	LH
	1:667	LHC
	1:168	NH

Palmer, Mrs. Joel, see
   Palmer, Sarah A   (Derbyshire)

Palmer, John Foster (Chemakum Indian)	188	ET
Palmer, Richard Mason	fol. pt. 2	SHB
Palmer, Sarah A (Derbyshire)	1:168	NH
Palmer, Wealthy (Titus)	3:725	SMS
Palmer, William F	fol. pt. 2	SHB
Palmer, William J	32	QT

Palouse Kamaiakan, see
   Tesh Palouse Kamaiakan

Pambrun, Maria, see
   Barclay, Maria (Pambrun)

Pamphlet, Thomas	140	LDM
Pandosy, Charles	175	WCS
Pantages, Alexander	57 no. 4:139	PN
Panter, Harry W	1943:157	ENC
Pape, Henry	399	LDM
Pape, Matthew H	3:913	FH
Paquet, Peter	1:532	NH
Parchen, Henry M	14 no. 3:264	MWH
	2:927	SM

Pardee, Jo, see
   Hallauer, Josephine (Pardee)

Pardun, David	195	LDM
Parish, Herbert	unp.	SAA
Park, George Hamilton	4:347	BHK
Park, Lucia (Darling)	5:187	MC

Park, Mrs. S   W , see
   Park, Lucia (Darling)

Parke, Philip	fol. title page	SHB
Parker, Aaron F	205	BR
_____	266	DSW
_____	286	HIT
	12:118 1929-30	IH
Parker, Blanche (Burnett)	1:11	D
Parker, Cyrus J	2:281	LHC
Parker, Emmett N	1922:34	WSP
Parker, Fred	1924:160	WSP
Parker, George LeRoy	86-87	KO
Parker, Hollon	1:175	HH
Parker, J G	55	LDM

Parker, Mrs. John Allen, see
   Parker, Blanche (Burnett)

Parker, John Allen	1:385	HH
_____	1:520	PHP

Parker, Matilda K , see
   Graves, Matilda K   (Parker)

Parker, Mertie	258	FF
Parker, Samuel	93, 197	DS
_____	26	EW
_____	1:28	NH
_____	1:469	PMO
Parker, Wilder W	1:524	NH

Parkhurst, Anna, see
   Stafford, Anna (Parkhurst)

Parkin, George	2:844-845	FH
_____	2:739	HHI

Parkin, Mrs. George, see
   Parkin, Sarah (Wilkinson)

Parkin, Sarah (Wilkinson)	2:844-845	FH
_____	2:739	HHI
Parkinson, Thomas	1943-44:75	OO
_____	1945-46:83	OO
Parkinson, W J	3 no. 9:439	PM
Parkison, W H	4:229	MC
Parks, Edwin B	2:451	CHW
Parks, Julia (West)	3:377	HHI
Parks, Samuel C	190	BHSI
Parks, William	3:376	HHI

Parks, Mrs. William, see
   Parks, Julia (West)

Parnell, W R	54	BN
Parr, Thelma (Cayuse Indian)	[13]	HN
Parr, William	348	JNT
Parrett, R D	45	LHN
Parrett, Mrs. R D	45	LHN
Parrington, Vernon Louis	120-121	GA
_____	44 no. 3:100	PN
_____	53 no. 3:107	PN
Parrish, Josiah L	1:32	NH
_____	6	OS
_____	1:410	PMO

Parrott, Catharine, see		
Rhoades, Catharine (Parrott)		
Parry, R P	3:517	BEA
Parry, Will H	unp.	VU
Parshley, Tamson, see		
Egan, Tamson (Parshley)		
Parson, A C	2:481	BHK
Parson, Henry G	1911:70-71	YB
Parsons, A H	177	PL
Parsons, Benjamin	104	PSW
Parsons, Berkley J	2:1226	SM
Parsons, Galusha	5:260	SH
Parsons, Harry H	3:1683	SM
Parsons, John	306	AC
Parsons, Reginald Hascall	4:13	BHK
————	3:147	BHS
————	1941:56	EN
————	3:58	PH
Parsons, Robert (Nez Percé Indian) 212		BR
————	127	DTI
Partridge, Emily Dow, see		
Young, Emily Dow (Partridge)		
Partridge, Frank	2:front. 1924	BCHA
Pascoe, Richard H	1120	SIH
Passmore, John W	6:382-383	MC
Patch, Leroy Vernon	3:340	BEA
————	2:591	FH
————	2:185	HHI
Paterson, James Venn	6:90	SH
Paterson, Thomas Frank	3:11	BCF
————	fol. pt. 2	SHB
Paterson, Thomas Wilson	2:281	BCF
————	fol. pt. 1	SHB
————	1911:6-7, 70-71	YB
Patkanim, Snoqualmie chief	1:76	NH
Patrick, Archibald Stewart	2:193	HWW
Patrick, H C	1:372	HHT
————	2:164	HHT
Patrick, Joseph	fol. pt. 2	SHB
Patten, Charles Edward	4:75	BHK
————	5:358	SH
Patten, Edwin H van, see		
Van Patten, Edwin H		
Patten, L W fol. title page		SHB
Patterson, (Captain)	167	LDM
Patterson, A W	1:104	NH
Patterson, Alexander R	6:382-383	MC
Patterson, Alvah W	1895:172	OO
Patterson, Amanda C (Olinger)	2:479	CHW
Patterson, Andrew W	2:479	CHW
Patterson, Mrs. Andrew W , see		
Patterson, Amanda C (Olinger)		
Patterson, Carrie (Hurst)	2:1268	SM
Patterson, Dugald Campbell	4:811	BCF
Patterson, Isaac Lee	1895:83	OO
————	75	TUR
Patterson, James O	2:1268	SM
Patterson, Mrs. James O , see		
Patterson, Carrie (Hurst)		

Patterson, Lee	1943-44:75	OO
————	1945-46:83	OO
Patterson, Orin L	1895:108	OO
Patterson, Paul L	1945-46:83	OO
————	96	TUR
Patterson, W H	236	LDM
Patterson, W J	16:137 1911	WBP
————	17:front. 1912	WBP
————	18:23 1913	WBP
Pattison, John	1:440	NH
Patton, B M	1937:3	S
Patton, Edward Burrell	3:232	BEA
Patton, F R	39	MG
Patton, H W	2:283	HWW
Patton, M M	37	MG
Patton, Matthew	1:456	GP
————	1:644	NH
Patton, Mrs. Matthew, see		
Patton, Mrs. Polly G		
Patton, Mrs. Polly G	1:644	NH
Patton, Priscilla, see		
Watson, Priscilla (Patton)		
Patton, Thomas McF	1:356	NH
Pattullo, Alexander Smith	1943:224	ENC
Patullo, Thomas Dufferin	218	JAC
Paul, C E	2:373	HH
Paul, George	3:833	SMS
Paul, George W	2:883	FH
Paul, John P	2:277	HH
Paul Miki, Sister	124	PI
Paulhamus, W H	55 no. 1:20	PN
————	[87]	RLX
————	1910:51	TDL
Paulsen, Albert Walter	3:194-195	BEA
Paulsen, Mrs. Albert Walter, see		
Paulsen, Rachel (Miller)		
Paulsen, Rachel (Miller)	3:194-195	BEA
Pauly, Fred M	1905-06:[46]	RLW
————	[102]	RLX
Pauly, Peter	2:340	SMS
Pauwelyn, Cyril	310, 366	PI
————	352, 436	PIW
————	2:214	SMS
Pavel, Frank	32	THI
Paxton, Henry	431	LDM
Paxton, Ossian Franklin	2:539	GP
————	1895:103	OO
Payne, Clifton E	64:324	OHQ
Payne, Martin	2:250	NH
Payne, Roy Alpha	1943:107	ENC
Paynter, Isaac N	2:835	HHI
Paynton, Eliza, see		
Hart, Eliza (Paynton)		
Pearce, Lot L	2:445	PMO
Pearce, Robert	3:1029	SMS
Pearce, Mrs. Robert, see		
Morris, Jennie M (Chilton) Pearce		
Pearce, Sidney J	4:315	BCF
Pearl, Guy H	22:64 1917	WBP

Pearne, T   H   456   AG
Pearse, Benjamin William   4:1071   BCF
                            fol. title page SHB
Pearson, Daniel O   2:330   NH
Pearson, F   S   332   AG
Pearson, John P   250   HA
Pearson, T   C   3:839   HHI
Pearson, Thomas Davies   3:123   BCF
Pearson, Thomas Robson   3:141   BCF
                            fol. pt. 1   SHB
Pearson, Walter E   1935-36:50   OO
                            1937-38:62   OO
                            1939-40:7   OO
                            1941-42:62   OO
Pearson, Walter J   1943-44:79   OO
                            1945-46:83   OO
Pearsons, Daniel K   272   NM
                            164   NW
Pease, Archie L   253   LDM
Pease, Fellows D   239   LHM
                            3:1050   SMS
Pease, George A   27   LDM
Pease, George H   1:258   GP
Pease, Henry A   609   LHM
Peasley, Edwin H   2:421   HHI
                            18:53 1941-42   IH
                            21:10 1947-48   IH
Peays, Clara (Tredinick)   3:948   SMS
Peays, William Henry   3:948   SMS
Peays, Mrs. William Henry, see
    Peays, Clara (Tredinick)
Peck, Albert D   2:469   HHI
                            4:68   MC
Peddycord, George W   [114]   RLX
                            23:112 1918   WBP
                            24:64 1919   WBP
                            25:128 1920   WBP
                            26:front. 1921   WBP
Pederson, L   H   306   AC
Pederson, Mary Ann, see
    Anderson, Mary Ann (Pederson)
Pedicord, T   J   258   E
Pedro, Felix   152   BET
                            278-279   HU
                            209   WOY
Peebler, George D   177   PL
Peebles, Margaret, see
    Manson, Margaret (Peebles) McNaughton
Peek, Della, see
    Furnell, Della (Peek)
Peer, Lily M   , see
    Blewett, Lily M   (Peer)
Peers, Alexander   3:64   BCF
Peers, Mrs. Alexander, see
    Peers, Margaret (Wells)
Peers, Brenda   2:front. 1924 BCHA
Peers, Margaret (Wells)   3:65   BCF

                            24:128 1919   WBP
Peet, Lucy Abigail, see
    Cowley, Lucy Abigail (Peet)
Peets, W   Finley   unp.   SAA
Pefley, P   J   58 no. 4:cover   PN
Peigne, Puyallup chief   610   USCI
Peirce, Joshua   1910:18   TDL
Pelly, John Henry   258   MH
Peltier, Joseph   3:816   SMS
Peltier, Mrs. Joseph, see
    Peltier, Lottie (Adams)
Peltier, Lottie (Adams)   3:816   SMS
Pemberton, Augustus Frederick 4:95   BCF
                            1897:42   YB
Pemberton, C   C   2:front. 1924 BCHA
                            3:14 1925   BCHA
Pemberton, Frederick Bernard 3:153   BCF
                            2:front. 1924   BCHA
                            fol. pt. 2   SHB
Pemberton, Joseph Despard   1:542   BCF
                            4:35   BCF
                            front.   LCT
                            fol. title page SHB
                            1897:103   YB
Pemberton, William Young   68   MI
                            2:897   SM
Pence, Arthur   3:1099   FH
Pence, Nell   1:917   LHC
Pence, Peter   2:865   FH
                            2:275   HHI
Pencier, Adam Urias de   3:233   BCF
Pender, Peter Alexander   2:160   SMS
Pendleton, Frank R   6:54   SH
Pendleton, Grant W   3:1152   FH
Pendleton, Posey Lewis   3:203   HHT
Penfield, E   S   1:210-211   GP
Pennock, W   J   41   MG
Pennoyer, Sylvester   1:292   NH
                            65:266   OHQ
                            48   TUR
Penny, Elizabeth   2:368-369   EPD
Penrose, Stephen Beasley Linnard 264   NM
                            182   NW
                            24   PC
                            1 no. 10:17   WN
Pentecost, Levi J   3:295   HHT
Penwell, M   W   2:294   SMS
Peo (Cayuse Indian)   93   JM
Peo, Umatilla chief   4:230   LH
                            1:121   PMO
                            568   USCI
Peo-peo-mox-mox, Walla Walla chief
                            fol. 705 (no. 9) JO
                            4:50   LH
                            359   SK
                            28   SKA
                            204   WCS
Peo-peo-Tholekt, Nez Percé chief 140   AI

	1:525	HHI
Pepin, Exzelia J	3:750	SMS
Pepoon, J B	74	MHS
Pepper, Maud	26	RO
Percival, D F	1:388	NH
Percival, Monty	3:711	BH
Perham, Josiah	108	BOO
Perkins, Charlton Bristow	2:282	PMO
Perkins, Dean	2:176	FSB
Perkins, Elsina, see		
Johnson, Elsina (Perkins)		
Perkins, Harry E	2:101	SMS
Perkins, James Allen	2:85	HH
Perkins, Juliet, see		
Johnson, Juliet (Perkins)		
Perkins, Raymond	4:235	BHK
Perkins, Sidney Albert	3:173	HHT
————	3:4	HWW
————	6:60	SH
————	1895-96:140	SSS
Perkins, William David	6:96	SH
Perkins, William T	172-173, 196	HA
Perky, K I	2:38	FSB
Perouse, Jean Francois de Galaup, see		
Laperouse, Jean Francois de Galaup,		
Comte de		
Perpetua, Mother	247	PIW
Perrenoud, Armand	259	E
Perret, Charles Jacob	4:175	BHK
Perrigo, Matilda (Thayer)	3:799	BHS
Perrigo, Warren Wentworth	3:1023	BHS
Perrigo, William P	1:481	BHK
————	3:799	BHS
Perrigo, Mrs. William P , see		
Perrigo, Matilda (Thayer)		
Perrine, I B	1:348	FH
Perrine, James W	3:740	SMS
Perrine, Mrs. James W , see		
Perrine, Mrs. Lillian M		
Perrine, Jane, see		
Travis, Jane (Perrine)		
Perrine, Mrs. Lillian M	3:740	SMS
Perry, David	55	BN
Perry, Herb B	unp.	SAA
Perry, J D	1939-40:31	OO
————	1941-42:66	OO
————	1943-44:79	OO
Perry, John Mansfield	1941:49	EN
Perry, Matthew C	62:13	OHQ
Perry, Percy J	1 no. 4:287	WM
Peschka, Caroline	66	MG
Pessemier, C M	3:449	BH
Peter (Aleut), see		
Old Peter (Aleut)		
Peter, Brother of Iron Bull, Crow chief		
	216	PI
	248	PIW
Peter, Jim	389	BF
Peter, Klickitat, see		
Klickitat Peter		
Peter Gaucher, see		
Left Handed Peter (Flathead Indian)		
Peter Umpqua, see		
Umpqua Peter		
Peters, Charles	48	LS
Peters, Francis White	4:501	BCF
Peters, John Lambert	3:349	BEA
Peters, R Frank	1931-32:41	OO
	1945-46:93	OO
Petersen, Christean	3:973	FH
Petersen, John S	4:621	PH
Petersen, Soren	4:710	PH
Peterson, A F	303	E
Peterson, Andrew A	178	GL
Peterson, Andrew F	409	GL
Peterson, Mrs. Andrew F , see		
Jones, Hannah (Christensen)		
Peterson, Mary Ann (Pherson)		
Peterson, C	159	WOY
Peterson, C A	426	AG
Peterson, C O	2:203	CHW
Peterson, Canute	11	GL
Peterson, Mrs. Canute, see		
Peterson, Sarah Ann (Nelson)		
Peterson, Chriss	234	FF
Peterson, Ervin L	1945-46:14	OO
Peterson, Frank Millard	1:461	HH
Peterson, Mrs. Frank Millard, see		
Peterson, Mary A (Tanger)		
Peterson, Gus	1112	SIH
Peterson, Hannah (Christensen), see		
Jones, Hannah (Christensen)		
Peterson, Henry E	1943-44:79	OO
————	1945-46:87	OO
Peterson, J Oscar	42	SCC
Peterson, Maren Eline, see		
Fjeld, Maren Eline (Peterson)		
Peterson, Marshall W	3:285	BHS
Peterson, Mary A (Tanger)	1:471	HH
Peterson, Mary Ann (Pherson)	408	GL
Peterson, Nels	300	HA
Peterson, Sarah Ann (Nelson)	88	GL
Pethtel, Frances Ellen (LeValley)	3:513	HHI
Pethtel, George M	3:513	HHI
Pethtel, Mrs. George M , see		
Pethtel, Frances Ellen (LeValley)		
Pethtel, Sarah Louisa (Goul)		
Pethtel, Sarah Louisa (Goul)	3:513	hHI
Pe-tow-ya (Cayuse Indian)	2:257	WT
Petroff, Ivan	59 no. 1:3	PN
Petterson, W H	2:494	NH
Pettibone, George	59 no. 1:26	PN
Pettibone, Nathaniel B	58	BR
————	562	SIH
Pettijohn, Clive A	1924:129	WSP

Pettit, Mae Marguerite, see				Pickett, Mrs. Moroni, see		
Hay, Mae Marguerite (Pettit)				Pickett, Frances A	(Clegg)	
Pettygrove, Francis W	1:206-207	GP		Pickman, H Derby	428	MI
	1:112	NH		Picotte, Jesse G	390	BF
	2:329	PMO		Piedalue, Joseph	2:312	SMS
	3:98	SH		Pier, Stanhope S	1939-40:31	OO
Pfaus, Albert	6:420-421	MC			1941-42:66	OO
Pfeufer, Joseph	562	SIH			1943-44:79	OO
Pfister, Fred	3:153	MC			1945-46:87	OO
Pfueller, Ernest E	4:609	PH		Pierce, Benjamin Butler	147	PL
Phelps, Byron	3:381	BHS		Pierce, Elias D	137	BHSI
	unp.	SEA			1:101	HHI
Phelps, E J	2:463	BCF		Pierce, Frank Richardson	4:357	BHK
Phelps, F I	1895-96:103	SSS		Pierce, Margaret, see		
Phelps, Mary A (Jones), see				Young, Margaret (Pierce)		
Hawthorne, Mary A (Jones) Phelps				Pierce, Robert G	147	PL
Phelps, Mrs. Moses A , see				Pierce, Walter Edgar	1:20	FSB
Phelps, Netta Wells (Sheldon)				Pierce, Walter M	53 no. 2:71	PN
Phelps, Netta Wells (Sheldon) 1:12		D			72	TUR
Pherson, Mary Ann, see				Pierre, Alec, see		
Peterson, Mary Ann (Pherson)				Alec Pierre (Spokan Indian)		
Phifer, David	908	SIH		Piers, Arthur	361	GI
Philips, Charles	206	BHSS		Pierse, Allen	2:558	SMS
Phillip, Carl D	44:338	OHQ		Pietila, John J	2:224	SMS
Phillip, Grace A (Weston) 3:1558		SM		Pietrzycki, Marcellus Marcus 2:114		NH
Phillip, William J	3:1558	SM		Pigot, Creswell T	1941:187	EN
Phillip, Mrs. William J , see				Pigott, W T	4:114	MC
Phillip, Grace A (Weston)				Pigott, William	5:282	SH
Phillips, Charles	181	GL			unp.	VU
Phillips, John	2:17	HBT		Pike, William	180	SRW
Phillips, Mary E	29:97	PNLA		Pike, Zebulon Montgomery	2:286	LH
	32 no. 1:3	PNLA		Piles, Samuel H	1905-06:[33]	RLW
Phillips, Moses (Spokan Indian) 58		LC			[82]	RLX
Phillips, Portugee, see					1 no. 3:162	WM
Phillips, John				Pilgrim, Rebecca, see		
Phillips, Samuel	3:1063	SMS		Goates, Rebecca (Pilgrim)		
Phillips, Thomas Neil	4:427	BCF		Pilgrim, W F	172-173	HA
Philpott, Cory A	3:29	HHI		Pillsbury, A B	194	LDM
Phinney, Guy Carleton	6:4	SH		Pinchot, Gifford	49 no. 2:51	PN
Phipps, C A	189	PSW		Pinckney, J J	1924:113	WSP
Picani, Salvador	2:72	HHT		Pine, Mrs. Hiram S	1:210-211	GP
Pickard, James A	2:24	CPD		Ping, Elisha	1:504	NH
Pickard, Mary (Hunt-Beeson) 2:24		CPD		Pings, Frank H	3:1334	SM
Pickard, Nancy Emmaline, see				Pingston, A F	138	LDM
Cochran, Nancy Emmaline (Pickard)				Pinieo, (Doctor)	1:917	LHC
Pickens, Russell M	3:191	PH		Pinkham, Joseph	2:53	HHI
Pickering, William	829	HI			282	IHI
	19	MAG		Pinney, James Alonzo	2:682	FH
	26	ME		Piper, A W	172-173	HA
	34 no. 4:400-401	PN		Piper, Alexander	69:243	OHQ
	[45]	RLX		Piper, Charles Vancouver	219	BHSS
	unp.	SE			254	MMR
Pickett, F L	445	BHSS			57:116	OHQ
Pickett, Frances A (Clegg) 2:967		HHI			1 no. 4:268	WM
Pickett, George Edward	488	CIR		Piper, George U	[106]	RLX
	4:52	SH			1895-96:147	SSS
Pickett, Moroni	2:966	HHI		Pipes, Martin Luther	139	PL

	16	TO
Pipeshear, (Yakima Indian)	41:154	OHQ
Pitchford, Charles	30	THI
Pitney, William McClure	2:232	CHW
Pitt, Mrs. George, see		
Pitt, Penelope (Atkins)		
Pitt, John	244	MV
Pitt, Penelope (Atkins)	292	MV
Pittman, Anna Maria, see		
Lee, Anna Maria (Pittman)		
Pittock, Georgiana M (Burton)	2:114	PMO
Pittock, Harry L	1:498	GP
Pittock, Henry Lewis	1:584-585	GP
	2:29	GP
	66:250	OHQ
	2:114, 343	PMO
Pittock, Mrs. Henry Lewis, see		
Pittock, Georgiana M (Burton)		
Pius XI	5	MG
	xxii	OB
Piva, Pete	3:430	BEA
Pixley, Minnie	57:349	OHQ
Pizey, Paul	3:807	HHI
Place, Victor Morton	3:1017	BHS
Planta, Albert Edward	4:305	BCF
Plenty Coups, Crow chief	256	PIW
	361	USCI
Plenty Grizzly Bears, Pend d'Oreille chief		
fol. 512 (no. 28)		BUR
Plomondon, Mary Ann, see		
St. Germain, Mary Ann (Plomondon)		
Plomondon, Simon	1:122	HWW
Plummer, Alfred A , Jr.	2:250	NH
Plummer, Alfred A , Sr.	1:160	NH
Plummer, Charles	1:60	BHK
Plummer, O P S	1:253	GP
	1:260	NH
Plumridge, James	4:143	BCF
Pogue, Joseph Irwin	418	FF
	1905-06:[42]	RLW
	[97]	RLX
Pohle, L H	408	BHSS
Poindexter, Miles	53 no. 3:116	PN
Poka-Billy Ann (Okanogan Indian)	367	FF
Poland, H E	281	E
Poland, J S	110-111	HCM
Polet, Antonio	326	HA
Poling, C C	unp.	SOU
Pollen, Clement Hungerford	fol. pt. 2	SHB
Pollinger, E M	5:110	MC
Pollock, John Robert	fol. pt. 2	SHB
Pollock, Nate	20	WOY
Polmere, John	2:257	BCF
Polson, Alexander	2:133	HWW
	1:346	PHP
	[100]	RLX
Polson, Robert	2:253	HWW
	3:350	PH

Pomeroy, Albert E	3:657	HHI
Pomeroy, Allan	unp.	SEA
Pomeroy, Charles W	4:32	MC
Pomeroy, Joseph M	1:115	HH
Pomeroy, Stephen Loren	3:146	BEA
Pond, Enoch (Nez Percé Indian)	212	BR
	414	DS
	127	DTI
Pond, Lysander C	2:796	FH
Pond, Mary A , see		
Buxton, Mary A (Pond)		
Ponischil, Adolph	3:71	HWW
Pontiac, Ottawa chief	1:74	HG
Pool, Anna	42:32 1930	WSGP
Poole, Rose M	1945-46:87	OO
Pooley, Charles Edward	2:293	BCF
	4:91	BCF
	264	KB
	fol. pt. 1	SHB
	1897:104	YB
	1911:70-71	YB
Poorman, John M	2:434	PMO
Pope, Annie, see		
Laswell, Annie (Pope)		
Pope, Bob (Quinault Indian)	6 no. 1:188	UV
Pope, Mrs. Bob (Hoh ")	6 no. 1:188	UV
Pope, Charles	1:77	PMO
Pope, Mrs. Charles, see		
Pope, Sarah E (Archer)		
Pope, George	1:82	PMO
Pope, James Pinckney	2:643	FH
Pope, John Henry	289	GI
Pope, Joseph	2:463	BCF
	2:97	SMS
Pope, Sarah E (Archer)	1:77	PMO
Pope, Seth	1:77	PMO
Pope, W H	329	LDM
Pope, William Henwood	1:77	PMO
Popham, George	58	BR
Porter, Allie	31	DH
Porter, Clarence D	3:265	LHC
Porter, Fannie (McCartney)	2:395	GP
Porter, Freeman B	263	HA
Porter, J	front.	LCT
Porter, James	2:front. 1924	BCHA
Porter, Mrs. James	2:front. 1924	BCHA
Porter, John Gray	2:394	GP
Porter, Mrs. John Gray, see		
Porter, Fannie (McCartney)		
Porter, Johnson D	69:301	OHQ
Porter, Joseph	1:542	BCF
	1897:103	YB
Porter, L L	2:457	PMO
Porter, William D	2:239	LHC
Porterfield, R E	1924:112	WSP
Portlock, Nathaniel	3	LDM
	1:266	LH
Post, Frank Truman	5:388	SH

	1919:front.	WSP
Post, Frederick	1:271	HH
	829	SIH
Post, Homer L	1924:40	WSP
Postill, Alfred	4:71	BCF
Potter, John	623	LHM
Potter, Joseph C	31	DH
Potter, Mrs. Joseph C	31	DH
Potter, Thad S	480	PL
Pottinger, James	2:front. 1924	BCHA
Potts, Benjamin Franklin	10 no. 1:63	F
	4:106	MC
	1:410	SMS
Potts, W G	1905-06:[49]	RLW
	[103]	RLX
Pounder, R J	135	MLO
Poundmaker, Cree chief	286	GI
Pounds, Earl C	185	MSG
Powell, A O	25	SA
Powell, Esther Ann (Ashton)	414	GL
Powell, Frank Abram	unp.	SOU
Powell, Henry W	74	AL
Powell, Israel Wood	11 no. 1:38	BCH
	fol. title page	SHB
	1897:42	YB
Powell, James Q	154	GL
Powell, Mrs. James Q	413	GL
Powell, James T	235	GL
Powell, Joab	1:665	CHW
Powell, John H	312	SIH
Powell, John Wesley	fol. 207 (no. 40)	SHI
Powell, Leonard Jackson	18-19	GA
Powell, Thaddeus	413	GL
Powell, Mrs. Thaddeus, see		
Powell, Esther Ann (Ashton)		
Powelson, Howard	1:154-155	EPD
Power, Thomas C	1941:12	EN
	803	MI
	2:998	SM
Powers, Clara	67	MG
Powers, Francis F	50:51 1949	WDT
Powers, Henry C	3:858	HHI
Powers, Mrs. Henry C , see		
Powers, Isabel (Gray)		
Powers, Ira F	3:581	GP
Powers, Isabel (Gray)	3:859	HHI
Powers, James	125	JNT
	1905-06:[28]	RLW
Powers, Leland E	50:23 1949	WDT
Powers, M T	14	SSP
Powers, Orlando W	267	GLS
Powers, Trueman	2:42	NH
Poxeitner, Charles J	1:442-443	EPD
Poyns, Jesse C	1905-06:[58]	RLW
Prahl, Fred	44:338	OHQ
Prando, Peter P	28	JJ
	216, 230	PI
	248	PIW
Prather, Leander Hamilton	237	HI
Pratt, Bela Lyon	499	CIR
Pratt, Charles A	2:417	HHT
Pratt, Charles H	6:350	MC
Pratt, Dudley	94	IN
Pratt, John W	1895-96:146	SSS
Pratt, L E	135	LDM
Pratt, Louis W	2:164	HHT
Pratt, Orson	110	BU
Pratt, Willard N	1:534	HHT
Pratt, William H	1924:128	WSP
Praxedes of Providence, Mother	35	MG
Pray, Charles P	1945-46:47	OO
Prefontaine, Francis Xavier	240	BE
	3:240	SH
Prentice, James Douglas	fol. pt. 1	SHB
Prentiss, Harriet, see		
Jackson, Harriet (Prentiss)		
Prentiss, Harvey Pratt	81	DW
Prentiss, Narcissa, see		
Whitman, Narcissa (Prentiss)		
Prescott, Augustus	2:493	CHW
Prescott, Charles Harrison		
	12 no. 6:583	MWH
	2:458	NH
Prestbye, Christ	2:628	SMS
Prestbye, Mrs. Christ, see		
Prestbye, Mathilde (Christensen)		
Prestbye, Martin	2:629	SMS
Prestbye, Mathilde (Christensen)	2:628	SMS
Preston, Harold	1924:16	WSP
Preston, Josephine (Corliss)	1 no. 7:11	WN
	1 no. 11:13	WN
Preston, William B	203	BHI
Pretty, Charles Fenn	3:195	BCF
Prettyman, Henry W	2:278	PMO
Pretty-Shield (Crow Indian)	13 no. 1:78	F
Prevost, James	63	LDM
Prevost, Jules L	14	PJ
	151	WOY
Price, A R	1895:87	OO
Price, Andrew	1 no. 8:15	WN
Price, Bruce	341	GI
Price, Con	1:174	ACR
Price, G W	36	HA
Price, Ivan	473	BHSS
Price, J C	2:133	CHW
Price, J T	172-173	HA
Price, James H	1895-96:59	SSS
Price, John E	unp.	VU
Price, Johnny	front.	BI
Price, Mabel	207	BHSS
Price, Sara (Elliott), see		
Wolheter, Sara (Elliott) Price		
Price, Susie	207	BHSS
Price, Vashti Larkin, see		
Meikle, Vashti Larkin (Price)		

Prichard, Arthur Gilman	2:377	HHT
Prichard, E R	105	PSW
Prichard, Louise	18:9	PNLA
Prickett, H E	213	DL
Pride, D P B	42	HIT
Pridham, Thomas Hill	2:470	SMS
Priest, Arthur Ragan	1:unp. 1900-01	WDT
	6:23 1906	WDT
Prim, Paine Page	1:156	NH
Pringle, Alexander	6:424-425	MC
Pringle, George	3:1467	SM
Pringle, J Arthur	50:23 1949	WDT
Prior, Edward Gawler	2:451	BCF
	3:69	BCF
_____	146	JAC
_____	270	KB
_____	fol. pt. 1	SHB
_____	1897:110	YB
_____	1911:70-71	YB
Pritchard, "Jakey"	456	BR
Pritchard, William Hugh	2:121	HH
	13 no. 3:290	MWH
Pritts, Truman W	147	PL
Procter, T G	fol. pt. 2	SHB
Proctor, A Phimister	20:232	OHQ
Proctor, Israel O	3:699	SMS
Proctor, Mrs. Israel O , see		
Proctor, Louisa (Klaue)		
Proctor, Louisa (Klaue)	3:699	SMS
Proctor, Thomas	4 no. 2:86	BCH
Proctor, W A	1931-32:41	OO
Proebstel, George W	2:456	PMO
Proff, Charles	287	BHSS
Prosch, Charles	1:214	HWW
	51 no. 4:177	PN
Prosch, Mrs. Charles, see		
Prosch, Mrs. Susan		
Prosch, Mrs. Susan	1:214	HWW
Prosch, Thomas W	1:687	BHK
	2:836	BHS
_____	2:162	HHT
_____	458	MP
_____	16	PC
Prosser, William Farrand	1:103	HH
	2:82	NH
_____	1:front.	PHP
_____	1905-06:[28]	RLW
_____	5:270	SH
Proulx, Emil A	261	GG
Proulx, Peter S	231	GG
Prouty, Fred	190	JNT
Provencher, Joseph	1:116	MCC
Provinse, Henry Clay	2:1253	SM
Provost, Mrs. Dena	31	THI
Provot, Etienne	257	HCC
Prudhomme, William Edward	2:443	GP
Pruyn, Edward	1926:20	WSP
Ptarmigan	1897:171	YB
Puccio, Gaspare	2:607	BHK
Puckett, W H	514	IHI
Pue, Galen D	3:1555	SM
Pugh, Arthur B	484	PL
Pugh, Catharine (Entz)	2:143	CHW
Pugh, David H	2:143	CHW
Pugh, Mrs. David H , see		
Pugh, Catharine (Entz)		
Pugh, Francis McKinney	2:145	HH
Pugh, John Harlan	1941:380	EN
Pulaski, Edward C	18:26 1941-42	IH
Pulse, John J	556	SIH
Puntenny, Charles S	320	SIH
Purcell, Michael F	3:1112	SMS
Purcell, Patrick Francis	3:343	BHS
	6:206	SH
Purcell, Thomas J	2:745	HHI
Purdy, Charles H	2:270	HHT
Purdy, Ernest W	3:389	HWW
	13:174 1908	WBP
_____	16:21 1911	WBP
_____	24:96 1919	WBP
Purinton, Harriet Newell, see		
Reed, Harriet Newell (Purinton)		
Purkeypile, Irus Ward	1943:162	ENC
Purser, Phoebe, see		
Foss, Phoebe (Purser)		
Purvis, Allan	4:1089	BCF
Puter, Stephen A Douglas	37, 294	PL
Putnam, Edward A	361	PL
Putnam, Marguerite E	18:9	PNLA
	30:202	PNLA
_____	26:42 1925	WDT
Putnam, Rex	1939-40:7	OO
_____	1941-42:13	OO
_____	1943-44:17	OO
_____	1945-46:29	OO
Putullo, Thomas R	2:257	BCF
Pybus, Henry	4 no. 2:86	BCH
Pyke, Robert Samuel	3:473	BCF
Pyle, John E	6:305	MC
Pyle, Mrs. John E	6:358	MC
Pyles, Jacob Phillis	3:637	BH
Pyper, William B	3:1349	SM

Q

Quackenbush, Edward	3:263	GP
Quackenbush, Louis B	3:497	HWW
Quahat, see		
Ollokot, Nez Percé chief		
Quarnberg, Andrew A	3:29	LHC
Quenell, Edward	139	LDM
Quevli, C	114	SS
Quickenden, Henry	6:420-421	MC
Quigley, Clarke H	1941:131	EN

Quigley, Edward Albert   4:625   BCF
Quille, Mary   title page   SO
Quimette, Esdras N   2:354   NH
Quinlan, W   E   [116]   RLX
Quinn, F   M   260   E
Quinn, Max F   215   GG
Quinn, Pauline   4 no. 12:28   C
Quinn, W   H   , Jr.   172-173   HA
Quivey, Charlotte Irene, see
    Coffin, Charlotte Irene (Quivey)

                        R

Raabe, George   232   LDM
Rabbeson, Antonio B   1:564   NH
Rabbit-Skin-Leggins (Nez Percé Indian) 20 AC
                                250   BR
_____   2:124-125   CN
_____   94-95   DGC
_____   82   DS
_____   42   FW
_____   129   GBS
_____   313   NM
_____   1:121   PHP
Racker, Frederick E   284   GL
Racker, William E   317   GL
Rackliff, William E   32   LDM
Radebaugh, R   F   2:164   HHT
Radelsheimer, Mollie, see
    Blumauer, Mollie (Radelsheimer)
Rader, Carey M   3:175   PH
Rader, L   E   1895-96:105   SSS
Rader, Melvin   50:45 1949   WDT
Rader, Ralph   290   BHSS
Rae, John   267   MH
Raff, George   6:382-383   MC
Rahskopf, Horace G   50:40 1949   WDT
Rainey, Joe   366   BF
Rainier, Peter   302   MMR
                                98   MV
_____   312   WCS
Rain-in-the-Face, Sioux chief 70   KY
                                323   VT
Rains, Grace, see
    Robinson, Grace (Rains)
Raitt, Effie   120-121   GA
Raleigh, George H   3:231   BH
                    1 no. 10:27 1928   WN
Raley, James H   2:462   NH
                                1895:85   OO
Ralph, Jacob   1:372   HHT
Ralph, William Alfred   4:703   BCF
Ralston, Caroline (Hood)   1:216   HHT
Ralston, Mrs. Joseph R   , see
    Ralston, Caroline (Hood)
Ralston, William C   244   QT

Ramage, L   M   1943-44:79   OO
Ramsay, Claude Clinton   1:481, 487   BHK
                                2:323   BHK
_____   3:557   BHS
_____   [133]   RLX
_____   6:146   SH
Ramsey, Frank C   397   IHI
Ramsey, John Marshall   2:882   SM
Ramsey, Robert M   6:416-417   MC
Ramstedt, Axel P   1941:151   EN
                                2:122   FSB
Rance, Bill   1:116   ACR
Rand, Charles D   fol. pt. 2   SHB
Rand, Edward Ethelbert   4:845   BCF
                                fol. pt. 2   SHB
Rand, Irving   1943-44:75   OO
                                1945-46:83   OO
Rand, John Langdon   2:91   CHW
_____   1941:38   EN
_____   1931-32:8   OO
_____   1935-36:34   OO
_____   1937-38:7   OO
_____   1939-40:7   OO
_____   1941-42:14   OO
Rand, Robert   1:917   LHC
Randall, Charles Carroll   3:633   HHI
Randle, Nellie   26   RO
Randolph, Catherine (Breckenridge)
                                3:357   BHS
Randolph, Frank Fitz   2:559   BHK
Randolph, John F   128   MCO
Randolph, Simon Peter   3:356   BHS
Randolph, Mrs. Simon Peter, see
    Randolph, Catherine (Breckenridge)
Rands, Edward McKeever   1905-06:[48]   RLW
_____   [89]   RLX
_____   6:46   SH
Range, J   W   1895-96:77   SSS
Ranges, Elise, see
    Otten, Elise (Ranges)
Rankin, A   A   3:691   BH
Rankin, Donald   2:123   BCF
Rankin, Egbert A   3:357   GP
Rankin, George Stroud   6:178   SH
Rankin, James   2:123   BCF
Rankin, Jeannette   55 no. 1:cover PN
Rankin, Mary (Burns)   2:730-731   FH
Rankin, Wellington D   2:1280   SM
Rankin, William Allen   2:730-731   FH
Rankin, Mrs. William Allen, see
    Rankin, Mary (Burns)
Rankin, William C   1935-36:51   OO
Ransom, Reno P   43 no. 2:136   PN
Ranum, Arthur   1:unp. 1900-01 WDT
Rappagliosi, Philip   188   PI
Rash, Matt   182-183   KO
Rasher, Huber   1905-06:[45]   RLW
Rasmussen, John Peter   3:757   GP

	2:701	LHC
Ratcliffe, C A	1905-06:[59]	RLW
Ratcliffe, William E	248	SIH
Rathbone, Edward J	385	LDM
Rathbun, C W	1924:160	WSP
Rathbun, John C	2:104	PHP
Raught, Al, Jr.	134	MLO
Ravalli, Anthony	fol. 512 (no. 13)	BUR
_____	25	CCA
_____	47	GG
_____	15	JJ
_____	16	LHM
_____	54	PI
_____	front.	PIW
Ravenswaay, Charles van, see		
Van Ravenswaay, Charles		
Rawlins, John A	23:113	DH
Rawson, A	172-173	HA
Rawson, William Franklin	2:872	FH
Rawson, Zephaniah B	3:369	BHS
Ray, Charles	1:219	GP
Ray, Mrs. Ed, see		
Ray, Emma (Ott) Corbett		
Ray, Emma (Ott) Corbett	50	CBC
Ray, Edward C	956	SIH
Rayburn, James	6:440-441	MC
Raymond, Alfred	2:229	BHK
	5:422	SH
Raymond, H A	2:289	HH
Raymond, John	3:1085	BCF
Raymond, Walter H	3:609	LHC
Raymond, Winthrop	2:976	SM
Rea, John	51	PSW
Rea, Sarah A (Hudson)	849	LHM
Rea, William F	849	LHM
Rea, Mrs. William F , see		
Rea, Sarah A (Hudson)		
Read, Benjamin H	2:697	HHI
Read, Hamilton	3:403	BCF
Read, William M	50:23 1949	WDT
Reading, H W	1924:160	WSP
Ready, Peter H	562	SIH
Rear, James S	4:1095	BCF
	fol. pt. 2	SHB
Reardon, Ruth	1941:336	EN
Reat, Lois	6:386	MC
Reavis, Edna, see		
Ross, Edna (Reavis)		
Reavis, G S	2:435	PMO
Reavis, James B	1:392	NH
Reavis, T A	3:19	LHC
Reber, R E	172-173	HA
Rebhan, W C	2:465	CHW
Rebmann, James	73	GG
_____	146-147, 366	PI
_____	164, 436	PIW
_____	9	SCH
Records, Golden	66	MG

Red Cloud, chief of the Oglala Teton Sioux		
	230	GR
_____	1:front.	HBT
_____	2:201	HBT
Red Feather, see		
Adolphe, Flathead chief		
Insula, Flathead chief		
Red Heart, Jesse (Nez Percé Indian)		
	fol. 705 (no. 24)	JO
Red Horn (Nez Percé Indian)	232	BR
Red Night, Flathead chief, see		
Alee, Flathead chief		
Red Plume, Flathead chief		
	fol. 512 (no. 23)	BUR
Red Wolf, Nez Percé chief		
	fol. 705 (no. 7)	JO
Redding, Charles W	1945-46:92	OO
Redding, George Herbert Huntington	363	HA
Reddoch, Charles F	2:717	FH
Reddoor, Clide	6:432-433	MC
Redenzel, A	1:372	HHT
Redfern, Charles Edward	2:293	BCF
_____	4:691	BCF
_____	2:front. 1924	BCHA
Redfield, F M	2:505	CHW
Redford, Walter	1945-46:75	OO
Redington, J W	135	BN
Redman, John T	2:606	NH
Redwing, Edward O	3:710	SMS
Redwood, F W	172-173	HA
Reece, Jonathan	2:139	BCF
Reed, Barbara A (Steiner)	2:234	NH
Reed, Belinda, see		
Hill, Belinda (Reed)		
Reed, Charles B	2:574	NH
Reed, Charles F	6:442-443	MC
Reed, Charles J	285	PL
Reed, Charles S	59	SSP
Reed, Cyrus A	1:242	GP
Reed, Duffy Edward	3:68	BEA
Reed, Ella (Cartee)	9:6 1923-24	IH
_____	19:15 1943-44	IH
Reed, Esther (DeBerdt)	1:70	D
Reed, Fred R	3:1301	FH
Reed, George Henry	3:224	HHT
	5:346	SH
Reed, Mrs. George Henry, see		
Reed, Harriet Newell (Purinton)		
Reed, George W , Jr.	9:6 1923-24	IH
Reed, Granville	125	LDM
Reed, Harriet Newell (Purinton)	3:225	HHT
Reed, Mrs. Hayter	340	GI
Reed, Henry E	2 no. 1:42	WM
Reed, J T	172-173	HA
Reed, John	240	MI
_____	50 no. 3:85	PN
Reed, John M	1905-06:[28]	RLW

Reed, Mrs. Joseph, see			
Reed, Esther (DeBerdt)			
Reed, Lydia (MacMillan)	1:12	D	
Reed, S B	37	DH	
Reed, Simeon G	1:402-403	GP	
	353	QT	
	130	SHP	
Reed, T M	172-173	HA	
	1905-06:[28]	RLW	
Reed, Thomas B	1146	SIH	
Reed, Walter J	2:234	NH	
	1905-06:[45]	RLW	
	[97]	RLX	
Reed, Mrs. Walter J , see			
Reed, Barbara A (Steiner)			
Reed, Mrs. Walter James, see			
Reed, Lydia (MacMillan)			
Reed, William R	343	LHM	
Reeder, Levi B	2:450	PMO	
Reese, Henry L	1:unp. 1900-01	WDT	
Reese, Mark Anthony	3:163	BHK	
Reese, T M	59	AG	
Reeves, A I	3:1443	SM	
Reeves, Mrs. Belle	1 no. 7:11	WN	
Reeves, Biddle	751	LHM	
Reeves, Charles Francis	1:unp. 1900-01	WDT	
Reeves, Charles H	1088	SIH	
Reeves, Frank	1914:front.	WSP	
Reeves, George Willis	307	MI	
Reeves, Webber N	3:1004	FH	
Refior, William	6:416-417	MC	
Regan, John M	2:533	HHI	
Regan, Timothy	1:42	FSB	
	2:7	HHI	
Reger, E L	39	MG	
Reichenbach, Charles	2:445	HH	
Reichle, W A	39	MG	
Reid, Alice, see			
Bacon, Alice (Reid)			
Reid, E	172-173	HA	
Reid, George Thomas	1941:433	EN	
	3:71	HHT	
	1905-06:[66]	RLW	
	[127]	RLX	
Reid, James	4:697	BCF	
	216	FT	
	6:386	MC	
	324	MHN	
	1897:109	YB	
Reid, James Clement	75	PSW	
Reid, John	51	PSW	
Reid, John, Jr.	6:416-417	MC	
Reid, Robie Lewis	9 no. 2:82	BCH	
Reid, W King	43 no. 2:137	PN	
Reid, William	1:299	GP	
	2:129	LHC	
	612	SHP	
Reid, William H	3:1363	SM	

Reid, William Thomas	3:559	BCF	
Reidy, Daniel	332	SCH	
Reierson, P H	44	MG	
Reigel, H D	38	LHN	
Reigel, Mrs. H D	38	LHN	
Reiley, J A	172-173	HA	
Reilly, Joe	64	KT	
Rein, Jacob	3:523	HHI	
Rein, Mrs. Jacob, see			
Rein, Sarah C (Goble) Shuler			
Rein, Sarah C (Goble) Shuler	3:522	HHI	
Reinhart, C S	1924:145	WSP	
Reinhart, Ernest E	836	SIH	
Reinhart, S D	190	JNT	
Reinhart, William E	836	SIH	
Reinig, Leonard Louis	4:45	BHK	
	6:220	SH	
Reinig, Mrs. Leonard Louis, see			
Reinig, Margarethe (Schafer)			
Reinig, Margarethe (Schafer)	4:49	BHK	
Reinking, Floyd B	1943:194	ENC	
Reins, John P	2:1005	SM	
Reiter, E D	1905-06:[55]	RLW	
Reiter, W H	2:637	SMS	
Reith, Alexander	3:265	HHT	
Rekdahl, Benedick B	680	SIH	
Rekdahl, Mrs. Benedick B , see			
Rekdahl, Martha (Gunderson)			
Rekdahl, Martha (Gunderson)	680	SIH	
Remi, Sister	126	PI	
Remington, Arthur	1926:20	WSP	
Remington, P A	41	MG	
Remsberg, C E	39	SA	
Rene, John B	117	GG	
	28	JJ	
	216	PI	
	248	PIW	
Renick, Frank H	[133]	RLX	
Rennie, A	1935-36:51	OO	
	1937-38:62-63	OO	
	1939-40:31	OO	
	1941-42:66	OO	
	1943-44:79	OO	
Renshaw, Fred E	3:1820	SM	
Renton, William	57 no. 4:165	PN	
	4:354	SH	
Reuth, Felix van, see			
Van Reuth, Felix			
Reynolds, A H	1:244	NH	
Reynolds, Charles B	1895-96:105	SSS	
Reynolds, Edward B	67	LDM	
Reynolds, Lloyd T	1:563	CHW	
	2:83	CHW	
Reynolds, Maryan E	33 no. 4:35	PNLA	
	34 no. 4:3	PNLA	
Reynolds, R R	48	LS	
Reynolds, William A	3:23	PH	

Name	Page	Code
Reynolds, William P	2:511	HHT
Rezanoff, Nicholas P	80	AN
	278-279	HU
Rhoades, Catharine (Parrott)	2:241	HH
Rhoades, Lewis Henry	2:241	HH
Rhoades, Mrs. Lewis Henry, see		
Rhoades, Catharine (Parrott)		
Rhoads, Ella, see		
Higginson, Ella (Rhoads)		
Rhoads, Jay	53	NL
Rhodehamel, Harry E	1941:117	EN
	37	MG
Rhodes, Albert J	2:239	BHK
Rhodes, Alonzo D	58	GL
Rhodes, D L	2:433	HHI
Rhodes, Henry Abraham	6:192	SH
	1910:43	TDL
Ribbach, F A	15	SSP
Riblett, Frank	2:569	HHI
Ricardo, W Crawley	fol. pt. 2	SHB
Rice, A E	1924:41	WSP
Rice, Alonzo F	3:1429	SM
	2:454	SMS
Rice, Carrie (Shaw)	1899:112	SSS
Rice, Dexter	2:441	PMO
Rice, Edmund	[123]	RLX
Rice, George S	146	PSW
Rice, Joseph Lee	3:1529	SM
Rice, Lindley Marshall	3:805	BHS
Rice, Lucius Cozzens	259	IHI
Rice, Robert E	3:960	SMS
Rice, Samuel B	955	LHM
Rich, Mrs. Charles, see		
Rich, Mrs. Melinda M		
Rich, Charles C	176	BHI
	266	HIT
	680	IHI
Rich, Joseph C	266	HIT
	693	IHI
Rich, L C	261	E
Rich, Mrs. Melinda M	5:316	MC
	6:325	MC
Rich, Roscoe C	3:494	BEA
Rich, Samuel J	2:679	FH
	638	IHI
Richards, Albert Norton	2:277	BCF
	fol. pt. 1	SHB
	1897:63	YB
	1911:70-71	YB
Richards, Charles L	6:301	MC
Richards, Emily, see		
Wilton, Emily (Richards)		
Richards, Frank H	172-173, 354	HA
Richards, Franklin D	169	BHI
Richards, George W	138	HIT
Richards, Grace Alice (De Lin)	1:14	HHT
Richards, James Heber	2:764	FH
	1:88	FSB
	2:161	HHI
	311	IHI
Richards, John S	18:9	PNLA
	20:11, 169	PNLA
Richards, Mrs. John T , see		
Richards, Grace Alice (De Lin)		
Richards, Joseph R A	4:531	BCF
Richards, N C	1918:front.	WSP
Richards, Nellie, see		
Harrington, Nellie (Richards) Hathaway		
Richards, Warrington	2:448	SMS
Richards, Willard	112-113 (xviii)	PR
Richardson, Alonzo L	2:702	FH
	19:5 1943-44	IH
Richardson, Charles	3:113	HHT
	1:336	PHP
	5:192	SH
	June 1909:60	TDL
	1910:75	TDL
Richardson, Charles, 1850- .	314	LDM
Richardson, F D	1:313	HH
Richardson, George Thomas	3:257	PH
Richardson, H G	2:80	PHP
Richardson, Harry M	1112	SIH
Richardson, Hedley T	4 no. 2:86	BCH
Richardson, Ida Olivia (Meacham)	3:257	PH
Richardson, James A	1:304	NH
Richardson, John Franklin	4:1083	BCF
Richardson, Len, see		
Richardson, Alonzo L		
Richardson, Mary, see		
Walker, Mary (Richardson)		
Richardson, Oliver H	26:57 1925	WDT
Richardson, Mrs. Thomas, see		
Richardson, Ida Olivia (Meacham)		
Richer-Lafleche, Louis Francois, see		
Lafleche, Louis Francois Richer		
Richmond, Mrs. America Talley	110	AC
	1:27	BH
	515	MP
Richmond, Francis	110	AC
	515	MP
Richmond, John P	110	AC
	1:27	BH
	515	MP
	8	PC
Richmond, Mrs. John P , see		
Richmond, Mrs. America Talley		
Richmond, Oregon	110	AC
Richmond, Thomas J	3:809	BHK
Richmond, Volney	5	KI
Richter, E T	37	MG
Richter, Francis Xavier	fol. title page	SHB
Rickard, Sarah E , see		
Conger, Sarah E (Rickard)		
Rickard, Tex	404	WOY
Rickards, Albert	338	LDM
Rickards, John E	153	MI
Ricklefs, Sophie, see		
Wassem, Sopnie (Ricklefs)		
Ricks, Nathan	2:131	HHI

Ricksecker, Eugene	2:100	HHT
Ricksecker, S E	97	DH
Riddell, Arthur Murchie	2:546	SMS
Riddell, C F	1924:49	WSP
Riddell, Crockett Morgan	3:487	BH
———	May 1907:38	TDL
Riddle, (Captain)	78	LDM
Riddle, Glenn N	1935-36:51	OO
———	1937-38:62-63	OO
———	1939-40:31	OO
Rider, Blackfoot chief	10:60	MC
Rider, Josephine, see		
Martin, Josephine (Rider) Adams Wright		
Riel, Louis	149, 282	GI
———	2:28, 74	MCC
Riel, Louis "David", see		
Riel, Louis		
Ries, J P	3:433	HHI
Rigdon, Winfield Taylor	1941:99	EN
Riggin, Francis A	359	LHM
Riggin, Mrs. Francis A , see		
Riggin, Ida I (Jordan)		
Riggin, Ida I (Jordan)	359	LHM
Riggs, Arthur	91	AL
Riggs, Henry Chiles	2:643	HHI
Riggs, Laura, see		
Slocum, Laura (Riggs)		
Riggs, Timothy Ambrose	2:172	PMO
Riggs, William S	27	GL
Rigley, Ann W , see		
Jaggar, Ann W (Rigley)		
Rigney, John	1:145	BH
Rigney, Mrs. John	1:145	BH
Riley, George	1911:70-71	YB
Riley, Leonard William	2:383	CHW
Riley, W T	138	HIT
Rinearson, G O	1895:111	OO
Rinehart, James H	1:408	NH
Rinehart, William V , Jr.		
———	172-173, 346	HA
Rinehart, William Vance	60:95	OHQ
———	65:18	OHQ
Ring, D B	1897:124	YB
Ringer, L M	1:313	HH
———	1:296	NH
Rininger, E M	172-173, 76	HA
Ripley, T E	1910:2	TDL
Riplinger, John	191	E
———	1905-06:[68]	RLW
Rising, Fred W	2:895	FH
Rising, Martin	3:825	SMS
Risley, Charles W	3:201	LHC
Risley, John F	3:137	LHC
Ritchie, Willis A	3 no. 4:300	PM
Rithet, Robert Paterson	fol. pt. 1	SHB
———	1897:108	YB
Rittenhouse, Irvin	213	PL
Ritz, Philip	161	BOO

———	1:134	HHT
Ritz, W A	108	BHSS
Rivers, Lady, see		
Pitt, Penelope (Atkins)		
Rixon, Frederick Panton	1941:477	EN
Rizer, Robert Inskeep	3:1793	SM
Robbins, Carl W	2:355	CHW
Robbins, Earl	43 no. 1:16-17	PN
Robbins, Herbert E	2:540	PHP
Robbins, Milton N	1:709	BHK
Robbins, Orlando	193	AI
———	11	BSC
———	115	DL
———	270	DSW
———	10:33 1925-26	IH
Robbins, Rube, see		
Robbins, Orlando		
Robbins, William L	2:540	PHP
Roberts, A S	2:432	PMO
Roberts, Andrew	1:632	NH
Roberts, B	3:691	SMS
Roberts, Brigham H	405	GLS
Roberts, E R	2:212	HHT
Roberts, Ebenezer L	3:601	HHT
Roberts, Edward J	211	GG
Roberts, Edward M	3:949	FH
Roberts, George	322	LDM
Roberts, George Barber	63:101	OHQ
Roberts, J L	1895-96:77	SSS
Roberts, Joe	3:153	MC
Roberts, John	12	TMP
Roberts, John, Jr.	280	GL
Roberts, John A	247	GG
Roberts, John H	69:314	OHQ
Roberts, John W	unp.	VU
———	1924:65	WSP
Roberts, Joseph Dana	2:457	BHK
Roberts, Mrs. Joseph Harvey, see		
Roberts, Mabel (Van Tromp)		
Roberts, Laura, see		
Clark, Laura (Roberts)		
Roberts, Logan H	1924:128	WSP
Roberts, Loren	24	LT
Roberts, Mabel (Van Tromp)	3:385	GP
Roberts, Milnor	6:28 1906	WDT
———	26:58 1925	WDT
———	36:23 1935	WDT
———	1 no. 10:18	WN
Roberts, Morley	267	GI
Roberts, Sam Alfred	1943:182	ENC
Roberts, Samuel W	1905-06:[62]	RLW
Roberts, William J	3:441	BH
———	219	BHSS
Roberts, William Milnor	116	BOO
Robertson, Alexander Rocke	2:337	BCF
———	1897:132	YB

	1911:70-71	YB
Robertson, Harry C	217	PL
Robertson, James	320	LDM
Robertson, Mrs. Jessie	6:397	MC
Robertson, John	171	LDM
Robertson, Keith	34 no. 1:32	PNLA
Robertson, T	2:front. 1924	BCHA
Robertson, Thomas	4:1143	BCF
	1:300	PMO
Robertson, W A	2:337	BCF
Robertson, Wilbur Wade	42 no. 2:112	PN
	52 no. 4:146	PN
	1 no. 6:17	WN
Robie, Edward W	464	SIH
Robie, Mrs. Edward W , see		
Robie, Isabella (Benedict)		
Robie, Isabella (Benedict)	464	SIH
Robins, Charles Armington	21:4 1947-48	IH
Robinson, Barton	4:418	PH
Robinson, Mrs. Barton, see		
Robinson, Katherine (Gorman)		
Robinson, Christopher	2:463	BCF
Robinson, Clyde	36:16 1935	WDT
Robinson, David	154	LDM
Robinson, Doran	3:45	BEA
Robinson, Emeline (Barnum)	2:641	LHC
Robinson, Frank Bruce	3, 32	RSA
Robinson, Mrs. Frank Bruce	4	RSA
Robinson, Fred K	3:251	BEA
Robinson, Mrs. Fred K , see		
Robinson, Grace (Rains)		
Robinson, George G	417	GL
Robinson, Grace (Rains)	3:251	BEA
Robinson, Grant	2:140	SMS
Robinson, James	2:337	BCF
Robinson, John	2:1293	SM
Robinson, John Moore	fol. pt. 1	SHB
Robinson, John Thomas	3:815	BCF
	fol. pt. 2	SHB
Robinson, Katherine (Gorman)	4:418	PH
Robinson, Leo	383	SCH
Robinson, Reuben F	2:22	PMO
Robinson, Reuben S	4:418	PH
Robinson, Mrs. Reuben S , see		
Robinson, Sarah Angeline (Arthur)		
Robinson, Sarah Angeline (Arthur)	4:418	PH
Robinson, Mrs. Statira E	166	BHSI
Robinson, Thomas Emery	3:291	BEA
Robinson, Walter J	3:27	PH
Robinson, William Fears	2:288	PHP
Robinson, William J	2:641	LHC
Robinson, Mrs. William J , see		
Robinson, Emeline (Barnum)		
Robison, Charles William	3:585	LHC
Robling, John S	25:34	PNLA
Robnett, V W	177	PL
Robson, E	1897:44	YB
Robson, John	2:337, 451	BCF
	3:997	BCF

	76	JAC
	42	KB
	fol. pt. 1	SHB
	96-97	SHL
	1897:64, 124	YB
	1911:70-71	YB
Rochester, Junius A	3 no. 8:424	PM
Rock, H H	89, 135	MLO
Rockliff, James A	53	GG
Rockwood, A J	2:493	HHI
Rockwood, Mrs. A J , see		
Rockwood, Mary (Dilley)		
Rockwood, Mary (Dilley)	2:493	HHI
Rocky, Eli	1:481	BHK
Rodger, Allan	41	LHN
Rodgers, John A	65	PSW
Rodman, James A	1941-42:66	OO
Rodman, Millard D	1935-36:51	OO
Roe, Watkin Lewis	3:1104	FH
Roeder, Henry	1:176	NH
	3:130	SH
Roeder, Otto B	2:368	PHP
	May 1907:68	TDL
Roediger, Richard	2:162	HHT
Roesli, Anton	3:563	BH
Rogers, A A	1945-46:18	OO
Rogers, A B	2:425	BCF
	217	GI
Rogers, A L	1	TF
Rogers, Benjamin Tingley	4:23	BCF
Rogers, Clarence Henry	4:389	BCF
Rogers, E R	2:390	NH
Rogers, George B	405	IHI
Rogers, Isaac	97	DH
Rogers, J H	12	DA
Rogers, Jay	1:481	BHK
Rogers, John C	3:909	FH
Rogers, John Rankin	168	BHSS
	43	MAG
	84	ME
	34 no. 4:400-401	PN
	60 no. 4:cover, 185	PN
	[67]	RLX
	unp.	SE
	1895-96:105	SSS
	1899:front.	SSS
Rogers, Lincoln	3:731	BCF
Rogers, Moses	47	LDM
Rogers, N L	159	LDM
Rogers, Nelson S	1945-46:32	OO
Rogers, Roger R	74-75	GA
	unp.	WD
Rogers, Samuel A	fol. title page	SHB
	1897:108	YB
Rogers, Susannah, see		
Bagley, Susannah (Rogers)		
Rogers, Thomas Hesperian	1:254	PMO
	unp.	SOU

Rogers, Will   1:228   ACR
Rohn, J   J   192   MCO
Rohrer, Pius A   247   GG
Rolfe, Lydia M   , see
    Stewart, Lydia M   (Rolfe)
Roller, Benjamin F   6:29 1906   WDT
                      1 no. 4:306   WM
————
Rollinson, William   262   E
Romaine, J   W   [137]   RLX
Romano, Leonard   3:173   BHK
Rommel, William C   6:301   MC
Ronald, J   T   unp.   SEA
                      58   SSP
————
Ronan, Peter   3:143   MC
                      156   PIW
                      1:206   SMS
————
Roney, Lord Nelson   61:155   OHQ
Roork, J   H   60   OS
Roos, John P   31   THI
Root, Milo A   1926:20   WSP
Roote, Jesse B   3:1598   SM
Roper, Eglantine L   3:764   SMS
Roper, William   3:47   HHI
Roper, William James   2:293   BCF
                      4:739   BCF
                fol. title page   SHB
————
Rorison, Robert Douglas   4:823   BCF
Rorison, Walford Douglas Somerled   3:55   BCF
Roscoe, Christopher Theophilus   2:295   HH
                      1924:81   WSP
————
Rose, Aaron   1:596   NH
Rose, Benjamin V   191   LDM
Rose, Elmer Lee   3:641   HHI
Rose, Mrs. Elmer Lee, see
    Rose, Sarah Mabel (Harrison)
Rose, F   L   3:189   HHI
Rose, Mrs. F   L   , see
    Rose, Grace (Vanderburg)
Rose, Grace (Vanderburg)   3:189   HHI
Rose, Sarah Mabel (Harrison)   3:641   HHI
Rose, Vera (Crisler)   1943:30   ENC
Rose, William Lewis   2:433   CHW
Rose of Cimarron   314   SW
Rosecrans, Anita Dolores   5:439   MC
Rosellini, Albert Dean   unp.   SE
Rosencranz, Mose   325   HA
Rosene, John   3:783   BHS
                      6:92   SH
                      unp.   VU
————
Rosenhaupt, Harry   [103]   RLX
Rosenthal, S   E   37   MG
Roser, Louis M   304   E
Rosling, Eric Edward   118   SS
Ross, Alexander   65   BF
                      65   BHSI
                      531   CIR
                      1:48   FI
                      3:784   SMS

Ross, Branson M   864   SIH
Ross, Mrs. Branson M   , see
    Ross, Susan A   (Terhune)
Ross, C   Ben   3:36   BEA
                      284   BR
Ross, Mrs. C   Ben, see
    Ross, Edna (Reavis)
Ross, Charles F   3:1020   FH
Ross, Clara Chase, see
    Young, Clara Chase (Ross)
Ross, Donald   4:685   BCF
                      110   PSW
Ross, E   L   1935-36:51   OO
                      1937-38:62   OO
Ross, Edna (Reavis)   3:36   BEA
Ross, Edward Wesley   3:419   LHC
                      135   MLO
                      [83]   RLX
                      6:184   SH
Ross, Edwin Byron   4:643   BCF
Ross, Ethel M   (Thomas)   3:407   BHS
Ross, Frances Eleanor, see
    Linfield, Frances Eleanor (Ross)
Ross, Frank C   2:306   HHT
Ross, James   251   GI
Ross, James Delmage   3:71   BHK
Ross, Jane (Stevenson), see
    Clark, Jane (Stevenson)
Ross, John   532   CIR
Ross, John D   3:736   SMS
Ross, John David   3:301   BCF
Ross, John E   418   GL
                      1:200   NH
————
Ross, Lucena K   , see
    Oatman, Lucena K   (Ross)
Ross, Lyman   1939-40:15   OO
Ross, Marcellus   2:356   HHT
Ross, Mrs. Marcellus, see
    Ross, Martha A   (Kellogg)
Ross, Martha A   (Kellogg)   2:357   HHT
Ross, Mrs. R   C   , see
    Ross, Ethel M   (Thomas)
Ross, Sarah E   , see
    Lamb, Sarah E   (Ross)
Ross, Mrs. Stephen W   , see
    Clark, Jane (Stevenson)
Ross, Susan A   (Terhune)   864   SIH
Ross, William Roderick   2:547   BCF
                      fol. pt. 1   SHB
                      1911:6-7, 70-71   YB
————
Rossi, Alexander   2:622   FH
Rossi, Herman J   1941:206   EN
Rosslyn, 1st earl of, see
    Wedderburn, Alexander
Rossman, George   1931-32:8   OO
                      1935-36:34   OO
                      1937-38:7   OO
————

Rosson, Hugh E — 1939-40:7 OO
— 1941-42:14 OO
— 1943-44:21 OO
— 1945-46:33 OO
Rosson, Hugh E — 1945-46:58 OO
Rotchford, Robert L — 37 — MG
Roth, Charles — 1905-06:[61] RLW
Roth, Paul E — 1937-38:62-63 OO
Rothstein, Samuel — 25:179 PNLA
— 27:23 PNLA
— 28:5 PNLA
————
Rothwell, Edwin James — 4:79 BCF
Rotten Tail, Crow chief — 10:114 MC
Rottler, Clarence T — 3:297 BHK
Roudebush, Rex S — 1924:128 WSP
Round, Eliza, see
   Russon, Eliza (Round)
Rounds, Nelson — 40 OS
Rounsefell, Frances William — 3:297 BCF
Rouse, Daniel E — 459 LHM
Rouse, Mrs. Daniel E , see
   Rouse, Susan E (Hitchcock)
Rouse, Susan E (Hitchcock) — 459 LHM
Rowand, John — 1:164 MCC
Rowe, Gordon — unp. SAA
Rowe, Lewis Solomon — 3:299 BHS
Rowe, Peter Trimble — 42 AL
— front., 47 PJ
Rowe, William — 3:680 SMS
Rowell, Fred Rice — 1:unp. 1900-01 WDT
Rowland, Dix H — 1924:129 WSP
Rowland, Gershom C — 43 no. 2:137 PN
Rowland, Green L — unp. SOU
Rowland, H G — May 1907:39 TDL
— 1924:176 WSP
Rowland, L L — 1:596 NH
Rowley, Edson M — 2:627 GP
Rowley, John — 2:41 SMS
Rowling, Henry S — 3:27 BCF
Rowntree, Jennie I — 50:32 1949 WDT
Roy, Andrew T — 4 no. 2:86 BCH
Royal, James Henry Bascom — 52 AG
Royle, Henry Moroni — 38 GL
Rozisky, Augusta — 311 BHSS
Ruark, James D — 3:89 HHI
Ruble, William Kent — 1941:362 EN
Rucker, J (Morris) — 2:184 PHP
Rucker, Mrs. Wyatt, see
   Rucker, J (Morris)
Rudd, George R — 26 DS
Ruddy, Charles A — 1:unp. 1900-01 WDT
Rude, H P — 59, 88 SS
Rudene, Bessie J (Wallace) Cornelius
— 4:515 PH
Rudene, J O — 1905-06:[64] RLW
Rudene, Mrs. John O , see
   Rudene, Bessie J (Wallace) Cornelius
Rudio, William M — 1905-06:[55] RLW

Rudkin, F H — 1926:20 WSP
Rudlin, George — 121 LDM
Rue, Alfred Welch — 3:923 SMS
Ruff, George C — 2:355 HH
Ruffner, Sanford — 5:315 MC
Rugh, Sam — 2:125 CHW
Rumel, Rosa, see
   Warner, Rosa (Rumel)
Rumley, Charles — 3:21 MC
Rummens, George H — 1924:96 WSP
— 1926:103 WSP
Rumsey, John W — 3:368 PH
Runner, W E — 1895-96:105 SSS
Running Crane, Piegan chief — 170 PI
— 204 PIW
Rupert, count Palatine of Rhine, see
   Rupert, Prince
Rupert, Prince — 8:front. HBR
— front. MH
————
Rupert, prince of Bavaria, see
   Rupert, Prince
Rupp, Otto B — 1920:front. WSP
Rupp, Werner A — 74-75 GA
— unp. WD
———— — 36:19 1935 WDT
———— — 1 no. 7:24 WN
Russel, James R — 6:303 MC
Russell, Charles — 2:463 BCF
Russell, Charles Marion — 1:passim ACR
— 535 CIR
———— — 119 NL
Russell, Charles Silas — 1:3, 206 ACR
Russell, David — 3:266 PH
Russell, Mrs. David, see
   Russell, Margaret (O'Connor)
Russell, Emma, see
   Crow, Emma (Russell)
Russell, George — May 1907:68 TDL
Russell, Harry J — 2:205 SMS
Russell, Israel Cook — 159 MMR
— fol. 207 (no. 17) SHI
————
Russell, James E — 896 SIH
Russell, James S — 2:409 HHI
Russell, Joanna Maria (Welch) — 4:145 BHK
Russell, John E — 4:569 PH
Russell, Joseph A — 3:47 BCF
Russell, Margaret (O'Connor) — 3:266 PH
Russell, Mary (Mead) — 1:3 ACR
Russell, May O , see
   Bast, May O (Russell)
Russell, Nancy (Cooper)
— 1:140, 154, 198, 228 ACR
Russell, Robert — 4:145 BHK
— 6:416-417 MC
————
Russell, Mrs. Robert, see
   Russell, Joanna Maria (Welch)
Russell, S S — 1905-06:[50] RLW

Russell, Sarah Jane (Gallagher)   200   BE
Russell, Mrs. Thomas S   , see
     Russell, Sarah Jane (Gallagher)
Russell, William   4:523   BCF
Russell, William H   167   HOM
Russell, William W   261   GG
Russon, Eliza (Round)   419   GL
Russon, Lot   276, 419   GL
Russon, Mrs. Lot, see
     Russon, Eliza (Round)
Rust, Correll Elisha   2:750   FH
Rust, Henry Arthur   4:730-731   PH
Rust, Marcia Maie, see
     Nicholson, Marcia Maie (Rust)
Rust, William Ross   3:9   BH
                            4:730-731   PH
Rustgard, John   290   HA
Ruth, A   S   1905-06:[48] RLW
                            [99]   RLX
Ryan, Edward P   36:19 1935   WDT
Ryan, John E   1924:41   WSP
Ryan, Joseph Gerald   4:640   PH
Ryan, Myrtle, see
     Bunger, Myrtle (Ryan)
Ryan, Paul M   247   GG
Ryan, Sarah A   , see
     Spinning, Sarah A   (Ryan)
Ryan, Timothy   3:307   BHS
Ryberg, Charles Elliott   359   HA
Ryder, William H   11   MLO
Ryland, A   S   1924:80   WSP
Rynning, J   L   116   SS

S

Sabin, Ella   1:402-403   GP
Sabiston, John, Jr.   324   LDM
Sabiston, John F   42   LDM
Sacajawea (Shoshone Indian) front., 21 BHSI
                            7   BR
                            1:320a   CGO
                            179   CHO
                            1:57   GP
                            70   LBT
                            16   NW
                            58 no. 1:cover PN
                            1:127   WT
Sachs, Adam   6:112   SH
Sage, Walter Noble   17 no. 1-2:1 BCH
Sager, Elizabeth, see
     Helm, Elizabeth (Sager)
Sager, Matilda J   , see
     Delaney, Matilda J   (Sager)
Sailors, R   L   134   MLO
St. Cyr, Ezra   3:719   BH

St. Germain, Mrs. Henri, see
     St. Germain, Mary Ann (Plomondon)
St. Germain, Mary Ann (Plomondon)
                            1:128   HWW
St. John, G   E   1:unp. 1900-01 WDT
St. Paul, Captain, see
     Lolo, Jean Baptiste (Shuswap Indian)
St. Vincent, earl of, see
     Jervis, John
Saldern, Lawrence J   O   3:739   GP
                            2:189   LHC
Sales, James   1:28   HHT
Saling, Francis M   1072   SIH
Saling, Mrs. Francis M   1072   SIH
Saling, Isham E   2:190   NH
Sallosalton, David (Salish Indian) 208 CAA
Salmond, Colin   305   LDM
Salomon, Edward S   25   MAG
                            42   ME
                            34 no. 4:400-401 PN
                            [53]   RLX
Salsberg, S   305   BR
Salter, John   1:317   BH
Salter, Lenore   67   MG
Saltice, see
     Seltice, Coeur d'Alene chief
Sam, Annie (Snoqualmie (?) Indian)
                            4 no. 1:fol. 83 UV
Samet, Rudolph   4:605   PH
Sammis, Charles W   3:1562   SM
Sample, W   A   81   PSW
Sampson, Betsey M   , see
     McDonald, Betsey M   (Sampson)
Sampson, H   C   215   BHSS
Sampson, John   3:899   BCF
Sampson, Julia, see
     Gage, Julia (Sampson)
Sampson, Lammon E   2:208   PHP
Samson, J   A   3:850   SMS
Samson, S   124   SS
Samson, Sam   3:389   PH
Samuels, H   F   56 no. 1:27 PN
Samuels, S   Maimon   3:699   BHK
Sanborn, I   B   309   LDM
Sanborn, John Carfield   3:43   BEA
Sandahl, C   N   70   SS
Sandegren, T   131   SS
Sanders, Edward H   1897:43   YB
Sanders, Edwin   4:557   BCF
Sanders, Helen Fitzgerald   1:front.   SM
Sanders, J   Fred   4:613   BCF
Sanders, James U   9:22   MC
Sanders, S   D   1 no. 1:30   WN
Sanders, Thomas   3:415   BHK
Sanders, Wilbur Fisk   194   BV
                            32-33   LHM

────────	808	MI
	2:front.	SM
Sanders-Husted, Mrs. Mary	2:60	PMO
Sanderson, Joseph W	6:311	MC
Sands, Alva C	3:305	HHT
Sandstrom, Emma	12	SS
Sanford, Arthur N	146	PSW
Santee, Eva	18:11	PNLA
Sanvik, Ole	3:787	SMS
Sapp, K	202	BHSS
Sappington, Henry H	3:806	SMS
Sappington, Mrs. Henry H , see		
Sappington, Ruphema J (Van Camp)		
Sappington, Ruphema J (Van Camp)		
	5:193	MC
	3:807	SMS
────────		
Sappington, William D	3:465	GP
Sard-Khom (Chehalis Indian), see		
Jackson, Robert J		
Sargeant, W P	1895-96:77	SSS
Sargent, Harry Otis King	3:247	GP
Sargent, Mollie Emily (Stockton) Leonard		
	2:119	HHI
Sargent, Nelson	132	MP
Sargent, Ralph C	3:531	HHT
Satank (Kiowa Indian)	354	SW
Satanta (Kiowa Indian)	358	SW
Satterfield, Ammon Y	3:507	BEA
Satterthwaite, J W	70	AG
Sauer, Adam	3:141	HHI
Sauer, Paul P	165	GG
Saul, Joe (Cree Indian)	34-35	MCK
Saul, William	fol. title page	SHB
Sault, George W	2:331	LHC
Saunders, James C	1:127	HH
Saunders, Robert Chancellor	3:873	BHS
Savage, Annie F (Sibley)	1:104	HWW
Savage, David	12	GL
Savage, Mrs. David, see		
Savage, Mary A (White)		
Savage, E H	unp.	SAA
Savage, Ethel Frances, see		
Clark, Ethel Frances (Savage)		
Savage, George Milton	3:133	HHT
	6:38	SH
────────		
Savage, Mrs. George Milton, see		
Savage, Annie F (Sibley)		
Savage, Mary A (White)	25	GL
Savage, Tony	176-177	GA
Savage, William	1:144	NH
Savery, William B	6:25 1906	WDT
Savidge, Clark V	1 no. 3:11	WN
Savier, Thomas A	1:210-211	GP
	2:591	GP
	1:130	PMO
────────		
	3:1373	SM
Sawyer, Caleb M	2:338-339	BCF
Sawyer, Charles A	226	LDM
Sawyer, Ladowich Latham	282	HA
Sawyer, Mary B	311	BHSS
Saxa, Francis, see		
Old Ignace (Flathead Indian)		
Saxman, S A	252	PSW
Saxton, Gertrude	215	BHSS
Saylor, Conrad G	1:500	NH
	1:360	PMO
Saylor, Fred H	1:192	PMO
Saylor, William H	568	SHP
Scafe, Charles R	143	PSW
Scallon, P J	263	E
Scalzo, Thomas C	2:541	BHK
Scanlan, Joseph D	1941:80	EN
Scanlan, Lawrence	323	HCC
Scanlan, William J	374	HA
Scanland, J M	3:1611	SM
Scarf, Oscar	447	LDM
Schafer, Margarethe, see		
Reinig, Margarethe (Schafer)		
Scharschmidt, Percy F	4:941	BCF
Schatzlein, Charles J	1:187	ACR
	2:1164	SM
Schaupp, Arthur W	1931-32:41	OO
Scheifflin, Ed	99	WOY
Schell, J	172-173	HA
Schempp, George C	3:461	HHT
Schenck, John Sylvester	2:259	LHC
Schermanson, Eric A	247	GG
Schick, Brown Macurdy	3:142	PH
Schill, Charles	1152	SIH
Schinner, A F	70:331	OHQ
Schively, John H	59 no. 3:133	PN
	1895-96:113	SSS
Schmadeka, George	567	IHI
Schmaltz, Nicholas	2:313	CHW
Schmeer, R W	14:4 1909	WBP
Schmershall, John F	3:952	FH
Schmidt, Ben	1:442-443	EPD
Schmidt, Carl	2:409	BHK
Schmidt, Grover C	unp.	HOF
Schmidt, Jacob	2:484	SMS
Schmidt, Mrs. Jacob, see		
Schmidt, Margaret (Miller)		
Schmidt, Joseph	167	OB
Schmidt, Margaret (Miller)	2:485	SMS
Schmidt, William Frederick	3:164	BEA
Schmieding, Samuel B	2:277	CHW
Schmitt, J H	44	MG
Schmitten, Fred W	3:72	PH
Schmitz, Henry	120-121	GA
Schnabel, Charles Joseph	2:199	LHC
Schnebly, David J	1:100	NH
Schnebly, Mrs. David J , see		
Schnebly, Margaretta (Painter)		
Schnebly, Eliza (Cooke)	3:170	PH
Schnebly, Margaretta (Painter)	1:102	D

134

Schnebly, Philip Henry	3:170	PH
Schnebly, Mrs. Philip Henry, see		
Schnebly, Eliza (Cooke)		
Schneider, Albert	207	HA
Schneider, C C	255	GI
Schneider, Daniel D	1924:97	WSP
Schofield, Edward Richard	2:351	LHC
Schofield, George D	338	HA
Schofield, James Hargrave	1911:70-71	YB
Scholl, Louis	67:325	OHQ
Schons, Mary Lyle	42:32 1930	WSGP
Schooley, Albert	1905-06:[28]	RLW
Schoonover, John A	3:501	BEA
Schorr, George F	2:630	NH
Schottland, Charles I	4 no. 8:3	C
Schow, Anton C	323	HA
Schow, Celestia (Willes)	422	GL
Schow, George Peter	421	GL
Schow, Mrs. George Peter, see		
Schow, Celestia (Willes)		
Schow, Mrs. Peter	87	GL
Schrader, Frank C	fol. 207 (no. 31)	SHI
Schram, John	2:169	BHK
Schram, Lloyd W	50:22 1949	WDT
Schramm, Arthur	1924:49	WSP
Schreiber, Adolph F	2:853	FH
Schrenk, Ernest Earl	2:41	CHW
Schricker, W E	2:420	PHP
	8:40 1903	WBP
Schroeder, John H	3:1299	SM
Schrunk, Terry	67:204	OHQ
Schubert, James	2:front. 1924	BCHA
Schue, Peter	1112	SIH
Schuebel, Christian	2:521	LHC
Schuler, Matthias	293	HA
Schulmerich, Edward	1931-32:40	OO
Schultz, F W	24:128 1919	WBP
Schultz, Joseph A	232	SIH
Schultz, Samuel Davies	4:457	BCF
Schultz, William	3:593	HHI
Schulze, Paul	1:109	HH
Schumacher, Henry J	3:1633	SM
Schumacher, Matilda French	5:191	MC
Schumann, Irma (Lum)	3:68	D
Schumann, Mrs. Oscar Robert, see		
Schumann, Irma (Lum)		
Schumann, Otto	2:437	PMO
Schuster, Gustav	3:509	BH
Schuyler, Philip Church	2:575	GP
Schuyver, William James van, see		
Van Schuyver, William James		
Schwab, Samuel	675	LHM
Schwab, Samuel B	3:821	GP
Schwachheim, Aug	3:985	SMS
Schwatk	9	HEG
Schwatka, Frederick	278-279	HU
	fol. 207 (no. 19)	SHI
Schweberger, John	3:367	LHC
Schwendiman, Fred	3:1166	FH
Schweppe, Alfred John	4:479	PH
Schwinn, H J	3:191	BH
	May 1907:68	TDL
Scobey, John O'B	1895-96:113	SSS
Scofield, George	6:48	SH
Scofield, Thomas Donaldson	2:109	HH
Sconce, Nancy, see		
Elliott, Nancy (Sconce)		
Scotch Jennie, see		
Allen, Mrs. Janet		
Scott, Abigail, see		
Duniway, Abigail (Scott)		
Scott, Anne (Roelofson)	14:104	OHQ
Scott, C G	unp.	SOU
Scott, C H	1895-96:107	SSS
Scott, Ella	70:251	OHQ
Scott, Elmon	1895-96:145	SSS
Scott, Francis Marion	3:1150	FH
Scott, Frank T	288	E
Scott, Golden	380	BF
Scott, Harvey Whitefield	1:4, 498	GP
	2:35	GP
	14:passim	OHQ
	34:191	OHQ
	70:197, 224, 232	OHQ
	1:584	PMO
	2:342	PMO
	1:front., 30, 60, 120	SHO
	2:front.	SHO
	3:front.	SHO
	4:front.	SHO
	5:front.	SHO
	154	SHP
	16	TO
Scott, Hugh L	118	LBT
Scott, J H	1895:98	OO
Scott, J N	299	E
Scott, James H E	1931-32:41	OO
	1935-36:51	OO
Scott, James W B	1924:160	WSP
Scott, John B	70:251	OHQ
Scott, John H	2:635	BHK
Scott, John N	1895-96:139	SSS
Scott, John Tucker	1:332	NH
	14:96	OHQ
	1:130	PMO
	4:449	BCF
Scott, Joseph		
Scott, Joseph N	1931-32:41	OO
Scott, Leslie M	1941-42:13	OO
	1943-44:17	OO
	1945-46:21	OO
Scott, Levi	1:278	NH
Scott, Mary, see		
Stewart, Mary (Scott)		

Scott, Perry	231	LDM
Scott, R	1:641	CHW
Scott, Richard	2:713	GP
Scott, Thomas	172-173	HA
Scott, Thomas A	321	QT
Scott, Thomas Fielding	1:673	CHW
_____	1:208-209	GP
_____	17	JP
_____	4:298	LH
_____	1:44	NH
_____	1:566	PMO
Scott, U B	1:258	GP
_____	211	LDM
Scott, W D	1905-06:[65]	RLW
_____	[91]	RLX
Scott, William	unp.	SOU
Scoullar, Edwin Sayre	276	KB
Scoy, T van, see		
Van Scoy, T		
Scranton, John Hart	45 no. 3:76	PN
Scrim, Walter George	4:101	BCF
Scruby, Wilbur William	3:249	PH
_____	43 no. 1:16-17	PN
Scudder, Lulu Dean, see		
Hildreth, Lulu Dean (Scudder)		
Scully, John A	3:819	BHK
Scurry, John G	3:975	BHS
Scurry, Matthew Edward	3:974	BHS
Seaborg, B A	1:265	HH
Seaborn, Henry G	3:333	PH
Seabury, William B	234	LDM
Sealth, see		
Seattle, chief of the Suquamps		
Sealth, Kick-is-om-lo, see		
Angeline, Princess		
Seaman, N G	41:154	OHQ
Seaman, Sarah A , see		
Luce, Sarah A (Seaman)		
Searing, W H	59	SSP
Searl, Albert	1895-96:149	SSS
Sears, Alfred	1:307	GP
Sears, Fred B	248	SIH
Sears, George C	1895:174	OO
Seaton, (Captain)	439	LDM
Seaton, R W	1935:5	S
_____	1936:3	S
_____	1937:3	S
Seattle, chief of the Suquamps	88	AG
_____	1:78	BHS
_____	1:82	D
_____	1:112	HWW
_____	2:4	NH
_____	1:221	PHP
_____	3:124	SH
_____	unp.	VU
_____	32	WCS
Seavey, Alice (Stewart)	2:445	CHW
Seavey, James	1:196	NH

Seavey, John H	2:445	CHW
Seavey, Mrs. John H , see		
Seavey, Alice (Stewart)		
Sebastian, Cloah C , see		
Cowling, Cloah C (Sebastian)		
Secrest, John Howard	3:519	LHC
_____	89	MLO
Secretan, James Henry Edward	136	SC
Seely, Jasper B	2:1147	SM
Seetin, Oliver	3:707	HHI
Seevers, E E	1895-96:107	SSS
Sefrit, Frank I	1 no. 10:14	WN
Seghers, Charles John	216	MHC
_____	70:325	OHQ
_____	199	OP
_____	194	OPC
_____	358	PI
_____	424	PIW
_____	59 no. 4:193	PN
_____	176	SG
Sehlbrede, C A	1895:104	OO
Seibert, Arthur D	unp.	SOU
Seibert, Weldon Earl	unp.	SOU
Seiffert, G	172-173	HA
Seis, F L	151	OB
Selck, William W , Jr.	3:609	HHI
Selden, J W	85	LDM
Selkirk, 5th earl of, see		
Douglas, Thomas		
Selleck, W H	118	AG
Sellwood, James R W	1:44	NH
_____	1:566	PMO
Seltice, Coeur d'Alene chief		
_____	fol. 512 (no. 8)	BUR
_____	16	CK
_____	224	MCO
_____	70:161	OHQ
Seltis, Andrew, see		
Seltice, Coeur d'Alene chief		
Selway, Ernest O	2:1014	SM
Selway, Herbert B	2:1054-1055	SM
Selway, James	2:1054-1055	SM
Selway, John Lloyd	3:1017	SMS
Selway, John R	5:323	MC
Semlin, Charles Augustus	2:337, 451	BCF
_____	110	JAC
_____	fol. pt. 1	SHB
_____	1897:105	YB
_____	1911:70-71	YB
Semon, Henry	1935-36:51	OO
_____	1937-38:62-63	OO
_____	1939-40:31	OO
_____	1941-42:66	OO
_____	1943-44:79	OO
_____	1945-46:87	OO
Semple, A	2:front. 1924	BCHA
Semple, Eugene	33	MAG

	64	ME
——— ———	1:580	NH
	2:534	PHP
	34 no. 4:400-401	PN
	59 no. 2:79	PN
	[61]	RLX
	unp.	SE
Senkler, John Harold	4:1101	BCF
	fol. pt. 2	SHP
Senter, Almon S	212	IHI
Serjeantson, Charles R	3:1015	BCF
Serra, Junipero	103	HCC
Serrurier, P M	23:64 1918	WBP
Service, Robert W	63	AL
Settergren, G E	2:143	SMS
Settlemeier, Bob	63:321	OHQ
Settlemier, J H	1:104	NH
Settlemier, Mary A , see		
Allen, Mary A (Settlemier)		
Severance, George	446	BHSS
Severe, Deseret, see		
Cummins, Deseret (Severe)		
Severyns, W B	7, 41, 60	SSP
Sewall, A M	[125]	RLX
Sewall, Russell E	2:16	PMO
Seward, Fred W	278-279	HU
Seward, William Henry	292	AC
	464	AG
	78	BET
	278-279	HU
Sewell, Amy P , see		
Stacy, Amy P (Sewell)		
Sewell, Frank C	fol. pt. 2	SHB
Sewell, J K	172-173	HA
Sewell, John R	359	LDM
Sexton, Charles J	3:1083	BHS
Sexton, Frank	243	GG
Sexton, Frank J	3:1041	BHS
Seymore, W B	395	LDM
Seymour, Frederick	2:167, 277	BCF
	fol. title page	SHB
	96-97	SHL
	1897:63	YB
	1911:70-71	YB
Seymour, H C	1945-46:194	OO
Seymour, Joseph Richard	4:857	BCF
Seymour, Walter R	2:799	HHI
Shaaks, see		
Shakes, Stikine chief		
Shadden, Thomas J	1:96	NH
Shaefer, George W	1924:176	WSP
Shaff, C W	32	SPI
Shaffer, C Will	1924:96	WSP
Shakes, Stikine chief	26	CT
	179	JA
	282	KB
Shakespeare, Noah	1924:112	WSP
Shank, Corwin Sheridan	3:294	PH
Shannahan, W T	1:470	GP
Shannon, George D	1:508	NH
Shannon, James	3:349	BHS
Shannon, Mike	1:292	ACR
Shapard, Henry Louis	3:1504	SM
Shaplish, Charlie, see		
Whirlwind (Umatilla Indian)		
Sharai, Wellington F	888	SIH
Sharon, William	244	QT
Sharp, Charles E	2:805	HHI
Sharp, E M	231	PSW
Sharpe, Ebenezer	6:339	MC
Sharpstein, E L	1905-06:[28]	RLW
Shatford, Lytton Wilmot	1911:70-71	YB
Shatford, Walter T	fol. pt. 1	SHB
Shattuck, Erasmus D	1:554	GP
	241	HIO
———	1:212	NH
Shattuck, Lewis	1 no. 1:15	WN
Shaub, O P	3:585	BH
Shaughnessy, T G	352, 371	GI
	194	SC
Shaver, Delmer	3:907	LHC
Shaver, George M	399	LDM
	3:906	LHC
Shaver, George Washington	3:897	LHC
	2:341	PMO
Shaver, James W	3:187	GP
	366	LDM
	3:901	LHC
Shaver, Lincoln	366	LDM
	3:911	LHC
Shaw, A J	289	E
Shaw, Alexander	3:885	BCF
Shaw, Benjamin F	1:464	NH
	3:492	SH
	1895-96:77	SSS
Shaw, C R	2:660	FH
Shaw, DeVota	66	MG
Shaw, F A	172-173	HA
Shaw, James P	1:572-573	GP
	3:763	GP
Shaw, James Pearson	fol. pt. 1	SHB
	1911:70-71	YB
Shaw, John, 1863-	4:629	BCF
Shaw, John	177	PL
Shaw, Katie	2:292	PMO
Shaw, Ralph	21:31	PNLA
Shaw, Samuel	76	DT
Shaw, Mrs. Sarah	1:464	NH
Shaw, Thomas C	1:260	NH
Shaw, W M	9:116 1904	WBP
Shaw, Wilfred W	135	PSW
Shaw, William	1:464	NH

Shay, Oren Everett 1943:216 ENC
Shea, John Francis 3:535 LHC
Shearer, Guy Harrison 3:121 BEA
Shearer, W W 48 LS
She-ca-yah, Cayuse chief 292 WCS
Shedd, Solon 175, 215 BHSS
Shee-at-ston, Sarah (Salish Indian) 128 CAA
Sheehan, John F 2:198 NH
Sheehan, Luke 151 OB
Sheehan, Mike 63 LT
Sheets, J H 1905-06: [58] RLW
 [126] RLX
Sheets, Mary Jane (Cochran) 2:24 CPD
Sheffield, William M May 1907:37 TDL
 unp. VU
Shelby, Annie Blanche 1:537 PMO
Sheldon, E L 1924:113 WSP
Sheldon, Netta Wells, see
 Phelps, Netta Wells (Sheldon)
Shelekov, Gregorii Ivanovich 44 AN
 41 BET
 278-279 HU
Shelley, Troy 1:917 LHC
 3:349 LHC
Shelton, David 1:420 NH
Shelton, Harriet 48 ST
Shelton, John A 3:1557 SM
Shelton, Joseph M 2:122 NH
Shelton, Mrs. Joseph M , see
 Shelton, Missouri C (Jones)
Shelton, Missouri C (Jones) 2:122 NH
Shelton, William (Snohomish Indian)
 front., 38 ST
 4 no. 1:fol. 83 UV
Shemanski, Alfred 4:690 PH
 36:19 1935 WDT
Shepard, Charles Edward 3:585 BHS
 1:unp. 1900-01 WDT
 1924:161 WSP
Shepherd, Harold 36:21, 26 1935 WDT
Shepherd, William 177 PL
Sheppard, Harry Peter 1941:199 EN
Shepperd, Ruth 67 MG
Sheridan, John 69:146 OHQ
Sheridan, Philip Henry 31 DH
 2:252 FI
 4:226 LH
 1:68 NH
Sherlock, Rosetta (Whale) 1:354 PMO
Sherlock, Samuel 3:173 GP
 1:354 PMO
 2:341 PMO
Sherlock, Mrs. Samuel, see
 Sherlock, Rosetta (Whale)
Sherlock, William 2:553 GP
 1:354 PMO
 2:333 PMO
Sherman, Evangeline (Fullmer) 3:63 D

Sherman, Fred 355 LDM
Sherman, Nora K (Daugherty) 3:819 SMS
Sherman, W P 3:818 SMS
Sherman, Mrs. W P , see
 Sherman, Nora K (Daugherty)
Sherman, William Tecumseh 31 DH
 331 VT
Sherrieb, F C 1:917 LHC
Sherrill, "Bunch" 7:122 MC
Sherrill, T C 7:122 MC
Sherwood, Charles 32 KT
Shields, E C 447 LDM
Shields, Elmer E 1924:64 WSP
Shields, James H 132 PSW
Shields, William 447 LDM
Shields, William W 2:569 BHK
Shillestad, Frank William 3:189 BHS
Shilling, Watson N 3:1026 FH
Shinn, Benny 2:24 CPD
Shinn, Mrs. Ethel 2:24 CPD
Shinn, Frank 252 JNT
Shinn, Ray 2:24 CPD
Shinn, Mrs. Ray, see
 Shinn, Mrs. Ethel
Shinn, William P 2:551 HHI
Shipley, A R 1:210-211 GP
Shipley, Mrs. A R 1:210-211 GP
Shipley, Brice 2:882 FH
Shipley, E A 48 LS
Shipley, John J 2:438 PMO
Shipley, Louis 58 BR
Shipley, Whitfield 2:181 SMS
Shipman, Allen W unp. SAA
Shippen, Joseph 3 no. 8:422 PM
Shirley, Charles B 2:842 FH
Shissler, Mrs. Bertha 2:208-209 EPD
Shissler, Mrs. Frances 2:208-209 EPD
Shissler, Frank 2:442-443 EPD
Shober, John H 185 LHM
Shoemaker, Mrs. Ida 59 MHS
Shoemaker, William B 43 no. 1:17 PN
Shofner, Henry B 3:385 LHC
Shofner, Webb C 3:323 LHC
Shorey, Mary E (Bonney) 2:1227 BH
Shorrock, Ebenezer 43 no. 1:16 PN
 unp. VU
Short, Mrs. Esther 1 no. 6:9 WN
Short, Joseph M 3:193 LHC
Short, Miles 235 LDM
Short, O F 3:159 HHI
Short, Sherman V 251 LDM
Short, W P 335 LDM
Short, William Mackie 3:215 PH
 57 no. 4:152 PN
Shorter, Fred 59 no. 2:96 PN
Shorthill, David R 7:83 MC

Shot-in-the-Head, see
    Ho-sus-pa-ow-yun (Nez Percé Indian)
Shotwell, Harvey E   3:917   BHS
Shoudy, John A   1905-06:[28]   RLW
Shoudy, W   H   unp.   SEA
Shoup, George Laird   3:41   BEA
    _____   307   DSW
    _____   1941:8   EN
        17:3 1939-1940   IH
Shoup, James M   1:120   FSB
Shoup, Richard Marvin   3:224   BEA
Shoup, William Henry   3:224   BEA
Show-a-Way, Paul, Umatilla chief
    1:568-569   GP
    1:120   PMO
Shrader, E   Von, see
    Von Shrader, E
Shultz, William   1905-06:[62]   RLW
    [136]   RLX
Shuluskin, Yakima chief   339   SK
    344   SKA
Shumway, Emma A   200   BE
Shupe, James R   3:1059   FH
Shutrum, George   1895:105   OO
Shutt, Calvin H   3:153   HWW
Shutt, R   D   May 1907:84   TDL
Shy, Maggie S   , see
    Simpson, Maggie S   (Shy)
Sibbits, William   3:891   SMS
Sibley, Annie F   , see
    Savage, Annie F   (Sibley)
Sicade, Henry (Nisqualli Indian)   1:38   HHT
Sichel, Sigmund   2:578   NH
Siddoway, James Clarence   3:268   BEA
    2:787   HHI
    _____   3:171   HHI
Siddoway, James W
Sidebotham, Robert A   3:1242   FH
Sidey, Thomas K   6:27 1906   WDT
Sieg, Lee Paul   120-121   GA
    36:front. 1935   WDT
Siegel, A   W   264   E
Siegel, Victor   2:553   SMS
Siegle, John Charles   1941:241   EN
Sieh, Magdalena, see
    Traeger, Magdalena (Sieh)
Sievers, John R   E   3:1576   SM
Sievert, Goswin   680   SIH
Sieward, H   F   447   LDM
Silcock, William Massey   4:7   BCF
Silcott, Jane (Nez Percé Indian)   105   BR
Silcott, John M   107   BR
    152   DSW
    _____   1:555   HHI
    _____   119   IHI
Silcott, Mrs. John M   , see
    Silcott, Jane (Nez Percé Indian)
Silverwood, J   F   (probably)
    2:368-369   EPD

Simineo, Joseph S   2:208   SMS
Simmonds, Henry   129   GL
Simmonds, Mrs. Henry   115   GL
Simmons, Daniel W   1:355   HH
Simmons, Hubert Alfred   1941:44   EN
    2:69   SMS
Simmons, Michael Troutman   1:108   HHT
    _____   1:102   HWW
    _____   232   MP
    _____   1:20   NH
    _____   44 no. 2:62   PN
    _____   46 no. 2:55   PN
    _____   3:front.   SH
    _____   49   WCS
Simmons, Mrs. Michael Troutman   1:103   HWW
Simms, Samuel   3:885   SMS
Simon, Joseph   1895:74   OO
    326   PL
    _____   1:300   PMO
Simon, Rose Emma, see
    Gwinn, Rose Emma (Simon)
Simons, Daniel Page   5:410   SH
Simonson, Katie, see
    Donley, Katie (Simonson)
Simplot, John Richard   3:2   BEA
Simpson, A   M   74   LDM
Simpson, Charles M   3:1360   SMS
Simpson, Mrs. Charles M   , see
    Simpson, Maggie S   (Shy)
Simpson, George   263   CHO
    62, 94   GI
    _____   1:front.   HBR
    _____   2:360   LH
    _____   174, 175   MH
    _____   34   MHN
    _____   2:402   SH
    _____   45   WTH
    _____   1897:18   YB
Simpson, Harry Percy   3:1103   BCF
Simpson, Hugh James   4:493   BCF
Simpson, Isaac M   2:448   PMO
Simpson, John P   4:573   PH
Simpson, Louis   1:372   HHT
Simpson, Maggie S   (Shy) 3:1360   SMS
Simpson, Robert Niel   319   HA
Simpson, Samuel L   1:545   CHW
    1:603   GP
    _____   4:354   LH
    _____   1:79   PMO
Simpson, T   W   3:1178   SMS
Simpson, Thomas   266   MH
Simpson, William   319   LDM
Sims, D   121   WOY
Sims, Edgar Albert   3:38   PH
Sims, James Howard   3:345   BEA
Sinclair, Bartlett   554   IHI

Sinclair, Clarence W   306   LDM
Sinclair, James   66:144   OHQ
Sinclair, James William   3:839   BCF
Sinclair, Temple Frederick   4:835   BCF
Sinclair, Walter   1895:170   OO
Singiser, T F   22   HIT
Sinnott, N J   1:423   LHC
Sinsel, Charles J   2:725   FH
Sisson, A A   89   MLO
Sistine Craig (Umatilla Indian)   212   AI
Sitting Bull, Sioux chief   322   AM
_____   302-303   HCM
_____   70   KY
_____   373   VT
Sitting Eagle, see
    Jones, Evan
Sitton, Charles E   2:517   GP
Sitton, Mrs. L W   1:386   GP
Sitton, N K   2:74   NH
Siyaka (Sioux Indian)   front.   DAI
Skahan, Winifred   66   MG
Skak-ish-tin (Tlingit Indian)   27   CTL
Skalet, Ole O   3:1078   FH
Skandoo, Chilkat chief   7   WOY
Skansie, Mitchell   1941:352   EN
Skeffington, Leo T   255   GG
Skelton, Oscar D   1:634   BCF
Skelton, William   3:1295   SMS
Skene, J L   fol. pt. 2   SHB
Skidmore, R M   172-173   HA
Skinner, David Edward   3:396   PH
Skinner, Eugene F   1:392   NH
Skinner, Harry J   2:495   SMS
Skinner, John M   141   PSW
Skinner, R J   1897:42   YB
Skinner, Thomas   344   LDM
Skinner, Thomas James   1:542   BCF
_____   front.   LCT
_____   1897:103   YB
Skipworth, G F   1945-46:92   OO
Skloo, Yakima chief   202   WCS
Skonnord, Bernt O   1152   SIH
Skylstead, Olaf G   3:752   SMS
Slack, Emma C , see
    Dickinson, Emma C (Slack)
Slacum, Clowwewalla (?) chief 7   BD
Slade, Jack   166   SW
Sladen, J A   119   PL
Slater, Bruce E   74   AL
Slater, Hannah, see
    Bone, Hannah (Slater)
Slater, James Harvey   4:318   LH
Slater, Joseph   131   GL
Slattery, William Charles   2:311   GP
Slaughter, Mary (Wells)   1:171   BH
_____   1:309   PH
Slaughter, William Alloway   1:171   BH
_____   1:309   PH

Slaughter, Mrs. William Alloway, see
    Slaughter, Mary (Wells)
Slayden, James Wesley   3:479   BH
_____   3:641   HHT
_____   [127]   RLX
_____   6:208   SH
Slemmer, Adam   31   DH
Slemmons, Arthur L   1895-96:134   SSS
_____   1926:20   WSP
Sligh, James M   2:300   SMS
Sloan, A D   290   E
Sloan, George Washington   1:566   BH
_____   152   PSW
Sloan, John M   369   HA
Sloan, W F   1167   LHM
Sloan, William   3:773   BCF
Sloan, William James   3:657   BCF
Sloan, William N   6:350   MC
Slocum, Charles Wilbur   2:526   GP
Slocum, Mrs. Charles Wilbur, see
    Slocum, Laura (Riggs)
Slocum, Laura (Riggs)   2:527   GP
Sloggy, Charles V   265   E
Sloop, Jacob A   848   SIH
Sloper, Chester O   2:457   CHW
Sloper, Willard A   2:421   CHW
Sloss, Louis   31   KI
Sloviaczek, Mike   2:144-145   EPD
Slugamus Koquilton, see
    Koquilton, Slugamus
Sluyter, Catherine, see
    Davis, Catherine (Sluyter)
Sluyter, Westol H   872   SIH
Slyke, J A van, see
    Van Slyke, J A
Slyke, Lee van, see
    Van Slyke, Lee
Slyter, George W   3:751   BH
Slyter, Mrs. George W , see
    Slyter, Theresa (Tobey)
Slyter, Theresa (Tobey)   3:751   BH
Small, Mary A , see
    Dunphy, Mary A (Small)
Small, Rainie (Adamson)   3:122   HWW
_____   2:154   PHP
Small, Wallace Franklin   3:123   HWW
Small, Mrs. Wallace Franklin, see
    Small, Rainie (Adamson)
Smalley, M A   [118]   RLX
Smedley,   (Fraser Valley) 2:139   BCF
Smeed, Florence (Beckmann)   3:415   BEA
Smeed, John W   3:415   BEA
_____   2:841   HHI
Smeed, Mrs. John W , see
    Smeed, Florence (Beckmann)
Smelser, Guy Weatherly   92   SRW

Name	Reference	Source
Smet, Pierre Jean de	284	BF
	99	BHSI
_____	fol. 512 (no. 7, 14)	BUR
_____	9	CCA
_____	9	CK
_____	130	DSW
_____	1:64	FI
_____	2:88	FI
_____	45	FM
_____	15	GG
_____	1:85	GP
_____	267	HCC
_____	unp.	HOF
_____	3	JJ
_____	3:422	LH
_____	16	LHM
_____	passim	LL
_____	3:201	MC
_____	front.	MF
_____	1:40	NH
_____	111	OP
_____	58	OPC
_____	1:192	PH
_____	24	PI
_____	32	PIW
_____	1:524	PMO
_____	9	SCH
_____	2:164	SH
_____	1:front., 150, 253	SLL
_____	3:839, 903	SLL
_____	4:front., 1592	SLL
_____	1:214	SMS
_____	149	VT
Smiley, A L	172-173	HA
Smith, (Captain)	439	LDM
Smith, Mrs. A	2:front. 1924	BCHA
Smith, A C	1:534	HHT
Smith, A J	2:485	HH
Smith, Alexander	6:330-331	MC
Smith, Alexander Malcolm	1941:466	EN
Smith, Alfred Wellington	1897:108	YB
Smith, Alleck C	189	BHSI
Smith, Alvin T	134	DO
Smith, Andrew	46	JNT
Smith, Andrew C	2:455	PMO
Smith, Ann (Coleman)	424	GL
Smith, Anne	42:32 1930	WSGP
Smith, Archibald Erskine	3:511	BCF
Smith, Arethusa E (Lynn)	1:392	NH
Smith, Atherton N	140	PSW
Smith, Betsy, see		
Goodwin, Betsy (Smith)		
Smith, Britt	46	LT
Smith, C A	307	PL
Smith, C J	unp.	VU
Smith, Carroll	37	MG
Smith, Charles	936	SIH
Smith, Charles J	576	SHP
Smith, Charles L	unp.	SEA
Smith, Charles McKeivers		
	fol. title page	SHB
Smith, Charles W	1924:161	WSP
Smith, Charles Wesley	12:19	PNLA
_____	26:42 1925	WDT
_____	36:23 1935	WDT
Smith, Chester A	front.	BM
Smith, Cleveland	1895-96:107	SSS
Smith, Cornelius B	1895:100	OO
Smith, D A	unp.	SOU
Smith, Mrs. Daisy	1:154-155	EPD
Smith, David	3:248	BEA
Smith, David, 1844-	112-113 (xii)	PR
Smith, David K	856	SIH
Smith, Delazon	1:415	CHW
_____	4:310	LH
_____	1:182	PMO
Smith, Donald Alexander	2:427	BCF
_____	front., 148, 298, 302	GI
_____	290	MH
_____	250	SC
Smith, E Deane	215	BHSS
Smith, E E	1905-06:[57]	RLW
Smith, E L	1:596	NH
Smith, Earl R	63:263	OHQ
Smith, Edmund Augustine	6:212	SH
Smith, Edward Lincoln	5:294	SH
Smith, Edward Loomis	12:243	MWH
Smith, Edward S	2:214	NH
Smith, Elizabeth	1:563	CHW
Smith, Ella M	1:462	GP
Smith, Elmer	49	LT
_____	59 no. 2:93	PN
Smith, Elmer H	3:229	LHC
Smith, Elmo E	99	TUR
Smith, Ephraim	3:1039	FH
Smith, Ernest C	1931-32:41	OO
Smith, Eugene D	2:163	HH
_____	1:376	NH
Smith, Eva Cline	1:456	GP
Smith, F R	37	OS
Smith, Fannie, see		
Goble, Fannie (Smith)		
Smith, Ferdinand C	70:60	OHQ
Smith, Frank S	248	HA
Smith, G William H	116	PSW
Smith, George	126	CBC
Smith, George	6:424-425	MC
Smith, George A	111	BU
Smith, Mrs. George D	163	BR
Smith, George Grantham	6:290	MC
_____	6:301	MC
Smith, George Otis	241	MMR
Smith, George Venable	3:281	HWW
_____	48	LS

Smith, Gilbert F   2:839   FH
Smith, Glynn Elliott   3:170   BEA
Smith, Green B   1:278   NH
Smith, Green Clay   4:100   MC
Smith, H   A   368   JNT
Smith, Mrs. H   F   6:436   MC
Smith, Mrs. Hannah M   1:312   NH
Smith, Harlan I   2 no. 1:74   WM
Smith, Harry C   3:1704   SM
Smith, Harry E   36:23 1935   WDT
Smith, Hedley Fletcher   3:1340   SM
Smith, Mrs. Helen (Indian name: Celiast)
                                2:110   NH
Smith, Henry, 1856-   232   HA
Smith, Henry   190   LDM
Smith, Henry A   1:79   BHK
————   2:846   BHS
————   12:243   MWH
————   2:354   NH
                                2:444   PMO
Smith, Henry T   6:436   MC
                                3:1266   SMS
Smith, Hiram   1:308   NH
Smith, Hiram F   44 no. 2:67   PN
Smith, Hyrum   112-113 (xiv)   PR
Smith, Ira S   1895:94   OO
Smith, Irene   212   SG
Smith, J   2:front. 1924   BCHA
Smith, J   A   1895:83   OO
Smith, J   Allen   120-121   GA
————   46 no. 3:69   PN
————   53 no. 2:51   PN
————   1:unp. 1900-01   WDT
                                6:22 1906   WDT
Smith, Mrs. J   F   2:front. 1924   BCHA
Smith, J   H   172-173   HA
Smith, J   L   2:front. 1924   BCHA
Smith, Mrs. J   L   2:front. 1924   BCHA
Smith, J   L   (Captain) 295   LDM
Smith, J   Miller   6:350   MC
Smith, J   N   2:440   PMO
Smith, J   W   11, 15   SSP
Smith, James C   53   PSW
Smith, James H   5:329   MC
Smith, Jane (Bell), see
    Coble, Jane (Bell)
Smith, Jeanette (Herrick)   836   SIH
Smith, Jefferson Randolph   18, 20   WOY
Smith, John   16 no. 1-2:74   BCH
Smith, John, 1781-1854   112-113 (xxxvi)   PR
Smith, John, 1832-   112-113 (xxxvi)   PR
Smith, John C   159   WOY
Smith, John E   38   LC
Smith, John James   1905-06:[50]   RLW
                                5:419   SH
Smith, John Jones   2:860   FH
Smith, John L   2:894   FH
Smith, John Randolph   94   LHN

Smith, John T   16   LHM
————   2:1100   SM
Smith, John W   637   LHM
Smith, Mrs. Joseph, Sr., see
    Smith, Lucy (Mack)
Smith, Joseph, 1805-1844   573   CIR
————   front.   FU
————   8   GMM
————   112-113 (xiv)   PR
Smith, Mrs. Joseph, see
    Willes, Melissa (Lott) Smith
Smith, Joseph, 1832-1914   573   CIR
————   112-113 (xi)   PR
Smith, Joseph E   N
                                fol. title page   SHB
Smith, Joseph Fielding   573   CIR
————   57   CWW
Smith, Joseph Johnson   39   GL
Smith, Mrs. Joseph Johnson, see
    Smith, Ann (Coleman)
    Smith, Sarah Ann (Liddiard)
Smith, Joseph K   1 no. 3:217   WM
Smith, Joseph Schoewalter   106   SHP
Smith, L   C   1:487   BHK
Smith, Leo   1939-40:31   OO
————   1941-42:66   OO
————   1943-44:79   OO
Smith, Leonard P   unp.   SEA
Smith, Lewis A   3:1537   SM
Smith, Lois A   , see
    Bushman, Lois A   (Smith)
Smith, Lotta C   1931-32:41   OO
Smith, Lucinda   70:60   OHQ
Smith, Lucy, see
    Cox, Lucy (Smith)
Smith, Lucy (Mack)   22   GLS
————   112-113 (xiii)   PR
Smith, Madison C   2:656   FH
————   2:853   HHI
Smith, Margaret E   (Watkins) 1:124   PMO
Smith, Mary, see
    Oldham, Mary (Smith)
Smith, Melissa (Lott), see
    Willes, Melissa (Lott) Smith
Smith, Mollie, see
    Mounce, Mollie (Smith)
Smith, Peter J   3:435   BHK
Smith, Phil   2:front. 1924   BCHA
Smith, Preston Carter   2:487   GP
Smith, Ralph   1911:70-71   YB
Smith, Rebecca, see
    Standring, Rebecca (Smith)
Smith, Reuben   28   LDM
Smith, Rex   1 no. 4:307   WM
Smith, Richard F   3:1039   SMS
Smith, Robert   2:337   BCF
————   126   CBC

Smith, Robert B — 4:68 — MC
———— — 332 — MI
Smith, Robert G — 1895:98 — OO
Smith, Robert T — 94 — HEH
Smith, Rufus H — 3:31 — BHS
———— — 5:418 — SH
Smith, S T — 1905-06:[44] — RLW
———— — [104] — RLX
Smith, Samuel Cameron — fol. pt. 2 — SHB
Smith, Samuel D — 2:605 — GP
———— — 1:124 — PMO
Smith, Mrs. Samuel D , see
   Smith, Margaret E (Watkins)
Smith, Samuel L — 836 — SIH
Smith, Mrs. Samuel L , see
   Smith, Jeanette (Herrick)
Smith, Samuel Thaddeus N — 2:625 — FH
Smith, Sanford — 1:917 — LHC
Smith, Sarah Ann (Liddiard) — 425 — GL
Smith, Mrs. Silas B — 2:110 — NH
Smith, Soapy, see
   Smith, Jefferson Randolph
Smith, Solomon Howard — 2:110 — NH
Smith, Mrs. Solomon Howard, see
   Smith, Mrs. Helen
Smith, Stevenson — 26:58 1925 — WDT
Smith, T Fleming — 1895:101 — OO
Smith, T K — fol pt. 2 — SHB
Smith, T V — 27 — LDM
———— — 1 — TM
Smith, Thelma — 42:32 1930 — WSGP
Smith, Thomas — 65 — BHSS
———— — 28 — LDM
———— — 1:392 — NH
———— — 1:428 — NH
Smith, Mrs. Thomas, see
   Smith, Arethusa E (Lynn)
Smith, Thomas B — 2:505 — HHI
Smith, Thomas John — fol. pt. 2 — SHB
Smith, W Egbert — 233 — LHM
Smith, W Parry — 3:895 — BHS
Smith, W Tyler — 2:454 — PMO
Smith, Warren D — 1945-46:187 — OO
Smith, Wilber Stanley — 4:483 — BCF
Smith, Wilfred A — 2:577 — HHT
Smith, William — 123 — LDM
Smith, William, 1854- — 2:451 — PMO
Smith, William Alexander, see
   De Cosmos, Amor
Smith, William K — 3:225 — GP
Smith, Mrs. William Lewis, see
   Coble, Jane (Bell)
Smithe, William — 2:335, 337 — BCF
———— — 62 — JAC
———— — fol. pt. 1 — SHB
———— — 1897:64 — YB
———— — 1911:70-71 — YB

Smither, Russell — 4:301 — BCF
Smithers, Erasmus M — 1:749 — BHK
Smitley, George Albert — 4:434 — PH
Smits, Paul — 2:163 — HWW
Smock, P Monroe — 2:820 — FH
———— — 1:136 — FSB
Smohalla (Sokulk Indian) — 3:44 — FI
———— — 2:4 — NH
Smoot, Isaac Albert — 2:167 — HHI
Smoot, Reed — 215 — GLS
———— — 60 no. 3:156 — PN
Smurthwaite, Richard J , Jr.
———— — 1935-36:51 — OO
Smylie, Robert E — 24:4 1953-54 — IHD
Snead, J L S — 60:8 — OHQ
Snead, Jack, see
   Snead, J L S
Snell, Earl W — 1931-32:41 — OO
———— — 1935-36:34 — OO
———— — 1937-38:7 — OO
———— — 1939-40:7 — OO
———— — 1941-42:13 — OO
———— — 1943-44:17 — OO
———— — 1945-46:17 — OO
———— — 88 — TUR
Snell, Francis M — 2:227 — HHI
Snell, George D — 2:263 — HHI
Snell, James H — 112 — NL
Snell, Marshall K — 1:361 — HH
———— — 13 no. 4:413 — MWH
———— — May 1907:39 — TDL
Snell, T C — 172-173 — HA
Snell, William Hedding — 1:319 — HH
———— — 3:93 — HHT
———— — May 1907:39 — TDL
———— — June 1909:48 — TDL
Snellbacher, J W — 2:203 — SMS
Snellstrom, John R — 1943-44:79 — OO
———— — 1945-46:87 — OO
Snider, P M — 32:32 1927 — WBP
Snider, Warner B — 1935-36:51 — OO
Snidow, Thomas Ash — 2:217 — SMS
Snively, H J — 1924:145 — WSP
Snively, Susan, see
   Young, Susan (Snively)
Snook, Charlotte Louise (Clayson) — 3:410 — BEA
Snook, Herbert Ernest — 3:1089 — BHS
Snook, John Wilson — 3:410 — BEA
———— — 2:685 — FH
———— — 2:32 — FSB
Snook, Mrs. John Wilson, see
   Snook, Charlotte Louise (Clayson)
Snow, Anna E — 75 — AL
Snow, Eliza Roxey, see
   Young, Eliza Roxey (Snow)

Snow, George T 74 AL
Snow, Joseph 163 LDM
Snow, William 92 GL
Snowden, Clinton A 2:26, 164 HHT
———— 5:212 SH
———— 1910:12 TDL
Snyder, Burt K 1939-40:31 OO
———— 1941-42:66 OO
———— 1943-44:79 OO
———— 1945-46:87 OO
Snyder, David M 3:397 BH
Snyder, Levi 216 LDM
Snyder, William 172-173 HA
Snyder, Wilson McLean 2:452 PHP
———— 19:160 1914 WBP
———— 20:80 1915 WBP
Soden, Sarah Ann, see
    Hovenden, Sarah Ann (Soden)
Soelberg, Axel H 66 SS
———— 1 no. 3:240 WM
Soelen, A   C   van, see
    Van Soelen, A   C
Sohns, Louis 1905-06:[28] RLW
Solner, Nordahl Brune 172-173, 203 HA
Solomon, Edward S unp. SE
Solomon, Old, see
    Old Solomon
Som-kin (Umatilla Indian) 271 WCS
Sommers, Alfred L 1910:2 TDL
Sonnefield, Henry F 713 LHM
Sonnemann, George Adolph 1941:356 EN
Soots, Orpheus C 1 no. 6:28 WN
———— 1 no. 8:20 WN
———— 1 no. 12:29 WN
Sophie (Pend d'Oreille Indian) 7 JJ
Sorensen, C   L 1935:5 S
Sorensen, Edna, see
    Millar, Edna (Sorensen)
Sorenson, Al 473 BHSS
Sorenson, George 353 PL
Sorenson, John C 2:1188 SM
Sorenson, Niels P 2:1095 SM
Sorenson, Peter C 944 SIH
Sorlie, A   G 22 LBT
Souders, Samuel Mott 3:1654 SM
———— 2:234 SMS
Soues, Frederick fol. title page SHB
Soule, Elizabeth S 120-121 GA
———— 50:62 1949 WDT
Soule, Ida, see
    Kuhn, Ida (Soule)
Soule, John A 1924:48 WSP
Soule, William H 4:27 BCF
Southmayd, LeRoy 2:532 SMS
Southward, A   E 172-173 HA
Southward, J   W 172-173 HA
Southwick, Ann Maria (Taylor) 430 GL
Southwick, Edward 429 GL

Southwick, Mrs. Edward, see
    Southwick, Ann Maria (Taylor)
Southwick, Edward, Jr. 311 GL
Southwick, William 276, 427 GL
Southworth, Wilbur D 3:980 FH
Sower, Forrest Lindsay 3:488 BEA
Spalding, Amelia Lorene, see
    Brown, Amelia Lorene (Spalding)
Spalding, Eliza, see
    Warren, Eliza (Spalding)
Spalding, Henry Harmon 257 BF
———— 94 BHSI
———— 36 BR
———— 1:134 BS
———— passim DS
———— 124 DSW
———— 95 DTI
———— 217 DW
———— 58 EW
———— 126 FW
———— 1:825 HHI
———— fol. 705 (no. 16) JO
———— 3:144 LH
———— 1:28 NH
———— 144 NM
———— 1:469 PMO
———— 15, 231 PSW
———— 2:120 SH
———— front. WMW
Spalding, Martha Jane, see
    Wigle, Martha Jane (Spalding)
Spalding, Warner R 93 DC
Spangler, James Williams 3:51 BHK
———— 31:16 1926 WBP
———— 32:front. 1927 WBP
———— 1 no. 1:12 WN
Spani, Magdalena, see
    Fox, Magdalena (Spani)
Spankie, James Ernest 3:387 BCF
Spannagel, Hugo 31 SCC
Spath, J   L 266 E
Spaulding, Charles K 1931-32:40 OO
———— 1935-36:50 OO
———— 1937-38:62 OO
Spaulding, William Wallace 525 HIO
———— 520 SHP
Spear, Arnold C 48 LS
Specht, Joseph 60 PI
Speck, George R 4:363 BCF
Speck, R   D 267 E
Spector, Mrs. Marion 45 no. 2:49 PN
Speer, Richard Alexander 3:87 BEA
Spencer, Mrs. Almon, see
    Spencer, Margaret Ann (Stitt)
Spencer, Almon Clark 2:166 SMS

Spencer, Bessie, see		
Evans, Bessie (Spencer)		
Spencer, Chris	2:front. 1924	BCHA
Spencer, Mrs. Chris	2:front. 1924	BCHA
Spencer, Ernest W	231	LDM
Spencer, Israel P	3:257	LHC
Spencer, Mrs. Israel P , see		
Spencer, Sarah A (Tindle) Gillahan		
Spencer, John Wood	3:480	BEA
Spencer, Laura E , see		
Howey, Laura E (Spencer)		
Spencer, Lloyd	2:front.	PH
Spencer, Margaret Ann (Stitt)	6:408-409	MC
Spencer, Matthew Lyle	120-121	GA
	26:59 1925	WDT
	1 no. 10:16	WN
Spencer, P K	1895-96:107	SSS
Spencer, Robert R	2:868	BHS
Spencer, Sarah A (Tindle) Gillahan		
	3:257	LHC
Sperling, Rochfort Henry	4:775	BCF
	fol. pt. 2	SHB
Sperry, Charles	192	LDM
Spicer, Elton F	143	PSW
Spike, W D C	1:566	BH
Spillman, W J	219	BHSS
Spinning, Charles Hadley	1:45	BH
	1:560	NH
Spinning, Mrs. Charles Hadley, see		
Spinning, Mildred Durley (Stewart)		
Spinning, Frank R	3:239	BH
Spinning, Mrs. Frank R , see		
Spinning, Sarah A (Ryan)		
Spinning, Mildred Durley (Stewart)	1:45	BH
Spinning, Sarah A (Ryan)	3:239	BH
Spirk, Charles A	1924:80	WSP
Spithill, Alexander	2:410	PHP
Splawn, Andrew Jackson	42 no. 2:112	PN
	1905-06:[51]	RLW
	6:198	SH
	front.	SK
	front.	SKA
Splawn, John A	2:226	NH
Split Lip Jim	front.	BI
Spofford, Judson	2:499	HHI
Spogen, Dominic	3:712	SMS
Spokane Garry, Spokan chief	65	AI
	6	CK
	1:118	D
	3:52	D
	148	DE
	126	DTI
	2:192	FI
	fol. 705 (no. 2)	JO
	front., 24, 32, 48	LC
	4:220	LH
	96	MCO

Spot (Puyallup Indian)	1:3	BH
Spotted Dog	2:19	DN
Spotted Eagle, Nez Percé chief		
	fol. 705 (no. 5)	JO
Sprague, Charles Arthur	1939-40:7	OO
	1941-42:13	OO
	85	TUR
Sprague, Franklin B	60:94	OHQ
Sprague, John W	1:190	HHT
	1:238	HWW
Sprague, Robert W	43 no. 2:136-137	PN
Spratt, Joseph	175	LDM
Spreckels, John D	321	QT
Sprice, Anthony	3:923	BCF
Spriggs, S R	252, 286	PSW
Spriggs, Mrs. S R	286	PSW
Spring, Charles	426	LDM
Spring, William	426	LDM
Springer, C H	2:120	PHP
Springer, Warren D	2:313	HHI
Sprott, John Hardie	4:527	BCF
Sproule, James A	1910:8	TDL
Sprowl, F G	39	MG
Squa-ha-lish Jim Yelo-kan-um (Nooksack Indian)	11	JNT
Squier, Hazen	368	SIH
Squire, Watson Carvosso	1:599	BHK
	3:505	BHS
	31	MAG
	58	ME
	11 no. 3:front	MWH
	2:479	PHP
	34 no. 4:400-401	PN
	[59]	RLX
	unp.	SE
	5:80	SH
Stack, Patrick J	151, 159, 167	OB
Stacy, Amy P (Sewell)	2:84	HHT
Stacy, F A	3:1230	FH
Stacy, Mrs. Fitch B , see		
Stacy, Amy P (Sewell)		
Stacy, Ralph S	18:64 1913	WBP
	20:16 1915	WBP
	21:front. 1916	WBP
	24:80 1919	WBP
Stadelman, Charles H	2:320	PHP
Stadelman, P J	1937-38:62	OO
	1939-40:15	OO
	1941-42:62	OO
	1943-44:75	OO
	1945-46:83	OO
Stafford, Mrs. Allis E	W	
	6:420-421	MC
Stafford, Anna (Parkhurst)	2:751	HHI
Stafford, George D	2:751	HHI

Stafford, Mrs. George D , see
   Stafford, Anna (Parkhurst)
Stafford, Mrs. John L , see
   Ellis, Telitha J (Arnett) Stafford
Stafrin, Conrad 2:659 CHW
Stairley, Wallace 1:53 ACR
Staley, John J 1943:232 ENC
Staley, Mrs. Rebecca (Rittman) Carr
   1:100 HHT
Staley, Walter I 1941:282 EN
Stalker, Hugh 120 LDM
Stallcup, John C 2:121 HH
Stamp, Jonas (Puyallup Indian) 1:3 BH
Stampfler, Jules 2:98 HHT
   ————— 1910:6 TDL
Stancliffe, Thomas A 6:442-443 MC
Standage, Henry front. GMM
Standring, Edwin 141 GL
Standring, Mrs. Edwin, see
   Standring, Rebecca (Smith)
Standring, Rebecca (Smith) 244 GL
Standrod, Drew W 3:1145 FH
Stanfield, Robert N 68:131 OHQ
Stanford, Leland 80 BOO
   ————— 204 QT
Stanford, Thomas C 3:1118 FH
Stanger, Christina, see
   Munroe, Christina (Stanger)
Stanley, Calvin 1895:96 OO
Stanley, Edwin J 355 LHM
Stanley, J C 172-173 HA
Stanley, James 119 LDM
Stanley, Mary Eliza (Grimes) 3:651 LHC
Stanley, Reginald 221 LHM
Stanley, Mrs. Samuel K , see
   Stanley, Mary Eliza (Grimes)
Stanly, Edward 51 no. 1:15 PN
Stannup, Puyallup chief 606 USCI
Stansbery, John E 3:809 GP
Stansell, M E 1905-06:[43] RLW
Stanton, George H 3:1357 SM
Stanton, Richard H 51 no. 1:14 PN
Staples, George W 100 LDM
Staples, Isaac E 1931-32:40 OO
   ————— 1935-36:50 OO
   ————— 1937-38:62 OO
   ————— 1939-40:15 OO
Staples, V B 1935-36:51 OO
   ————— 1937-38:62-63 OO
   ————— 1939-40:31 OO
   ————— 1941-42:66 OO
   ————— 1943-44:79 OO
   ————— 1945-46:87 OO
Stapleton, George W 302 MI
   ————— 2:886 SM
Stapleton, George Washington 2:631 LHC
Star Robe, Blackfoot chief 10:54 MC
Starbird, John Henry 3:725 BHS

Stark, Benjamin 1:655 LHC
   ————— 2:330 PMO
Stark, James fol. pt. 2 SHB
Stark, Roy Allen 2:409 SMS
Stark, William M 3 no. 4:227, 238 BCH
Stark, Mrs. William M 3 no. 4:238 BCH
Starks, Edwin Chapin 1:unp. 1900-01 WDT
Starkweather, Harvey Gordon 3:275 LHC
Starr, Belle 318 SW
Starr, Clyde Gideon 3:300 BEA
Starr, William S 3:997 FH
Starrett, Lee 234 FF
Stateler, L B 901 LHM
Statloth, Cowichan chief 35 HF
Stauff, Vendla [34] HN
Stauffer, Joseph E 2:424 PHP
Staunton, Michael D 2:584 SMS
Staver, George W 634 SHP
Stearns, A Ella (Stoughton) 1:242 PMO
Stearns, Mrs. D H , see
   Stearns, A Ella (Stoughton)
Stearns, John W 108, 255 BHSS
Stearns, Joseph O , Jr. 3:127 LHC
Stearns, Loyal B 2:159 LHC
Stedman, Livingston Boyd 2:333 BHK
   ————— 5:298 SH
Stedman, Louie W 1160 SIH
Steel, Mrs. David (Weatherford) 1:242 PMO
Steel, George A 1:260 NH
   ————— 476 SHP
Steel, Harry G 375 HA
Steel, James 298 SHP
Steel, W G 1:626 GP
Steele, E N 1924:80 WSP
Steele, F A 172-173 HA
Steele, Mrs. H N , see
   Steele, Janet (Elder)
Steele, Janet (Elder) 1:124 HHT
Steele, John W 6:442-443 MC
Steele, Lawrence W 2:282 SMS
Steele, Martha J , see
   Foster, Martha J (Steele)
Steele, Samuel B 286 GI
Steele, William A 139 LDM
Steele, William L 110 BV
   ————— 14 no. 2:216 MWH
Steelhammer, John F 1939-40:31 OO
   ————— 1941-42:66 OO
   ————— 1943-44:79 OO
   ————— 1945-46:87 OO
Steere, Eugene A 6:424-425 MC
Steers, Andrew 4:626 PH
Steeves, B L 2:55 CHW
Steffen, John F 245 LDM
Stein, Edward 2:523 HHI
Stein, Edward Wanek 3:185 BEA
Steinbach, E May 1907:73 TDL

Steiner, Barbara A   , see
   Reed, Barbara A   (Steiner)
Steiner, Joseph   [139]   RLX
Steinhauser, William   1:154-155   EPD
Steinweg, William Lewis   6:58   SH
————   19:160 1914   WBP
————   25:128 1920   WBP
————   26:128 1921   WBP
————   27:97 1922   WBP
Steiwer, W   H   1935-36:50   OO
————   1937-38:62   OO
————   1939-40:15   OO
————   1941-42:62   OO
————   1943-44:75   OO
Steiwer, Winlock W   1895:86   OO
————   2:458   PMO
Stellmon, George W   191   SIH
Steltella, see
   Thunder, Kutenai chief
Stenberg, Oscar   39   MG
Stephen, George   198, 212, 302 GI
————   88   SC
Stephen, Lord Mount, see
   Stephen, George
Stephens, Bessie (Thompson) 3:71   D
Stephens, E   M   [135]   RLX
Stephens, Eleanor Sharpless 1945-46:43   OO
————   23:133   PNLA
Stephens, Elizabeth (Walker) 1:224   NH
————   2:334   PMO
Stephens, Mrs. Frank, see
   Stephens, Bessie (Thompson)
Stephens, I   N   [118]   RLX
Stephens, James B   1:224   NH
————   2:334   PMO
Stephens, Mrs. James B   , see
   Stephens, Elizabeth (Walker)
Stephens, John H   2:124   SMS
Stephens, LaRele J   3:420   BEA
Stephens, Philip   270   MV
Stephenson, David   3:913   BCF
Stephenson, James, Jr.   2:706   FH
Stephenson, Ralph O   1937-38:62-63 OO
Steptoe, Edward J   21   AI
————   3:4   FI
————   front.   MCO
Steptoe, Nannie, see
   Eldridge, Nannie (Steptoe)
Sterling, Frederick Thorne 2:349   SMS
Sternberg, W   A   172-173   HA
Stetson, W   F   289   LDM
Stettin, Carlis J   unp.   SAA
Steunenberg, Albert K   2:679   HHI
Steunenberg, Frank   357   BHSI
————   1:208   FSB
————   11:38, 39 1927-28 IH
————   58 no. 1:27   PN
Stevens,   (Judge)   68   MHS

Stevens, A   A   38:front.   G
Stevens, DeWitt   320   SIH
Stevens, Edwin Bicknell   36:20 1935   WDT
Stevens, Mrs. Finette F   66   MHS
Stevens, George G   320   SIH
Stevens, H   A   1:372   HHT
Stevens, Hazard   1:146   HHT
————   2:183   HWW
————   94   MMR
Stevens, Henry Herbert   4:923   BCF
————   fol. pt. 1   SHB
Stevens, Horace   397   PL
Stevens, Irving   87   LDM
Stevens, Isaac Ingalls   176   BHSS
————   48   BOO
————   589   CIR
————   1:127   D
————   2:188   FI
————   159   GBS
————   1:front.   HH
————   1:134   HWW
————   fol. 705 (no. 15) JO
————   224   LBT
————   4:178   LH
————   13   MAG
————   4   ME
————   229   MP
————   1:24   NH
————   1:277   PH
————   1:205   PHP
————   34 no. 4:400-401 PN
————   44 no. 2:62, 65 PN
————   [39]   RLX
————   unp.   SE
————   1:front.   SH
————   258   WCS
Stevens, Jess H   3:871   SMS
Stevens, John Frank   155   AM
————   187   BOO
————   18   KS
————   238, 254   LBT
————   56 no. 2:83, 84 PN
Stevens, Robert L   290   PL
Stevens, Sylvanus Harlow   308   HA
————   404   WOY
Stevens, Thomas E   7:92   MC
Stevenson, Albert M   3:1024   SMS
Stevenson, Arthur   fol. title page SHB
Stevenson, David Osborn   2:674   FH
Stevenson, Edward A   296   DSW
Stevenson, George F   fol. pt. 2   SHB
Stevenson, George H   1905-06:[28]   RLW
Stevenson, Mrs. Grace   26:18   PNLA
Stevenson, J   M   1905-06:[58]   RLW
————   [120]   RLX
Stevenson, Jane, see
   Clark, Jane (Stevenson)

Stevenson, John R   197   PL
_____   [104]   RLX
Stevenson, Robert   3:77   BCF
_____   243   WSE
Stevenson, Robert G   3:111   BHK
Stevenson, Robert M   6:311   MC
Stevenson, Mrs. Robert M   6:438-439   MC
Stevenson, Samuel   6:416-417   MC
Stevenson, Thad A   1 no. 8:21   WN
Stevenson, Walter A   147   PSW
Stevenson, William   248   SIH
Stewart, A B   1:219   GP
Stewart, A Williamson   56   PSW
Stewart, Alexander Bruce   unp.   VU
_____   1 no. 7:18, 19, 28, 32   WN
Stewart, Alexander Campbell   284   HA
Stewart, Alice, see
   Seavey, Alice (Stewart)
Stewart, Calvin W   3:377   HHT
Stewart, Carey L   2:444   PHP
_____   1905-06:[46]   RLW
Stewart, Claiborne H   2:361   CHW
Stewart, Donald Malcolm   3:149   BCF
Stewart, E B   268   E
Stewart, Frederick LeRoy   6:210   SH
Stewart, George Harlan   3:938   FH
_____   176   IHI
Stewart, Horatio A   1941:262   EN
Stewart, J   2:front 1924   BCHA
Stewart, James   2:203   HWW
Stewart, James B   2:113   CHW
Stewart, Mrs. James B , see
   Stewart, Margaret (Cole)
Stewart, James J   157   GG
Stewart, James L   2:319   HHI
Stewart, James P   2:178   NH
Stewart, John   433   GL
Stewart, Mrs. John, see
   Stewart, Lydia M (Rolfe)
Stewart, John   2:654   NH
Stewart, Mrs. John, see
   Stewart, Mary (Scott)
Stewart, John A   2:379   HH
Stewart, John Thomas   2:796   BHK
Stewart, Mrs. John Thomas, see
   Stewart, Nancy H (Faucett)
Stewart, Mrs. Lou Stocking   unp.   HOF
Stewart, Lydia M (Rolfe)   433   GL
Stewart, Malcolm D   3:859   BHS
Stewart, Margaret (Cole)   2:113   CHW
Stewart, Mary (Scott)   2:654   NH
Stewart, Mathew   2:447   PMO
Stewart, Mildred Durley, see
   Spinning, Mildred Durley (Stewart)
Stewart, Nancy H (Faucett)   2:797   BHK
Stewart, Peter G   1:655   LHC
_____   1:500   NH

_____   1:6   PMO
_____   5   TUR
Stewart, Ray, see
   Stewart, Horatio A
Stewart, S L   1931-32:41   OO
Stewart, Samuel Vernon   1941:41   EN
Stewart, Thomas Pettigrew   3:1669   SM
Stewart, William Francis   3:881   BCF
Stewart, William M   222   JNT
Sticker, Mrs. Lucy   18:68 1941-42   IH
Sticklin, Louis J   1:460   PHP
Stiles, Charles T   2:502   NH
Stiles, G L   1905-06:[28]   RLW
Stiles, Theodore L   2:458   NH
_____   1926:20   WSP
Stillwell, James B   3:659   BHK
Stillwell, William D   2:658   NH
Stilson, Leroy   1905-06:[57]   RLW
Stimpson, Herbert E   3:263   BH
Stimson, Charles Douglas   4:397   BHK
_____   4:426   PH
_____   5:398   SH
_____   unp.   VU
Stimson, F S   266   BHSS
Stimson, Thomas Douglas   4:428   PH
Stinson, F L   1:223   HH
Stinson, Ulmer   2:235   HH
_____   1:480   NH
Stirling, Sarah (Livingston)   1:73   D
Stirrat, James Raeside   3:567   BHK
Stites, A   393   BHSS
Stites, W Scott   6:339   MC
Stitt, Margaret Ann, see
   Spencer, Margaret Ann (Stitt)
Stivers, Daniel Gay   2:594   SMS
Stock, John Laing   fol. pt. 2   SHB
Stockdale, W E   1931-32:41   OO
Stockett, Julia C   6:74   PNLA
_____   12:136   PNLA
Stocking, Clark   200   SW
Stocking, Margaret (Henry)   172   LHM
_____   2:587   SMS
Stocking, Winfield Scott   173   LHM
_____   2:586   SMS
Stocking, Mrs. Winfield Scott, see
   Stocking, Margaret (Henry)
Stockman, Lowell   1943-44:13   OO
_____   1945-46:13   OO
Stockslager, Charles O   218   IHI
Stockton, Mollie Emily, see
   Sargent, Mollie Emily (Stockton) Leonard
Stoddard, Birdie   233   GL
Stoddard, Joseph McNett   3:224   PH
_____   1 no. 9:11   WN
Stoddard, Robert   269   GL

Stoddard, Sarah, see
    Brown, Sarah (Stoddard)
Stoddart, David A   1897:108   YB
Stoddart, Thomas   3:863   BCF
Stodden, William T   2:418   SMS
Stoeckl, Edouard de   278-279   HU
Stoker, John   257   GL
Stokes, Caroline, see
    Cullen, Caroline (Stokes)
Stokes, Elvira, see
    McCollum, Elvira (Stokes)
Stoller, Robert   3:372   PH
Stolz, Gideon   2:153   CHW
Stone, Ben   3:153   MC
Stone, Corliss P   unp.   SEA
    6:110   SH
Stone, Elbert Homer   3:705   SMS
Stone, Franklyn L   6:330-331   MC
Stone, George Henry   3:103   HHT
    6:64   SH
    1910:2   TDL
Stone, J E   3:379   PH
Stone, Mrs. Malvina L   6:420-421   MC
Stone, Margaret, see
    Lang, Margaret (Stone)
Stoneman, George   47 no. 2:34   PN
Stoney, George M   fol. 207 (no. 24)   SHI
Stooptoopnin (Nez Percé Indian) 54   MW
Storey, J O   2:413   GP
Stork, Louise   137   LHN
Story, Ellen, see
    Story, Helen (Trent)
Story, George L   2:442   PMO
Story, Helen (Trent)   127   LHM
Story, Nelson   126   LHM
    5:314   MC
    741   MI
    2:867   SM
Story, Mrs. Nelson, see
    Story, Helen (Trent)
Stotler, Floyd L   1922:125   WSP
Stoughton, A Ella, see
    Stearns, A Ella (Stoughton)
Stout, Edward   4:505   BCF
    fol. title page   SHB
    51   WSE
Stout, J L   1:144   NH
Stout, Ned, see
    Stout, Edward
Stout, Tom   1:front.   SMS
Stover, Henry   1:412   NH
Stowell, Helen   42:32 1930   WSGP
Stowell, Hollis L   1:223   HH
Strahan, R S   1:368   NH
Strahorn, Robert Edmund   235   BOO
    3:180   FI
    59 no. 1:38   PN
    5:194   SH

Straight, J A   138   HIT
Stranahan, C T   114   BR
    front., 8   SPI
    30   THI
Stranahan, Mrs. C T , see
    Stranahan, May L (Bostwick)
Stranahan, May L (Bostwick) front.   SPI
    31   THI
Strand, A L   1945-46:71   OO
Strandberg, Arthur Morris   3:235   BHK
Strang, James   92   LDM
Strange, F G   113   PSW
Strathcona and Mount Royal, 1st baron, see
    Smith, Donald Alexander
Stratton, C C   44   OS
Stratton, Howard W   1:252   NH
Strayer, W H   1931-32:40   OO
    1935-36:50   OO
    1937-38:62   OO
    1939-40:15   OO
    1941-42:62   OO
    1943-44:75   OO
    1945-46:83   OO
Street, Thornton A   6:330-331   MC
Streeter, Alice M (Kellar) 1941:423   EN
Streeter, John O   1941:423   EN
Streib, Philip   2:371   LHC
Streitz, E E   305   BR
Strevell, Helen, see
    Miles, Helen (Strevell)
Strevell, Jason W   6:401   MC
Strevell, Mrs. Jason W   6:401   MC
Strever, William J   2:196   SMS
Stricker, Herman   3:1126   FH
    3:230   HHI
Stricker, Mrs. Herman, see
    Stricker, Lucy (Wolgamott)
Stricker, Lucy (Wolgamott) 3:231   HHI
Strickland, H P   5:412   SH
Stricklin, Charles E   1945-46:27   OO
Stringer, Cortis D   1935-36:50   OO
    1937-38:62   OO
Stringer, Isaac O   42   AL
Stripp, Albert Edward   2:154   SMS
Strobridge, H L   1905-06:[70]   RLW
    [135]   RLX
Stromberg, Augusta   12   SS
Stromberg, Lottie   12   SS
Strong, Frank   1:639   CHW
Strong, J F A   16   AL
    44, 172-173   HA
Strong, James R   648   SIH
Strong, Mrs. Kuria   311   BHSS
Strong, W B   311   BHSS
Strong, William   1:552-553   GP
    2:238   NH
    62:60   OHQ

_____	64:292	OHQ
_____	94	SHP
Strong, William B	261	QT
Strowbridge, Joseph Alfred	2:170	GP
_____	1:260	NH
_____	1:416	PMO
_____	2:339	PMO
_____	238	SHP
Strowbridge, Mrs. Joseph Alfred, see		
Strowbridge, Mary H (Bodman)		
Strowbridge, Justus M	2:163	GP
_____	1:372	PMO
_____	2:340	PMO
Strowbridge, Mary H (Bodman)	2:171	GP
Struve, Frederic Karl	2:752	BHS
_____	5:421	SH
Struve, Henry G	1:599	BHK
_____	2:750	BHS
_____	3 no. 8:419	PM
_____	unp.	SEA
_____	4:154	SH
Stuart, David	9 no. 4:277	BCH
Stuart, Elbridge Amos	4:546	PH
_____	5:264	SH
Stuart, Granville	175	MI
_____	1:front.	SFY
_____	2:873	SM
Stuart, James	1:front.	MC
_____	1:168	SM
_____	1:136	SMS
Stuart, James Duff-, see		
Duff-Stuart, James		
Stuart, John	54	GI
_____	114	MH
Stuart, John, 3rd earl of Bute	222	MV
Stuart, L J	14	SSP
Stuart, Mary J , see		
Nesbitt, Mary J (Stuart)		
Stuart, Robert	2:480a	CGO
_____	64-65	LCRH
Stuart, W S	3:239	HHI
Stubbs, R S	1:130	HHT
Stuck, Hudson	114, 115	PJ
Stuckey, Alfred J	4:387	BHK
Stufft, W F	3:1304	SMS
Stump, Mrs. Martin, see		
Hamilton, Anna (Balch) Stump Morrell		
Stump, Thomas J	107	LDM
_____	1:191	LHC
Sturdevant, R M	1924:113	WSP
Sturdevant, Robert F	2:182	NH
_____	1905-06:[28]	RLW
Sturgis, Sarah Jane, see		
Anderson, Sarah Jane (Sturgis)		
Sturtevant, Cullen Kittredge	136-137	SRW
Su-a-lis, "Captain John" (Salish Indian)		
_____	208	CAA
Sublette, John	93	DCW
Suksdorf, H F	1905-06:[28]	RLW
Suksdorf, Wilhelm N	57:116	OHQ
Sulktashkosha, see		
Moses, Sinkiuse chief		
Sulliger, Mrs. Eliza C	438	AG
Sulliger, S S	405	AG
Sullivan, Arthur W	215	GG
Sullivan, C H	1905-06:[28]	RLW
Sullivan, E P	172-173	HA
Sullivan, Edward	353	LDM
Sullivan, Harvey E	215	GG
Sullivan, Isaac Newton	2:48	FSB
_____	182	IHI
Sullivan, Jere	499	LHM
Sullivan, John B	151	GG
Sullivan, John S	680	SIH
Sullivan, Joseph T	272	HA
Sullivan, Katherine	42:32 1930	WSGP
Sullivan, Michael J	291	HA
Sullivan, Nellie (Cronin)	2:440	SMS
Sullivan, P C	172-173	HA
Sullivan, Potter C	3:397	HHT
_____	1905-06:[28]	RLW
_____	1923:103	WSP
Sullivan, T J	219	PSW
Sullivan, William Aloysius	3:31	PH
Summers, Clyde Earl	2:847	HHI
Summers, Owen	1:578-579	GP
_____	2:169	LHC
_____	1:236	PMO
Summers, Sara	67	MG
Sumner, Charles	278-279	HU
Sumner, Leslie Curtis	3:103	BEA
Sumner, Thomas Boyd	2:428	PHP
_____	1905-06:[44]	RLW
_____	[89]	RLX
Sumpkin, Captain, see		
Te-low-kike (Cayuse Indian)		
Sunday, Billy	87	MLO
Sunde, Carl Johan	4:225	BHK
_____	4:650	PH
Sundown, Jackson (Nez Percé Indian)	21	DSW
Surber, William Harvey	3:87	BHS
_____	6:142	SH
_____	59	SSP
Suren, Fred	243	GG
Survant, John	3:1503	SM
Sutcliffe, H	unp.	SOU
Suter, C C	172-173	HA
Suter, Louis W	172-173, 314	HA
Sutherland, James	120	RO
Sutherland, Mrs. Margaret	6:410-411	MC
Sutherland, William Henry	fol. pt. 2	SHB
Sutro, Adolph	244	QT
Sutton, Albert	3:45	BH
Sutton, John	204	LDM
Sutton, Wakeman	3:1364	SM

Sutton, William John	fol. pt. 1	SHB
Suzzallo, Henry	120-121	GA
	139	MLO
————	50 no. 3:103, 104	PN
————	unp.	WD
————	26:10, 61 1925	WDT
Svenson, August	3:501	BH
Svenson, Mrs. August, see		
Svenson, Laura A (Malm) Frick		
Svenson, Laura A (Malm) Frick 3:501		BH
Sverdrup, Ingvard Berner	249	HA
Swain, Arthur J	2:784	FH
	2:915	HHI
Swain, Walter	369	LDM
Swallow, George Clinton	6:339	MC
Swalwell, J A	20:48 1915	WBP
	21:32 1916	WBP
————	22:front. 1917	WBP
	24:80 1919	WBP
	1 no. 1:21	WN
Swalwell, William G	2:502	PHP
Swan, Edgar M	1924:81	WSP
Swan, James Gilchrist	1:620	NH
	3:284	SH
————	front.	SWA
Swaney, A W	3:1275	SMS
Swanson, Almin L	3:159	BH
Swanson, August	3:81	HWW
Swanson, John	49	LDM
Swanton, Frank W	172-173, 281	HA
Swasey, George O	136-137	SRW
Swearingen, Philip B	2:469	HHT
Swee, John P	2:403	SMS
Sweek, Alex	2:457	PMO
Sweek, C L	1945-46:93	OO
Sweeney, Charles T	6:416-417	MC
Sweeney, John M	153	LHM
Sweeney, William	3:789	GP
Sweeny, Campbell	fol. pt. 2	SHB
Sweeny, Charles	1905-06:[34]	RLW
	5:424	SH
Swee-o-lum (Chiliwist Indian) 330		FF
Sweet, Edward S	572	SIH
Sweet, Ensign	1:48	ACR
Sweet, Ralph L	3:649	BHK
Sweet, William N	2:331	HHI
Sweet, William T	2:481	SMS
Sweetland, Scott	1895-96:145	SSS
Swem, Blanche (Cooper)	3:66	D
Swem, Mrs. Daniel Roy, see		
Swem, Blanche (Cooper)		
Sweney, E R	43 no. 2:136-137	PN
Swenson, Leon Hughie	3:200	BEA
Swift, A V	1931-32:41	OO
Swift, E A	288	LDM
Swift, George Wilkins	3:837	BHS
Swift, J H	188	LDM
Swift, Louis Fuller	1943:25	ENC

Swigart, Leslie, see		
Kent, Leslie (Swigart)		
Switzer, John	2:front. 1924	BCHA
Sword, Colin Buchanan	1897:108	YB
Sybert, Edward M	2:245	SMS
Sylvester, Edmund	3:64	SH
Sylvester, Frank	10 no. 1:43	BCH
Symms, Darwin	3:451	BEA
Symms, Robert Doyle	3:451	BEA

T

Taché, Alexander Antonin	1:250	MCC
	2:144	MCC
————		
Tackaberry, J D	103	LDM
Taelman, Louis	239	GG
	175	SCH
————		
Taggart, Edward Thomas	2:451	LHC
Tagish (Skookum) Jim	72	DM
Tail Feathers Coming Over The Hill, Piegan		
chief	170	PI
	204	PIW
Tait, Charles William	3:421	BCF
Tait, V B	2:141	BCF
Talbert, John A	2:446	PMO
Talbot, E A	2:909	HHI
Talbot, Ethelbert	front.	TMP
Talbot, Guy Webster	2:189	GP
Talbot, Harry G	2:329	CHW
Talbot, Robert	180	TMP
Talbot, Truxton	1:25	FSB
Talbot, William Chaloner	3:249	BHS
————	5:124	SH
Talkington, Albert W	1:154-155	EPD
Talkington, Henry L	16:10 1937-38	IH
Talley, Mrs. America, see		
Richmond, Mrs. America Talley		
Tallman, Boyd J	3:81	BHS
	134	E
————	1924:145	WSP
Tally, war chief of the Utes 106-107		HCC
Tamootsin of Alpowa, see		
Timothy, Nez Percé chief		
Tanger, Mary A , see		
Peterson, Mary A (Tanger)		
Tangney, Frank	243	GG
Tangney, Thomas J , Jr. 255		GG
Tannahill, George W	1:112	FSB
Tannatt, T R	108	BHSS
Tanner, A H	215	PL
Tanner, James Whitmer	3:96	HHI
Tanner, Mrs. James Whitmer, see		
Tanner, Millie Grace (Cook)		
Tanner, Lewis B	172-173, 252	HA
Tanner, Millie Grace (Cook) 3:97		HHI

Tanzer, Gottwerth Lebrecht	3:425	BHS
Tarpley, Daniel W	64	PL
Tarr, Effie (Mercer)	3:744	HHI
Tarr, Raymond P	1910:19	TDL
Tarr, Thomas W	3:744	HHI
Tarr, Mrs. Thomas W , see		
Tarr, Effie (Mercer)		
Tartar, Herman V	50:47 1949	WDT
Tarte, James W	220	LDM
Tarte, John F	223	JNT
Tarte, John F , Jr.	349	JNT
Taschereau, George Louis	4:727	BCF
Tassell, Philip van, see		
Van Tassell, Philip		
Tate, C M	287	AG
	2:front. 1924	BCHA
Tate, D'Arcy	fol. pt. 2	SHB
Tate, David Gekeler	3:27	BEA
Tate, John P	3:10	HHI
Tatlow, Robert Garnett	fol. pt. 1	SHB
	1911:6-7	YB
Tatro, Burr E	3:99	LHC
Tatro, Joseph F	3:995	FH
Tats-Homi (Warm Springs)	4:260	LH
	66:320	OHQ
Tattan, John W	2:461	SMS
Tatton, James	380	LDM
Taufen, Peter L	211	GG
Tauitau, Cayuse chief	fol. 705 (no. 11)	JO
Tauscher, Frank A	3:855	LHC
Tavernier, Emmelie, see		
Gamelin, Mother		
Tawis Geejumnin, see		
No-Horns-On-His-Head (Nez Percé Indian)		
Ta-wis-sis-sim-nim, see		
No-Horns-On-His-Head (Nez Percé Indian)		
Ta-wits-poo	121	WCS
Tawits-tsi-tsim-nin, see		
No-Horns-On-His-Head (Nez Percé Indian)		
Taw-wa-toi (Umatilla Indian)	205	AI
Taya, Carrier chief	256	FT
	15	MHN
Taylor, Alonzo S	2:520	PHP
	6:82	SH
Taylor, Andrew J	512	SIH
Taylor, Ann Maria, see		
Southwick, Ann Maria (Taylor)		
Taylor, Arthur J	2:638	NH
Taylor, C B , see		
Cary, C B (Taylor)		
Taylor, C E	3:335	BH
Taylor, Delbert G	3:207	BEA
Taylor, Douglas W	2:352	PMO
Taylor, Edward W	1895-96:79	SSS
Taylor, Esther (DeArmon)	1:344	NH
Taylor, Eva, see		
Green, Eva (Taylor)		
Taylor, Frank E	2:395	CHW
Taylor, Fred T	1895-96:109	SSS
Taylor, George E	24:147	PNLA
	50:37 1949	WDT
Taylor, George W	87	LDM
Taylor, Glen H	60 no. 1:12	PN
Taylor, Glenn O	1935-36:51	OO
Taylor, Gordon J	1931-32:41	OO
Taylor, Howard D	55 no. 1:25	PN
	[129]	RLX
Taylor, Isaac	224	GL
Taylor, J C	1895-96:109	SSS
Taylor, J D	5:316	MC
Taylor, J Hopkins	6:305	MC
Taylor, J W	48	LS
Taylor, James, 1809-	1:344	NH
Taylor, Mrs. James, see		
Taylor, Esther (DeArmon)		
Taylor, James	1 no. 4:28	WN
Taylor, James Madison	front.	CBC
Taylor, James W	242	GL
Taylor, Mrs. James W	96	GL
Taylor, John	127	CWW
	112-113 (xviii)	PR
Taylor, John Sanford	3:527	BHS
Taylor, Martha Ann (Fox)	436	GL
Taylor, Mary, see		
Livesley, Mary (Taylor)		
Taylor, Mary J , see		
Graeter, Mary J (Taylor)		
Taylor, Matt, see		
Taylor, James Madison		
Taylor, O C	3:667	BHS
Taylor, Oliver Hazard Perry	88	MCO
Taylor, Peter	1:244	GP
Taylor, R E	134	MLO
Taylor, Renwick W	May 1907:68	TDL
Taylor, Sam F	66	CBC
Taylor, Samuel Rogers	234	GL
Taylor, Mrs. Samuel Rogers, see		
Taylor, Martha Ann (Fox)		
Taylor, Stephen D	1:122	FSB
Taylor, Thomas	2:547	BCF
———	3:1145	BCF
———	56, 224	GL
———	fol. pt. 1	SHB
———	1911:6-7, 70-71	YB
Taylor, Thomas Clarkson	2:341	LHC
Taylor, W H	2:394	NH
Taylor, William E	2:880	FH
Taylor, William Whitehead	186	GL
Taylor, Zebulon Bryant	3:315	HHT
	1:323	PHP
Teade, Edith	67	MG
Teague, John	2:front. 1924	BCHA
Teague, William	2:139	BCF
———	4:221	BCF

	fol. title page	SHB
Teal, George Coleman	1941:202	EN
Teal, Joseph	1:372	PMO
Teal, Joseph N	20:234	OHQ
Teats, Governor	1:504	PHP
_____	May 1907:39	TDL
	1924:48	WSP
Tebay, John F	2:929	SM
Tebbetts, Frank P	3:435	LHC
Teck, Frank Carleton	1:524	HWW
Teddy Blue, see		
Abbott, Edward C		
Teeples, Glen H	3:132	BEA
Teeter, Charles Nelson	13:24 1931-32	IH
Teeter, Darius	13:34 1931-32	IH
Teeters, Charles A	278-279	KO
Tefft, Bertram W	272	SIH
Tefft, Mrs. Bertram W , see		
Tefft, Catherine (Hendrickson)		
Tefft, Catherine (Hendrickson)	272	SIH
Teh-wes-in-pilpt, see		
Red Horn (Nez Percé Indian)		
Tekahionwake, see		
Johnson, Emily Pauline (Mohawk Indian)		
Telford, George	4:237	BCF
Telford, Robert	4:251	BCF
Te-low-kike (Cayuse Indian)	23	BSC
	10:45 1925-26	IH
_____		
Temple, G W	1895-96:109	SSS
Temple, I U	1931-32:41	OO
Templeman, John L	2:400	SMS
Templeman, William	1911:70-71	YB
Templeton, Harry S	84	PSW
Templeton, W A	1895:102	OO
Tendoy, Lemhi chief	216	AI
	249	BHI
_____	30	BHSI
_____	1:537	HHI
	4:208	MC
Tendoy, Lemhi chief, wife of	31	BHSI
Tennant, Charles	18	SSP
Tennant, J D	11, 23	MLO
	1 no. 6:26	WN
_____		
Tennant, John A	328	AG
	129, 131	JNT
Tepyahlahnah Temoni, see		
Spotted Eagle, Nez Percé chief		
Terhune, Susan A , see		
Ross, Susan A (Terhune)		
Terrace, Frank	1:481	BHK
	3:507	BHK
_____	3:82	PH
Terrell, Margaret E	50:23 1949	WDT
Terrell, Robert M	3:981	FH
Terrill, Anna M (Adamson)	3:1160	FH
Terrill, Frank J	3:1160	FH
Terrill, Mrs. Frank J , see		
Terrill, Anna M (Adamson)		
Terry, C T	1895-96:109	SSS
Terry, Charles C	1:69	BHK
	1:180	NH
Terry, Henry B	23	DH
Terwillegar, R J	300	E
Terwilliger, Charlotte, see		
Cartwright, Charlotte (Terwilliger) Moffett		
Terwilliger, James	3:67	GP
_____	413	HIO
_____	1:188	PMO
	2:333	PMO
Tesh Palouse Kamaiakan (Yakima Indian)		
	128	SK
	124	SKA
Testerman, William A	248	SIH
Tetacú, Nootka chief	1:182	BCF
Teton, Oliver	387	BF
Teutsch, William	63:9	OHQ
Thaanum, William	2:343	BHK
Thacker, Gus L	1924:113	WSP
Thalburt, E	1:unp. 1900-01	WDT
Thaler, Joseph A	2:431	SMS
Thatcher, Frank H	172-173, 245	HA
Thatcher, Joseph L	1895-96:119	SSS
Thatcher, Moses	312	GLS
Thatcher, R W	483	BHSS
Thayer, Andrew Jackson	1:512	NH
Thayer, Mrs. Andrew Jackson, see		
Thayer, Melissa D (Chandler)		
Thayer, Eli	16:313	OHQ
Thayer, Matilda, see		
Perrigo, Matilda (Thayer)		
Thayer, Melissa D (Chandler)	1:512	NH
Thayer, William Wallace	1:368	NH
	42	TUR
_____		
Theresa, Mother	1:451	GP
Therkelson, Laurits Walse	584	SHP
Theunte, Clement M	488	PIW
Thibault, Jean-Baptiste	1:170	MCC
Thiel, Fred	1941-42:66	OO
Thiele, A L	35:62 1930	WBP
Thiele, Henry	1943:255	ENC
Thielsen, H	653	HIO
Thisted, Andrew	1941:445	EN
Thomas (Carrier Indian)	23	MHN
Thomas, Tanana chief	278-279	HU
Thomas, Alfred L	2:39	SMS
Thomas, Ann (Moorehead)	36	GL
Thomas, Cabot T	3:1391	SM
Thomas, Charles W	669	HI
Thomas, Christy	1 no. 8:21	WN
Thomas, Claiborne	20	GL
Thomas, Mrs. Claiborne, see		
Thomas, Mrs. Jane		
Thomas, Daniel Stillwell	60	GL

Thomas, Mrs. Daniel Stillwell, see
    Thomas, Martha Pane (Jones)
Thomas, Daniel White   224   GL
Thomas, David James   3:919   BCF
Thomas, Mrs. David James, see
    Thomas, Mary Ann (Morris)
Thomas, David P   2:889   FH
Thomas, Elizabeth, see
    White, Elizabeth (Thomas)
Thomas, Ethel M   , see
    Ross, Ethel M   (Thomas)
Thomas, Frances Ann, see
    White, Frances Ann (Thomas)
Thomas, George D   626   LHM
Thomas, Mrs. George D   , see
    Thomas, Lucy A   (Alexander)
Thomas, Mrs. Harrison Ayers, see
    Thomas, Ann (Moorehead)
Thomas, J   D   919   LHM
Thomas, J   E   3 no. 10:suppl. 12   PM
Thomas, Jack   206   BHSS
Thomas, James   394   IHI
Thomas, James William   3:823   BHS
Thomas, Mrs. Jane   20   GL
Thomas, Jesse Olmsted, Jr.   1943:203   ENC
Thomas, John D   3:406   BHS
Thomas, John M   2:142   NH
Thomas, John T   86   LDM
Thomas, Lucy A   (Alexander) 626   LHM
Thomas, Lyle D   1935-36:51   OO
————   1937-38:62-63   OO
————   1939-40:31   OO
————   1941-42:66   OO
    1945-46:87   OO
Thomas, Martha Pane (Jones) 437   GL
Thomas, Mary Ann (Morris)   3:919   BCF
Thomas, Matilda Ann, see
    Evans, Matilda Ann (Thomas)
Thomas, Owen   431   LDM
Thomas, Robert Pennell   2:298   PHP
Thomas, Tuberville   4:61   BCF
Thomas, W   R   269   E
Thompson, Asa B   2:443   PMO
Thompson, Bessie, see
    Stephens, Bessie (Thompson)
Thompson, Carl N   3:1240   SMS
Thompson, Charles   110-111   HCM
Thompson, Charles W   2:280   PHP
Thompson, D   2:front. 1924 BCHA
Thompson, D   M   [112]   RLX
Thompson, David P   2:195   GP
————   3:891   LHC
    1:22   PMO
Thompson, Mrs. David P   1:143   PMO
Thompson, Mrs. E   1:404   NH
Thompson, E   H   1895:95   OO
Thompson, Esther (Abercrombie) 4:433   BCF
Thompson, F   B   4 no. 1:19   PM

Thompson, Francis M   4:91   MC
Thompson, George Herbert   fol. pt. 2   SHB
Thompson, Gordon G   2:827   BHK
Thompson, H   Y   534   SHP
Thompson, J   172-173   HA
Thompson, J   A   421   LDM
Thompson, J   S   2:463   BCF
    1897:42   YB
Thompson, James   4:433   BCF
Thompson, Mrs. James, see
    Thompson, Esther (Abercrombie)
Thompson, Mrs. Jesse, see
    Thompson, Ruth A   (Whiteside) Kilbury
Thompson, John   263   LDM
————   3:790   SMS
Thompson, John A   2:619   GP
Thompson, John R   320   AG
Thompson, L   L   1921:112   WSP
Thompson, Levant F   1:129   BH
————   2:178   NH
Thompson, Mrs. Levant F   , see
    Thompson, Susan (Kincaid)
Thompson, M   E   2:448   PMO
Thompson, Mary Anna (Cook) 1:536   GP
————   2:735   GP
Thompson, Nicholas   3:545   BCF
Thompson, Orval N   1941-42:66   OO
Thompson, Mrs. Reuben, see
    Thompson, Mary Anna (Cook)
Thompson, Robert R   80   LDM
————   1:655   LHC
————   353   QT
Thompson, Rufus B   2:137   SMS
Thompson, Ruth A   (Whiteside) Kilbury
    848   SIH
Thompson, S   A   147   SS
Thompson, Samuel H   4:467   BCF
Thompson, Seth B   1945-46:41   OO
Thompson, Susan (Kincaid)   1:129   BH
Thompson, Thomas G   50:46 1949   WDT
Thompson, Thomas H   304   SIH
Thompson, W   H   [117]   RLX
Thompson, Walter J   2:115   HH
    2:354   NH
Thompson, William   110-111   HCM
————   951   LHM
    230   MI
Thompson, William J   143   PSW
Thomsen, Moritz   5:336   SH
Thomson, Arthur D   3:402   BEA
Thomson, David   120-121   GA
————   6:25 1906   WDT
————   26:59 1925   WDT
    36:20 1935   WDT
Thomson, Earl Alexander   3:379   BEA
Thomson, Francis A   430   BHSS

Thomson, Henry Broughton   3:433   BCF
                                1911:70-71   YB
_____   190   PSW
Thomson, James M
Thomson, James Wolsely   4:1131   BCF
Thomson, Reginald Heber   1:481, 637   BHK
                                2:93   BHK
_____   2:820   BHS
Thorkelson, Jacob   2:365   SMS
Thorn, C   C   172-173   HA
Thorn, Charles   137   LDM
Thorn, John Charles   3:807   BCF
Thorn, Jonathan   64-65   LCRH
Thornber, W   S   529   BHSS
Thornburgh, John A   1931-32:41   OO
Thorne, Chester   5:126   SH
Thornquest, J   T   172-173   HA
Thornton, Charles W   221   HA
Thornton, Harrison Robertson
                                54 no. 4:169   PN
Thornton, J   Q   2:696   CP
                                1:92   NH
_____
Thornton, John C   Calhoun 251   MI
Thornton, John W   4:229   BCF
Thornton, Sarah, see
    Coleman, Sarah (Thornton)
Thoroughman, Robert Perry   3:729   SMS
Thorp, Fielden M   2:78   NH
Thorp, Mrs. Fielden M   , see
    Thorp, Margaret (Bound)
Thorp, Leonard   25:35   PNLA
Thorp, Leonard L   2:166   NH
Thorp, Mrs. Leonard L   , see
    Thorp, Philena W   (Hanson)
Thorp, Margaret (Bound)   2:78   NH
Thorp, Philena W   (Hanson) 2:166   NH
Thorpe, John C   6:27 1906   WDT
Thorpe, Philip   5:323   MC
Thramer, John   2:173   CHW
Three Feathers, Nez Percé chief 153, 232   BR
                                1:76   NH
_____
Throckmorton, Arthur   57 no. 4:182   PN
Thronson, Joel A   1:355   HH
Thuland, Conrad M   336   HA
Thunder, see
    Fidelis, Flathead chief
Thunder, Kutenai chief fol. 512 (no. 20) BUR
Thunder Eyes, see
    James, Nez Percé chief
Thunder Strikes, see
    James, Nez Percé chief
Thunder Traveling to Loftier Mountain
    Heights, see
    Joseph, Nez Percé chief
Thurlow, 1st baron, see
    Thurlow, Edward
Thurlow, Edward   246   MV
Thurman, George William   214   GL
Thurman, Samuel R   219   GL
Thurston, John M   219   PL

Thurston, June   25:34   PNLA
Thurston, Samuel Royal   1:127   GP
_____   3:404   LH
_____   1:56   NH
_____   15:153   OHQ
Thwaite, Thomas, Jr.   270   E
Thyng, William S   215   BHSS
Tibbals, Henry L   112   LDM
                                1:352   NH
_____
Tibbetts, C   C   135   MLO
Tibbetts, George W   3:557   BHK
                                2:660   NH
_____   1905-06:[28, 51]RLW
_____   [130]   RLX
_____
Tibbits, George, see
    Tibbetts, George W
Tibbits, Milton Orlando   6:156   SH
Tidball, Ben W   4 no. 11:5   C
Tidy, Harry   4:681   BCF
Tiffin, John Butler   4:15   BCF
Tigard, C   F   1895:102   OO
Tigert, Allen H   3:202   BEA
Tilghman, William   284   SW
Tiloukaikt, Cayuse chief   400-401   DW
Tilsley, John H   1120   SIH
Tilton, George E   92   SRW
Tilton, George F   18   HA
Tilton, Howard   2:217   HH
Tilton, William   3:905   BCF
Timanus, Clarence S   front.   BM
Timms, Herbert   4:441   BCF
Timothy, Nez Percé chief   32   AI
                                279   BR
_____   214   DS
_____   158   DTI
_____   fol. 705 (no. 4) JO
Timotsk, Klikitat chief   1:58   GP
Tindle, Sarah A   , see
    Spencer, Sarah A   (Tindle) Gillahan
Tindoy, see
    Tendoy, Lemhi chief
Tingley, Frederick Chipman 4:715   BCF
Tingley, Robert S   3:667   SMS
Tingley, Stephen   4:41   BCF
                                fol. title page SHB
_____
Tinker, Frederick A   2:689   FH
Tinn, Robert Thompson   4:745   BCF
Tin-tin-mit-si (Cayuse Indian) 52   JM
Tisdall, Charles Edward   1911:70-71   YB
Titcomb, Harvey A   3:163   HWW
Titcomb, Luke   127   GL
Titus, Wealthy, see
    Palmer, Wealthy (Titus)
Tobel, Edward von, see
    Von Tobel, Edward
Tobey, Franke M   , see
    Jones, Franke M   (Tobey)

Tobey, Theresa, see
    Slyter, Theresa (Tobey)
Tobias, David Sampsol   4:522   PH
Tod, Eliza (Waugh)   18 no. 3-4:144   BCH
Tod, Emmeline Jane, see
    Newton, Emmeline Jane (Tod)
Tod, John   1:391   BCF
    ————   18 no. 3-4:133, 144   BCH
    ————   232   MHN
    ————   fol. title page   SHB
    ————   59   WTH
    ————   1897:18   YB
Tod, Mrs. John, see
    Tod, Eliza (Waugh)
Todd, C   2:337   BCF
Todd, C C   430   BHSS
Todd, Ella M   76   PC
Todd, Hugh C   298   BHSS
Todd, Olga   410   BHSS
Todd, T J   513   LHM
Todd, Thomas N   6:398   MC
Todd, William H   499   LHM
Tokalin, Charley, see
    Twa-ka-kite (Walla Walla Indian)
Tola-Tsomy, see
    Tolo (Nez Percé Indian)
Tola-Tsonmy, see
    Tolo (Nez Percé Indian)
Tolman, James Clark   1:332   NH
Tolman, Warren Winfield   1941:483   EN
    ————   1924:8   WSP
Tolmie, John Work   3:787   BCF
    ————   fol. title page   SHB
Tolmie, Simon Fraser   4:1053   BCF
    ————   206   JAC
Tolmie, William Fraser   162   AC
    ————   2:337   BCF
    ————   4:651   BCF
    ————   156   DW
    ————   6   MMR
    ————   449   MP
    ————   1:16   NH
    ————   2:56   PMO
    ————   2:396   SH
    ————   fol. title page   SHB
    ————   45   WCS
    ————   1897:18   YB
Tolo (Nez Percé Indian)   207   BHSI
    ————   183   BR
    ————   261   DSW
    ————   1:368-369   EPD
    ————   145   IHI
    ————   60   SIH
Tolo, great granddaughter of Tolo (Nez Perce
    Indian)   1:368-369   EPD
Tomahas (Cayuse Indian)   400-401   DW
Tomasket, Nez Percé chief   240   USCI
Tomlinson, Ralph   3:155   LHC

Tompkins, Morton   1931-32:41   OO
Toner, Ethelyn   50:22 1949   WDT
Tonetex, Hunt (Klikitat Indian)   1:76   LHC
Tonkin, F H   [130]   RLX
Tonneson, C A   1910:51   TDL
Tooker, John S   74   MI
Too-lah, see
    Tolo (Nez Percé Indian)
Toole, Edwin Warren   181   LHM
        6:445   MC
    ————   14 no. 2:163   MWH
Toole, John R   2:1288   SM
Toole, Joseph Kemp   1941:317   EN
        3:front.   MC
    ————   4:148   MC
    ————   23   MI
    ————   156   PIW
    ————   1:444   SMS
Tooze, Walter L   1945-46:92   OO
Torrance, Roscoe C   176-177   GA
Torrance, "Torchy", see
    Torrance, Roscoe C
Torre, Louie   3:327   BHK
Tosten, Thomas   1167   LHM
Totten, Joseph Phelps   136-137   SRW
Totten, Oscar B   447   LHM
Totten, William P   1924:64   WSP
Tourtellotte, J E   2:138   FSB
Tout, Charles Hill-, see
    Hill-Tout, Charles
Tower, F P   76   OS
Towle, Walter R   872   SIH
Townsend, Elizabeth, see
    Meagher, Elizabeth M J   (Townsend)
Townsend, John Kirk   31:front.   OHQ
Townsend, William Borridaile   290   KB
Townshend, 1st marquis, see
    Townshend, George
Townshend, George   94   MV
Townshend, H H   6:404-405   MC
Tox-e-lox (Cayuse Indian)   1:578, 579   PMO
Tracy, George L   3:1346   SM
Tracy, Harry   182-183   KO
Tracy, William H   637   LHM
Traeger, Gottlieb   2:899   BHK
Traeger, Mrs. Gottlieb, see
    Traeger, Magdalena (Sieh)
Traeger, Magdalena (Sieh)   2:899   BHK
Train, George Francis   32   QT
Trane, Eliza Maria (Howes)   442   GL
Trane, Thomas F   441   GL
Trane, Mrs. Thomas F   , see
    Trane, Eliza Maria (Howes)
Traphagen, Delmar H   280   HA
Traphagen, Frank W   6:386   MC
Trapp, Thomas John   3:101   BCF

	fol. pt. 1	SHB
Trask, Ray H	3:343	HHI
Trask, Tirzah (Umatilla Indian)	78	LCR
Traver, George Washington	2:26	HHT
	13 no. 4:419	MWH
Traver, L N	2:395	CHW
Travers, S E , see		
Morrow, S E (Travers)		
Travis, J J	1905-06:[28]	RLW
Travis, James	3:670	SMS
Travis, Mrs. James, see		
Travis, Jane (Perrine)		
Travis, Jane (Perrine)	3:670	SMS
Treadwell, George T	1935:5	S
	1936:3	S
	1937:3	S
	unp.	SAA
Treat, Harry Whitney	5:420	SH
Tredinick, Clara, see		
Peays, Clara (Tredinick)		
Trego, Byrd	374	BF
Tremblay, L	364	PI
	432	PIW
Tremper, C W	172-173	HA
Tremper, Henry S	1924:128	WSP
Trent, Helen, see		
Story, Helen (Trent)		
Trevett, T (Brooks)	1:210-211	GP
Trevitt, Victor	3:487	GP
	1:813	LHC
Trimble, Frank	3:769	BCF
Trimble, Hank	334	BR
Trimble, J G	55	BN
Trimble, James	2:337	BCF
	fol. pt. 1	SHB
	1897:42	YB
	1911:70-71	YB
Trimble, Mrs. S A , see		
Trimble, Sarah (Benson) Allen		
Trimble, Sarah (Benson) Allen	1:572	NH
	1:588	PMO
Trimble, William Pitt	2:860	BHS
	5:304	SH
	1924:160	WSP
Triplett, W T	22:128 1917	WBP
	23:112 1918	WBP
	24:64 1919	WBP
	32:16 1927	WBP
	33:front. 1928	WBP
Trites, Amos Bliss	fol. pt. 2	SHB
Trites, Wycliffe Steves	3:891	BCF
Trodden, James	3:671	BCF
Trodick, Alfred J	3:702	SMS
Tromp, Mabel van, see		
Roberts, Mabel (Van Tromp)		
Troup, Charles	287	LDM
Troup, Claud	335	LDM

Troup, James W	183	LDM
Troup, William H	43	LDM
Trowbridge, May, see		
Blakeslee, May (Trowbridge)		
Trowbridge, Willis Chester	3:161	PH
Troy, D S	255	BHSS
	[125]	RLX
Troy, John Weir	1943:44	ENC
Troy, Preston Marion	3:106	PH
	1923:front.	WSP
Troyer, Nelson	3:475	BHK
Truax, Daniel W	2:151	HH
True, Mark C	2:175	HH
Trueblood, Donald V	3:527	BHK
Truitt, L W	3:1178	SMS
Trullinger, John Corse	1:552	NH
	1:248	PMO
Trump, Philemon Beecher Van, see		
Van Trump, Philemon Beecher		
Truscott, Matthew H	544	SIH
Trutch, Joseph William	2:277	BCF
	fol. pt. 1	SHB
	96-97	SHL
	1897:63, 124	YB
	1911:70-71	YB
Tshusick (Ojibway Indian)	100	GBS
Tubbs, Charles C	3:900	SMS
Tuchscherer, Walter	243	GG
Tucker, E E	44:338	OHQ
Tucker, Franklin	54	LDM
Tucker, Orville A	1905-06:[47]	RLW
Tucker, Wilmon	1916:front.	WSP
Tuekakas, Nez Percé chief		
	fol. 705 (no. 1)	JO
Tueller, Rudolph	3:825	HHI
Tufts, James	4:102	MC
Tulk, A Edward	3:175	BCF
Tull, Francis M	1895-96:111	SSS
Tullis, Amos F	2:214	NH
Tullux Holiquilla, Warm Springs chief		
	228	LCR
Tunin, E N	1:466	PHP
Tunstall, Simon John	4:385	BCF
Tupper, Charles Hibbert	2:463	BCF
	fol. pt. 1	SHB
Turgoose, Fred	2:front. 1924	BCHA
Turnbull, James	65	LDM
Turnbull, William R	126	LDM
Turner, A W	271	E
Turner, Charles A	1924:112	WSP
Turner, Charles H	2:823	FH
Turner, D A	1:911	LHC
Turner, Edward L	120-121	GA
	50:60 1949	WDT
Turner, Frank B	238	LDM
Turner, George	2:113	BCF

_____	4:271	BCF
_____	1:151	HH
_____	1905-06:[28]	RLW
_____	5:110	SH
_____	1926:20	WSP
Turner, H H	19:64 1914	WBP
_____	21:160 1916	WBP
Turner, Harry W	3:1496	SM
Turner, Henry T	4 no. 6:177	PM
Turner, Herbert Spencer	2:303	BHK
Turner, Horace	114	RO
Turner, Howard W	1937-38:62-63	OO
_____	1939-40:31	OO
_____	1943-44:79	OO
Turner, John Herbert	2:451	BCF
_____	98	JAC
_____	48	KB
_____	1897:64, 104	YB
_____	1911:6-7, 70-71	YB
Turner, John W	496	SIH
Turner, Julia Ann, see		
Littlejohn, Julia Ann (Turner)		
Turner, Raymond	1:26-27	EPD
Turner, Robert	275	LDM
Turner, William H	3:922	FH
Turner, William S	44:338	OHQ
Tuttle, Christian	396	JNT
Tuttle, Daniel S	109	BHSI
_____	9:43 1923-24	IH
_____	5:289	MC
Tuttle, Mrs. Daniel S	5:308	MC
T'Vault, William G	1:127	GP
_____	16	TO
Twa-ka-kite (Walla Walla Indian) 23		BSC
_____	10:45 1925-26	IH
Tweedie, Arch C	283	E
Tweney, George H	33 no. 4:36	PNLA
Twichell, Frank A	2:325	HH
_____	1905-06:[70]	RLW
Twilliger, Porter	58	BR
Two Belly (Crow Indian)	361	USCI
Two Moon (Nez Percé Indian)	1:533	HHI
Two Moon, Cheyenne chief	313	AM
Twogood, James H	2:770	FH
Twohy, D W	24:96 1919	WBP
Twohy, Edmund	211	GG
Twohy, John D	215	GG
Ty-Hee, Bannock chief	26	BHSI
Tyler, Adin Parker	3:359	HHI
Tyler, Columbus Tyler	3:829	BHS
Tyler, O S	3:851	HHI
Tyler, Richard G	36:22 1935	WDT
Tyler, William D	13 no. 3:295	MWH
Tyrer, Thomas	393	BHSS
Tyrwhitt-Drake, Montague William 4:289		BCF
_____	fol. pt. 1	SHB
_____	1897:124, 136	YB
_____	1911:70-71	YB

Tyson, Arthur Ralph	1943:78	ENC
Tyson, James	900	SIH

U

Udell, C E	1924:65	WSP
Uehren, Frank	2:179	HHI
Uhl, Willis L	36:22 1935	WDT
Uhle, Margaret, see		
Stocking, Margaret (Henry)		
Uhlman, C Paul	25:128 1920	WBP
_____	26:128 1921	WBP
_____	27:97 1922	WBP
Uhlman, Charles T	2:458	NH
_____	[139]	RLX
Uhlman, Wesley C	unp.	SEA
Ulbrickson, Al M	176-177	GA
Ulrich, O J	3:789	LHC
Ulsh, J A	1905-06:[56]	RLW
_____	[122]	RLX
U-ma-pine, Umatilla chief	208	AI
_____	4:120	LH
Umpqua Peter, chief	1:195	PMO
Underwood, David C	60:94	OHQ
Underwood, George W	334	BR
_____	248	SIH
Underwood, J J	1 no. 8:4	WN
Unsinger, Peter	48	LS
Upton, Jay H	1931-32:40	OO
Upton, Robert Jarvis	2:503	GP
U'Ren, William S	1:565	GP
_____	68:198	OHQ
Urquhart, Alex	2:front. 1924	BCHA
Urquhart, Mrs. Alex	2:front. 1924	BCHA
Urquhart, James	1:340	NH
Urquhart, William M	1:424	PHP
Usher, Joseph J	unp.	SAA
Utter, Darwin A	3:1299	FH
Utterback, Clarence B	3:433	BH
Utterback, Clinton L	50:49 1949	WDT
Utz, Benjamin Edward	3	US
Utz, Mrs. Benjamin Edward, see		
Utz, Mrs. Cora		
Utz, Mrs. Cora	3	US

V

Vail, Curtis C D	50:39 1949	WDT
Vail, E E	48	LS
Vail, G W	48	LS
Valentine, Albert L	373	HA
Van Anda, Emma	1:917	LHC

Van Asselt, Henry   2:500   NH
Van Auken, Henry   322   LDM
Van Ausdeln, Howard C   3:946   FH
Van Bokkelen, J   J   H   1:124   NH
Van Brocklin, John Wesley   3:777   BHS
Van Buskirk, Philip Clayton 50 no. 2:49   PN
Van Camp, Charles   5:191   MC
Van Camp, Ruphema J   , see
    Sappington, Ruphema J   (Van Camp)
Vance, Frank   1 no. 4:311   WM
Vance, J   A   2:637   HWW
Van Cleve, Richard   50:36 1949   WDT
Van Cott, Mary, see
    Young, Mary (Van Cott)
Vancouver, George   1:157   BCF
_____   2:149   BCF
_____   67   GBS
_____   45   GI
_____   front.   GV
_____   7   LDM
_____   1:334   LH
_____   1   MMR
_____   front.   MV
_____   1:593   PMO
_____   1:184   SH
_____   fol. title page   SHB
_____   1:16   WI
_____   1897:17   YB
_____   1911:70-71   YB
Vancouver, John   170   GV
Vandall, Frank E   4:663   BCF
Vandenberg, David R   1945-46:93   OO
Van Den Broeck, Victor   309   PI
Vanderburg, Grace, see
    Rose, Grace (Vanderburg)
Vanderburg, W   S   1895:88   OO
Vandercock, Eliza, see
    Cooke, Eliza (Vandercock)
Vandercook, Wesley   11, 17   MLO
Vanderford, Thomas Sylvester 3:406   BEA
Van der Veer, Charles   1:unp. 1900-01   WDT
Vanderveer, George   23   LT
Van der Velden, Aloysius   214   PI
_____   164   PIW
Van Deusen, Dudley H   2:631   HHI
Van de Ven, H   J   366   PI
_____   436   PIW
Van Doren, John W   3:1329   SM
Van Doren, Mrs. Nancy L   120, 219   BHSS
Van Doren, Seaton   206   BHSS
Van Duser, Oliver   70   LDM
Van Dyke, Frank J   1943-44:79   OO
                             1945-46:87   OO
Van Dyke, John B   3:391   BHK
Van Eaton, Nellie (Appleby) 3:333   BH
Van Eaton, Thomas C   3:533   BH
                             6:108   SH
_____   1895-96:117   SSS

Van Eaton, Mrs. Thomas C   , see
    Van Eaton, Nellie (Appleby)
Van Epps, Theodore C   1:612   NH
Van Gorp, Leopold   141   GG
_____   288   PI
_____   308   PIW
Van Gundy, J   E   583   LHM
Van Hoomissen, Joseph   235   GG
Van Horn, Francis Joseph   3:601   BH
Van Horne, William Cornelius 2:427   BCF
_____   230, 302, 327   GI
_____   96   SC
Van Houten, B   C   1895-96:79   SSS
Van Houten, Walter John   fol. pt. 2   SHB
Van Iorns, William   2:887   FH
Van Laken, Peter John   2:57   SMS
Van Lennep, David   23   DH
Van Lente, Annie, see
    Nienhuis, Annie (Van Lente)
Van Name, J   F   1905-06:[28]   RLW
Van Orsdel, William Wesley   1:242   ACR
_____   5, 10, 94   LHN
_____   217   VT
Van Patten, Edwin H   4:533   PH
Van Ravenswaay, Charles   66:292   OHQ
Van Reuth, Felix   2:769   HHI
Van Schuyver, William James 3:157   GP
Van Scoy, T   72   OS
Van Slyke, J   A   20:80 1915   WBP
Van Slyke, Lee   1905-06:[60]   RLW
Van Soelen, A   C   1924:81   WSP
Van Tassell, Philip   158   LDM
Van Tromp, Mabel, see
    Roberts, Mabel (Van Tromp)
Van Trump, Philemon Beecher 1:146   HHT
Van Vleet, Elisabeth A   (Coffey)
                             2:637   GP
Van Vleet, Lewis   2:636, 637   GP
Van Vleet, Mrs. Lewis, see
    Van Vleet, Elisabeth A   (Coffey)
Van Winkle, I   H   1931-32:8   OO
_____   1935-36:34   OO
_____   1937-38:7   OO
_____   1939-40:7   OO
_____   1941-42:13   OO
_____   1943-44:17   OO
Van Zante, Arthur B   138   PSW
Varley, William   3:1090   FH
Varnum, Charles A   110-111   HCM
Vashon, James   144   MV
Vasquez, Tiburcio   134   SW
Vassar, S   H   3:303   HHI
Vaughan, Elbert   3:883   LHC
Vaughan, Elisha Cutts   3:85   BH
Vaughan, Thomas   67:200, 204   OHQ
Vaughan, William D   1:63   BH

Vaughn, Andrew 48 KT
Vaughn, Christine 42:32 1930 WSGP
Vaughn, Clara, see
  Cary, Clara (Vaughn)
Vaughn, Hank 110 BR
Vaughn, Jane Mariah (Brain) 444 GL
Vaughn, Lena 6:386 MC
Vaughn, Michael 443 GL
Vaughn, Mrs. Michael, see
  Vaughn, Jane Mariah (Brain)
Vaughn, Michael, Jr. 224 GL
Vaughn, Robert 288 MI
———— 2:956 SM
———— front. VT
Veatch, Marion 2:69 CHW
Veazie, Walter C 40 BCC
Veblen, John 26:18 PNLA
———— 29:112 PNLA
Veit, Katherine, see
  Wood, Katherine (Veit) Hagenbarth Murphy
Velikanje, E B 1924:144 WSP
Veness, J A 1905-06:[41] RLW
———— [94] RLX
Veniaminov, Ivan 278-279 HU
———— fol. 92 SHE
Venneman, John J 352 PIW
Venosta, E Viconti 2:463 BCF
Verendrye, Pierre Gaultier de Varennes, see
  La Verendrye, Pierre Gaultier de Varennes
Vergowe, George E [126] RLX
Verhagen, A 48 MG
Vernon, Forbes George 60 KB
———— 1897:132 YB
Vernon, J F 144 PSW
Vernon, James Mercer 2:304 PHP
Verschoyle, W Denham 4:319 BCF
Vertrees, Mary J , see
  Johns, Mary J (Vertrees)
Vesser, Samuel 864 SIH
Vest, George G 160 PIW
Vickers, Alonzo 116 LDM
Vickers, Elias 319 LDM
Vickers, Robert A 2:1013 SM
Victor, Flathead chief, see
  Lodge Pole, Flathead chief
Victor, Frances (Fuller) 1:596 GP
———— 62:309 OHQ
———— 45 no. 4:108 PN
Victor, Mrs. Henry Clay, see
  Victor, Frances (Fuller)
Victoria (Clallam ? Indian) 18 WCS
Vidal, James Henry 3:253 BCF
Vigelius, A 2:front. 1924 BCHA
Vigus, Joel 39 LHN
Villard, Henry 144 BOO
———— 1:519 CHW
———— 1:294 GP
———— 400 QT
————

———— 1 no. 11:10 WN
Vinal, William A 295 HA
Vincent, Coeur d'Alene chief
  fol. 512 (no. 32) BUR
Vincent, A W 2:430 PMO
Vincent, Mrs. Ed 1:154-155 EPD
Vincent, L A 1926:20 WSP
Vincent, S B 197 PL
Vincent, W D 13:16 1908 WBP
———— 17:209 1912 WBP
———— 18:128 1913 WBP
———— 19:80 1914 WBP
———— 24:80 1919 WBP
Virges, William 1910:2 TDL
Virtue, George Alexander 3:925 BHS
———— 24 SRW
Visby, Niels J 640 SIH
Visscher, William Lightfoot 2:162 HHT
Vogal, L A 177 PL
Voght, William fol. title page SHB
Vogtlin, George H 1905-06:[63] RLW
Voight, Mina (Wengel) 3:457 BHS
Voight, William 3:456 BHS
Voight, Mrs. William, see
  Voight, Mina (Wengel)
Volkert, Fred 2:1140 SM
Vollmer, John P 3:1006 FH
———— front. SIH
Von Alvensleben, Constantin Alvo, see
  Alvensleben, Constantin Alvo von
Von Boecklin, August 3:471 HHT
———— 1910:2 TDL
Von Falde, Catharina Elizabeth, see
  Linnemann, Catharina Elizabeth
  (Von Falde)
Von Shrader, E 1:372 HHT
Von Tobel, Edward 2:705 BHK
Von Wrangel, Ferdinand Petrovich, see
  Wrangel, Ferdinand Petrovich von
Voris, Bernard D 3:607 BHS
Votaw, H L June 1909:62 TDL
Vowell, Arthur W fol. title page SHB
Vuicich, William Dukin 1943:146 ENC

W

Waddell, Hugh 24:32 1919 WBP
Wade, A M [123] RLX
Wade, Alfred H 3 AT
Wade, C H Stuart 3:519 BCF
Wade, Decius S 121 LHM
———— 4:110 MC
———— 102 MI
———— 14 no. 1:front. MWH
————

	1:428	SMS	
Wade, F M	1:534	HHT	
Wade, Ira	472	PL	
Wade, Justus	2:452	PMO	
Wade, Mark S	fol. pt. 1	SHB	
Wade, W H H	177	PL	

Wade, Wilhelmina, see
   Ellis, Wilhelmina (Wade)

Wadsworth, Benjamin Schallenberger 3:87	PH
Waggoner, David	272	PSW
Wagner, Alexander	3:741	BCF
Wagner, Billy	1:401	BH
Wagner, Harold	332	SCH
Wagner, Henry	3:407	GP
Wagner, Jack	1937-38:62-63	OO
Wagner, Lou	3:601	LHC

Wagner, Louisa, see
   Kaiser, Louisa (Wagner)

Wahlstrom, Nelson A	50:22 1949	WDT
Wainwright, Louis C	6:440-441	MC
Wair, Donald	1945-46:62	OO
Wait, Aaron E	1:56	NH
Waite, Charles W	3:928	SMS
Waite, John D	2:175	SMS
Waitt, Warren A	3:637	LHC
Waitt, William I	82	LDM
Wakefield, Duron Whittlesey	2:61	GP
Wakefield, George W	2:978	SM
Wakefield, William J C	5:302	SH
Wakema (Klikitat Indian)	157, 161	WCS
Wakeman, Edgar	100	LDM
Wakeman, Mrs. Emma J	1:448	GP
Wakeman, Maurice B	3:31	GP
Walbran, John T	351	LDM
Waldorf, John Taylor	197	PL
Waldron, John	159	WOY
Waldron, Rodney K	30:5	PNLA
	34 no. 1:33	PNLA
Wale, Billy	2:front. 1924	BCHA
Walgamot, Frank H	149	PL

Walgamot, Leather Stocking, see
   Walgamot, Frank H

Walkem, George Anthony	2:191, 335, 337	BCF
	30	JAC
	fol. pt. 1	SHB
	286	WSE
	1897:64, 135, 136	YB
	1911:70-71	YB
Walkem, William Wymond	front.	WSE
	1897:108	YB
Walker, Ute chief	133	BHI
Walker, (Captain)	163	LDM

Walker, Mrs. A M , see
   Walker, Abba Beatrice (Creel)

Walker, Abba Beatrice (Creel)	6:358	MC

Walker, Abigail Boutwell, see
   Karr, Abigail Boutwell (Walker)

Walker, Amy Gertrude (Littlehale)	3:67	D
	3:919	LHC

Walker, Arlie G	1945-46:93	OO
Walker, Chester B	3:781	HHI
Walker, Cyrus	1:661	BHK
	3:37	BHS
	5:120	SH
Walker, Cyrus Hamlin	1:249	CHW
	240, 248	DE
	1:124	PMO
Walker, David D	2:1089	SM
Walker, Dean H	1935-36:50	OO
	1937-38:62	OO
	1939-40:15	OO
	1941-42:62	OO
	1943-44:75	OO
	1945-46:83	OO
Walker, E A	177	PSW
Walker, E C	unp.	SOU
Walker, Elizabeth	25:35	PNLA

Walker, Elizabeth, see also
   Stephens, Elizabeth (Walker)

Walker, Elkanah	front., 240-241	DE
	197	DS
	41	EI
	290	EW
	1:28	NH
	1:469	PMO
	2:136	SH

Walker, Mrs. Elkanah, see
   Walker, Mary (Richardson)

Walker, Flora A (Bredes)	1:7, 14	D
Walker, Frank	3:1348	SM
Walker, Fred	1:26-27	EPD
Walker, I N	2:561	SMS

Walker, Mrs. James Greig, Jr., see
   Walker, Amy Gertrude (Littlehale)

Walker, John	248	DE
Walker, Joseph	248	DE
Walker, Joseph C	6:364	MC
Walker, Levi	248	DE
Walker, M L	3:35	HHI
Walker, Marcus	248	DE
Walker, Mary (Richardson)	1:133	D
	227, 240-241, 248	DE
	1:66	PMO
Walker, Noble M	2:1039	SM
Walker, Robert	3:61	BH
Walker, Robert C	273	LHM
Walker, Samuel C	2:643	SMS
Walker, Samuel T	248-249	DE
Walker, Sharpless	3:1664	SM
Walker, Thomas B	435	PL
Walker, Thomas J	2:1185	SM
Walker, William	2:103	BHK
	3:487	BHS
	5:414	SH

Walker, Mrs. William Sherman, see
   Walker, Flora A (Bredes)

Wall, Edward	2:front. 1924	BCHA

Wall, Harry   3:435   BEA
Wall, Harry E   4:615   PH
Wall, Joseph   43   LDM
Wall, Patrick   3:1383   SM
Wallace, Bessie J   , see
    Rudene, Bessie J   (Wallace) Cornelius
Wallace, Charles   1:917   LHC
Wallace, Collin A   unp.   SOU
Wallace, David O   368   LDM
Wallace, E   W   unp.   SOU
Wallace, G   D   110-111   HCM
Wallace, Hugh C   1895-96:124   SSS
Wallace, James L   3:1755   SM
Wallace, Leo Gus   2:539   HHT
Wallace, Lew   1935-36:51   OO
_____   1939-40:15   OO
_____   1941-42:62   OO
_____   1943-44:75   OO
_____   1945-46:83   OO
Wallace, N   G   1935-36:50   OO
Wallace, Robert Bruce   1:618   SM
                                1:646   SMS
Wallace, William Henson   186   BHSI
_____   front.   DL
_____   1:147   HHI
_____   17   MAG
_____   22   ME
_____   1:560   NH
_____   60 no. 2:79   PN
_____   [43]   RLX
Waller, A   Orville   2:167   CHW
                                1937-38:62-63 OO
Waller, Alvin F   88   AC
_____   41   EI
_____   1:32   NH
_____   front.   OS
_____   2:56   PMO
Waller, Henry Edwin   3:633   BCF
Waller, Osmar L   327   BHSS
                                1941:87   EN
Wallgren, Monrad C   61   MAG
                                unp.   SE
Wallin, Charles C   3:1725   SM
Wallingford, John Noble   180   SRW
Wallis, C   R   44:338   OHQ
Wallis, James Harknett   1:69   FSB
Walrath, Mrs.   99   LHN
Walsh, D   H   89   MLO
Walsh, James J   159, 167   OB
Walsh, John Raphael   247   GG
Walsh, Mollie   51   AL
Walsh, Thomas J   55 no. 1:3, 7 PN
                                56 no. 3:117   PN
                                1911:146   WSP
Walsh, Walter William   3:533   BCF
Walsh, William   2:1290   SM
Walsh, William E   1941-42:62   OO
                                1943-44:75   OO
                                1945-46:83   OO

Walters, Amelia, see
    Wold, Amelia (Walters)
Walters, Augustus   1:236   HHT
Walters, Carl O   178   SS
Walters, Edward A   1:115   FSB
Walters, Frank L   1924:81   WSP
Walters, N   P   2:515   SMS
Walters, Samuel J   3:639   BHK
Walters, Theodore A   54 no. 1:16   PN
Walther, William E   3:49   LHC
Walton, Arthur Leland   3:205   BEA
Walton, Hiram F   2:440   PHP
Walton, Joshua J   1:639   CHW
                                2:318   NH
Waltz, Ray M   1945-46:63   OO
Wal-wa-ma, Nez Percé chief 153   BR
Wanamaker, Clarence I   3:253   HWW
Wand, John B   151   OB
Wanlass, William   189   GL
Wann, James H   272   SIH
Warburton, Elizabeth, see
    Harrison, Elizabeth (Warburton)
Warburton, Stanton   2:439   HHT
                                2:16   PHP
_____   May 1907:39   TDL
Ward, George W   3:733   BHS
Ward, Irving   59   SSP
Ward, J   F   2:857   BHK
Ward, Mary Ann, see
    Webb, Mary Ann (Ward)
Ward, May Dunn   36:25 1935   WDT
Ward, Moses   1:71   BH
Ward, Sarah E   , see
    Bell, Sarah E   (Ward)
Ward, William Curtis   fol. title page SHB
Wardall, Norman M   24   PIG
Warden, John Weightman   3:1079   BCF
Ware, Marie, see
    McKinley, Marie (Ware)
Ware, S   M   129   PSW
Warncke, Ruth   30 no. 4:cover PNLA
Warner, C   H   1905-06:[28]   RLW
Warner, C   V   1926:20   WSP
Warner, Charles Dudley   90   DT
Warner, Charlie (Spokan Indian) 58   LL
Warner, Matt, see
    Warner, Willard Christiansen
Warner, Rosa (Rumel)   182-183   KO
Warner, Willard Christiansen 182-183   KO
Warner, Mrs. Willard Christiansen, see
    Warner, Rosa (Rumel)
Warren, A   235   AG
Warren, Mrs. A   J   , see
    Warren, Eliza (Spalding)
Warren, Althea   8:127   PNLA
Warren, Amelia, see
    Crooks, Amelia (Warren)
Warren, Andrew   1:380   NH

Warren, Berle J   80   WMW
Warren, Charles S   457   MI
Warren, Daniel K   3:527   LHC
Warren, Eliza (Spalding)   98   BHSI
_____   55   CW
_____   310   DS
_____   1:20   FH
_____   1:52   NH
_____   1:62   PMO
                         32, 49, 80, 128   WMW
Warren, F   H   172-173   HA
Warren, Felix   196, 199   BR
_____   13   SPI
Warren, Henry L   4:102   MC
Warren, J   F   59   SSP
Warren, James D   168   LDM
Warren, James H   80   WMW
Warren, Ledelle   80   WMW
Warren, Minnie, see
     Illsley, Minnie (Warren)
Warren, Otey Yancey   1941:23   EN
Warren, William L   unp.   SOU
Washakie, Shoshone chief   41   BHI
_____   654   CIR
_____   185   EP
_____   216   GR
_____   181   HB
_____   30   TMP
Washburn, Henry D   5:375   MC
Washburn, R   C   1895-96:79   SSS
Washburn, Volney W   844   SIH
Washburne, Betsey (Wright)   1:98   D
Washburne, Mrs. James, see
     Washburne, Betsey (Wright)
Washikie, Shoshone chief, see
     Washakie, Shoshone chief
Washington, Mrs. Augustine, see
     Washington, Mary (Ball)
Washington, George   82   BT
_____   front.   CC
_____   2   MV
Washington, Mary (Ball)   1:62   D
Washkin, see
     Waskin (Nez Percé Indian)
Waskin (Nez Percé Indian)   23   BR
_____   19   SPI
Wassem, George F   556   SIH
Wassem, Mrs. George F   , see
     Wassem, Sophie (Ricklefs)
Wassem, Sophie (Ricklefs)   556   SIH
Wasserman, Paul   30 no. 4:cover   PNLA
Wassler, Ernest P   3:107   BEA
Wassmuth, A   J   1:282-283   EPD
Wassmuth, Clara   1:282-283   EPD
Wassmuth, Lawrence   1:282-283   EPD
Wasson, Andrew   4 no. 4:125   PM
Waterman, Catharine (Boyle)   2:946   SM
Waterman, Christopher H   2:946   SM

Waterman, Mrs. Christopher H   , see
     Waterman, Catharine (Boyle)
Waterman, Mrs. Max   6:408-409   MC
Waters, Ela Collins   2:918   SM
Waters, James A   3:1018   FH
Waters, Mrs. John M   6:325   MC
Waters, Julius Spencer   153   IHI
Waters, Lydia   42:32 1930   WSGP
Waters, Thomas R   1924:80   WSP
Wat-is-kow-kow (Umatilla Indian) 243   AI
_____   22   BSC
_____   10:44 1925-26   IH
Watkins, Charles F   3:1048   SMS
Watkins, Frank E   3:877   LHC
Watkins, George E   3:333   GP
Watkins, Margaret E   , see
     Smith, Margaret E   (Watkins)
Watkins, Robert Morton   4:759   PH
Watkins, Walter William   3:1379   SM
Watkins, William H   1:536   GP
_____   1:304   NH
Watson, A   L   1905-06:[48]   RLW
                                 [101]   RLX
Watson, Adam   3:681   BCF
Watson, Alexander R   , Jr. 2:367   HHT
Watson, Alice, see
     Overman, Alice (Watson)
Watson, Chandler B   66:172   OHQ
Watson, Charles Hubert   3:283   BCF
Watson, Coverdale   3:199   BCF
Watson, Daniel M   2:443   PMO
Watson, Edward Byers   2:85   GP
Watson, Mrs. Emma L   115   PL
Watson, Harry   3:201   BHS
Watson, Henry Holgate   1911:70-71   YB
Watson, J   Howard   1895-96:147   SSS
Watson, John Mallery   3:611   BCF
Watson, Malcolm Vau   1941:61   EN
Watson, Mrs. Maria L   6:420-421   MC
Watson, Priscilla (Patton) 1:644   NH
Watson, Thomas G   88   PSW
Watson, Mrs. Tom   2:front. 1924   BCHA
Watson, William   2:front. 1924   BCHA
Watson, William H   6:420-421   MC
Watson, William Penn   1:644   NH
Watson, Mrs. William Penn, see
     Watson, Priscilla (Patton)
Watson, William W   2:1217   SM
Watt, George H   215   BHSS
Watt, Joseph   1:242   GP
Watt, P   H   172-173, 304   HA
Watt, Vivien   207   BHSS
Watt, W   B   172-173   HA
Watt, William H   262   IHI
Watters, Dennis Alonzo   2:531   LHC
Watters, Mrs. Dennis Alonzo, see
     Watters, Lucy E   (McKever)

Watters, Lucy E (McKever)	2:531	LHC	
Watts, George Eliot	3:403	LHC	
Watts, James G	274	IHI	
Waubish, Klikitat chief	front.	BL	
Waud, Orrin S	232	LDM	
Waugh, Eliza, see			
Tod, Eliza (Waugh)			
Waughop, John W	2:98	NH	
Wead, Eva, see			
Gove, Eva (Wead)			
We-ark-koomt, see			
Looking Glass, Sr., Nez Percé chief			
We-as-kush, Nez Percé chief	153	BR	
	1:76	NH	
Weatherbee, Martha Ann, see			
Foster, Martha Ann (Weatherbee)			
Weatherford, F M	1905-06:[66]	RLW	
Weatherford, J K , Jr.	1931-32:41	OO	
Weatherford, James K	2:fol. 516	CHW	
Weatherford, M (Harris)	2:74	NH	
Weatherford, Mark V	2:675	CHW	
Weatherford, William	2:74	NH	
Weatherford, Mrs. William, see			
Weatherford, M (Harris)			
Weatherly, George W	3:671	LHC	
Weatherwax, John M	2:93	HWW	
Weaver, Albert E	2:481	HHI	
Weaver, Charles Russell	3:303	BEA	
Weaver, David B	7:73, 83	MC	
Weaver, John	4:905	BCF	
Weaver, Samuel C	2:133	SMS	
Weaver, Samuel P	1924:176	WSP	
Webb, Ann Eliza, see			
Young, Ann Eliza (Webb)			
Webb, Beulah (Allen)	3:665	HHI	
Webb, George	232	GL	
Webb, Mrs. George, see			
Webb, Mary Ann (Ward)			
Webb, H J	58	BHSS	
Webb, Hannah (Grace)	447	GL	
Webb, Harriet (Grace)	448	GL	
Webb, Horatio	2:front. 1924	BCHA	
Webb, John Stokes	446	GL	
Webb, Mrs. John Stokes, see			
Webb, Hannah (Grace)			
Webb, Mary Ann (Ward)	445	GL	
Webb, Thomas	299	GL	
Webb, William	448	GL	
Webb, Mrs. William, see			
Webb, Harriet (Grace)			
Webb, William H	2:475	SMS	
Webb, Willis	3:665	HHI	
Webb, Mrs. Willis, see			
Webb, Beulah (Allen)			
Webber, Albert	277	BR	
Weber, John J	260	GG	
Weber, William H	1905-06:[58]	RLW	
	[115]	RLX	

Webster, E E	unp.	VU	
Webster, Edgar J	2:486	NH	
Webster, J P	272	E	
Webster, John	1:201	BHK	
	2:772-773	BHS	
Webster, Mrs. John	2:772-773	BHS	
Webster, John McA	47 no. 2:46	PN	
Webster, N H	3:300	MC	
Webster, Richard	2:463	BCF	
Webster, S H	219	BHSS	
Webster, Valter C	4:433	BHK	
Wedderburn, Alexander	230	MV	
Weed, Alfred B	1:217	HH	
Weed, Elbert Durkee	118	MI	
Weed, Gideon Allen	877	HI	
	unp.	SEA	
Weedin, Luther	4:215	BHK	
Weeks, Cecil L	2:973	HHI	
Weeks, Joseph E	2:903	HHI	
Weeks, Reuben	2:787	GP	
Wegener, O F	3:93	BHS	
Wegener, Theodore Henry	3:383	BEA	
	1941:166	EN	
Wegner, E E	430	BHSS	
Wehr, Leonard B	2:799	FH	
Wehrung, William H	2:454	PMO	
Weichbrodt, Irvin Arthur	3:177	BHS	
Weidler, George Washington	2:761	LHC	
Weikert, Andrew J	3:153	MC	
Weiler, Charles	2:front. 1924	BCHA	
Weiler, John	300	KB	
Weiler, Otto	2:front. 1924	BCHA	
Weinard, Phil	1:90, 206	ACR	
Weinel, Louis	3:187	PH	
Weinhard, Henry	2:289	GP	
	638	SHP	
Weinzirl, John	1941:257	EN	
Weir, Allen	2:130	NH	
	1905-06:[28]	RLW	
Weir, James	1905-06:[63]	RLW	
	[132]	RLX	
Weisbach, R Jacob	1:360, 372	HHT	
Weisenburger, J J	1905-06:[28]	RLW	
Weisenhorn, A	689	LHM	
Weiss, Karl	3:429	BCF	
Welahetum (Wasco Indian)	41:154	OHQ	
Welch, Daniel J	913	LHM	
Welch, Hiram U	3:463	LHC	
Welch, Joanna Maria, see			
Russell, Joanna Maria (Welch)			
Welchel, Herbert Edwin	4:407	BCF	
Weldon, George A	1924:112	WSP	
Weldon, Richard C	1:634	BCF	
Welker, Jesse R	3:229	BEA	
Wellcome, John Ball	3:1343	SM	
Weller, Kathleen	66	MG	

164

Wellhouser, Henry F	2:1020	SM
Wellman, Alfred C	282	E
Wellman, William	2:1266	SM
Wells, A C	2:139	BCF
Wells, George F	2:707	GP
Wells, Harvey	1931-32:41	OO
_____	1939-40:31	OO
_____	1941-42:66	OO
_____	1943-44:79	OO
	1945-46:87	OO
Wells, Hulet M	57 no. 4:150	PN
Wells, L B	534	MI
Wells, Lemuel H	78	BE
Wells, Margaret, see		
Peers, Margaret (Wells)		
Wells, Mary, see		
Slaughter, Mary (Wells)		
Wells, Max	287	BHSS
Wells, Merle W	3:520	BEA
Wells, Richard	208-209	SIH
Wells, Mrs. Richard, see		
Wells, Sallie M (Wilsey)		
Wells, Sallie M (Wilsey)	208-209	SIH
Wells, William Benjamin	38	LDM
	1:120	NH
Welsh, Charles A	4:617	BCF
Welsh, John T	1:400	PHP
	1905-06:[47]	RLW
Welsh, Martin C	1924:129	WSP
Wengel, Mina, see		
Voight, Mina (Wengel)		
Wentworth, Charles L	2:111	SMS
Wentworth, S H	1924:144	WSP
Werner, Adolph	2:366	HWW
Werner, Mrs. Adolph, see		
Werner, Josephine Ferrera		
Werner, Josephine Ferrera	2:367	HWW
Wernicke, C W	168	IHI
Wessinger, Henry W	3:783	LHC
Wessinger, Paul	3:309	GP
Wessman, Harold E	50:54 1949	WDT
West, Arnold J	2:263	HWW
_____	1905-06:[28]	RLW
West, Charles M	3:1313	SMS
West, George F	158	AG
West, J R	43	SA
West, Josiah	3:797	LHC
West, Julia, see		
Parks, Julia (West)		
West, O J	3:517	BHK
West, Oswald	66:250, 342	OHQ
	68:133	OHQ
_____	337	PL
_____	63	TUR
Westby, J A	172-173	HA
Westby, Jacob A	218	HA
Westby, Nels	3:417	HHI
Westcott, C J	3:80	BEA

Westendorf, Thomas Paine	60 no. 1:26	PN
Wester, George	439	LDM
Westerman, Robert G	3:549	BHS
Westfal, Carl	2:48-49	EPD
Westfall, Jasper	63:286	OHQ
Westfall, L L	1924:48	WSP
Westgate, George A	299	PL
Westman, Edward Emil	3:286	PH
Weston, Edward Oscar	4:471	BCF
Weston, Grace A , see		
Phillip, Grace A (Weston)		
Westover, Peter	4:509	BCF
Westover, Willie	[139]	RLX
Westwood, Elizabeth Clara, see		
Dick, Elizabeth Clara (Westwood)		
Wetzel, John B	26	LHN
Wetzell, W A	2:318	NH
Wevley, M C	273	E
Wexler, Herbert	290	BHSS
Weythman, Verna	42:32 1930	WSGP
Whale, Rosetta, see		
Sherlock, Rosetta (Whale)		
Whalley, John William	2:475	GP
Wharton, Jesse R	6:382-383	MC
Whatcom, Napoleon (Puyallup Indian)	1:3	BH
Wheatman, John Thomas	3:1053	BHS
_____	1941:285	EN
Wheelan, J W	23	DH
Wheeler, Mrs. Amelia (Nez Percé Indian)		
	200	PSW
Wheeler, Burton K	54 no. 1:23	PN
Wheeler, H C	1931-32:40	OO
_____	1935-36:50	OO
_____	1937-38:62	OO
_____	1939-40:15	OO
_____	1941-42:62	OO
_____	1943-44:75	OO
_____	1945-46:83	OO
Wheeler, H E	41	MG
Wheeler, Henry Sibley	4:21	MC
Wheeler, Hial A	2:27	CHW
Wheeler, J D	135	JNT
Wheeler, John B	144	DL
Wheeler, W A	2:16	PMO
Wheeler, William (Nez Percé Indian)	212	BR
_____	414	DS
_____	127	DTI
_____	200	PSW
Wheeler, Mrs. William, see		
Wheeler, Mrs. Amelia (Nez Percé Indian)		
Wheeler, William Carleton	3:167	BH
Wheeler, William Edward	3:1065	FH
Wheeler, William Fletcher	341	LHM
_____	3:27	MC
Wheelwright, John	278-279	KO

Wheelwright, Shorty, see
    Wheelwright, John
Whelan, George   fol. title page   SHB
Whillock, Henry Westerman 3:39   BEA
Whipkey, A   J   268   PSW
Whipkey, Mrs. A   J   268   PSW
Whipple, Charles Amos   2:1234   SM
Whipple, Lucie, see
    Carr, Lucie (Whipple)
Whipple, Robert John   449   GL
Whipple, Mrs. Robert John, see
    Whipple, Susie (Winn)
Whipple, Susie (Winn)   450   GL
Whipps, William C   2:1174   SM
Whirlwind (Umatilla Indian) 242   AI
                    14   BSC
             10:36 1925-26 IH
                 104   JM
Whitcomb, Fred J   293   LDM
Whitcomb, George A   293   LDM
Whitcomb, James H   293   LDM
Whitcomb, James P   293   LDM
Whitcomb, James William 248   SIH
Whitcomb, Mrs. James William, see
    Whitcomb, Sallie (Nelson)
Whitcomb, Lot   4:270   LH
Whitcomb, Sallie (Nelson) 248   SIH
Whitcomb, Wes P   293   LDM
Whitcomb, William H   293   LDM
White, A   K   832   SIH
White, Benjamin Franklin 144   DL
               2:315   SMS
White, C   F   unp.   VU
White, Charles   274   E
White, Charles D   9   MG
                332   SCH
White, Coral B   1 no. 2:100 WM
White, E   J 2:front. 1924 BCHA
White, E   M   50   LDM
White, Eben W   3:179   PH
White, Elijah   668   CIR
White, Elizabeth (Thomas) 19   GL
White, Eugene D   1:480   PMO
White, Floyd Corey   2:661   HHI
White, Frances Ann (Thomas) 14   GL
White, Francis A   2:524   PHP
White, G   144   DL
White, Harry   1:325   HH
              2:456   PHP
              unp.   SEA
White, Harry K   1 no. 3:23 WN
White, Horace   96   LS
White, J   J   275   E
White, Joel William   14   GL
White, Mrs. Joel William, see
    White, Frances Ann (Thomas)
White, John W   184   SIH
White, Joseph   45   DW
White, Joseph C   3:905   FH

White, Leonard   81   LDM
White, Lily E   2:22   PMO
White, Mary A   , see
    Savage, Mary A   (White)
White, O   H   1:105   BH
White, Mrs. O   H 1:105   BH
White, R   B   195   AT
White, Raymond LeRoy 3:271   BEA
White, Rhoda M   346   BHSS
White, Richard Mansfield 3, 27   DA
White, Robert J   3:31   HWW
White, S   S   26   LDM
              1:188   PMO
White, Mrs. Samuel, see
    White, Elizabeth (Thomas)
White, T   172-173   HA
White, T   A   unp.   SOU
White, Thomas Henry   4:799   BCF
              fol. pt. 1   SHB
White, W   H   3 no. 8:419 PM
White Bird (Crow Indian) 360   USCI
White Bird, Nez Percé chief 118 AI
               196   BR
White Bull, Cheyenne chief 238 KY
White Calf, Piegan chief 170   PI
               204   PIW
White Grass, Piegan chief 170   PI
               204   PIW
White Thunder, see
    Yellow Wolf, Nez Percé chief
Whiteaker, John   4:302   LH
              1:12   PMO
               28   TUR
Whitehead, A   T   172-173   HA
Whitehead, Cabell   148   HA
Whitehead, Mortimer 25:front. 1913 WSGP
Whitehead, Reah M   1924:145 WSP
Whitehill, Sarah B   6:438-439 MC
Whitehouse, Benjamin Gardner 3:429 GP
Whitehouse, Morris Homans 1943:121 ENC
Whiteley, J   J   447   LDM
Whiteley, W   H   447   LDM
Whitesell, Elizabeth Agnes, see
    Lane, Elizabeth Agnes (Whitesell)
Whitesell, Henry   3:703   BH
Whitesell, Mrs. Henry, see
    Whitesell, Mrs. Margaret
Whitesell, Mrs. Margaret 3:703 BH
              3:433   HHT
Whiteside, Ruth A   , see
    Thompson, Ruth A   (Whiteside) Kilbury
Whitfield, A   J   200   AG
Whitfield, George 2:front. 1924 BCHA
Whitfield, Mrs. I   G   443   AG
Whitfield, Jay A   1924:81 WSP
Whitfield, Wilmot   399   AG
Whitford, O'Dillon B   945   LHM

_____	795	MI
	2:936	SM
Whitham, Paul Page	3:499	BHS
	43	SA
Whitlatch, J W	683	LHM
Whitlow, M W	[113]	RLX
Whitman, Alice, see		
Wisewell, Alice (Whitman)		
Whitman, Alice (Green)	25	DW
Whitman, Augustus	24-25	DW
Whitman, Mrs. Beza, see		
Whitman, Alice (Green)		
Whitman, Henry	24-25	DW
Whitman, Marcus	1:134	BS
	1:87	D
_____	front., 400-401	DW
_____	front.	EW
_____	76	FW
_____	139	GBS
_____	42	GR
_____	1:front.	HM
_____	front., 72, 128	NM
_____	57, 118, 132, 152	NW
_____	1:186	PH
_____	44 no. 3:132	PN
_____	front., 13, 241	PSW
_____	front.	RW
Whitman, Mrs. Marcus, see		
Whitman, Narcissa (Prentiss)		
Whitman, Mrs. Martha (Nez Percé Indian)		
	200	PSW
Whitman, Narcissa (Prentiss)	80	DW
	112	FW
_____	137	GBS
_____	104	NM
_____	front.	RW
Whitman, Perrin	158	DTI
Whitman, Samuel	24-25	DW
Whitman, Silas (Nez Percé Indian)	212	BR
	414	DS
_____	127	DTI
_____	200	PSW
Whitman, Mrs. Silas, see		
Whitman, Mrs. Martha		
Whitman, Solomon (Nez Percé Indian)	414	DS
Whitmer, David	670	CIR
Whitney, Ira L	2:1199	SM
Whitney, J J	2:433	PMO
Whitney, Mrs. O C	443	AG
Whitney, William	54 no. 3:95	PN
Whitson, Edward	65	BHSS
	5:112	SH
_____	1926:20	WSP
Whittier, Mrs. A	2:front. 1924	BCHA
Whittle, George Vernon	4:125	BHK
Whittlesey, William H	2:590	NH
Whittren, J Potter	279	HA
Whitworth, F H	18-19	GA
Whitworth, George F	257	HI
_____	4	PC
_____	2:574	PHP
_____	23, 231	PSW
_____	4:222	SH
Whitworth, Joseph	2:1087	SM
Whymper, Frederick	86	WOY
Whyte, John J	3:928	FH
Whyte, William	331	GI
Whyuctan Swalamesett (Cowichan Indian)		
	front.	HF
Wiberg, Charles M	514	SHP
Wickersham, J H	18:3 1941-42	IH
Wickersham, James	1941:291	EN
_____	172-173	HA
_____	1:372	HHT
_____	406-407	HU
_____	1895-96:155	SSS
_____	front.	WOY
Wickes, Thomas A	6:398, 413	MC
Wickes, Mrs. Thomas A	6:438-439	MC
Wickes, William W	6:415	MC
Wickes, William W , Sr.	6:398	MC
Widger, M A , see		
Norton, M A (Widger)		
Widmer, Conrad	2:102	CHW
Widmer, Mrs. Conrad, see		
Widmer, Elizabeth (Ebler)		
Widmer, Elizabeth (Ebler)	2:102, 103	CHW
Wiechmann, Mark	3:493	BH
Wiedeman, George J	2:1219	SM
Wiesen, Allen	34 no. 1:32	PNLA
Wiggett, James Walter	1941:123	EN
Wiggins, William Bryson	2:491	LHC
Wiggins, William H	84	LDM
Wigle, Martha Jane (Spalding)	310	DS
	1:20	FH
_____	49	WMW
Wigle, Mrs. W S , see		
Wigle, Martha Jane (Spalding)		
Wike, Floyd V	884	SIH
Wilbur, James H	1:114	D
	1:208-209	GP
_____	1:32	NH
_____	19:1	OHQ
_____	70:148	OHQ
_____	46 no. 1:7	PN
_____	50 no. 4:137	PN
_____	326	SK
_____	331	SKA
Wilbur, Lot	1:431	HH
Wilbur, Rozel Millage	2:683	GP
Wilburn, Mary E , see		
Bennett, Mary E (Wilburn)		
Wilby, James	2:front. 1924	BCHA
Wilby, William	2:front. 1924	BCHA

Wilcox, Hyland D	7	GL
Wilcox, Mrs. Julia	1:219	GP
Wilcox, Ralph	1:367	GP
Wilcox, Mrs. Ralph, see		
Wilcox, Mrs. Julia		
Wilcox, Theodore Burney	2:29	LHC
Wilder, Walter R	1 no. 3:23	WN
Wilding, George C	245	AG
	2:26	HHT
Wiley, Bert E	2:621	SMS
Wiley, George P	19:64 1914	WBP
Wiley, Harry	1939-40:31	OO
Wiley, Joseph R	2:729	GP
Wilhelm, Charles C	2:255	SMS
Wilhelm, Fridolin	3:393	BHS
Wilhelm, Otto	3:601	HHI
Wilhite, Jennie, see		
Ellis, Jennie (Wilhite)		
Wilkerson, M Caroline, see		
Humble, M Caroline (Wilkerson)		
Wilkes, Charles	120	AC
	1:41	BH
	141	GBS
	13	MMR
	front.	PC
	1:94	PH
	2:182	SH
Wilkes, Jabez	1:570	GP
Wilkins, Warren C	286	HA
Wilkinson, Barnett	252	BR
Wilkinson, Edwin Eugene	1943:151	ENC
Wilkinson, H C	172-173	HA
Wilkinson, J A	1:313	HH
Wilkinson, Malcolm W	1937-38:62-63	OO
	1939-40:31	OO
Wilkinson, Sarah, see		
Parkin, Sarah (Wilkinson)		
Wilks, John W	31	THI
Wilks, Mrs. John W	32	THI
Will, Edward Gray	307	HA
Willard, Alexander H	1:123	WT
Willard, Asa	3:1640	SM
Willard, D F	14	SSP
Willard, E S	252	PSW
Willard, Mrs. E S	252	PSW
Willburn, John Polk	3:1008	FH
Willburn, Mrs. John Polk, see		
Willburn, Vianna Frances (Hudson)		
Willburn, Vianna Frances (Hudson) 3:1008		FH
Willert, J C	191	PSW
Willes, Alzina Lucinda (Lott)	454	GL
Willes, Celestia, see		
Schow, Celestia (Willes)		
Willes, Ira Jones	33	GL
Willes, Mrs. Ira Jones, see		
Willes, Melissa (Lott) Smith		
Willes, John S	282	GL
Willes, Melissa (Lott) Smith	451	GL

Willes, William Sidney Smith	69	GL
Willes, Mrs. William Sidney Smith, see		
Willes, Alzina Lucinda (Lott)		
Willey, Lafayette	2:90	PHP
Willey, Norman B	498	BR
William Moore, Crow chief, see		
Moore, William, Crow chief		
William Three Mountains (Spokan Indian)		
	58	LC
Williams, A H T	3:935	LHC
Williams, Adolphus	fol. pt. 1	SHB
	1897:108	YB
Williams, Albert	86-87	KO
Williams, Alexander T	6:303	MC
Williams, Alfred	3:137	BCF
Williams, Arnold	20:front. 1945-46	IH
Williams, Barrett	2:740-741	FH
Williams, Billy	218	FW
Williams, Carl Leslie	3:355	BEA
Williams, Charles	128	KT
Williams, Charles Henry	2:339	SMS
Williams, Chris	172	LDM
Williams, David Griffith	fol. pt. 2	SHB
Williams, E M	[105]	RLX
Williams, Edward Marshall	3:623	LHC
Williams, Elijah	1:300	PMO
Williams, Ellen, see		
Jones, Ellen (Williams)		
Williams, Frank E	2:157	SMS
Williams, Fred A	2:317	CHW
Williams, Frederick James	4:161	BCF
Williams, Frederick W	fol. pt. 1	SHB
	1911:70-71	YB
Williams, George	2:337	BCF
Williams, George Henry	1:519	CHW
	1:552-553	GP
	2:11	GP
	front.	HIO
	4:314	LH
	1:723	LHC
	1:304	NH
	14:192	OHQ
	70:224	OHQ
	1:22	PMO
	120	SHO
	82	SHP
	114	WRE
Williams, George T	257	HA
Williams, Gib	58	BR
Williams, H R	unp.	VU
Williams, J E	403	AG
Williams, James	78	BR
	224	BV
Williams, James, 1846-1900	3:867	BHS
Williams, John B	723	LHM

Williams, Jonathan Billy (Nez Percé Indian)		
	414	DS
Williams, Joseph	163	LDM
Williams, Lewis	3:17	HHI
Williams, Louis	48	LS
Williams, Mark (Nez Percé Indian)	199	PSW
Williams, Myra, see		
Clark, Myra (Williams)		
Williams, Parker	1911:70-71	YB
Williams, R T	2:front. 1924	BCHA
Williams, Richard	2:740-741	FH
	38	LDM
	310	SHP
Williams, Robert	3:801	GP
Williams, Robert (Nez Percé Indian)	212	BR
	127	DTI
	199	PSW
Williams, Solon T	1895-96:117	SSS
Williams, Speck, see		
Williams, Albert		
Williams, V E	408	BHSS
Williams, W R	1905-06:[59]	RLW
Williams, Walter Winston	3:399	BHS
Williams, William Thwaites	4:259	BCF
Williams-Nash, Mrs. A T	6:358	MC
Williamson, Charles B	840-841	SIH
Williamson, E L	3:165	LHC
Williamson, J R	218	LDM
Williamson, James T	157	LDM
Williamson, John N	346	PL
	2:451	PMO
Williamson, Ralph B	1926:25	WSP
Williamson, Thomas F	840-841	SIH
Williamson, William	218	LDM
Williard, John H	6:420-421	MC
Williard, Mrs. John H	6:420-421	MC
Willis, Bailey	142	MMR
Willis, Park Weed	4:285	BHK
Willis, S A (Sid)	1:116	ACR
Willis, S P	35	PSW
Willison, H C	1905-06:[28]	RLW
Willoughby, Charles H	104	LDM
Willoughby, Westel	45	DW
Willson, Davis	5:314	MC
	6:330-331	MC
Willson, Mrs. Davis	6:438-439	MC
Willson, Mrs. Emma	6:325	MC
Willson, Fred F	1941:35	EN
	2:319	SMS
Willson, Lester S	5:315	MC
Willson, Mrs. Lester S	5:316	MC
Willson, William Holden	55	DO
	3:302	LH
	50 no. 3:95	PN
Wilmer, F J	108	BHSS
Wilsey, Sallie M , see		
Wells, Sallie M (Wilsey)		

Wilson, Mrs. (Kathlamet Indian)		
	front.	BKT
Wilson, Albert	2:742	FH
Wilson, Benjamin W	3:1619	SM
Wilson, Charles	4:667	BCF
	fol. pt. 1	SHB
	2:72	SMS
Wilson, Charles R	2:293	HWW
Wilson, Cloyd J	3:83	HHI
Wilson, David	2:26	HHT
Wilson, E T	16:50 1911	WBP
Wilson, Edgar	312	DSW
Wilson, Fred	115	LDM
Wilson, Fred W	1945-46:93	OO
	1924:96	WSP
Wilson, G B	1905-06:[49]	RLW
Wilson, George H	3:193	HWW
Wilson, Harry L	2:47	SMS
Wilson, Herbert Goulding	3:417	BCF
Wilson, Mrs. Hugh	2:front. 1924	BCHA
Wilson, James	4:475	BCF
	147	IHI
Wilson, Mrs. James A , see		
Wilson, Martha Lydia (Martin)		
Wilson, James M	94	PSW
Wilson, James Marquis	125	PSW
Wilson, James W	3:271	HHI
Wilson, Jane W , see		
Critchfield, Jane W (Wilson)		
Wilson, Jesse C	6:394, 416-417	MC
Wilson, Joe	1943-44:79	OO
	1945-46:87	OO
Wilson, John	3:541	BCF
Wilson, John, 1826-1900	1:592-593	GP
	3:39	GP
Wilson, John J	77	AL
Wilson, John Lockwood	5:250	SH
	1895-96:54	SSS
Wilson, John M	66	LT
Wilson, Joseph Gardner	1:929	LHC
Wilson, Manley J	1941-42:66	OO
	1943-44:79	OO
	1945-46:87	OO
Wilson, Martha Lydia (Martin)	2:742	FH
Wilson, R C	1895-96:121	SSS
Wilson, R R	1:767	BHK
Wilson, Robert	1:138	DN
Wilson, Robert Bruce	3:17	GP
	1:519	LHC
	1:92	NH
	1:366	PMO
Wilson, Ruth M	50:34 1949	WDT
Wilson, Smith M	1935:5	S
	1936:3	S
	1937:3	S

Wilson, Thomas J   219   LDM
Wilson, Tom   236   GI
Wilson, Woodrow   57:314   OHQ
Wilson, Worrall   43 no. 1:16-17   PN
Wilton, Emily (Richards)   3:221   HHI
Wilton, Mark   3:221   HHI
Wilton, Mrs. Mark, see
    Wilton, Emily (Richards)
Wimberly, Carl E   1945-46:92   OO
Winans, P   M   18:48 1913   WBP
    24:128 1919   WBP
Winans, William Park   47 no. 1:19   PN
    219   PSW
Winant, J   J   245   LDM
Winch, Harold E   6:151   PNLA
Winchell, Virgil   3:395   LHC
Windebank, Hori   3:515   BCF
Winder, Hugh E   215   GG
Windham, Robert Edward   3:59   LHC
Windus, Walter V   2:175   HH
Wines, F   B   1 no. 6:31   WN
Wines, Josiah L   3:1527   SM
Winfree, W   H   1924:48   WSP
Wing, Frederick A   1895-96:111   SSS
Wing, John William   455   GL
Wing, Mrs. John William, see
    Wing, Martha (Goates)
Wing, John William, Jr.   457   GL
Wing, Mrs. John William, Jr., see
    Wing, Rachel (Evans)
Wing, Martha (Goates)   456   GL
Wing, Rachel (Evans)   457   GL
Wingard, Samuel C   5:236   SH
Wingate, Robert   1:272   NH
Winge, Albert M   3:1005   BHS
Winger, R   M   50:49 1949   WDT
Wininger, McClellan   2:634   SMS
Winkenwerder, Hugo   120-121   GA
    26:60 1925   WDT
    36:22 1935   WDT
Winn, Martha (Evans)   458   GL
Winn, Susie, see
    Whipple, Susie (Winn)
Winn, William Henry   207   GL
Winn, Mrs. William Henry, see
    Winn, Martha (Evans)
Winning, E   S   178   LDM
Winslow, George P   1931-32:41   OO
    1945-46:83   OO
Winslow, H   H   unp.   SOU
Winsoer, Helen M   , see
    Almy, Helen M   (Winsoer)
Winsor, Eunice (Huntington) 160   MP
Winsor, Henry   160   MP
    1905-06:[28]   RLW
Winsor, Mrs. Henry, see
    Winsor, Eunice (Huntington)
Winston, Joseph   202   BHSS

Winter, Fitz Henry   2:1067   SM
Winterbotham, H   J   347   LDM
Wintermute, James S   14 no. 3:278   MWH
Winters, William   6:168   SH
Winther, Oscar Osburn   58 no. 4:184   PN
Winthrop, Theodore   34   MMR
    xix, xxi   WCS
Wipperman, Louis W   1939-40:15   OO
    1941-42:62   OO
    1943-44:75   OO
Wire, F   B   1945-46:206   OO
Wirt, Susan M   (Kimball) 55   CW
    1:52   NH
    1:62   PMO
Wisewell, Alice (Whitman)   24-25   DW
Wisner, Albert G   288   SIH
Wisner, W   O   41   MG
Wiswall, Robert Davis   3:625   GP
Witherspoon, Herbert   43 no. 1:16-17   PN
Witherspoon, Thomas Casey   2:863   SM
    3:1211   SMS
Withycombe, James   66   TUR
Witmer, Martin A   2:1059   SM
Witney, Charles J   3:425   HWW
Witt, George M   1895-96:111   SSS
Witt, James   512   SIH
Witt, Maud   163   PL
Witt, William   2:33   SMS
Wittard, H   S   172-173   HA
Wittenberg, Caroline (Blas) 64:260   OHQ
Wittenberg, David   64:260   OHQ
Wittenberg, Minnie   64:260   OHQ
Wiyitooyi (Yakima? Indian) 339   SK
    344   SKA
Wolcott, J   Herman   2:248   SMS
Wold, Amelia (Walters)   3:599   BHK
Wold, Ingebright A   3:599   BHK
Wold, Mrs. Ingebright A   , see
    Wold, Amelia (Walters)
Wolf, John H   3:127   GP
    109   LDM
    1:422   PMO
Wolf Voice (Gros Ventre Indian) 139   VT
Wolfe, Adolphe   1:614-615   GP
Wolfe, John H   , see
    Wolf, John H
Wolfenden, R   2:113   BCF
    1911:70-71   YB
Wolgamott, Lucy, see
    Stricker, Lucy (Wolgamott)
Wolheter, Sara (Elliott) Price 696   SIH
Wolheter, Washington   696   SIH
Wolheter, Mrs. Washington, see
    Wolheter, Sara (Elliott) Price
Wolverton, Charles E   261   PL
Wolverton, Newton   fol. pt. 2   SHB

Womack, Isaac   3:877   HHI
Womack, Mrs. Isaac, see
    Womack, Purlia Cordelia (Bradford)
Womack, Purlia Cordelia (Bradford) 3:877 HHI
Wongee, Charles   2:464-465   EPD
Wood, Alanson Dean   3:133   HWW
Wood, Alexander   328   LDM
Wood, Charles Erskine Scott 135   BN
_____   70 no. 1:cover OHQ
_____   70 no. 2:101   OHQ
_____   50 no. 3:81, 88 PN
Wood, Mrs. David, see
    Wood, Katherine (Veit) Hagenbarth Murphy
Wood, Frank E   4:409   BHK
Wood, Frederick J   2:352   PHP
Wood, Fremont   2:94   FSB
                                 2:221   HHI
_____   263   LDM
Wood, George W
Wood, Harriet, see
    Carter, Harriet (Wood)
Wood, James A   unp.   VU
Wood, John   fol. title page   SHB
Wood, Katherine (Veit) Hagenbarth Murphy
                                 56   CBC
Wood, L   B   276   E
Wood, Lovett Mortimer   3:651   BHS
Wood, Lyman   2:322   NH
Wood, Mary, see
    McCleery, Mary (Wood)
Wood, N   B   144   DL
Wood, Mrs. Nellie   48   LS
Wood, Sterling M   1941:183   EN
Wood, T   L   1897:43, 124   YB
Wood, Thomas   fol. title page   SHB
Wood, Thomas A   909   HIO
                                 1:130   PMO
Wood, W   D   unp.   SEA
Wood, William B   25:81   PNLA
Woodard, Charles Henry   2:561   GP
                                 1895:84   OO
Woodbury, L   S   3:1070   SMS
Woodbury, M   Cerula   3:1072   SMS
Woodcock, C   Harold   2:581   CHW
Woodcock, Gertrude   45 no. 2:49   PN
Woodcock, Milton E   2:617   CHW
Woodcock, Milton Sherman   2:553   CHW
Woodfield, Francis William   66:329   OHQ
Woodhouse, Charles C   , Jr. 1:277   HH
Woodhouse, John   168   GL
Woodin, Scott Percy   3:1117   BHS
Woodley, William J   89   LDM
Woodmansee, Charles H   2:65   HHI
Woodruff, Charles A   7:105   MC
Woodruff, Wilford W   685   CIR
                                 177   CWW
                                 262   GLS
Woods, Dennis   287   BHSS

Woods, E   M   N   16 no. 3-4:134   BCH
Woods, Edward P   235   LDM
Woods, Mrs. George   1:470   GP
Woods, George Lemuel   1:292   NH
                                 2:172   PMO
_____   34   TUR
Woods, Owen   May 1907:38   TDL
Woods, Rufus   52 no. 4:140   PN
                         1 no. 8:13   WN
Woods, William   1941:158   EN
Woodside, Frank E   3:1003   BCF
Woodson, Mattie, see
    Moss, Mattie (Woodson)
Woodsworth, James   front.   WTY
Woodward, A   P   1:364   NH
Woodward, C   A   4:558   PH
Woodward, Charles   fol. pt. 1   SHB
Woodward, Henry H   1:156   NH
Woodward, Tyler   468   SHP
Woodward, William F   1931-32:40   OO
Woodworth, Almon   1895-96:111   SSS
Woodworth, Charles   2:75   SMS
Woody, Frank H   287   LHM
_____   7:front.   MC
_____   709   MI
_____   2:870   SM
_____   1:432   SMS
Wool, John Ellis   67:317   OHQ
                                 46 no. 2:50   PN
Woolard, Alfred E   2:436   PHP
Woolery, James H   238   LDM
Woolfolk, Lizzie   6:386   MC
Woollen, William Watson   1:front.   WI
Woolley, Hiram S   3:1096   FH
Woolley, Hoyt Budge   3:283   BEA
Woolley, M   D   1945-46:66   OO
Woolman, Joseph P   195   LHM
Woolston, Howard B   26:60 1925   WDT
Wootton, E   E   2:front. 1924   BCHA
Wootton, Henry   6 no. 2:94   BCH
                         93   DC
Word, Lee   4:119   MC
Word, R   Lee, see
    Word, Lee
Word, Samuel   227   LHM
_____   91   MI
_____   14 no. 1:64   MWH
Worden, Francis L   , see
    Worden, Frank L
Worden, Frank L   827   LHM
_____   2:front.   MC
_____   1:224   SMS
Worden, Mrs. Frank L   , see
    Worden, Lucretia (Miller)
Worden, Lucretia (Miller) 827   LHM
Worden, Warren A   2:40   PHP

171

Work, John	4:1177	BCF
————	68	BHSI
————	1:216	FI
————	232	MHN
————	8	NF
————	1897:18	YB
Work, John F	2:971	SM
Works, Miriam, see		
Young, Miriam (Works)		
Worlton, Anna (Bronelson)	461	GL
Worlton, John	460	GL
Worlton, Mrs. John, see		
Worlton, Anna (Bronelson)		
Wormald, Joe	31	SCC
Worsfold, Cuthbert Coleman	3:595	BCF
Worth, Frank	283	LDM
Worthington, Mary M , see		
Elison, Mary M (Worthington)		
Worthington, P A	2:542	NH
Worthington, S R	3:1016	FH
Wortman, Hardy C	3:221	LHC
Wortman, Mary (Cochran)	2:24	CPD
Wotton, George A	Feb. 1906:27	TDL
Wrangel, Ferdinand Petrovich von	688	CIR
————	13	CTL
Wray, William	1924:64	WSP
Wright, Albert H	2:508	PHP
Wright, Annie (Davidson)	272	SIH
Wright, B Franklin	1:139	BH
Wright, Mrs. B Franklin	1:139	BH
Wright, Betsey, see		
Washburne, Betsey (Wright)		
Wright, Charles B	166	BOO
————	1:194	HHT
Wright, Charles W	272	SIH
Wright, Mrs. Charles W , see		
Wright, Annie (Davidson)		
Wright, Crispin	2:812	FH
Wright, Ellen	217	DSW
Wright, Elsia	unp.	SOU
Wright, Emily	1:139	BH
Wright, Ernest W	6:392	MC
Wright, Fannie V	front.	FC
Wright, George	49	AI
————	3:20	FI
————	front.	MCO
————	1:68	NH
Wright, George P	2:517	HHT
————	May 1907:38	TDL
Wright, George S	66	LDM
Wright, Harry	1911:70-71	YB
Wright, Henry Press	19 no. 3-4:123	BCH
Wright, J A	1895:99	OO
Wright, John T , Jr.	205	LDM
Wright, John T , Sr.	66	LDM
Wright, Max	41	MG
Wright, Minnie M , see		
Evans, Minnie M (Wright)		
Wright, Percy E	1 no. 10:24	WN
Wright, Reuben Bean	2:708	FH
Wright, Richard H	6:416-417	MC
Wright, Thomas	64	LDM
Wright, Mrs. Tom, see		
Martin, Josephine (Rider) Adams Wright		
Wright, W S	unp.	SOU
Wright, William T	216	DSW
————	2:510	NH
————	2:292	PMO
Wright, Zachary T	717	HIO
Wriglesworth, Joe	2:front. 1924	BCHA
Wyatt, J R	2:493	CHW
Wyatt, James B	1:210-211	GP
Wyeth, Joseph Henry	26:424	OHQ
Wyeth, Nathaniel Jarvis	front.	BF
————	78	BHI
————	79	BHSI
————	2:592	CAFT
————	132	DSW
————	2:128	FI
————	114	HC
————	3:100	LH
————	58:201	OHQ
————	2:386	PMO
————	2:14	SH
Wygant, Theodore	44	LDM
Wykoff, W	97	DH
Wylie, William W	6:323	MC
Wylie, Mrs. William W	6:325	MC
Wyman, Cyrus K	2:263	SMS
Wynkoop, Daniel J	283	HA
Wynkoop, Urban G	2:160	PHP
Wynn, James D	3:1589	SM
Wynn, Thomas	135	JNT
Wyrouck, Jacob	769	LHM
Wyrouck, Mrs. Jacob, see		
Wyrouck, M J (Howe)		
Wyrouck, M J (Howe)	769	LHM
Wythe, J H	16	OS

X - Y

Xavier Ross, Mother	294	PI
Yantis, J L	1:208-209	GP
Yard, H H	429	PL
Yarnell, Griff	266	HA
Yarnell, S	41	MG
Yates, Chris P	1895:104	OO
Yates, George W	110-111	HCM
Yates, Mrs. George W	110-111	HCM
Yates, J P	1931-32:41	OO
Yates, James	1:542	BCF
————	front.	LCT
————	1897:103	YB

Yates, John E   2:628   FH
                                 2:439   HHI
Yates, William   173   GL
Ya-tin-ow-itz, Cayuse chief 15 BSC
                                 10:37 1925-26   IH
Yealy, Lee James   1943:21   ENC
Yegen, Christian   2:1196-1197   SM
Yegen, Peter   1941:101   EN
                                 2:1196-1197   SM
Yelle, Cliff   3:110   PH
Yellow Bird, see
    Peo-peo-mox-mox, Walla Walla chief
Yellow Boy   5:207   MC
Yellow Bull, Nez Percé chief 186 BR
                                 2:368-369   EPD
                                 1:525   HHI
Yellow Fringe, Crow chief 216   PI
                                 248   PIW
Yellow Serpent, see
    Peo-peo-mox-mox, Walla Walla chief
Yellow Wolf, Nez Percé chief 1:525 HHI
Yellowstone Kelly, see
    Kelly, Luther Sage
Yeon, John B   66:250   OHQ
Yesler, Henry L   1:57   BHK
                                 2:708   BHS
                                 2:front.   HH
                                 65   MP
                                 11 no. 6:front.   MWH
                                 1:140   NH
                                 60 no. 3:cover   PN
                                 unp.   SEA
Yett, Porter W   3:487   LHC
Yi-yi-wa-som-way (Nez Percé Indian)
                                 1:541   HHI
Yocom, Joseph M   unp.   SOU
Yoder, Albert Henry   6:24 1906   WDT
Yonge, Emily, see
    Foster, Emily (Yonge)
York, Duke of, see
    James II, king of England, Scotland and
    Ireland
    Chetzemoka, Clallam chief
York, Lemuel A   3:65   BEA
Yorke, Philip   238   MV
Yorke, T F   2:front. 1924   BCHA
Yothers, Levi   896   SIH
Youmans, William W   3:497   HHI
Young, Abraham Coon   3:419   BH
Young, Ann Eliza (Webb)   272, 368   CB
                                 40   CY
Young, Augusta (Adams)   272   CB
                                 14a   CY
Young, Benjamin Franklin
                                 fol. title page   SHB
Young, Bernard A   1937-38:62-63   OO

Young, Brigham   108   BHI
                                 105   BHSI
                                 118   BU
                                 front., 36, 222, 272, 322   CB
                                 22   CWW
                                 8   CY
                                 1:205   DN
                                 52, 165   EP
                                 10   GL
                                 137   GLS
                                 120   GMM
                                 8   HB
                                 112-113 (xxxiv)   PR
                                 222   TMP
Young, Mrs. Brigham, see
    Young, Ann Eliza (Webb)
    Young, Augusta (Adams)
    Young, Clara (Decker)
    Young, Clara Chase (Ross)
    Young, Eliza (Burgess)
    Young, Eliza Roxey (Snow)
    Young, Emily Dow (Partridge)
    Young, Emmeline (Free)
    Young, Harriet (Barney)
    Young, Harriet Amelia (Folsom)
    Young, Harriet Elizabeth Cook (Campbell)
    Young, Lucy (Bigelow)
    Young, Lucy Ann (Decker)
    Young, Margaret (Pierce)
    Young, Martha (Bowker)
    Young, Mary (Van Cott)
    Young, Mary Ann (Angell)
    Young, Miriam (Works)
    Young, Naamah Kendell Jenkins (Carter)
    Young, Susan (Snively)
    Young, Zina Diantha (Huntington)
Young, Clara (Decker)   272   CB
                                 14a   CY
Young, Clara Chase (Ross)   272   CB
Young, Delbert A   3:213   HHT
Young, E   366   BF
Young, Ed   206, 408   BHSS
Young, Edward Thomas   2:402   NH
Young, Eliza (Burgess)   272   CB
Young, Eliza Roxey (Snow)   272   CB
                                 34   CY
                                 1:294   DN
Young, Emily Dow (Partridge)   272   CB
Young, Emmeline (Free)   272   CB
Young, Fannie E   (Kellogg)   231   JA
Young, Frederic George 11 no. 4:front. CR
                                 30:front.   OHQ
                                 48 no. 2:34   PN
Young, Harriet (Barney)   272   CB
                                 38   CY
Young, Harriet Amelia (Folsom)   272   CB
                                 38   CY

Young, Harriet Elizabeth Cook (Campbell)
        272 CB
_____   18 CY
Young, Henry Esson   2:547 BCF
_____   16 no. 3-4:151 BCH
_____   fol. pt. 1 SHB
_____ 1911:6-7, 70-71 YB
Young, James D   58 no. 1:19 PN
Young, John   120 DL
        165 EP
Young, Joseph   165 EP
Young, Joseph Taylor 2:83 HHI
Young, Kenneth B 1 no. 4:300 WM
Young, Lorenzo   165 EP
Young, Lucy (Bigelow) 272 CB
_____   30 CY
Young, Lucy Ann (Decker) 272 CB
_____   18 CY
Young, Margaret (Pierce) 272 CB
Young, Martha (Bowker) 272 CB
_____   30 CY
Young, Mary (Van Cott) 272 CB
_____   40 CY
Young, Mary Ann (Angell) 272 CB
_____   14 CY
Young, Miriam (Works) 272 CB
_____   14 CY
Young, Naamah Kendell Jenkins (Carter)
        272 CB
Young, Phineas   165 EP
Young, Pony, see
  Young, John
Young, R Herndon, Jr. 3:261 BEA
Young, R Herndon, Sr. 3:261 BEA
Young, S Hall 191, 231 JA
       252, 280 PSW
Young, Mrs. S Hall, see
  Young, Fannie E (Kellogg)
Young, Susan (Snively) 272 CB
Young, William H   280 SIH
Young, Winfield S   3:776 SMS
Young, Zina Diantha (Huntington) 34 CB
_____   34 CY
Young Bear Chief, Piegan chief 170 PI
       204 PIW
Young Boy (Cree Indian) 1:94 ACR
Young Chief, see
  Tauitau, Cayuse chief

Young Ignace (Flathead Indian) 22 PI
Younglove, Edward A 3:183 BH
Youngson, William Wallace 3:699 LHC
Yun-Cheng, Lu   24:147 PNLA

Z

Zabel, Oscar A   2:521 BHK
Zachariah   149 DE
Zachary, Mrs. Alex, see
  Zachary, Mrs. Sarah
Zachary, Lucetta, see
  Emerick, Lucetta (Zachary)
Zachary, Mrs. Sarah 1:236 NH
Zan, Frank   600 SHP
Zante, Arthur B van, see
  Van Zante, Arthur B
Zech, Raymond L   3:799 BHK
Zednick, Victor H 1 no. 2:88 WM
Zehner, Isaac   562 SIH
Zehner, R B   318 HA
Zeller, Phillip J   3:805 GP
Zent, W W   277 E
_____   1924:64 WSP
Zielinski, J P 2:163 CHW
Zielinski, Mrs. J P , see
  Zielinski, Lena (Andrews)
Zielinski, Lena (Andrews) 2:163 CHW
Zilly, Carroll Keith 3:817 LHC
Zimmerman, Clarence 393 BHSS
Zimmerman, Edward L 2:535 CHW
Zimmerman, H K 1945-46:93 OO
Zimmerman, Harriet Laura (Lamb) 134 GL
Zimmerman, John   134 GL
Zimmerman, Mrs. John, see
  Zimmerman, Harriet Laura (Lamb)
Zimmerman, Peter 1935-36:50 OO
Zoll, Sylvia, see
  Griswold, Sylvia (Zoll)
Zoohalitz   23 HF
Zurcher, C H 1939-40:15 OO
_____   1941-42:62 OO
_____   1943-44:75 OO
_____   1945-46:83 OO
Zweifell, Anna, see
  Gohn, Anna (Zweifell)

AC   Atwood, Albert. Conquerors: historical sketches of the American
         settlement of the Oregon country, embracing facts in the
         life and work of Rev. Jason Lee. Boston: Jennings and
         Graham, c1907

ACR   Adams, Ramon Frederick. Charles M. Russell, the cowboy artist.
         Collectors' ed. 2 v. Pasadena: Trail's End, c1948

AG   Atwood, Albert. Glimpses in pioneer life on Puget Sound.
         Seattle: Denny-Coryell, 1903

AI   Arnold, Royal Ross. Indian wars of Idaho. Caldwell: Caxton,
         c1932

AL   Alaska-Yukon gold book; a roster of the progressive men and
         women who were the argonauts of the Klondike gold stampede,
         and those who are identified with the pioneer days and sub-
         sequent development of Alaska and the Yukon Territory.
         Seattle: Sourdough Stampede Association, Inc., c1930.
         Selective indexing

AM   Abbott, Newton Carl. Montana in the making. 13th ed. rev.
         Billings: Gazette Printing Co., c1964

AN   Andrews, Clarence Leroy. Story of Alaska. Caldwell: Caxton,
         1944, c38

AT   Atkinson, Reginald Noel. Historical souvenir of Penticton,
         B. C., 1867 - 1967, on the occasion of the centenary of the
         Dominion of Canada. Okanagan Historical Society, Penticton
         Branch, with the cooperation of the City of Penticton,
         B. C., 1967. Selective indexing

AYP   Seattle. Alaska-Yukon-Pacific Exposition, 1909. Alaska-Yukon-
         Pacific Exposition, Seattle, Washington, June 1 to October 16,
         1909. Official publication. Seattle: Portland Postcard
         Company, 1909?

BCC   Brunner, Edmund de Schweinitz. Church and community survey of
         Pend Oreille County, Washington. Committee on Social and
         Religious Surveys. New York: Doran, c1922

BCF   British Columbia from the earliest times to the present. 4 v.
         Vancouver: Clarke, 1914

BCH   British Columbia historical quarterly. v.1 no.1 - v.20 no.1/2
         January 1937 - January/April 1956

BCHA   British Columbia Historical Association. Report. 4 v. in 1.
            Victoria: Banfield, 1923 - 1929

BCN   Blanchard, John. Caravans to the Northwest, by John Blanchard
            under the direction of the Northwest Regional Council,
            Portland, Oregon. Boston: Houghton, c1940

BD   Bushnell, David Ives. Drawings by George Gibbs in the far
            Northwest, 1849-1851. Smithsonian miscellaneous collections
            v.97 no.8. Washington: The Smithsonian Institution, 1938

BE   Bowden, Angie (Burt) Early schools of Washington Territory.
            Seattle: Lowman & Hanford, c1935

BEA   Beal, Merrill D. History of Idaho. 3 v. New York: Lewis
            Historical Publishing Co., c1959

BET   Becker, Ethel (Anderson) A treasury of Alaskana. Seattle:
            Superior, c1969

BF   Brown, Jennie Broughton. Fort Hall on the Oregon trail; a
            historical study...with Ferry Butte, by Susie Boice Trego.
            Caldwell: Caxton, c1932

BH   Bonney, William Pierce. History of Pierce County, Washington.
            3 v. Chicago: Pioneer Historical Publishing Co., c1927

BHI   Beal, Merrill D. A history of southeastern Idaho; an intimate
            narrative of peaceful conquest by empire builders...
            Caldwell: Caxton, c1942

BHK   Bagley, Clarence Booth. History of King County, Washington.
            4 v. Chicago: Clarke, 1929

BHS   Bagley, Clarence Booth. History of Seattle from the earliest
            settlement to the present time... 3 v. Chicago: Clarke,
            c1916

BHSI   Brosnan, Cornelius James. History of the state of Idaho. New
            York: Scribner's, c1918-48

BHSS   Bryan, Enoch Albert. Historical sketch of the State college of
            Washington, 1890-1925. Published by the Alumni and the
            Associated Students. Pullman: Author, c1928

BI   Bruseth, Nels. Indian stories and legends of the Stillaguamish, Sauks
            and allied tribes. 2nd ed. Arlington, Wash.: Arlington
            Times Press, c1926-50

BJ   Brosnan, Cornelius James. Jason Lee, prophet of the new
            Oregon. New York: Macmillan, c1932

BK   Bankson, Russell Arden. Klondike nugget. Caldwell: Caxton,
            c1935

BKT Boas, Franz. Kathlamet texts. Smithsonian Institution, Bureau of American Ethnology, Bulletin no.26. Washington: Government Printing Office, 1901

BM   Burns and McDonnell Engineering Co. Results of municipal electric systems; record of 758 cities under municipal ownership; rates in effect 1940-41. Kansas City, Mo.: Author, c1941

BN   Brady, Cyrus Townsend. Northwestern fights and fighters... New York: Doubleday, 1923, c1907

BO   Brogan, James M. Historical landmark: old mission church of the Coeur d'Alene Indians... Reprinted and revised from Gonzaga quarterly, November 20, 1926. Spokane: Gonzaga University, 1926

BOO Bryan, Enoch Albert. Orient meets Occident; the advent of the railways to the Pacific Northwest. Pullman: Students Book Corporation, c1936

BR   Bailey, Robert Gresham. River of no return (the great Salmon River of Idaho). A century of central Idaho and eastern Washington history and development; together with the wars, customs, myths and legends of the Nez Percé Indians. Lewiston: Bailey-Blake, c1935

BS   Bartlett, Laura Belle (Downey) Students' history of the Northwest and the state of Washington. Tacoma: Smith-Digby, c1922

BSC Brown, William Carey. The Sheepeater campaign, Idaho -- 1879. Reprinted from the tenth Biennial Report, Idaho Historical Society, 1926. Boise: Syms-York, c1926

BT   Brown, Henry. Taxation of church property; an appeal to the citizens of Washington. Spokane: Spokane Printing Co., 1892

BU   Beadle, John Hanson. Undeveloped West; or, Five years in the territories... Philadelphia: National Publishing Co., 1873

BUR Burns, Robert Ignatius. The Jesuits and the Indian wars of the Northwest. New Haven: Yale University Press, 1966

BV   Birney, Hoffman. Vigilantes... a chronicle of the rise and fall of the Plummer gang of outlaws in and about Virginia City, Montana in the early '60s; drawings by Charles Hargens. Philadelphia: Penn, c1929

C   Washington (State) State Department of Public Welfare. Coordinator. v.1 no.1-12 - v.4 no.14 October 15, 1934 - March 1938. Olympia

CAA Crosby, Thomas. Among the An-ko-me-nums; or, Flathead tribes of Indians of the Pacific Coast. Toronto: Briggs, 1907

CAF   Chittenden, Hiram Martin. American fur trade of the far West...
       3 v. New York: Harper, 1902, c 1901

CAFT   Chittenden, Hiram Martin. American fur trade of the far West...
       2 v. New York: Press of the Pioneers, c1935

CB   Cannon, Frank Jenne. Brigham Young and his Mormon empire; by
       Frank J. Cannon and George L. Knapp... New York: Revell,
       c1913

CBC   Clark, Barzilla Worth. Bonneville County in the making.
       Idaho Falls: Author, c1941

CC   Chandler, George. Textbook of civics for the state of Washing-
       ton. New York: American Book Co., c1910

CCA   Cody, Edmund R. History of the Coeur d'Alene mission of the
       Sacred Heart... Old mission, Cataldo, Idaho. Caldwell:
       Caxton, c1930

CES   Chittenden, Hiram Martin. History of early steamboat naviga-
       tion on the Missouri River; life and adventures of Joseph
       LaBarge... 2 v. New York: Harper, c1903

CGO   Carey, Charles Henry. General history of Oregon prior to 1861.
       2 v. Portland, Ore.: Metropolitan Press, c1935-1936

CHO   Carey, Charles Henry. History of Oregon. Authors ed. Chicago:
       Pioneer Historical Publishing Co., c1922

CHW   Clark, Robert Carlton. History of the Willamette Valley,
       Oregon. 3 v. Chicago: Clarke, c1927

CI   Carmichael, Alfred. Indian legends of Vancouver Island...
       illustrated by J. Semeyn. Toronto: Musson, c1922

CIR * Cirker, Hayward, ed. Dictionary of American portraits. 4045
       pictures of important Americans from earliest times to the
       beginning of the twentieth century. New York: Dover, c1967

CK   Crosby, Laurence E. "Kuailks Metatcopun" (Black Robe Three-
       Times-Broken)... Wallace: Wallace Press-Times, 1925

CM   Cross, Osborne & others. March of the Mounted Riflemen...
       Glendale: Clark, c1940

CMG   Cross, Osborne & others. March of the regiment of Mounted
       Riflemen to Oregon in 1849... Fairfield, Washington: Ye
       Galleon Press, 1967

CML   Campbell, Marjorie Wilkins. McGillivray; Lord of the Northwest.
       Toronto: Clarke, Irwin, c1962

CN   * Catlin, George. North American Indians; being letters and notes on their manners, customs, and conditions... With three hundred and twenty illustrations, carefully engraved from the author's original paintings. 2 v. Philadelphia: Leary, Stuart, 1913

CP   Clarke, Samuel A. Pioneer days of Oregon history. 2 v. Portland, Ore.: Gill, c1905

CPD   Cochran, John Eakin. Pioneer days in eastern Washington and northern Idaho. 2 v. Spokane: Knapp Book Store, 1942

CPP   Canse, John Martin. Pilgrim and pioneer; dawn in the Northwest. New York: Abingdon Press, c1930

CR   Commonwealth review of the University of Oregon. v. 1-3 January 1916-October 1918; n.s. v. 1-23 no. 2 1919-May 1941

CT   Corser, Harry Prosper. Totem lore of the Alaska Indians. 5th ed. Juneau: Nugget Shop, nd

CTL   Corser, Harry Prosper. Totem lore of the Alaska Indian, and the Land of the totem. New ed., rev. Wrangell: Bear Totem Store, c1932

CW   Cannon, Miles. Waiilatpu, its rise and fall, 1836-1847... Boise: Capital News Job Rooms, 1915

CWC   Clayton, William. William Clayton's journal; a daily record of the journey of the original company of "Mormon" pioneers from Nauvoo, Illinois, to the valley of the Great Salt Lake, pub. by the Clayton family association. Salt Lake City: Deseret News, 1921

CWW   Carlton, Ambrose B. Wonderlands of the wild West, with sketches of the Mormons. n. p., 1891

CY   Crockwell, James H., pub. Pictures and biographies of Brigham Young and his wives. Salt Lake City: Crockwell, 1896

D   Daughters of the American Revolution. Washington State Society. History and register. 3 v. 1924-61

DA   Davidson, Innes N. The Arctic Brotherhood; a souvenir history of the order. Pub. under the auspices of the Executive Building Board. Seattle: Acme, 1909

DAI   Densmore, Frances. American Indians and their music. rev. ed. New York: Womans Press, 1936-c26

DC   Deaville, Alfred Stanley. Colonial postal systems and postage stamps of Vancouver Island and British Columbia, 1849-1871... Archives of British Columbia, Memoir no. VIII. Victoria: Banfield, 1928

DCW   Dickson, Albert Jerome. Covered wagon days; a journey across
        the plains in the sixties, and pioneer days in the Northwest;
        from the private journals of Albert Jerome Dickson, edited by
        Arthur Jerome Dickson. Cleveland: Clark, c1929

DD   Defenbach, Byron. Red heroines of the Northwest; illustrated by
        original drawings and photographs. Caldwell: Caxton, 1929

DE   Drury, Clifford Merrill. Elkanah and Mary Walker; pioneers
        among the Spokanes. Caldwell: Caxton, c1940

DEA   De Armond, R. N. Founding of Juneau. Juneau, Alaska: Gastineau
        Channel Centennial Association, c1967

DGC   * Donaldson, Thomas Corwin. The George Catlin Indian gallery in
        the U. S. National Museum (Smithsonian Institution) with
        memoir and statistics. Washington: Government Printing
        Office, 1887

DH   Dodge, Grenville Mellen. How we built the Union Pacific rail-
        way. Council Bluffs: Monarch Printing Co., nd

DL   Donaldson, Thomas Corwin. Idaho of yesterday. Caldwell:
        Caxton, 1941

DM   Donnellan, Kenneth M., ed. Mining events and dividends, United
        States: Alaska: Canada: Mexico. Whittier, Cal.: Western
        Printing Corporation, 1933

DN   Dixon, William Hepworth. New America. 5th ed. rev. 2 v.
        London: Hurst & Blackett, 1867

DO   Dobbs, Caroline (Conselyea) Men of Champoeg; a record of the
        lives of the pioneers who founded the Oregon government.
        Portland, Ore.: Metropolitan Press, c1932

DS   Drury, Clifford Merrill. Henry Harmon Spalding. Caldwell:
        Caxton, c1936

DSR   Delaney, Matilda J. (Sager). Survivor's recollections of the
        Whitman massacre. Spokane: sponsored by Esther Reed Chapter,
        Daughters of the American Revolution, c1920

DSW   Defenbach, Byron. The state we live in, Idaho. Caldwell:
        Caxton, c1933

DT   Dyer, Charles Newell. History of the town of Plainfield, Hamp-
        shire County, Mass.; from its settlement to 1891, including
        a genealogical history of twenty-three of the original
        settlers and their descendants, with anecdotes and sketches.
        Northampton, Mass.: Press of Gazette Printing Co., 1891

DTI   Drury, Clifford Merrill. A tepee in his front yard; a biography
        of H. T. Cowley, one of the four founders of the city of
        Spokane, Washington. Portland, Ore.: Binfords & Mort, c1949

DU   Dryden, Cecil Pearl. Up the Columbia for furs. Illus. by
          E. Joseph Dreany. Caldwell: Caxton, c1949

DW   Drury, Clifford Merrill. Marcus Whitman, M. D., pioneer and
          martyr. Caldwell: Caxton, c1937

E   Elks of Washington; with a short account of the growth of the
          benevolent and protective order of Elks of the United States
          of America. Madison, Wis.: 1903

EI   Eells, Myron. History of Indian missions on the Pacific Coast.
          Oregon, Washington and Idaho, with introduction by Rev. A. H.
          Atkinson. Philadelphia: The American Sunday-School Union,
          c1882

EN   Encyclopedia of Northwest biography; W. S. Downs, ed. New York:
          American Historical Co., c1941

ENC   Encyclopedia of Northwest biography. Winfield Scott Downs, ed.
          New York: American Historical Co., c1943

EP   Egan, Howard. Pioneering the West, 1846 to 1878; Major Howard
          Egan's diary, also thrilling experiences of pre-frontier
          life among   Indians... Richmond, Utah: Howard R. Egan
          Estate, 1917

EPD   Elsensohn, Alfreda, Sister. Pioneer days in Idaho County. 2 v.
          Caldwell: Caxton, c1947-1951

ET   Eells, Myron. Ten years of missionary work among the Indians at
          Skokomish, Washington territory, 1874-1884. Boston: Congre-
          gational Sunday-School and Publishing Society, c1886

EW   Eells, Myron. Marcus Whitman, pathfinder and patriot. Seattle:
          Alice Harriman Co., c1909

F   Frontier. v. 3 no. 1 - v. 13 no. 4 November 1922 - May 1933.
          Lacks v. 3 no. 2, v. 4 no. 3, v. 6, v. 7 no. 2. Missoula:
          State University of Montana

FA   Frontier and midland. v. 14 no. 1 - v. 19 no. 4 November 1933 -
          Summer 1939. Missoula: State University of Montana

FC   Frances, pseud. Church in an early day. Lamoni, Iowa: 1891

FEE   Feerick, John D. and Emalie P. Vice-presidents of the United
          States. New York: Watts, c1967. Selective indexing

FF   Fries, Ulrich Englehart. From Copenhagen to Okanogan; the auto-
          biography of a pioneer, by U. E. Fries, with the assistance
          of Emil B. Fries. Ed. by Grace V. Stearns and Eugene F. Hoy.
          Caldwell: Caxton, c1949

FH   French, Hiram Taylor. History of Idaho: a narrative account of
          its historical progress, its people and its principal inter-
          ests. 3 v. Chicago: Lewis, 1914

FI   Fuller, George Washington. Inland empire of the Pacific Northwest: a history. 4 v. Spokane: Linderman, c1928

FM   Federal Writers' Project. Montana, a state guide book... Rev.
ed. New York: Hastings House, c1939-49

FO   Fiske, John. Unpublished orations: "The discovery of the Columbia River, and the Whitman controversy"... Boston: printed
for members only, Bibliophile Society, 1909

FR   Farnham, Mary Frances, comp. Catalogue of rare books from the
library of Pacific University exhibited at the Lewis and
Clark fair, 1905... Forest Grove: Pacific University, 1905

FRA   Franchère, Gabriel. Adventure at Astoria, 1810-1814. Trans-
lated from the French and edited by Hoyt C. Franchère.
Norman: University of Oklahoma Press, 1967

FSB   Flenner, John Davis. Syringa blossoms. 2 v. Caldwell: Caxton,
1912-1915

FT   Fifty years in western Canada, being the abridged memoirs of Rev.
A. G. Morice, O. M. I., by D. L. S. Toronto: Ryerson Press,
c1930

FU   Ferris, Benjamin G. Utah and the Mormons; the history, government, doctrines, customs, and prospects of the Latter-day
saints... New York: Harper, 1854

FW   Faris, John Thomson. Winning the Oregon country. New York:
Missionary Education Movement of the United States and
Canada, c1911

G   Grand Army of the Republic. Department of Washington and Alaska.
Journal of the proceedings of the annual encampment... v. 38.
June 16-18, 1920 (held in Yakima)

GA   Gates, Charles Marvin. First century at the University of
Washington, 1861-1961. Seattle: University of Washington
Press, c1961

GBS   Gould, Dorothy Wheaton (Fay). Beyond the shining mountains.
Portland, Ore.: Binfords & Mort, c1938

GE   Ghent, William James. Early far West; a narrative outline, 1540-
1850. New York: Longmans, Green, c1931

GG   Gonzaga University, Spokane, Wash. Gonzaga's silver jubilee; a
memoir. Spokane: Gonzaga University, 1912

GI   Gibbon, John Murray. Romantic history of the Canadian Pacific;
the Northwest passage of today. New York: Tudor, 1937, c35

GL   Gardner, Hamilton. History of Lehi, including a biographical
section... Salt Lake City: Deseret News, 1913

GLS   Gibbs, Josiah Francis. Lights and shadows of Mormonism. Salt
          Lake City: Salt Lake Tribune Publishing Co., c1909

GMM   Golder, Frank Alfred & others, eds. March of the Mormon battal-
          ion from Council Bluffs to California; taken from the journal
          of Henry Standage... New York: Century, c1928

GP   Gaston, Joseph. Portland, Oregon; its history and builders...
          3 v. Chicago: Clarke, 1911

GR   Ghent, William James. Road to Oregon; a chronicle of the great
          emigrant trail. London: Longmans, Green, 1929

GU   Gove, Jesse Augustus. Utah expedition 1857-1858... New Hampshire
          Historical Society, Collections v. 12. Concord: New Hampshire
          Historical Society, 1928

GUG   Gray, William Henry. Unpublished journal of William H. Gray from
          December 1836 to October 1837. From Whitman College quarterly
          v. XVI, no. 2. Walla Walla: 1913

GV   Godwin, George Stanley. Vancouver; a life, 1757-1798. Appleton,
          1931

HA   Harrison, Edward Sanford. Nome and Seward Peninsula; history,
          description, biographies and stories. Seattle: Metropolitan
          Press, c1905. Partially indexed

HB   Hickman, William A. Brigham's destroying angel... the notorious
          Bill Hickman, the Danite chief of Utah... New York: Crofutt,
          1872

HBC   Howay, Frederick William. British Columbia; the making of a
          province. Toronto: Ryerson Press, c1928

HBR   * Champlain Society, Toronto. Publications. Hudson's Bay Company
          series. 12 v. Toronto: Author, 1938-1949

HBT   Hebard, Grace Raymond & Brininstool, E. A. The Bozeman trail;
          historical accounts of the blazing of the overland routes into
          the Northwest, and the fights with Red Cloud's warriors...
          with an introduction by General Charles King... 2 v.
          Cleveland: Clark, 1922

HC   Hulbert, Archer Butler, ed. Call of the Columbia; iron men and
          saints take the Oregon trail... Stewart Commission on Western
          History of Colorado College, Overland to the Pacific v. 4.
          Stewart Commission of Colorado College and Denver Public
          Library, c1934

HCA   Hutton, Mrs. May Arkwright. The Coeur d'Alenes; or, A tale of
          the modern inquisition in Idaho. Wallace: Author, 1900

HCC   Harris, William Richard. Catholic church in Utah... Salt Lake
          City: Intermountain Catholic Press, c1909

HCM   Hanson, Joseph Mills. The conquest of the Missouri; being the story of the life and exploits of Captain Grant Marsh... with map and thirty-six illustrations. Chicago: McClurg, 1909

HCS   Mourning Dove (Humishuma). Coyote stories. Ed. and illus. by Heister Dean Guie... Caldwell: Caxton, 1933

HD   Hanna, Joseph A. Dr. Whitman and his ride to save Oregon. Los Angeles? 1903

HEG   Hegg, Eric A. Souvenir of Alaska and Yukon Territory. Seattle: E. A. Hegg, c1902

HEH   Howay, Frederick William. Early history of the Fraser River mines. British Columbia. Provincial Archives Department. Archives of British Columbia. Memoir no. 6. Victoria: Banfield, 1926

HF   Harris, Mrs. Martha Douglas, tr. History and folklore of the Cowichan Indians. Victoria: Colonist Printing and Publishing Co., 1901

HG   Howe, Henry. Historical collections of the great West... 2 v. in 1. Cincinnati: Howe, 1854

HH   Hawthorne, Julian, ed. and Brewerton, G. D. History of Washington, the Evergreen state, from early dawn to daylight. With portraits and biographies. ...assisted by Col. G. Douglas Brewerton. 2 v. New York: American Historical Publishing Co., 1893

HHI   Hawley, James H., ed. History of Idaho, the gem of the mountains. 4 v. Indexed v. 1-3 only. Chicago: Clarke, 1920

HHT   Hunt, Herbert. Tacoma, its history and its builders; a half century of activity. 3 v. Chicago: Clarke, 1916

HI   Hines, Harvey Kimball. Illustrated history of the state of Washington... Chicago: Lewis, 1893

HIO   Hines, Harvey Kimball. Illustrated history of the state of Oregon... Chicago: Lewis, 1893

HIT   History of Idaho Territory, showing its resources and advantages, with illustrations descriptive of its scenery... San Francisco: Elliott, 1884

HM   Hulbert, Archer Butler and Hulbert, Mrs. D. (P.) eds. Marcus Whitman, crusader. Stewart Commission on Western History of Colorado College, Overland to the Pacific v. 6-8. Stewart Commission of Colorado College and Denver Public Library, c1936-1941

HMS   Hamilton, William Thomas. My sixty years on the plains trapping, trading, and Indian fighting... edited by E. T. Sieber; with eight full page illustrations by Charles M. Russell. New York: Forest & Stream, 1905

HN   Sheldon, Henry Hargrave. Northwest corner; Oregon and Washington: the last frontier; photos by Henry Sheldon. Introduction and commentary by Stewart Holbrook. Garden City, N. Y.: Doubleday, 1948

HO   Hulbert, Archer Butler and Hulbert, Mrs. D. (P.) eds. Oregon crusade; across land and sea to Oregon... Stewart Commission on Western History of Colorado College, Overland to the Pacific v. 5. Stewart Commission of Colorado College and Denver Public Library, c1935

HOF   Harber, Nora E., pub. Our Fort Benton, "the birthplace of Montana"... Fort Benton: Nora E. Harber, 193-

HOM   Hafen, LeRoy R. Overland mail 1849-1869; promoter of settlement, precursor of railroads. Cleveland: Clark, 1926

HS   Halcombe, John Joseph. Stranger than fiction. 3rd ed. London: Society for Promoting Christian Knowledge, 1873

HSP   Hines, Harvey Kimball, comp. At sea and in port; or Life and experience of William S. Fletcher... Portland, Ore.: Gill, 1898

HU   Hulley, Clarence C. Alaska: past and present. 3rd ed. Portland, Ore.: Binfords & Mort, 1970, c53-70

HWW   Hunt, Herbert and Kaylor, F. C. Washington, west of the Cascades; historical and descriptive; the explorers, the Indians, the pioneers, the modern... 3 v. Chicago: Clarke, 1917

IH   Idaho State Historical Society. Biennial report of the board of trustees. v. 6-20 1917/18 - 1945/46. Boise: Author

IHD   Idaho. State Historical Department. Biennial report of the board of directors. v. 21-24 1947/48 - 1953/54. Boise: Author

IHI   Illustrated history of the state of Idaho... Chicago: Lewis, 1899

IN   * International Business Machines Corporation. Sculpture of the western hemisphere, Permanent collection... Author, c1942

JA   Jackson, Sheldon. Alaska, and missions on the north Pacific Coast. New York: Dodd, Mead, 1880

JAC   Jackman, S. W. Portraits of the premiers; an informal history of British Columbia.   Sidney, B. C.: Gray's, c1969

JJ   Jung, Aloysius M. Jesuit missions among the American tribes of the Rocky Mountain Indians. Spokane: Gonzaga University, 1925

JM   Judson, Katharine Berry. Myths and legends of the Pacific Northwest, especially of Washington and Oregon... Chicago: McClurg, 1910. With 50 illustrations from photographs

JNT   Jeffcott, Percival Robert. Nooksack tales and trails; being a collection of stories and historical events connected with the most northwest county in the United States -- Whatcom County, Washington. Ferndale: Sedro Woolley Courier Times, 1949

JO   Josephy, Alvin M., Jr. The Nez Percé Indians and the opening of the Northwest. New Haven: Yale University Press, c1965

JP   Jessett, Thomas Edwin. Pioneering God's country; the history of the Diocese of Olympia, 1853-1967. 2nd ed., enl. Seattle: Diocese of Olympia Press, 1967, 52-67

JV   Johnson, Emily Pauline. Legends of Vancouver... New ed. Toronto: McClelland & Stewart, 1924, c1922

KB   Kerr, J. B. Biographical dictionary of well-known British Columbians; with a historical sketch. Vancouver, B. C.: Kerr and Begg, 1890

KI   Kitchener, L. D. Flag over the north; the story of the Northern Commercial Company. Seattle: Superior, c1954

KO   Kelly, Charles. Outlaw trail... New York: Devin-Adair, 1959, c38-59

KS   Kerr, Duncan John. Story of the Great Northern Railway Company -- and James J. Hill. Newcomen Society, American Branch, a Newcomen address 1939. Princeton: Princeton University Press, c1939

KT   Kelley, Joseph. Thirteen years in the Oregon penitentiary, by Joseph (Bunko) Kelley. Portland, Ore.· n. p., 1908

KU   Kugelmass, J. Alvin. Roald Amundsen: a saga of the polar seas. Messner, c1955

KY   Kelly, Luther Sage. "Yellowstone Kelly": the memoirs of Luther S. Kelly, edited by M. M. Quaife, with a foreword by Lt.-General Nelson A. Miles, U. S. A. New Haven: Yale University Press, 1926

LBT   Laut, Agnes Christina. Blazed trail of the old frontier, being the log of the Upper Missouri historical expedition under the auspices of the governors and historical associations of Minnesota, North and South Dakota and Montana for 1925... with many illustrations from drawings by Charles M. Russell. New York: McBride, 1926

LC   Lewis, William Stanley. Case of Spokane Garry... Spokane Historical Society, Bulletin v. 1 no. 1. Spokane: Spokane Historical Society, 1917

LCR   Lyman, William Denison. Columbia River; its history, its myths, its scenery, its commerce... 3rd ed. rev. and enl. New York: Putnam, 1917, c09-17

LCRH   Lyman, William Denison. Columbia River; its history, its myths,
        its scenery, its commerce. 4th ed. Portland, Ore.: Binfords
        & Mort, 1963

LCT   Laut, Agnes Christina. Cariboo trail; a chronicle of the gold-
        fields of British Columbia. Toronto: Brook, 1920

LDL   Lowery, Woodbury. The Lowery collection. A descriptive list
        of maps of the Spanish possessions within the present
        limits of the United States, 1502-1820... Washington:
        Government Printing Office, 1912

LDM   Wright, E. W., ed. Lewis and Dryden's marine history of the
        Pacific Northwest... from the advent of the earliest naviga-
        tors to the present time, with sketches and portraits of a
        number of well known marine men. Reprint with corrections.
        New York: Antiquarian Press, 1961, 1895-1961

LH   Lyman, Horace Sumner. History of Oregon, the growth of an
        American state... 4 v. New York: North Pacific Publishing
        Society, 1903

LHC   Lockley, Fred. History of the Columbia River Valley from The
        Dalles to the sea... 3 v. Chicago: Clarke, 1928

LHM   Leeson, Michael A., ed. History of Montana, 1739-1885...
        Chicago: Warner, Beers, 1885

LHN   Logan, George. Histories of the North Montana Mission, Kalis-
        pell Mission and Montana Deaconess Hospital with some bio-
        graphical and autobiographical sketches. Author, 1909?

LI   Linderman, Frank Bird. Montana adventure; the recollections of
        Frank B. Linderman. Edited by H. G. Merriam. Lincoln:
        University of Nebraska Press, 1968

LL   Laveille, E. Life of Father de Smet, S. J. (1801-1873)...
        New York: Kenedy, 1915

LMM   Lee, John Doyle. Mormon chronicle: the diaries of John D. Lee,
        1848-1876... 2 v. San Marino, Calif.: Huntington Library,
        1955

LS   Lauridsen, Gregers Marius and Smith, A. A. Story of Port
        Angeles, Clallam County, Washington; an historical symposium.
        Seattle: Lowman & Hanford, c1937. Selective indexing

LSJ   Lockley, Fred. Story of the Journal, a picture story of how a
        great newspaper is made... and a bit of its history.
        Portland, Ore.: Journal, 1930?

LT   Lampman, Ben Hur. Centralia tragedy and trial. Joint publica-
        tion of Grant Hodge post no. 17, Centralia, Wn., and Edward B.
        Rhodes post no. 2, Tacoma, Wn., The American Legion. Tacoma:
        c1920

LW   Lindsay, Ernest Earl. State college of Washington; a land-grant
      college. Reprinted from Americana, v. 34 no. 2 April 1940.
      New York: American Historical Co., 1940

MAG   Magrini, Louis A. Meet the governors of the State of Washing-
      ton. Seattle: Author, 1946

MB   Murphy, Patrick Charles. Behind gray walls. Caldwell: Caxton,
      c1920

MC   Montana Historical Society. Contributions to the historical
      society of Montana; with its transactions, officers and mem-
      bers. v. 1-10   1876-1940. Helena

MCC   Morice, Adrien Gabriel. History of the Catholic church in
      western Canada, from Lake Superior to the Pacific (1659-1895)
      ... 2 v. Toronto: Musson, 1910

MCK   McCracken, Harold. Roughnecks and gentlemen. Garden City,
      N. Y.: Doubleday, 1968. Selective indexing

MCO   Manring, Benjamin Franklin. The conquest of the Coeur d'Alenes,
      Spokanes and Palouses; the expeditions of Colonels E. J.
      Steptoe and George Wright against the "northern Indians" in
      1858. Spokane: Inland Printing Co., 1912

ME   Meany, Edmond Stephen. Governors of Washington, territorial
      and state. Seattle: University of Washington, 1915

MF   Magaret, Helene. Father de Smet, pioneer priest of the Rockies.
      New York: Farrar & Rinehart, c1940

MG   Mary Leopoldine, Sister. ·Fifty golden years; a short history
      of Sacred Heart hospital, Spokane, Washington, years of jubi-
      lee, 1886-1936. Spokane: Acme Stamp & Printing Co., 1936

MH   MacKay, Douglas. Honourable company; a history of the Hudson's
      Bay Company. Indianapolis, New York: Bobbs-Merrill, c1936

MHC   Mary Theodore, Sister. Heralds of Christ, the King; missionary
      record of the North Pacific, 1837-1878. New York: Kenedy,
      1939

MHN   Morice, Adrien Gabriel. History of the northern interior of
      British Columbia, formerly New Caledonia (1660-1880) with
      map and illustrations. Toronto: Briggs, 1904

MHS   Mitchell, Rebecca. Historical sketches, pioneer characters, and
      conditions of eastern Idaho. Idaho Falls: B. F. Mill, 1905

MI   Miller, Joaquin. An illustrated history of the state of
      Montana, containing... biographical mention... of its pio-
      neers and prominent citizens. Chicago: Lewis, 1894

ML   Morice, Adrien Gabriel. Carrier language (Déné family); a gram-
      mar and dictionary combined... 2 v. Winnipeg: Author, 1932

MLO   McClelland, John M. Longview... the remarkable beginnings of a
            modern western city. Portland, Ore.: Binfords & Mort, c1949.
            Selective indexing

MMR   Meany, Edmond Stephen, ed. Mount Rainier: a record of explora-
            tion... New York: Macmillan, 1916

MP   Meeker, Ezra. Pioneer reminiscences of Puget Sound... Seattle:
            Lowman & Hanford, 1905

MS   Meeker, Ezra. Seventy years of progress in Washington.
            Seattle: 1921

MSG   Murphy, Patrick Charles. Shadows of the gallows. Caldwell:
            Caxton, c1928

MT   McCormick, Dell Jerome. Tall timber tales; more Paul Bunyan
            stories; illustrated by Lorna Livesley. Caldwell: Caxton,
            1939

MV   Meany, Edmond Stephen. Vancouver's discovery of Puget Sound...
            Portland, Ore.: Binfords & Mort, 1957, c07-35

MW   Mowry, William Augustus. Marcus Whitman and the early days of
            Oregon... New York: Silver, Burdett, c1901

MWH   * Magazine of western history. v. 1-14 November 1884-1891.
            Cleveland: Magazine of Western History Publishing Co.

MWHN   * National magazine; a monthly journal of American history.
            v. 15-17 1891/92, 1892, 1892/93. Preceded by Magazine of
            western history. Cleveland

NF   Nelson, Denys. Fort Langley, 1827-1927; a century of settle-
            ment in the valley of the lower Fraser River. Vancouver,
            B. C.: Evans & Hastings, 1927

NH   History of the Pacific Northwest: Oregon and Washington... 2 v.
            Portland, Ore.: North Pacific History Co., 1889

NL   Noyes, Alva Josiah. In the land of Chinook; or, The story of
            Blaine County, by Al J. Noyes (Ajax). Helena: State Publish-
            ing Co., 1917

NM   Nixon, Oliver Woodson. How Marcus Whitman saved Oregon...
            Chicago: Star Publishing Co., 1895

NT   Newton, William. Twenty years on the Saskatchewan, N. W.
            Canada. London: Elliot Stock, 1897

NW   Nixon, Oliver Woodson. Whitman's ride through savage lands,
            with sketches of Indian life. Chicago: Winona Publishing
            Co., 1905

OB   O'Connor, Dominic. Brief history of the Diocese of Baker City.
            Baker: Diocesan Chancery, 1930

OHQ   Oregon historical quarterly. v. 1 no. 1 - v. 70 no. 4 March 1900 - December 1969. Portland, Ore.: Oregon Historical Society

OO   Oregon. Secretary of State. Oregon blue book. Official directory of the state of Oregon. 1895, 1911-1946. Salem, Ore.

OP   O'Hara, Edwin Vincent. Pioneer Catholic history of Oregon. Portland, Ore.: Glass & Prudhomme, 1911

OPC   O'Hara, Edwin Vincent. Pioneer Catholic history of Oregon. Centennial ed. Paterson, N. J.: St. Anthony Guild Press, 1939

OS   Odell, Margaretta (Grubbs). Semi-centennial offering to the members and friends of Methodist Episcopal church, Salem, Oregon, 1884. Portland, Ore.: Swope & Taylor, 1885

PC   Pierce County Pioneer Association, Tacoma, Washington. Commemorative celebration at Sequalitchew Lake, Pierce County, Washington, July 5, 1906... Tacoma: Vaughan & Morrill

PH   Spencer, Lloyd and Pollard, Lancaster. A history of the state of Washington. 4 v. New York: American Historical Society, 1937

PHP   Prosser, William Farrand. History of the Puget Sound country... 2 v. New York: Lewis, 1903

PI   Palladino, Lawrence Benedict. Indian and white in the Northwest. Baltimore: Murphy, 1894

PIG   Pigott, H. C. History and progress of King County, Washington. Seattle: Hutchinson, 1916

PIW   Palladino, Lawrence Benedict. Indian and white in the Northwest; a history of Catholicity in Montana, 1831-1891... Lancaster, Pa.: Wickersham, 1922

PJ   Stuck, Hudson. Alaskan missions of the Episcopal church; a brief sketch, historical and descriptive. Preface by P. T. Rowe. Facsimile. Seattle: Shorey Book Store, 1968

PL   Puter, Stephen A. Douglas and Stevens, Horace. Looters of the public domain... Portland, Ore.: Portland Printing House, c1907

PM   Pacific magazine. v. 1 no. 2 - v. 4 no. 7 October 1889 - April 1892. Lacking v. 2 no. 4, v. 3 no. 6-7, v. 4 no. 5. (v. 1 through v. 3 no. 3 have title Washington Magazine) Seattle: Washington Magazine Co.

PMO   Oregon native son... v. 1 - v. 2 May 1899 - March 1901. Portland, Ore.: Native Son Publishing Co.

PMT   Prosch, Thomas Wickham. McCarver and Tacoma. Seattle: Lowman & Hanford, 1906

PN   Pacific Northwest quarterly. v. 27 - v. 60 no. 4 January 1936
          - October 1969. Preceded by Washington historical quarterly.
          Seattle: University of Washington

PNLA   Pacific Northwest Library Association. PNLA quarterly. v. 1 -
          v. 34 October 1936 - Summer 1970

PR   Piercy, Frederick Hawkins. Route from Liverpool to Great Salt
          Lake Valley. Ed. by Fawn M. Brodie. Cambridge, Mass.:
          Belknap Press of Harvard University Press, 1962

PSW   Presbyterian Church in the United States of America. Synod of
          Washington. History of the synod of Washington... 1835-1909.
          Seattle: The Synod, 1910?

QT   Quiett, Glenn Chesney. They built the West; an epic of rails
          and cities. New York: Appleton-Century, 1934

RA   Reid, Robie Lewis. The assay office and the proposed mint at
          New Westminster; a chapter in the history of the Fraser River
          mines. British Columbia. Provincial Archives Department.
          Archives of British Columbia. Memoir no. 7. Victoria:
          Banfield, 1926

RLW   Ryan, John Henry. Ryan's legislative manual, 1905-1906.
          Olympia: 1906

RLX   Ryan, John Henry. Ryan's legislative manual, tenth session,
          1907, state of Washington, historical, statistical, biograph-
          ical and illustrative... Tacoma: Ryan, c1907

RO   Redeman, Clara P. Our first forty years. Caldwell: Caxton,
          c1941

RSA   Robinson, Frank Bruce. Life story of Frank B. Robinson.
          Moscow: Review Publishing Co., c1934. Selective indexing

RW   Richardson, Marvin M. Whitman mission, the third station on the
          old Oregon trail. Walla Walla: Whitman, c1940

S   Port of Seattle yearbook; history and resources... 1914, 1919/
          20-1937. Seattle: Northwestern Publishing Co.

SA   Seattle. Port Commission. The port of Seattle, comprising all
          that great district embraced within the boundaries of King
          County: Farmer's day Saturday, Sept. 4, 1915... Seattle:
          H. C. Pigott, pr., 1915

SAA   Port of Seattle. Public Relations Dept. A look at the expand-
          ing port of Seattle; the fast great circle routes to the
          world. Seattle: 1949?

SC   Secretan, James Henry Edward. Canada's great highway: from the
          first stake to the last spike. London: Lane, 1924

SCC   Spokane. Charters. Charter of the city of Spokane, state of
Washington. Spokane: 1911

SCH   Schoenberg, Wilfred P. Gonzaga University; seventy-five years,
1887-1962. Spokane: Lawton, 1963

SE   Seattle Public Library. History Department. Robert T. McDonald
collection of pictures of the governors of Washington.
Uncatalogued collection of plates

SEA   Seattle Public Library. History Department. Robert T. McDonald
collection of pictures of the mayors of Seattle. Uncatalogued collection of plates

SFY   Stuart, Granville. Forty years on the frontier as seen in the
journals and reminiscences of Granville Stuart, goldminer,
trader, merchant, rancher and politician; edited by Paul C.
Phillips. 2 v. Cleveland: Clark, 1925

SG   Sisters of the Holy Names of Jesus and Mary. Province of
Oregon. Gleanings of fifty years; the Sisters of the Holy
Names of Jesus and Mary in the Northwest, 1859-1909.
Portland, Ore.: Glass & Prudhomme, 1909

SH   Snowden, Clinton A. History of Washington; the rise and progress of an American state... 6 v. New York: Century History
Co., 1909-1911

SHB   Scholefield, Ethelbert Olaf Stuart and Gosnell, R. E. History
of British Columbia... Vancouver, B. C.: British Columbia
Historical Association, 1913

SHE   Sherwood, Morgan B., ed. Alaska and its history. Seattle:
University of Washington Press, c1967

SHI   Sherwood, Morgan B. Exploration of Alaska, 1865-1900. New
Haven: Yale University Press, c1965

SHL   Shelton, W. George, ed. British Columbia and Confederation.
Victoria, B. C.: Published for the University of Victoria by
Morriss Printing Company, c1967

SHO   Scott, Harvey Whitefield. History of the Oregon country...
6 v. Cambridge: Riverside Press, 1924

SHP   Scott, Harvey Whitefield, ed. History of Portland, Oregon,
with illustrations and biographical sketches of prominent
citizens and pioneers. Syracuse: Mason, 1890

SIH   Illustrated history of north Idaho, embracing Nez Percés, Idaho,
Latah, Kootenai and Shoshone counties, state of Idaho.
Moscow: Western Historical Publishing Co., 1903

SK   Splawn, Andrew Jackson. Ka-mi-akin, the last hero of the Yaki-
mas. Portland, Ore.: Kilham Stationery and Printing Co., 1917

SKA   Splawn, Andrew Jackson. Ka-mi-akin, the last hero of the
          Yakimas. Portland, Ore.: Binfords & Mort, 1944

SLL   Smet, Pierre Jean de. Life, letters and travels of Father
          Pierre-Jean de Smet, S. J. 1801-73... by H. M. Chittenden
          and A. T. Richardson. 4 v. New York: Harper, c1904

SM   Sanders, Helen Fitzgerald. A history of Montana. 3 v.
          Chicago: Lewis, 1913

SMS   Stout, Tom, ed. Montana, its story and biography... 3 v.
          Chicago: American Historical Society, 1921

SO   Smet, Pierre Jean de. De Smet's Oregon missions and travels
          over the Rocky Mountains, 1845-46. New York: E. Dunigan,
          1847

SOU   Souvenir, G. A. R. encampment, 1899, McMinnville, Oregon

SPB   Shephard, Mrs. Esther. Paul Bunyan. Illus. by Rockwell Kent.
          Harcourt, c1924

SPI   Stranahan, C. T. Pioneer stories. Lewiston? Idaho: 1947

SRW   Sons of the American Revolution. Washington State Society.
          Register of the Washington state society... Seattle: Wash-
          ington State Society, 1916

SS   Stine, Thomas Ostenson. Scandinavians on the Pacific, Puget
          Sound. Seattle, Wash.? 1900

SSP   Seattle. Police Department. History of Seattle Police Depart-
          ment, 1923. Seattle: Grettner-Diers, 1923. Selective indexing

SSS   Washington (State) Legislature. Legislative manual. 1893/94,
          1895/96, 1899

ST   Shelton, William. Story of the totem pole; early Indian leg-
          ends. Everett: Kane & Harcus, c1923

STPB   Stevens, James. Paul Bunyan... woodcuts by Allen Lewis. New
          York: Knopf, 1925

SW   Sabin, Edwin Legrand. Wild men of the wild West. New York:
          Crowell, c1929

SWA   Swan, James Gilchrist. The Northwest coast; with an introduc-
          tion by W. A. Katz. Fairfield, Wash.: Ye Galleon Press, 1966

TDL   Tacoma daily ledger. Chamber of Commerce edition. 4 v. in 1.
          Tacoma: 1910. Includes Tacoma daily news, Annual edition,
          1906-1908, 3 v.

TF   Tax facts; State of Washington, official publication of State
          Federation of Taxpayers Associations. v. 1 - v. 2 no. 3
          January 1924 - March 1925. Seattle: State Federation of Tax-
          payers Associations

THI   Talkington, Henry Leonidas. Highlights in Lewiston history.
            Lewiston: Bailey, 1945

TM   Tobie, Harvey Elmer. No man like Joe; the life and times of
            Joseph L. Meek. Portland, Ore.: Binfords & Mort, c1949

TMP   Talbot, Ethelbert. My people of the plains... New York:
            Harper, 1906

TO   Turnbull, George Stanley. History of Oregon newspapers.
            Portland, Ore.: Binfords & Mort, c1939

TP   Turney, Ida Virginia. Paul Bunyan marches on; illustrated by
            Norma Madge Lyon. Portland, Ore.: Binfords & Mort, 1942

TUR   Turnbull, George Stanley. Governors of Oregon. Portland, Ore.:
            Binfords & Mort, 1959

US   Utz, Mrs. Cora, comp. History of Spokane University, opened
            September 15, 1913, closed June 8, 1933. Spokane: Leo's
            Studio, 1941

USCI * U. S. Census Office. 11th Census, 1890. Indians. Washington:
            Government Printing Office, 1894

UV   Washington (State) University. Publications in anthropology.
            v. 1 - v. 15 1920-1967. Lacking v. 2, 7, 10. Seattle:
            University of Washington Press

VT   Vaughn, Robert. Then and now; or, Thirty-six years in the
            Rockies... 1864-1900. Minneapolis: Tribune Printing Co.,
            1900

VU   Vulcan Iron Works, Seattle. Meet me in Seattle, 1909; general
            history, Alaska Yukon Pacific exposition. Seattle: 1908?

W   Washingtonian. v. 1 - v. 5 October 1908 - December 1911.
            Seattle: Washingtonian Company, University of Washington

WAS   Washington historical quarterly. v. 1 - v. 26 October 1906 -
            October 1935. Continued as Pacific Northwest quarterly

WBP   Washington Bankers' Association. Proceedings... annual conven-
            tion. v. 8 - v. 44 1903-1939. Lacking v. 11-12, 15, 38-39
            1906-07, 1910, 1933-34. Tacoma

WCS   Winthrop, Theodore. Canoe and the saddle; or, Klalam and
            Klickatat... Tacoma: J. H. Williams, 1913

WD   Washington (State) University. Alumni Association. Decennial
            banquet in honor of Henry Suzzallo, President, University of
            Washington, Olympic Hotel, November 6, 1925. Seattle: Lum-
            bermen's Printing Co.

WDT   Washington (State) University. Tyee. v. 1, 6, 26, 36, 50, 55
            1900-01, 1906, 1925, 1935, 1949, 1954. Seattle. Selective
            indexing

WFU   Wilbur, Earl Morse. History of the First Unitarian Church of
            Portland, Oregon, 1867-1892... Portland, Ore.: First Uni-
            tarian Church, 1893

WI   Woollen, William Watson. The inside passage to Alaska, 1792-
            1920... 2 v. Cleveland: Clark, 1924

WJ   Weibel, George F. Rev. Joseph M. Cataldo, S. J., a short
            sketch of a wonderful career. Reprinted from Gonzaga
            quarterly March 15, 1928. Spokane: 1928

WM   Washington magazine of industry and progress. March - November
            1906. Seattle: Washington Magazine Publishing Co.

WMW   Warren, Eliza (Spalding) ed. Memoirs of the West: the Spaldings.
            Portland, Ore.: Marsh, 1916

WN   Washingtonian, a state magazine of progress. v. 1 no. 1 - v. 2
            no. 2 January 1928 - April 1929. Seattle: Arthur H. Allen,
            publisher

WOY   Wickersham, James. Old Yukon; tales, trails and trials. Wash-
            ington, D. C.: Washington Law Book Co., 1938

WRE   Woodward, Walter Carleton. Rise and early history of political
            parties in Oregon 1843-1868. University of California,
            Thesis Ph.D. 1910. Portland, Ore.: Gill, 1913

WSE   Walkem, W. Wymond. Stories of early British Columbia. Illus-
            trated by S. P. Judge. Vancouver, B. C.: News-Advertiser,
            1914

WSGP   Patrons of Husbandry. Washington State Grange. Proceedings of
            the... annual session. v. 21 - v. 58, v. 68 1909 - 1947,
            1957. Lacking v. 29, 1917. Olympia

WSM   Wellcome, Henry Solomon. Story of Metla Kahtla. London:
            Saxon, 1887

WSP   Washington State Bar Association. Proceedings. v. 6 - v. 39
            1894 - 1927. Lacking v. 10, v. 13 1898, 1901

WT   Wheeler, Olin Dunbar. The trail of Lewis and Clark, 1804-
            1904... 2 v. New York: Putnam, 1926. Selective indexing

WTH   Wade, Mark Sweeten. The Thompson country; being notes on the
            history of southern British Columbia... Kamloops, B. C.:
            Inland Sentinel Print, 1907

WTY   Woodsworth, James. Thirty years in the Canadian North-West.
            Toronto: McClelland, Goodchild & Stewart, 1917

YB   Year book of British Columbia and manual of provincial informa-
            tion. 1897, 1911. Victoria

ALPHABETICAL

LIST OF BOOKS INDEXED

Abbott, Newton Carl. Montana in the making   AM
Adams, Ramon Frederick. Charles M. Russell, the cowboy artist   ACR
Alaska-Yukon gold book   AL
Andrews, Clarence Leroy. Story of Alaska   AN
Arnold, Royal Ross. Indian wars of Idaho   AI
Atkinson, Reginald Noel. Historical souvenir of Penticton, B. C.   AT
Atwood, Albert. Conquerors   AC
_____. Glimpses in pioneer life on Puget Sound   AG
Bagley, Clarence Booth. History of King County, Washington   BHK
_____. History of Seattle   BHS
Bailey, Robert Gresham. River of no return   BR
Bankson, Russell Arden. Klondike nugget   BK
Bartlett, Laura Belle (Downey). Students' history of the   BS
    Northwest
Beadle, John Hanson. Undeveloped West   BU
Beal, Merrill D. History of Idaho   BEA
_____. A history of southeastern Idaho   BHI
Becker, Ethel (Anderson). A treasury of Alaskana   BET
Birney, Hoffman. Vigilantes   BV
Blanchard, John. Caravans to the Northwest   BCN
Boas, Franz. Kathlamet texts   BKT
Bonney, William Pierce. History of Pierce County, Washington   BH
Bowden, Angie (Burt). Early schools of Washington Territory   BE
Brady, Cyrus Townsend. Northwestern fights and fighters   BN
British Columbia from the earliest times to the present   BCF
British Columbia Historical Association. Report   BCHA
British Columbia historical quarterly   BCH
Brogan, James M. Historical landmark: old mission church   BO
Brosnan, Cornelius James. History of the state of Idaho   BHSI
_____. Jason Lee   BJ
Brown, Henry. Taxation of church property   BT
Brown, Jennie Broughton. Fort Hall on the Oregon trail   BF
Brown, William Carey. The Sheepeater campaign -- 1879   BSC
Brunner, Edmund de Schweinitz. Church and community survey of   BCC
    Pend Oreille County, Washington
Bruseth, Nels. Indian stories and legends of the Stillaguamish   BI
Bryan, Enoch Albert. Historical sketch of the State college of   BHSS
    Washington, 1890-1925
_____. Orient meets Occident   BOO
Burns, Robert Ignatius. The Jesuits and the Indian wars of the   BUR
    Northwest
Burns and McDonnell Engineering Co. Results of municipal   BM
    electric systems
Bushnell, David Ives. Drawings by George Gibbs in the far   BD
    Northwest, 1849-1851
Campbell, Marjorie Wilkins. McGillivray; Lord of the Northwest   CML
Cannon, Frank Jenne. Brigham Young and his Mormon empire   CB
Cannon, Miles. Waiilatpu, its rise and fall, 1836-1847   CW
Canse, John Martin. Pilgrim and pioneer   CPP

Carey, Charles Henry. General history of Oregon prior to 1861   CGO
_____. History of Oregon   CHO
Carlton, Ambrose B. Wonderlands of the wild West   CWW
Carmichael, Alfred. Indian legends of Vancouver Island   CI
Catlin, George. North American Indians   CN
Champlain Society, Toronto. Publications. Hudson's Bay Company   HBR
    series
Chandler, George. Textbook of civics for the state of Washington   CC
Chittenden, Hiram Martin. American fur trade of the far West...   CAF
    c1901

_____. American fur trade of the far West... c1935   CAFT
_____. History of early steamboat navigation...   CES
Cirker, Hayward, ed. Dictionary of American portraits   CIR
Clark, Barzilla Worth. Bonneville County in the making   CBC
Clark, Robert Carlton. History of the Willamette Valley, Oregon   CHW
Clarke, Samuel A. Pioneer days of Oregon history   CP
Clayton, William. William Clayton's journal   CWC
Cochran, John Eakin. Pioneer days in eastern Washington and   CPD
    northern Idaho
Cody, Edmund R. History of the Coeur d'Alene mission of the   CCA
    Sacred Heart
Commonwealth review of the University of Oregon   CR
Corser, Harry Prosper. Totem lore of the Alaska Indians   CT
_____. Totem lore of the Alaska Indian, and the Land of   CTL
    the totem
Crockwell, James H., pub. Pictures and biographies of Brigham   CY
    Young and his wives
Crosby, Laurence E. "Kuailks Metatcopun"   CK
Crosby, Thomas. Among the An-ko-me-nums   CAA
Cross, Osborne & others. March of the Mounted Riflemen. c1940   CM
_____. March of the regiment of Mounted Riflemen to Oregon   CMG
    in 1849. 1967
Daughters of the American Revolution. Washington (State)   D
    History and register
Davidson, Innes N. The Arctic Brotherhood   DA
De Armond, R. N. Founding of Juneau   DEA
Deaville, Alfred Stanley. Colonial postal systems and postage   DC
    stamps of Vancouver Island and British Columbia
Defenbach, Byron. Red heroines of the Northwest   DD
_____. The state we live in, Idaho   DSW
Delaney, Matilda J. (Sager). Survivor's recollections of the   DSR
    Whitman massacre
Densmore, Frances. American Indians and their music   DAI
Dickson, Albert Jerome. Covered wagon days   DCW
Dixon, William Hepworth. New America   DN
Dobbs, Caroline (Conselyea). Men of Champoeg   DO
Dodge, Grenville Mellen. How we built the Union Pacific railway   DH
Donaldson, Thomas Corwin. The George Catlin Indian gallery   DGC
_____. Idaho of yesterday   DL
Donnellan, Kenneth M., ed. Mining events and dividends   DM
Drury, Clifford Merrill. Elkanah and Mary Walker   DE
_____. Henry Harmon Spalding   DS
_____. Marcus Whitman, M. D.   DW
_____. A tepee in his front yard   DTI
Dryden, Cecil Pearl. Up the Columbia for furs   DU
Dyer, Charles Newell. History of the town of Plainfield   DT
Eells, Myron. History of Indian missions on the Pacific Coast   EI

_____. Marcus Whitman, pathfinder and patriot   EW

_____. Ten years of missionary work among the Indians   ET
   at Skokomish

Egan, Howard. Pioneering the West, 1846 to 1878   EP

Elks of Washington   E

Elsensohn, Alfreda, Sister. Pioneer days in Idaho County   EPD

Encyclopedia of Northwest biography. c1941   EN

Encyclopedia of Northwest biography. c1943   ENC

Faris, John Thomson. Winning the Oregon country   FW

Farnham, Mary Frances, comp. Catalogue of rare books   FR

Federal Writers' Project. Montana, a state guide book   FM

Feerick, John D. and Emalie P. Vice-presidents of the United   FEE
   States

Ferris, Benjamin G. Utah and the Mormons   FU

Fifty years in western Canada   FT

Fiske, John. Unpublished orations   FO

Flenner, John Davis. Syringa blossoms   FSB

Frances, pseud. Church in an early day   FC

Franchère, Gabriel. Adventure at Astoria, 1810-1814   FRA

French, Hiram Taylor. History of Idaho   FH

Fries, Ulrich Englehart. From Copenhagen to Okanogan   FF

Frontier   F

Frontier and midland   FA

Fuller, George Washington. Inland empire of the Pacific Northwest   FI

Gardner, Hamilton. History of Lehi   GL

Gaston, Joseph. Portland, Oregon   GP

Gates, Charles Marvin. First century at the University of   GA
   Washington, 1861-1961

Ghent, William James. Early far West   GE

_____. Road to Oregon   GR

Gibbon, John Murray. Romantic history of the Canadian Pacific   GI

Gibbs, Josiah Francis. Lights and shadows of Mormonism   GLS

Godwin, George Stanley. Vancouver; a life, 1757-1798   GV

Golder, Frank Alfred and others, eds. March of the Mormon   GMM
   battalion from Council Bluffs to California

Gonzaga University, Spokane, Wash. Gonzaga's silver jubilee   GG

Gould, Dorothy Wheaton (Fay). Beyond the shining mountains   GBS

Gove, Jesse Augustus. Utah expedition 1857-1858   GU

Grand Army of the Republic. Dept. of Washington and Alaska.   G
   Journal of the... annual encampment. June 16-18, 1920

Gray, William Henry. Unpublished journal   GUG

Hafen, LeRoy R. Overland mail 1849-1869   HOM

Halcombe, John Joseph. Stranger than fiction   HS

Hamilton, William Thomas. My sixty years on the plains   HMS

Hanna, Joseph A. Dr. Whitman and his ride to save Oregon   HD

Hanson, Joseph Mills. The conquest of the Missouri   HCM

Harber, Nora E., pub. Our Fort Benton   HOF

Harris, Mrs. Martha Douglas, tr. History and folklore of the   HF
   Cowichan Indians

Harris, William Richard. Catholic church in Utah   HCC

Harrison, Edward Sanford. Nome and Seward Peninsula   HA

Hawley, James H., ed. History of Idaho   HHI

Hawthorne, Julian, ed. & G. D. Brewerton. History of Washington   HH

Hebard, Grace Raymond & E. A. Brininstool. The Bozeman trail   HBT

Hegg, Eric A. Souvenir of Alaska and Yukon Territory   HEG

Hickman, William A. Brigham's destroying angel   HB

Hines, Harvey Kimball, comp. At sea and in port   HSP

_____. Illustrated history of the state of Oregon   HIO

_____. Illustrated history of the state of Washington	HI
History of Idaho Territory	HIT
History of the Pacific Northwest: Oregon and Washington	NH
Howay, Frederick William. British Columbia	HBC
_____. Early history of the Fraser River mines	HEH
Howe, Henry. Historical collections of the great West	HG
Hulbert, Archer Butler, ed. Call of the Columbia	HC
_____ and Mrs. D. (P.) Hulbert, eds. Marcus Whitman, crusader	HM
_____. Oregon crusade	HO
Hulley, Clarence C. Alaska: past and present	HU
Hunt, Herbert. Tacoma, its history and its builders	HHT
_____ and F. C. Kaylor. Washington, west of the Cascades	HWW
Hutton, Mrs. May Arkwright. The Coeur d'Alenes	HCA
Idaho. State Historical Dept. Biennial report of the board of directors	IHD
Idaho State Historical Society. Biennial report of the board of trustees	IH
Illustrated history of north Idaho	SIH
Illustrated history of the state of Idaho	IHI
International Business Machines Corporation. Sculpture of the western hemisphere	IN
Jackman, S. W. Portraits of the premiers	JAC
Jackson, Sheldon. Alaska, and missions on the north Pacific Coast	JA
Jeffcott, Percival Robert. Nooksack tales and trails	JNT
Jessett, Thomas Edwin. Pioneering God's country	JP
Johnson, Emily Pauline. Legends of Vancouver	JV
Josephy, Alvin M., Jr. The Nez Percé Indians	JO
Judson, Katharine Berry. Myths and legends of the Pacific Northwest	JM
Jung, Aloysius M. Jesuit missions	JJ
Kelley, Joseph. Thirteen years in the Oregon penitentiary	KT
Kelly, Charles. Outlaw trail	KO
Kelly, Luther Sage. "Yellowstone Kelly"	KY
Kerr, Duncan John. Story of the Great Northern Railway Company	KS
Kerr, J. B. Biographical dictionary of well-known British Columbians	KB
Kitchener, L. D. Flag over the north	KI
Kugelmass, J. Alvin. Roald Amundsen	KU
Lampman, Ben Hur. Centralia tragedy and trial	LT
Lauridsen, Gregers Marius & A. A. Smith. Story of Port Angeles	LS
Laut, Agnes Christina. Blazed trail of the old frontier	LBT
_____. Cariboo trail	LCT
Laveille, E. Life of Father de Smet, S. J.	LL
Lee, John Doyle. Mormon chronicle	LMM
Leeson, Michael A., ed. History of Montana, 1739-1885	LHM
Lewis, William Stanley. Case of Spokane Garry	LC
Linderman, Frank Bird. Montana adventure	LI
Lindsay, Ernest Earl. State college of Washington	LW
Lockley, Fred. History of the Columbia River Valley	LHC
_____. Story of the journal	LSJ
Logan, George. Histories of the North Montana Mission	LHN
Lowery, Woodbury. The Lowery collection	LDL
Lyman, Horace Sumner. History of Oregon	LH
Lyman, William Denison. Columbia River... 3rd ed.	LCR
_____. Columbia River... 4th ed.	LCRH
McClelland, John M. Longview	MLO

McCormick, Dell Jerome. Tall timber tales; more Paul Bunyan   MT
    stories
McCracken, Harold. Roughnecks and gentlemen   MCK
MacKay, Douglas. Honourable company   MH
Magaret, Helene. Father de Smet, pioneer priest of the Rockies   MF
Magazine of western history   MWH
Magrini, Louis A. Meet the governors of the state of Washington   MAG
Manring, Benjamin Franklin. The conquest of the Coeur d'Alenes,   MCO
    Spokanes and Palouses
Mary Leopoldine, Sister. Fifty golden years   MG
Mary Theodore, Sister. Heralds of Christ, the King   MHC
Meany, Edmond Stephen. Governors of Washington, territorial   ME
    and state
_____. Mount Rainier; a record of exploration   MMR
_____. Vancouver's discovery of Puget Sound   MV
Meeker, Ezra. Pioneer reminiscences of Puget Sound   MP
_____. Seventy years of progress in Washington   MS
Miller, Joaquin. Illustrated history of the state of Montana   MI
Mitchell, Rebecca. Historical sketches   MHS
Montana Historical Society. Contributions   MC
Morice, Adrien Gabriel. Carrier language   ML
_____. History of the Catholic church in western Canada   MCC
_____. History of the northern interior of British Columbia   MHN
Mourning Dove (Humishuma). Coyote stories   HCS
Mowry, William Augustus. Marcus Whitman   MW
Murphy, Patrick Charles. Behind gray walls   MB
_____. Shadows of the gallows   MSG
National magazine   MWHN
Nelson, Denys. Fort Langley, 1827-1927   NF
Newton, William. Twenty years on the Saskatchewan   NT
Nixon, Oliver Woodson. How Marcus Whitman saved Oregon   NM
_____. Whitman's ride through savage lands   NW
Noyes, Alva Josiah. In the land of Chinook   NL
O'Connor, Dominic. Brief history of the Diocese of Baker City   OB
Odell, Margaretta (Grubbs). Semi-centennial offering to the   OS
    members and friends of Methodist Episcopal church
O'Hara, Edwin Vincent. Pioneer Catholic history of Oregon. 1911   OP
_____. Pioneer Catholic history of Oregon. 1939   OPC
Oregon. Secretary of State. Oregon blue book   OO
Oregon historical quarterly   OHQ
Oregon native son   PMO
Pacific magazine   PM
Pacific Northwest Library Association. PNLA quarterly   PNLA
Pacific Northwest quarterly   PN
Palladino, Lawrence Benedict. Indian and white in the   PI
    Northwest. 1894
_____. Indian and white in the Northwest. 1922   PIW
Patrons of Husbandry. Washington State Grange. Proceedings   WSGP
Pierce County Pioneer Association, Tacoma, Washington.   PC
    Commemorative celebration... July 5th, 1906
Piercy, Frederick Hawkins. Route from Liverpool to Great Salt   PR
    Lake Valley
Pigott, H. C. History and progress of King County, Washington   PIG
Port of Seattle. Public Relations Dept. A look at the   SAA
    expanding port of Seattle
Port of Seattle yearbook   S
Presbyterian Church in the United States of America. Synod of   PSW
    Washington. History

Prosch, Thomas Wickham. McCarver and Tacoma   PMT
Prosser, William Farrand. History of the Puget Sound country   PHP
Puter, Stephen A. Douglas and Stevens, Horace. Looters of the   PL
    public domain
Quiett, Glenn Chesney. They built the West   QT
Redeman, Clara P. Our first forty years   RO
Reid, Robie Lewis. The assay office and the proposed mint at   RA
    New Westminster
Richardson, Marvin M. Whitman mission   RW
Robinson, Frank Bruce. Life story of Frank B. Robinson   RSA
Ryan, John Henry. Ryan's legislative manual, 1905-1906   RLW
_____. Ryan's legislative manual, tenth session, 1907   RLX
Sabin, Edwin Legrand. Wild men of the wild West   SW
Sanders, Helen Fitzgerald. A history of Montana   SM
Schoenberg, Wilfred P. Gonzaga University   SCH
Scholefield, Ethelbert Olaf Stuart and Gosnell, R. E. History   SHB
    of British Columbia
Scott, Harvey Whitefield, ed. History of Portland, Oregon   SHP
_____. History of the Oregon country   SHO
Seattle. Alaska-Yukon-Pacific Exposition, 1909. Official   AYP
    publication
Seattle. Police Dept. History   SSP
Seattle. Port Commission. The port of Seattle   SA
Seattle Public Library. History Department. ...Governors of   SE
    Washington
_____. ...Mayors of Seattle   SEA
Secretan, James Henry Edward. Canada's great highway   SC
Sheldon, Henry Hargrave. Northwest corner   HN
Shelton, W. George, ed. British Columbia and Confederation   SHL
Shelton, William. Story of the totem pole   ST
Shephard, Mrs. Esther. Paul Bunyan   SPB
Sherwood, Morgan B. ed. Alaska and its history   SHE
_____. Exploration of Alaska, 1865-1900   SHI
Sisters of the Holy Names of Jesus and Mary. Province of Oregon.   SG
    Gleanings of fifty years
Smet, Pierre Jean de. De Smet's Oregon missions   SO
_____. Life, letters and travels   SLL
Snowden, Clinton A. History of Washington   SH
Sons of the American Revolution. Washington State Society.   SRW
    Register
Souvenir, G. A. R. encampment, 1899, McMinnville, Oregon   SOU
Spencer, Lloyd and Pollard, Lancaster. A history of the state   PH
    of Washington
Splawn, Andrew Jackson. Ka-mi-akin... 1917   SK
_____. Ka-mi-akin... 1944   SKA
Spokane. Charters. Charter of the city of Spokane   SCC
Stevens, James. Paul Bunyan   STPB
Stine, Thomas Ostenson. Scandinavians on the Pacific, Puget   SS
    Sound
Stout, Tom, ed. Montana, its story and biography   SMS
Stranahan, C. T. Pioneer stories   SPI
Stuart, Granville. Forty years on the frontier   SFY
Stuck, Hudson. Alaskan missions of the Episcopal church   PJ
Swan, James Gilchrist. The Northwest coast   SWA
Tacoma daily ledger   TDL
Talbot, Ethelbert. My people of the plains   TMP
Talkington, Henry Leonidas. Highlights in Lewiston history   THI

Tax facts; state of Washington   TF
Tobie, Harvey Elmer. No man like Joe   TM
Turnbull, George Stanley. Governors of Oregon   TUR
_____. History of Oregon newspapers   TO
Turney, Ida Virginia. Paul Bunyan marches on   TP
U. S. Census Office. 11th Census, 1890. Indians   USCI
Utz, Mrs. Cora, comp. History of Spokane University   US
Vaughn, Robert. Then and now   VT
Vulcan Iron Works, Seattle. Meet me in Seattle, 1909   VU
Wade, Mark Sweeten. The Thompson country   WTH
Walkem, W. Wymond. Stories of early British Columbia   WSE
Warren, Eliza (Spalding), ed. Memoirs of the West: the   WMW
    Spaldings
Washington (State) Legislature. Legislative manual   SSS
Washington (State). State Dept. of Public Welfare. Coordinator   C
Washington (State) University. Alumni Association. Decennial   WD
    banquet in honor of Henry Suzzallo
_____. Publications in anthropology   UV
_____. Tyee   WDT
Washington Bankers' Association. Proceedings   WBP
Washington historical quarterly   WAS
Washington magazine of industry and progress   WM
Washington State Bar Association. Proceedings   WSP
Washingtonian   W
Washingtonian, a state magazine of progress   WN
Weibel, George F. Rev. Joseph M. Cataldo, S. J.   WJ
Wellcome, Henry Solomon. Story of Metla Kahtla   WSM
Wheeler, Olin Dunbar. The trail of Lewis and Clark, 1804-1904   WT
Wickersham, James. Old Yukon; tales, trails and trials   WOY
Wilbur, Earl Morse. History of the First Unitarian Church of   WFU
    Portland, Oregon, 1867-1892
Winthrop, Theodore. Canoe and the saddle   WCS
Woodsworth, James. Thirty years in the Canadian North-West   WTY
Woodward, Walter Carleton. Rise and early history of political   WRE
    parties in Oregon 1843-1868
Woollen, William Watson. The inside passage to Alaska,   WI
    1792-1920
Wright, E. W., ed. Lewis and Dryden's marine history of the   LDM
    Pacific Northwest
Year book of British Columbia. 1897, 1911   YB

PACIFIC NORTHWEST

Beadle, John Hanson. Undeveloped West	BU
Blanchard, John. Caravans to the Northwest	BCN
Brady, Cyrus Townsend. Northwestern fights and fighters	BN
Bryan, Enoch Albert. Orient meets Occident	BOO
Burns, Robert Ignatius. The Jesuits and the Indian wars of the Northwest	BUR
Burns and McDonnell Engineering Co. Results of municipal electric systems	BM
Bushnell, David Ives. Drawings by George Gibbs in the far Northwest, 1849-1851	BD
Catlin, George. North American Indians	CN
Chittenden, Hiram Martin. American fur trade of the far West... c1901	CAF
_____. American fur trade of the far West... c1935	CAFT
_____. History of early steamboat navigation...	CES
Cirker, Hayward, ed. Dictionary of American portraits	CIR
Crosby, Thomas. Among the An-ko-me-nums	CAA
Cross, Osborne & others. March of the Mounted Riflemen. c1940	CM
_____. March of the regiment of Mounted Riflemen to Oregon in 1849. 1967	CMG
Defenbach, Byron. Red heroines of the Northwest	DD
Densmore, Frances. American Indians and their music	DAI
Dodge, Grenville Mellen. How we built the Union Pacific railway	DH
Donaldson, Thomas Corwin. The George Catlin Indian gallery	DGC
Donnellan, Kenneth M., ed. Mining events and dividends	DM
Dryden, Cecil Pearl. Up the Columbia for furs	DU
Dyer, Charles Newell. History of the town of Plainfield	DT
Eells, Myron. History of Indian missions on the Pacific Coast	EI
Egan, Howard. Pioneering the West, 1846 to 1878	EP
Encyclopedia of Northwest biography. c1941	EN
Encyclopedia of Northwest biography. c1943	ENC
Faris, John Thomson. Winning the Oregon country	FW
Farnham, Mary Frances, comp. Catalogue of rare books	FR
Frances, pseud. Church in an early day	FC
Frontier	F
Frontier and midland	FA
Fuller, George Washington. Inland empire of the Pacific Northwest	FI
Ghent, William James. Early far West	GE
_____. Road to Oregon	GR
Godwin, George Stanley. Vancouver; a life, 1757-1798	GV
Gould, Dorothy Wheaton (Fay). Beyond the shining mountains	GBS
Hafen, LeRoy R. Overland mail 1849-1869	HOM
Hamilton, William Thomas. My sixty years on the plains	HMS
Hanson, Joseph Mills. The conquest of the Missouri	HCM
Hebard, Grace Raymond and Brininstool, E. A. The Bozeman trail	HBT
Howe, Henry. Historical collections of the great West	HG
Hulbert, Archer Butler, ed. Call of the Columbia	HC
_____ and Hulbert, Mrs. D. (P.), eds. Oregon crusade	HO

International Business Machines Corporation. Sculpture of the western hemisphere	IN
Josephy, Alvin M., Jr. The Nez Percé Indians	JO
Jung, Aloysius M. Jesuit missions	JJ
Kelly, Charles. Outlaw trail	KO
Kelly, Luther Sage. "Yellowstone Kelly"	KY
Kerr, Duncan John. Story of the Great Northern Railway Company	KS
Laut, Agnes Christina. Blazed trail of the old frontier	LBT
Laveille, E. Life of Father de Smet, S. J.	LL
Lowery, Woodbury. The Lowery collection	LDL
Lyman, William Denison. Columbia River. 3rd ed.	LCR
_____. Columbia River. 4th ed.	LCRH
McCormick, Dell Jerome. Tall timber tales; more Paul Bunyan stories	MT
Magaret, Helene. Father de Smet, pioneer priest of the Rockies	MF
Magazine of western history	MWH
Mary Theodore, Sister. Heralds of Christ, the King	MHC
Meany, Edmond Stephen. Vancouver's discovery of Puget Sound	MV
Morice, Adrien Gabriel. Carrier language	ML
National magazine	MWHN
Oregon historical quarterly	OHQ
Pacific magazine	PM
Pacific Northwest Library Association. PNLA quarterly	PNLA
Pacific Northwest quarterly	PN
Puter, Stephen A. Douglas and Stevens, Horace. Looters of the public domain	PL
Quiett, Glenn Chesney. They built the West	QT
Sabin, Edwin Legrand. Wild men of the wild West	SW
Scott, Harvey Whitefield. History of the Oregon country	SHO
Seattle. Alaska-Yukon-Pacific Exposition, 1909. Official publication	AYP
Shelton, William. Story of the totem pole	ST
Shephard, Mrs. Esther. Paul Bunyan	SPB
Smet, Pierre Jean de. De Smet's Oregon missions	SO
_____. Life, letters and travels	SLL
Stevens, James. Paul Bunyan	STPB
Tobie, Harvey Elmer. No man like Joe	TM
Turney, Ida Virginia. Paul Bunyan marches on	TP
U. S. Census Office. 11th Census, 1890. Indians	USCI
Vulcan Iron Works, Seattle. Meet me in Seattle, 1909	VU
Washington historical quarterly	WAS
Washington (State) University. Publications in anthropology	UV
Wright, E. W., ed. Lewis and Dryden's marine history of the Pacific Northwest	LDM

ALASKA

Alaska-Yukon gold book	AL
Andrews, Clarence Leroy. Story of Alaska	AN
Bankson, Russell Arden. Klondike nugget	BK
Becker, Ethel (Anderson). A treasury of Alaskana	BET
Corser, Harry Prosper. Totem lore of the Alaska Indians	CT
_____. Totem lore of the Alaska Indian, and the Land of the totem	CTL

ALASKA, cont.

Davidson, Innes N. The Arctic Brotherhood   DA
De Armond, R. N. Founding of Juneau   DEA
Grand Army of the Republic. Dept. of Washington and Alaska.   G
    Journal of the... annual encampment. June 16-18, 1920
Harrison, Edward Sanford. Nome and Seward Peninsula   HA
Hegg, Eric A. Souvenir of Alaska and Yukon Territory   HEG
Hulley, Clarence C. Alaska: past and present   HU
Jackson, Sheldon. Alaska, and missions on the north Pacific   JA
    Coast
Kitchener, L. D. Flag over the north   KI
Kugelmass, J. Alvin. Roald Amundsen   KU
McCracken, Harold. Roughnecks and gentlemen   MCK
Sherwood, Morgan B., ed. Alaska and its history   SHE
_____. Exploration of Alaska, 1865-1900   SHI
Stuck, Hudson. Alaskan missions of the Episcopal church   PJ
Wickersham, James. Old Yukon; tales, trails and trials   WOY
Woollen, William Watson. The inside passage to Alaska, 1792-1920   WI

BRITISH COLUMBIA

Atkinson, Reginald Noel. Historical souvenir of Penticton, B. C.   AT
British Columbia from the earliest times to the present   BCF
British Columbia Historical Association. Report   BCHA
British Columbia historical quarterly   BCH
Campbell, Marjorie Wilkins. McGillivray; Lord of the Northwest   CML
Carmichael, Alfred. Indian legends of Vancouver Island   CI
Champlain Society, Toronto. Publications. Hudson's Bay   HBR
    Company series
Deaville, Alfred Stanley. Colonial postal systems and postage   DC
    stamps of Vancouver Island and British Columbia
Fifty years in western Canada   FT
Gibbon, John Murray. Romantic history of the Canadian Pacific   GI
Halcombe, John Joseph. Stranger than fiction   HS
Harris, Mrs. Martha Douglas, tr. History and folklore of the   HF
    Cowichan Indians
Howay, Frederick William. British Columbia   HBC
_____. Early history of the Fraser River mines   HEH
Jackman, S. W. Portraits of the premiers   JAC
Johnson, Emily Pauline. Legends of Vancouver   JV
Kerr, J. B. Biographical dictionary of well-known British   KB
    Columbians
Laut, Agnes Christina. Cariboo trail   LCT
MacKay, Douglas. Honourable company   MH
Morice, Adrien Gabriel. History of the Catholic church in   MCC
    western Canada
_____. History of the northern interior of British Columbia   MHN
Nelson, Denys. Fort Langley, 1827-1927   NF
Newton, William. Twenty years on the Saskatchewan   NT
Reid, Robie Lewis. The assay office and the proposed mint at   RA
    New Westminster
Scholefield, Ethelbert Olaf Stuart and Gosnell, R. E. History   SHB
    of British Columbia
Secretan, James Henry Edward. Canada's great highway   SC
Shelton, W. George, ed. British Columbia and Confederation   SHL

BRITISH COLUMBIA, cont.

Wade, Mark Sweeten. The Thompson country   WTH
Walkem, W. Wymond. Stories of early British Columbia   WSE
Wellcome, Henry Solomon. Story of Metla Kahtla   WSM
Woodsworth, James. Thirty years in the Canadian North-West   WTY
Yearbook of British Columbia. 1897, 1911   YB

IDAHO

Arnold, Royal Ross. Indian wars of Idaho   AI
Bailey, Robert Gresham. River of no return   BR
Beal, Merrill D. History of Idaho   BEA
_____. A history of southeastern Idaho   BHI
Brogan, James M. Historical landmark: old mission church   BO
Brosnan, Cornelius James. History of the state of Idaho   BHSI
Brown, Jennie Broughton. Fort Hall on the Oregon trail   BF
Brown, William Carey. The Sheepeater campaign -- 1879   BSC
Clark, Barzilla Worth. Bonneville County in the making   CBC
Cochran, John Eakin. Pioneer days in eastern Washington and   CPD
    northern Idaho
Cody, Edmund R. History of the Coeur d'Alene mission of the   CCA
    Sacred Heart
Crosby, Laurence E. "Kuailks Metatcopun"   CK
Defenbach, Byron. The state we live in, Idaho   DSW
Donaldson, Thomas Corwin. Idaho of yesterday   DL
Drury, Clifford Merrill. Henry Harmon Spalding   DS
Elsensohn, Alfreda, Sister. Pioneer days in Idaho County   EPD
Flenner, John Davis. Syringa blossoms   FSB
French, Hiram Taylor. History of Idaho   FH
Hawley, James H., ed. History of Idaho   HHI
History of Idaho Territory   HIT
Hutton, Mrs. May Arkwright. The Coeur d'Alenes   HCA
Idaho. State Historical Dept. Biennial report of the board   IHD
    of directors
Idaho State Historical Society. Biennial report of the board   IH
    of trustees
Illustrated history of north Idaho   SIH
Illustrated history of the state of Idaho   IHI
Mitchell, Rebecca. Historical sketches   MHS
Murphy, Patrick Charles. Behind gray walls   MB
_____. Shadows of the gallows   MSG
Robinson, Frank Bruce. Life story of Frank B. Robinson   RSA
Stranahan, C. T. Pioneer stories   SPI
Talbot, Ethelbert. My people of the plains   TMP
Talkington, Henry Leonidas. Highlights in Lewiston history   THI
Warren, Eliza (Spalding), ed. Memoirs of the West: the Spaldings WMW
Weibel, George F. Rev. Joseph M. Cataldo, S. J.   WJ

MONTANA

Abbott, Newton Carl. Montana in the making   AM
Adams, Ramon Frederick. Charles M. Russell, the cowboy artist   ACR

MONTANA, cont.

Birney, Hoffman. Vigilantes	BV
Dickson, Albert Jerome. Covered wagon days	DCW
Federal Writers' Project. Montana, a state guide book	FM
Harber, Nora E., pub. Our Fort Benton	HOF
Leeson, Michael A., ed. History of Montana, 1739-1885	LHM
Linderman, Frank Bird. Montana adventure	LI
Logan, George. Histories of the North Montana Mission	LHN
Miller, Joaquin. An illustrated history of the state of Montana	MI
Montana Historical Society. Contributions	MC
Noyes, Alva Josiah. In the land of Chinook	NL
Palladino, Lawrence Benedict. Indian and white in the Northwest. 1894	PI
_____. Indian and white in the Northwest. 1922	PIW
Sanders, Helen Fitzgerald. A history of Montana	SM
Stout, Tom, ed. Montana, its story and biography	SMS
Stuart, Granville. Forty years on the frontier	SFY
Vaughn, Robert. Then and now	VT
Wheeler, Olin Dunbar. The trail of Lewis and Clark, 1804-1904	WT

OREGON

Atwood, Albert. Conquerors	AC
Brosnan, Cornelius James. Jason Lee	BJ
Canse, John Martin. Pilgrim and pioneer	CPP
Carey, Charles Henry. General history of Oregon prior to 1861	CGO
_____. History of Oregon	CHO
Clark, Robert Carlton. History of the Willamette Valley, Oregon	CHW
Clarke, Samuel A. Pioneer days of Oregon history	CP
Commonwealth review of the University of Oregon	CR
Dobbs, Caroline (Conselyea). Men of Champoeg	DO
Franchère, Gabriel. Adventure at Astoria, 1810-1814	FRA
Gaston, Joseph. Portland, Oregon	GP
Gray, William Henry. Unpublished journal	GUG
Hines, Harvey Kimball, comp. At sea and in port	HSP
_____. Illustrated history of the state of Oregon	HIO
History of the Pacific Northwest: Oregon and Washington	NH
Judson, Katharine Berry. Myths and legends of the Pacific Northwest	JM
Kelley, Joseph. Thirteen years in the Oregon penitentiary	KT
Lockley, Fred. History of the Columbia River Valley	LHC
_____. Story of the Journal	LSJ
Lyman, Horace Sumner. History of Oregon	LH
O'Connor, Dominic. Brief history of the Diocese of Baker City	OB
Odell, Margaretta (Grubbs). Semi-centennial offering to the members and friends of Methodist Episcopal church	OS
O'Hara, Edwin Vincent. Pioneer Catholic history of Oregon. 1911	OP
_____. Pioneer Catholic history of Oregon. 1939	OPC
Oregon. Secretary of State. Oregon blue book	OO
Oregon historical quarterly	OHQ
Oregon native son	PMO
Scott, Harvey Whitefield, ed. History of Portland, Oregon	SHP
Sheldon, Henry Hargrave. Northwest corner	HN

Sisters of the Holy Names of Jesus and Mary. Province of Oregon.   SG
    Gleanings of fifty years
Souvenir, G. A. R. encampment, 1899, McMinnville, Oregon   SOU
Turnbull, George Stanley. Governors of Oregon   TUR
_____. History of Oregon newspapers   TO
Wilbur, Earl Morse. History of the First Unitarian Church of   WFU
    Portland, Oregon, 1867-1892
Woodward, Walter Carleton. Rise and early history of political   WRE
    parties in Oregon 1843-1868

UTAH

Cannon, Frank Jenne. Brigham Young and his Mormon empire   CB
Carlton, Ambrose B. Wonderlands of the wild West   CWW
Clayton, William. William Clayton's journal   CWC
Crockwell, James H., pub. Pictures and biographies of Brigham   CY
    Young and his wives
Dixon, William Hepworth. New America   DN
Ferris, Benjamin G. Utah and the Mormons   FU
Gardner, Hamilton. History of Lehi   GL
Gibbs, Josiah Francis. Lights and shadows of Mormonism   GLS
Golder, Frank Alfred and others, eds. March of the Mormon   GMM
    battalion from Council Bluffs to California
Gove, Jesse Augustus. Utah expedition 1857-1858   GU
Harris, William Richard. Catholic church in Utah   HCC
Hickman, William A. Brigham's destroying angel   HB
Lee, John Doyle. Mormon chronicle   LMM
Piercy, Frederick Hawkins. Route from Liverpool to Great Salt   PR
    Lake Valley

WASHINGTON

Atwood, Albert. Glimpses in pioneer life on Puget Sound   AG
Bagley, Clarence Booth. History of King County, Washington   BHK
_____. History of Seattle   BHS
Bartlett, Laura Belle (Downey). Student's history of the   BS
    Northwest and the state of Washington
Boas, Franz. Kathlamet texts   BKT
Bonney, William Pierce. History of Pierce County, Washington   BH
Bowden, Angie (Burt). Early schools of Washington Territory   BE
Brown, Henry. Taxation of church property   BT
Brunner, Edmund de Schweinitz. Church and community survey of   BCC
    Pend Oreille County, Washington
Bruseth, Nels. Indian stories and legends of the Stillaguamish   BI
Bryan, Enoch Albert. Historical sketch of the State college of   BHSS
    Washington, 1890-1925
Cannon, Miles. Waiilatpu, its rise and fall, 1836-1847   CW
Chandler, George. Textbook of civics for the state of Washington CC
Cochran, John Eakin. Pioneer days in eastern Washington and   CPD
    northern Idaho
Daughters of the American Revolution. Washington (State) History D
    and register

Delaney, Matilda J. (Sager). Survivor's recollections of the   DSR
    Whitman massacre
Drury, Clifford Merrill. Elkanah and Mary Walker   DE
_____. Marcus Whitman, M. D.   DW
_____. A tepee in his front yard   DTI
Eells, Myron. Marcus Whitman, pathfinder and patriot   EW
_____. Ten years of missionary work among the Indians at   ET
    Skokomish
Elks of Washington   E
Feerick, John D. and Emalie P. Vice-presidents of the United   FEE
    States
Fiske, John. Unpublished orations   FO
Fries, Ulrich Englehart. From Copenhagen to Okanogan   FF
Gates, Charles Marvin. First century at the University of   GA
    Washington, 1861-1961
Gonzaga University, Spokane, Wash. Gonzaga's silver jubilee   GG
Grand Army of the Republic. Dept. of Washington and Alaska.   G
    Journal of the... annual encampment. June 16-18, 1920
Hanna, Joseph A. Dr. Whitman and his ride to save Oregon   HD
Hawthorne, Julian, ed. & Brewerton, G. D. History of Washington   HH
Hines, Harvey Kimball. Illustrated history of the state of   HI
    Washington
History of the Pacific Northwest: Oregon and Washington   NH
Hulbert, Archer Butler and Hulbert, Mrs. D. (P.), eds. Marcus   HM
    Whitman, crusader
Hunt, Herbert. Tacoma, its history and its builders   HHT
_____ and Kaylor, F. C. Washington, west of the Cascades   HWW
Jeffcott, Percival Robert. Nooksack tales and trails   JNT
Jessett, Thomas Edwin. Pioneering God's country   JP
Judson, Katharine Berry. Myths and legends of the Pacific   JM
    Northwest
Lampman, Ben Hur. Centralia tragedy and trial   LT
Lauridsen, Gregers Marius & Smith, A. A. Story of Port Angeles   LS
Lewis, William Stanley. Case of Spokane Garry   LC
Lindsay, Ernest Earl. State college of Washington   LW
McClelland, John M. Longview   MLO
Magrini, Louis A. Meet the governors of the state of Washington   MAG
Manring, Benjamin Franklin. The conquest of the Coeur d'Alenes,   MCO
    Spokanes and Palouses
Mary Leopoldine, Sister. Fifty golden years   MG
Meany, Edmond Stephen. Governors of Washington, territorial   ME
    and state
_____, ed. Mount Rainier   MMR
Meeker, Ezra. Pioneer reminiscences of Puget Sound   MP
_____. Seventy years of progress in Washington   MS
Mourning Dove (Humishuma). Coyote stories   HCS
Mowry, William Augustus. Marcus Whitman   MW
Nixon, Oliver Woodson. How Marcus Whitman saved Oregon   NM
_____. Whitman's ride through savage lands   NW
Patrons of Husbandry. Washington State Grange. Proceedings   WSGP
Pierce County Pioneer Association, Tacoma, Washington.   PC
    Commemorative celebration... July 5, 1906
Pigott, H. C. History and progress of King County, Washington   PIG
Port of Seattle. Public Relations Dept. A look at the   SAA
    expanding port of Seattle

Port of Seattle yearbook   S
Presbyterian Church in the United States of America.   Synod   PSW
   of Washington.   History
Prosch, Thomas Wickham.   McCarver and Tacoma   PMT
Prosser, William Farrand.   History of the Puget Sound country   PHP
Redeman, Clara P.   Our first forty years   RO
Richardson, Marvin M.   Whitman mission   RW
Ryan, John Henry.   Ryan's legislative manual, 1905-1906   RLW
_____.   Ryan's legislative manual, tenth session, 1907   RLX
Schoenberg, Wilfred P.   Gonzaga University   SCH
Seattle.   Police Dept.   History   SSP
Seattle.   Port Commission.   The port of Seattle   SA
Seattle Public Library.   History Department.   ...Governors of   SE
   Washington
_____.   ...Mayors of Seattle   SEA
Sheldon, Henry Hargrave.   Northwest corner   HN
Snowden, Clinton A.   History of Washington   SH
Sons of the American Revolution.   Washington State Society.   SRW
   Register
Spencer, Lloyd & Pollard, Lancaster.   A history of the state of   PH
   Washington
Splawn, Andrew Jackson.   Ka-mi-akin.   1917   SK
_____.   Ka-mi-akin.   1944   SKA
Spokane.   Charters.   Charter of the city of Spokane   SCC
Stine, Thomas Ostenson.   Scandinavians on the Pacific, Puget   SS
   Sound
Swan, James Gilchrist.   The Northwest coast   SWA
Tacoma daily ledger   TDL
Tax facts; state of Washington   TF
Utz, Mrs. Cora, comp.   History of Spokane University   US
Washington (State) Legislature.   Legislative manual   SSS
Washington (State) State Dept. of Public Welfare.   Coordinator   C
Washington (State) University.   Alumni Association.   Decennial   WD
   banquet in honor of Henry Suzzallo
_____.   Tyee   WDT
Washington Bankers' Association.   Proceedings   WBP
Washington historical quarterly   WAS
Washington magazine of industry and progress   WM
Washington State Bar Association.   Proceedings   WSP
Washingtonian   W
Washingtonian, a state magazine of progress   WN
Winthrop, Theodore.   Canoe and the saddle   WCS

76701